# The Picturesque Prison

# The Picturesque Prison

## Evelyn Waugh and His Writing

### Jeffrey Heath

McGill—Queen's University Press · Kingston and Montreal

© McGill – Queen's University Press 1982
ISBN 0-7735-0377-3 (Cloth)
ISBN 0-7735-0407-9 (Paper)
Legal deposit 1st quarter 1982
Bibliothèque Nationale du Québec

This book has been published with the help of a grant from the Canadian Federation for the Humanities, using funds provided by the Social Sciences and Humanities Research Council of Canada.

Printed in Canada
Reprinted in 1983
First printing in paperback 1983.


CANADIAN CATALOGUING IN PUBLICATION DATA

Heath, Jeffrey M., 1943–
    The picturesque prison

Includes index.
ISBN 0-7735-0377-3
ISBN 0-7735-0407-9 PBK

1. Waugh, Evelyn, 1903 – 1966.  2.  Novelists, English – 20th century – Biography.  I. Title.

PR6045.A97Z7      823'.912      C81-095090-1

For my Mother and Father

*All things are double one against another.*
Marcias, in *Helena*

*Odi profanum vulgus et arceo.*
Horace, quoted in *Helena*

*Will is to grace as the horse is to the rider.*
Saint Augustine

# Contents

PREFACE                                          xi

ACKNOWLEDGEMENTS                                 xvii

  1.  Vocation                     1

  2.  God and Taste                30

  3.  The Artist                   37

  4.  The Man and the Critics      48

  5.  *Decline and Fall*           63

  6.  *Vile Bodies*               80

  7.  *Black Mischief*            91

  8.  *A Handful of Dust*         104

  9.  *Scoop*                     124

10.  *Work Suspended*                      139

11.  *Put Out More Flags*                  152

12.  *Brideshead Revisited*                161

13.  *Scott-King's Modern Europe*          184

14.  *The Loved One*                       188

15.  *Helena*                              198

16.  *Love Among the Ruins*                206

17.  The War Trilogy: Introduction         210

18.  *Men at Arms*                         217

19.  *Officers and Gentlemen*              228

20.  *Unconditional Surrender*             244

21. *The Ordeal of Gilbert Pinfold*                                    259

22. Epilogue                                                           266

TEXTUAL NOTE                                                           275

NOTES                                                                  279

INDEX                                                                  323

# Preface

"A combination of eccentric don and testy colonel": Waugh's description of Gilbert Pinfold aptly characterizes the gruff persona which he presented to the world in middle age. The face was often pinkly irascible, sometimes fiery red, and the prominent eyes glared with disapproval above the glowing, accusing cigar. It was the countenance of an irritable and quirky genius who had virtually invited his public to regard him as a crank. But behind the thick shell of masks and poses, like the oyster with its pearl, Waugh was an intensely serious artist who laboured with painstaking care to create fiction of lasting merit. This is a book about his career as a writer. It examines his evolving attitudes and ideas, shows how his view of the world helped shape his work, and explores the way he imaginatively transmuted his experiences, fascinated by what he deplored and repelled by what he admired. This study brings together information about Waugh and focuses on characteristic currents and patterns in his thought and writing; not least, it is an attempt to reinterpret his work and establish his reputation on a firmer basis than before.

With his scrupulous sense of tone and phrase, Waugh was an accomplished wordsmith who made language fulfil its appointed function, and he insisted that people and objects should do the same. One of his most remarkable traits was the desire, reflected in his work, to escape from the restrictive sanctuary of youth into the liberating confines of some adult vocation. Yet despite his ingrained commitment to his calling as a writer, he often struggled against it, perceiving it too as a potential prison. As Waugh aged he lost his joy in absurdity, abandoned his hard-won balance of gaiety and censure, and posed as a peevish diehard behind West Country ramparts. The reader who considers Waugh's declining years may well wonder whether the secluded artist found freedom in Piers Court and Combe Florey House or whether (like his own protagonists in their constricting Arcadias) he unexpectedly found only more irksome constraint.

My interest in Waugh and his work dates back some fifteen years to the time when I began a dissertation on his satiric method based on close reading of his fiction. The present book grew out of an examination of the manuscripts of Waugh's novels and diaries, and the questions I have asked this time are different from those I asked before, having been prompted by the conviction (supported, I think, in the following pages) that Waugh's life and writings are not at all as unrelated as he himself liked to maintain. In trying to shed new light on Waugh's work by combining the advantages of biography and aesthetic criticism, I have been motivated by the belief that—if treated with the proper tact—an author's experience and his art may validly offer mutual illumination. Although I begin and end with biographical considerations, my interest is ultimately in Waugh's novels, which I have examined in sequence in order to trace the formation of his preoccupations and techniques. I have treated his work as a developing whole which displays an organic consistency; the chapter on *Brideshead Revisited* is the book's centre, both a destination and a point of departure. Where it has seemed useful, I have supplied information drawn from the manuscripts and variant editions (see the Textual Note) and from interviews with Waugh's contemporaries. While the chapters of literary analysis may be read individually, they will make better sense if read consecutively, as parts of an unfolding history, in the light of the chapters which frame them.

Waugh's career as a man of letters was not exceptionally long (he died in his sixty-third year), and toward the end it was darkened by illness and melancholy; nevertheless, his life's work was extensive and various. In all, he wrote seventeen novels, three collections of short stories, eight travel books, three biographies, the first volume of an unfinished autobiography, and hundreds of articles, reviews, and prefaces. In his youth he produced diaries, letters, cartoons, woodcuts, bookplates, sketches, dust-jackets, stories, editorials, essays, plays, poems, and the script of a comic film. In addition to all this, he was a tireless and prolific correspondent (Mark Amory's excellent edition of the letters contains only 840 of the 4,500 available, with many others lost or withheld), and he kept a diary throughout his life, including a highly illegal journal during his years as a gentleman at arms.

Ever since he came of age as a novelist in 1928 with the publication of *Decline and Fall*, Waugh has been the subject of intense critical interest. A. A. De Vitis, Christopher Hollis, Frederick J. Stopp, Malcolm Bradbury, and Stephen Jay Greenblatt all wrote significant studies before Waugh's death, and the books of James F. Carens, Paul A. Doyle, William

J. Cook, Jr., David Lodge, and Gene D. Phillips followed soon after.
More recently, the publication of Waugh's diaries, selected journalism,
and letters has led to an explosion in the number of essays, evaluations,
and longer critiques; as the present study goes to press, a book by Robert
Murray Davis, which unfortunately I have not seen, is about to appear. A
full-length biography by Christopher Sykes and books of reminiscence by
Alec Waugh, Frances Donaldson, Dudley Carew, Alan Pryce-Jones, and
John St. John have also been published, and Waugh's name appears with
increasing frequency in the memoirs of the period. There have been hundreds of scholarly articles about different aspects of his work, and a
newsletter provides a forum for discussion of his fiction. A 1972 checklist
by Robert Murray Davis, Paul A. Doyle, Heinz Kosok, and Charles E.
Linck, Jr. cites some 1,300 items about Waugh, while a forthcoming annotated bibliography of criticism compiled by David Dooley and Margaret Morriss refers to over 1,500 representative and selected pieces. I
have found much of this work very useful, and have tried to acknowledge
the assistance of other writers where I have been aware of it. Whatever
Waugh himself might have said about this proliferation of criticism, there
can be no doubt that his reputation has come far (though not always in
the right direction) since 1928, when T. Sturge Moore in *TLS* mistook
the unknown author of *Rossetti* for "a dainty Miss of the Sixties."

In examining Waugh's life and work, I have noticed a broad range of
recurring interests and a variety of characteristic techniques which go together to compose a distinctive "figure in the carpet." Above all, I have
stressed Waugh's interest in religion. I have not done so because I think
he is a narrowly doctrinaire "Catholic writer" (one mistaken view of
Waugh) but because I hope to counteract two other widespread misconcep-
ceptions: that is, that Waugh wholly approved of the bizarre world he
chronicled, and that he produced his best writing when he had no convictions. I have tried to show that his hilarious comedy is at the same time
serious business and that its complex temper arises out of his deep ambivalence toward experience. In Waugh's work as in his life, a pronounced moral dimension coexists with a deep strain of the most untamed anarchy; and although there can be no question that he became
sterner as he aged, it is evident that he was a moralist at least as early as
*Decline and Fall*. In my view, Waugh's novels are satires rooted in a
Christian and ultimately a Roman Catholic vision of history, in which the
contemporary world is a hollow caricature of an unseen realm and a
bleak parody of the more substantial past.

My primary purpose in this study has been to show how Waugh's novels work, but implicit in that aim has been the opinion that they fully
repay such close attention. I believe that they will endure because of their

stylistic vivacity and comic inventiveness, and because of the underlying seriousness which removes them from the world of "entertainments" and places them firmly in the tradition of Christian moralists like More and Swift. Waugh's novels document an age and they contain a share of human truth. They dramatize, often in a mode of fantasy which cuts closer to the bone than realism can, the desolate world of routine betrayals and casual injustice, and they do so in the measured language of civilized outrage. They expose incompetence and corruption, pretentiousness and fraud, but not without implying alternatives. In their insistence on order, taste, responsibility, reason, and faith, they promote virtues which, if not in Waugh's view widely practised, are not for that reason out of date. No doubt there are many ways of reacting to the knowledge that Waugh himself sometimes failed to demonstrate these same virtues; some of us, perhaps, will respond with the *caritas* which Waugh struggled so painfully to approach.

Needless to say, this is only one of many possible books about Waugh. There were many routes which might have been taken, but in the end this is the book which got itself written. In preparing it I was fortunate to have the assistance and support of friends and colleagues who listened patiently, gave unstintingly of their time and efforts, and made many useful suggestions. David Dooley helped me see the religious basis of Waugh's satire and carefully read an early draft of this book. John Baird, Bob Bilan, Melba Creelman, Paul Doyle, and Lee Patterson all read portions of the manuscript and offered helpful suggestions. Michael Millgate's advice on a number of points was extremely valuable. In London, Catharine Carver gave guidance and encouragement which was crucially important. David Wykes and James Gindin read late versions of the book and furnished detailed and helpful criticism. Margaret Morriss provided useful bibliographical information, and E. C. Beer copy-edited the manuscript with meticulous care. In expressing my gratitude for all this help, which has resulted in a much stronger piece of work, I wish to add that any errors or shortcomings which persist are, of course, entirely my own.

For generously offering information which has been of great value in forming this book's biographical dimension, I am deeply grateful to the friends and relatives of Waugh who took the time to write to me or who agreed to meet me in conversation. I wish to thank Lady Diana Cooper, Lady Pansy Lamb, and Dudley Carew, and to express my gratitude to the memory of Cecil Beaton, Sir Maurice Bowra, Father Martin D'Arcy, s.j., Tom Driberg, Henry Yorke, Lord Kinross, Nancy Mitford and Laura Waugh.

I should like to thank Eileen Dunlap and her staff at the Humanities Research Center, University of Texas at Austin, for their friendly assistance during the research periods of this project. Joan Gibbs at the Paleography Room, University of London Library, gave generously of her time and advice, and the staff of the British Library was efficient and cooperative as usual. For their cheerful and reliable help I am particularly grateful to my typists, Rosemary Nelson, Jean Gunn, Elizabeth MacGregor, Jane Widdicombe, and Judy Broughton. I also wish to thank Jane Widdicombe for assisting me with the index.

This project was generously supported at various stages by the Social Sciences and Humanities Research Council of Canada. I am especially grateful to the Council for providing me with a Leave Fellowship in 1976–77, when most of this book came into being. I also wish to thank the Canadian Federation for the Humanities, which helped fund the publication of this book, and the University of Toronto Office of Research Administration, which provided other assistance along the way.

Lastly, and most important of all, I wish to express my deep gratitude to those who were there even when the going was not good. They have my warmest thanks.

# Acknowledgements

Passages from the following works are reprinted by permission of A. D. Peters and Co., Ltd., and by permission of Little, Brown and Co.: *Decline and Fall*, copyright 1928, 1956, and 1962 by Evelyn Waugh; *Vile Bodies*, copyright 1930, 1958, 1965 by Evelyn Waugh; *Black Mischief*, copyright 1932, 1960, 1962 by Evelyn Waugh; *A Handful of Dust*, copyright 1934, 1962, 1964 by Evelyn Waugh; *Scoop*, copyright 1934, 1938, 1964, 1965, 1966 by Evelyn Waugh; Mr. *Loveday's Little Outing and Other Sad Stories*, copyright 1936 by Evelyn Waugh; *Put Out More Flags*, copyright 1942, 1966 by Evelyn Waugh and 1970 by Laura Waugh; *Brideshead Revisited: The Sacred and Profane Memories of Captain Charles Ryder*, copyright 1944, 1945, 1960 by Evelyn Waugh and 1972, 1973 by Laura Waugh; *When the Going Was Good*, copyright 1946 by Evelyn Waugh; *Scott-King's Modern Europe*, copyright 1947, 1949 by Evelyn Waugh; *The Loved One*, copyright 1948, 1965 by Evelyn Waugh and 1976 by Auberon Waugh; *Helena*, copyright 1950 and 1962 by Evelyn Waugh and 1978 by Auberon Waugh; *Men at Arms*, copyright 1952 and 1965 by Evelyn Waugh and 1980 by Auberon Waugh; *Officers and Gentlemen*, copyright 1955 and 1965 by Evelyn Waugh; *Unconditional Surrender* (American title: *The End of the Battle*), copyright 1961 and 1965 by Evelyn Waugh; *Love Among the Ruins*, copyright 1953 and 1954 by Evelyn Waugh; *The Ordeal of Gilbert Pinfold*, copyright 1957 by Evelyn Waugh; *The Life of the Right Reverend Ronald Knox* (American title: *Monsignor Ronald Knox*), copyright 1959 by Evelyn Waugh; *The Diaries of Evelyn Waugh*, copyright the Estate of Evelyn Waugh, 1976, copyright in the introduction and compilation Michael Davie, 1976.

Passages from the following works are reprinted by permission of A. D. Peters and Co., Ltd.: *Labels: A Mediterranean Journal* (American title: *A Bachelor Abroad: A Mediterranean Journal*), copyright Evelyn

Waugh, 1930; *Remote People* (American title: *They Were Still Dancing*), copyright 1931 and 1932 by Evelyn Waugh; *Ninety-Two Days: The Account of a Tropical Journey through British Guiana and Part of Brazil*, copyright 1934 by Evelyn Waugh; *Waugh in Abyssinia*, copyright 1936 by Evelyn Waugh; *Robbery Under Law: The Mexican Object-Lesson* (American title: *Mexico: An Object-Lesson*), copyright 1939 by Evelyn Waugh; *Work Suspended*, copyright 1942 by Evelyn Waugh; "Compassion," copyright 1949 by Evelyn Waugh; *The Holy Places*, copyright 1952 by Evelyn Waugh; *A Tourist in Africa*, copyright 1960 by Evelyn Waugh; *Rossetti: His Life and Works*, copyright 1928 by Evelyn Waugh; *Edmund Campion*, copyright 1935, 1947, 1961 by Evelyn Waugh; *Basil Seal Rides Again*, copyright 1963 by Evelyn Waugh; *A Little Learning*, copyright 1964 by Evelyn Waugh; *The Letters of Evelyn Waugh*, copyright the Estate of Laura Waugh 1980; copyright in the introduction and compilation Mark Amory 1980 (passages from *The Letters* are reprinted in the United States by permission of Ticknor and Fields). I am also indebted to A. D. Peters and Co. for permission to quote from Waugh's juvenilia, journalism, prefaces, and from extensive unpublished material located at the Humanities Research Center, the University of Texas at Austin.

I am grateful to the University of London Library and Riette Sturge Moore for giving me permission to quote from the T. Sturge Moore and Arthur Waugh collections, and I should like to express my particular appreciation to the Humanities Research Center, the University of Texas at Austin, for giving me permission to quote from Waugh's unpublished manuscripts.

Small sections of this book appeared in *English Studies* 55 (December 1974):529, and 56 (June 1975):227; *English Studies in Canada* 2 (Fall 1976):330–31; and in different form in *Evelyn Waugh Newsletter* 7 (Spring 1973):9; 7 (Winter 1973):7–8; 11 (Spring 1977):4–5; 13 (Autumn 1979):5–7. I thank the editors of these journals for permitting me to reprint this material.

## CHAPTER 1

# Vocation

Looking back over his life from the vantage-point of his sixtieth year, Evelyn Waugh recalled his boyhood fascination with the "derelict furnace-house" and "old kitchen-garden" of his aunts' house at Midsomer Norton: "This cellar and this wilderness I took as my special province, thus early falling victim to the common English confusion of the antiquated with the sublime, which has remained with me; all my life I have sought dark and musty seclusions, like an animal preparing to whelp." [1] Like much of what Waugh says about himself the remark sounds facetious, but it points to an essential truth about his character: he searched all his life for a refuge where he need not compromise with the world around him. During Waugh's declining years, that refuge was his house at Combe Florey in Somerset, where he barricaded himself away from modernity, inveighing against it in crusty letters to *The Times* and the *Spectator* and energetically repelling all intrusions upon his privacy. But Waugh's love of the sequestered life began much earlier. As a little boy he loathed the "trippers" who invaded his solitude when he was on vacation, and as a youth he often recoiled fastidiously from the too-coarsely communal life of Lancing College. At Lancing Waugh was intensely ambitious and ardently wished to make his mark on the world, but at the same time he needed a retreat from the arena of action. Although he drove himself to participate fully in the life of the college, with its boxing competitions, rugger, cross-country racing, debates, and literary societies, he found a refuge from the clamour of "public life" in the workshop of a strange, reclusive aesthete named Francis Crease. Crease taught Waugh the fine art of manuscript lettering and illumination, and his retiring, almost furtive character stands in sharp contrast to those of the glaringly public figures who influenced Waugh at other times.

Waugh eventually outgrew the influence of his cloistered mentor, for he saw that Crease's type of retirement was inadequate and even dangerous.

But he never gave up his desire for a sanctuary, and he embarked upon a lifelong quest for the right kind of seclusion. His search was so urgent that it inevitably carried over into his novels, where it became a major motif, and if we examine the refuges in Waugh's fiction we may discern a pattern which illuminates the very core of his work and personality.

In the novels before *Brideshead Revisited* Waugh's protagonists typically find solitary refuges which are false—not unlike Francis Crease's—while in the fiction of later date they discover the correct refuge which has been adumbrated by the false ones: the Household of the Faith. To express the pattern in other terms, the characters—more properly, the personae—of Waugh's early fiction try to take refuge in the barbarous and essentially immature City of Man; later they find the authentic sanctuary they seek in the City of God. Until they do so they are mere shadows capering in a debased realm which is a parody of the real world and a travesty of the richer past.

William Boot's "lush place" at Boot Magna is perhaps the most memorable false refuge, but there are many others. They include Paul Pennyfeather's Oxford, the various houses of the past which Adam Symes visits, Tony Last's Hetton and Amazon jungle, John Plant's Morocco, Ambrose Silk's tower of "pure art," Brideshead House, Dennis Barlow's Hollywood, Scott-King's Neutralia, and Guy Crouchback's Castello. There are other examples, but the important thing to notice about them is that they all seem to offer boundless freedom and utopian ease; they all appear to be places of relaxation and tolerance where there are no laws, no constraints, and no irksome discipline. They are places where, to quote Dr. Kakophilos in "Out of Depth," "Do what thou wilt shall be the whole of law."[2] Only lax, lenient fathers dwell here—often no fathers at all. Yet paradoxically these lotus-lands of self-indulgence lead to, or prove to be, prisons.

In keeping with the magical law of inversion which governs Waugh's fiction, the false, merely secular refuge of his early novels looks like a Camelot but turns out to be a jail, for the abundant material ease it affords is always purchased at the price of spiritual bondage. The Wonderland logic of Waugh's first novel, *Decline and Fall*, illustrates that the false refuge and the prison are only different sides of the same coin. Dislodged by an act of barbarism from his placid cul-de-sac at Oxford, Paul Pennyfeather seeks a substitute refuge in schoolteaching and high society, but banal Llannabba College and King's Thursday are so chaotic that they prove to be prisons in all but name. Like England itself, they are prisons of the spirit, and (the figurative becoming literal, in characteristic Waugh fashion) they lead Paul to actual imprisonment at Blackstone Gaol and Egdon Heath. Normally in Waugh sanctuaries prove to be prisons, but at Blackstone a prison proves to be a sanctuary, like the asylums which shelter happy Mr. Loveday and, later, the contented madmen in *Brideshead Revisited*. Paul enjoys his incarceration, and after other adventures in other apparent refuges he returns to Oxford pretending to be his own cousin. But despite its reassuringly stable appearance, Scone College is only one more in the novel's circle of spiritually restrictive lush places, for it harbours aging Peter Pans, Bacchic excesses, and false doctrine. Paul complacently resumes his studies there as an Anglican ordinand; he condemns the heretical Bishop of Bithynia and the ascetic Ebionites, but he is unwittingly a heretic himself. Since Paul perseveres in his failure to recognize correct spiritual values, he makes no moral advance—a fate which often befalls Waugh's early protagonists. He begins and ends his adventures in the prison of heresy: only the names of the prisons change, and because he has no real (that is, no supernatural) option Paul never achieves the maturity and the vocation that he seeks.

In novel after novel, seductive false refuges prove to be prisons as the pattern of *Decline and Fall* recurs. In *A Handful of Dust* Tony Last loves his cloistered life at neo-Gothic Hetton Abbey, but he "can't possibly get away" from it; later, he seeks the "radiant sanctuary" of a fabulous Eldorado, but achieves only permanent slavery in Mr. Todd's bleak house, reading about the Marshalsea and other prisons. In *Work Suspended* John Plant's permissive life in the *quartier toléré* of Fez issues in his arrest, but in an important later development, he resists the temptation to buy the "Composed Hermitage in the Chinese Taste," in an engraving of which "a curiously complacent malefactor" receives the bastinado. In *Put Out More Flags* Ambrose Silk tries to retreat like a muezzin to the Ivory Tower of "pure art," but he soon finds himself immured in an Irish fishing village. Other examples could be mentioned, but the point is clear: Waugh regarded the world as a seductive bower which would prove a prison to the man who failed to outgrow its blandishments. The "doom of youth," to borrow Wyndham Lewis's phrase,[3] was imprisonment in one's own immaturity. Evelyn Waugh was indeed part of the "Youngergenerationism" that Lewis attacked, but he by no means unambiguously loved the condition he wrote about.[4]

*Brideshead*, Waugh's pivotal novel, adds an important extra dimension to the metaphor of the lush place: while false refuges continue to be prisons, imprisonment emerges as a necessary stage on the road to the true refuge. So it is that Charles Ryder passes through the low door in the garden wall towards an enchanted life with Sebastian at Brideshead House, a life which is really a form of spiritual incarceration; in fact, their excesses actually lead the two youths to jail. Brideshead House itself, as the imagery shows, emerges as an elaborate false sanctuary,[5]

but—and here is the central development in Waugh's fiction—imprisonment in the secular lush place is now seen as a necessary forerunner of the
*right* kind of imprisonment, which consists of the discipline imposed by
the Church, the true refuge. Instead of constricting Charles Ryder's existence, religious discipline amplifies it; like Milton, Waugh believed that
unrestrained freedom was slavery, while the right sort of constraint could
be liberating. The same thing happens to Guy Crouchback in the War
Trilogy, where Eldoret and the Castello Crouchback are false refuges
which imprison, while the austere life at Broome is a restraint which
frees. Even in novels where the false refuges are not explicitly linked with
imprisonment, they are shown to be fraught with menace. Thus in *Black
Mischief* Azania becomes a peaceful protectorate, but waves lap ominously at its shores. And in *Scoop* gentle William Boot retires for the
night at Boot Magna, but the sinister imagery insinuates that his serenity
will be brief.

In the fiction before *Brideshead* Waugh's personae fail to see how pernicious their false refuges are, and they "mysteriously disappear"; this
early fiction is governed by fate, fortune, and circumstance. In the later
fiction, which is ruled by Providence, they see their danger and make
good their escapes. In *The Loved One* Dennis Barlow seems destined to
succumb to the deathly blandishments of Hollywood, but he cleverly escapes that bone-littered strand. Similarly Scott-King sees the dangerous
truth behind utopian Neutralia and, passing briefly through a prison-like
displaced persons' camp, he escapes—to the Holy Land. Helena, asking
Constantius whether "the City" might not one day break out, sees that
worldly security can be a trap and avoids it, while emperor after emperor
goes to prison and to death. After living in a cell-like cabin in a pleasure-
ship named for the bestial Caliban, Mr. Pinfold eludes his "voices" by
taking personal responsibility for them. However, not all of the later novels show a successful escape from immaturity. *Love Among the Ruins* is
not typical, for its spiritually undernourished protagonist finds no authentic alternative for his lush prison and escapes only into death. And
*Basil Seal Rides Again* playfully inverts the pattern. Here, the elderly
Basil's pose as a respectable citizen drives him to confine himself in a
posh retreat in the hope of *recovering* his youth. There, like a "convicted
felon," he "examines his conscience" and realizes that fatherhood has
caused a debilitating "deviation into rectitude" which has perverted his
"destiny" and has made him a mere "parody" of an old buffer. In order to
get back in touch with his true self he uses a trick worthy of the young
Basil Seal to escape his confining fraudulence and to drive out Albright,
his young rival and double. The story, Waugh's last, is a minor work, but

it demonstrates that despite his desire to escape from youth and anarchy, there was always a part of him which cherished them right to the end.

Ostensibly ample and paradisal, Waugh's lush place is in fact an emblem of the confining City of Man, the beckoning but dangerous realm of the pagan god, Pan. Like the seductive domain glimpsed by T. S. Eliot's "Ash-Wednesday" climber at the first turning of the third stair, it is charming but meretricious, a Bower of Bliss in which spiritual adolescents may hide from maturity and identity. Deflected thus from their purpose in life, and arrested by their apostasy, the neo-pagan inmates of Waugh's surrogate Edens are wraiths who pass the time playing charades and "analogies" in an infantile shadowland. The lush places, then, are images of perversion itself: they are overwhelmingly attractive and, if they are loved as ends in themselves, they are fatally dangerous. Yet if these Arcadias are loved with the right love as means to a divine end, they are beneficial, indeed, necessary.

Waugh's nostalgia for the lush places of this world shows how deeply he longed for their sensuality, solitude, self-indulgence, immaturity, and heterodoxy; his ruthless rejection of them shows how intensely he needed to impose order and stability upon his wayward impulses. As things turned out, Waugh never wholly exorcised his immature love of the profane world; in the end, indeed, his long struggle to purge himself of the unripe and the untrue only drove the two sides of his cleft nature even further apart. The deep rift in Waugh's psyche between the worldly and the other-worldly made him unhappy, but it also generated the tensions which sustain his art and give it its characteristic quirky complexity. Waugh both feared and loved the lush places, and despite his lifelong attack on immaturity he could not root it out of his own heart. Although he tried to exorcise them, Paul, Adam, William Boot, Ambrose Silk, and Basil Seal probably remain closer to the essential Evelyn Waugh than Charles Ryder and Guy Crouchback. In later life Waugh adopted the outward pose of a patriarchal country gentleman who abominated the world, but that orderly patriarch harboured in his soul a Dionysiac youth who was fascinated by what he loathed. Insistent on the Augustan graces though he was, Waugh never overcame his Petronian impulses; to the end he was always partly in thrall to memories of an age without restraint.

What induced Waugh habitually to view life as a seductive trap, and to seek a true discipline to counteract life's blandishments? The answer seems to be, in part, that his riotous life at Oxford taught him to distrust his own unguided impulses. There, he learned that complete freedom was its own form of imprisonment. Undoubtedly because of the anarchy which he sensed not far below the surface of his own nature, Waugh frequently argued that discipline, or "imprisonment," was beneficial to the creative faculties. As early as 1929, in a sharp attack on the aimless "younger generation," he prescribed "the imposition by rigid discipline . . . of the standards of civilization. . . . The muscles which encounter the most resistance in daily routine are those which become most highly developed and adapted. It is thus that the restraint of a traditional culture tempers and directs creative impulses. Freedom produces sterility."[6] If freedom dulls the aesthetic ability, discipline sharpens it. In "A Call to the Orders" (1938) Waugh observed that the fantasies of the Augustan designers were liberated by their strict adherence to the Palladian orders,[7] and as early as 1927 he noted, "In writing, once the barest respect has been paid to the determining structure of the letter, the pen is free to flourish and elaborate as it will."[8]

But if discipline imparted direction and purpose in aesthetic matters, it was even more effective, Waugh argued, in spiritual matters. Here, purpose came from submission to God. In "Palinurus in Never-Never Land," Waugh spoke of "an all-wise God who has a particular task for each individual soul, which the individual is free to accept or decline at will, and whose ultimate destiny is determined by his response to God's vocation."[9] In "Fan-Fare" he claimed that each human being is "God's creature with a defined purpose."[10] In "St. Helena Empress" he wrote, "What we can learn from Helena is something about the workings of God; that He wants a different thing from each of us, laborious or easy, conspicuous or quite private, but something which only we can do and for which we were each created."[11] And in a letter of the same date to John Betjeman he wrote, "Each individual has his own peculiar form of sanctity which he must achieve or perish."[12] In spiritual as in aesthetic (and other) affairs, liberation and fulfilment came from discipline (or "imprisonment") of the right kind. In short, Waugh believed that heterodoxy was slavery while orthodoxy was freedom: compare Orwell's *1984*, where "freedom is slavery."

In an unpublished section of *Decline and Fall* Paul Pennyfeather laments that he is "the creature of chaos" while his incarcerated self is "the creature of order and purpose." "Why am I here?" he asks, his imprisonment generating concern about his *raison d'être*.[13] Waugh deleted the passage, but it shows clearly that as early as 1928, nearly two years before his conversion, Waugh was asking questions about purpose—or, to borrow the title of his first novel's first chapter, vocation. A concern for vocation dominates *Decline and Fall*, and the same concern integrates all of Waugh's subsequent fiction. Waugh's use in *Decline and Fall* of the word "vocation" seems merely facetious, but it is in fact deeply serious, for it heralds his lifelong quest to discover and actualize the "particular task," the "defined purpose" for which he believed God had created him. In Waugh's view, each individual's potential is unique, and he fulfils his vocation when he develops his possibilities to the utmost by performing the thing "which only we can do and for which we were each created."

How can a person know what his special purpose is? Waugh's world-view rests upon the conviction that behind contingency there stands a design which reveals itself when individuals exchange their self-centred perspectives on the world for a God-centred perspective. A man's place in God's design becomes clear when he exchanges his false refuge for a true one in which he can become genuine. "Come inside," Waugh wrote in 1949. "You cannot know what the Church is like from outside. However learned you are in theology, nothing you know amounts to anything in comparison with the knowledge of the simplest actual member of the Communion of Saints."[14] If a man wishes to discover his role in the universal design, he must first perceive that such a design exists; and his right seeing will depend on right believing. Orthodoxy is the key to the achievement of purpose and vocation.

It is easier to understand Waugh's treatment of vocation—and good taste—if we trace his attitudes to their source in Augustine's pronouncements on ends and means. According to Augustine, each person or thing has its own God-given nature and purpose, and each nature is in itself good as long as it occupies its proper place in the universal order:

> All natures, then, are good simply because they exist and, therefore, have each its own measure of being, its own beauty, even in a way, its own peace. And when each is in the place assigned by the order of nature, it best preserves the full measure of being that was given to it. Beings not made for eternal life, changing for better or worse according as they promote the good and improvement of things to which, by the law of the Creator, they serve as means, follow the direction of Divine Providence and tend toward the particular end which forms a part of the general plan for governing the universe. This means that the dissolution which brings mutable and mortal things to their death is not so much a process of annihilation as a process toward something they were designed to become.[15]

According to Augustine most natures, being transient, are not ends in themselves but means to an end which is above them: union with God. Created beings may turn upward towards God (conversion) or downward (aversion) towards the body and merely human concerns. Lower things are not in themselves evil, since all things are good; rather, it is the *decision to turn away* from a higher thing to a lower thing which is evil. Evil results from "a desertion from God." [16] When the lower thing, rightly a means, becomes an end in itself, then its particular purpose is perverted and the person who prefers it to the higher thing injures himself: "In a word, anyone who loves perversely the good of any nature whatsoever and even, perhaps, acquires this good makes himself bad by gaining something good and sad by losing something better." [17] All things have a capacity for union with God, and perversion is the thwarting of this capacity. The City of Man is an example of perversion: it is composed of individuals who have the capacity for a higher union but who choose instead to devote themselves to merely human matters.

Thus, although all created things are good in themselves, they are perverted if they are used for an end other than that which "they were designed to become." A man actualizes his identity when he turns toward God, and he perverts and loses his identity when he turns away. When a man accepts his unique vocation, he submits his own design for himself to a larger design; he ceases to be an end in himself and becomes a means to a more important end. He is mature. Vocation is a question of spiritual good taste: like an object in nature or like an *objet d'art*, a man's soul has a distinct identity and a "defined purpose." And just as ordinary good taste depends upon acknowledging the "right properties of things," [18] so the fulfilment of one's vocation depends upon acknowledging one's true identity and "right properties." Waugh may have held this view as early as 1922, when he remarked in a letter to Dudley Carew that other people's characters are "like designs" and "are not to be tampered with." [19] Vocation is the acceptance of God's design. It is spiritual decorum, spiritual maturity, and to attain it a man must abandon the false refuges of his childhood.

Like F. Scott Fitzgerald, his American counterpart, Waugh insisted on outgrowing the illusions of youth through a realistic attitude to time— and like Fitzgerald he loved the immaturity he castigated. [20] "Growing up is a disagreeable process for most men," he told his son Auberon in 1956, [21] but as early as 1929 he was urging certain aging "Peter Pans of Bloomsbury" to grow up and give way to the younger generation. [22] After the Conservative defeat in the 1945 general election, he recorded in his diary the advice he gave to Randolph Churchill: "I attempted to explain to Randolph that he had reached a grave climacteric in his life and must now grow up or perish. He will perish." [23] But if the failure to mature is lethal, so in a different sense is maturation itself, for it involves the painful death of a familiar and easy way of life. Charles Ryder's early life is annihilated by an avalanche of grace; maturity overtakes Guy Crouchback as he slowly and painfully rejects his romantic illusions about war and comes to grips with the question of charity. Because spiritually coming of age is such a cruel rite of passage, Waugh's characters often evade maturity and struggle fiercely against their vocations. Waugh's early satires depict a resolutely immature and unregenerate world which rejects any suggestion of a purpose beyond itself, if indeed it has ever heard of one. The denizens of Waugh's early "comic" world are ends in themselves, savagely autonomous; like Eliot's wastelanders, they do not want to sprout. But unlike the wastelanders, they do not know what they dread; all they experience is a vague malaise. From Charles Ryder onwards, Waugh's protagonists know what it is that they fear, and they struggle violently against it. But they yield to their vocations in the end, unlike the early protagonists, who remain woefully unenlightened. The central conflict in Waugh's fiction, then, is man's struggle to escape his divinely ordained identity by hiding in an immature and (Waugh would say) perverted world. Waugh's central theme is the flight from vocation into a false refuge. Yet here we encounter a central contradiction in Waugh: even while attacking immaturity, Waugh loved it; he advocated growth and responsibility, but it would be idle to argue that he did not at the same time resent the repressive adult world as stodgy, boring, and—above all, perhaps—unstylish.

Waugh's vocation was a lifelong preoccupation. Although his novels appear to be anything but personal—a notion which he himself carefully fostered—they reflect Waugh's unceasing quest to find his own "defined purpose" in life. Before 1945 Waugh vacillated between the life of action and the retiring life of taste. Accordingly, few of his personae find successful vocations: Paul Pennyfeather returns to his stultifying existence at Scone College; Adam Fenwick-Symes slumps forlornly on a devastated battlefield; Tony Last hopelessly reads Dickens to a madman, and William Boot returns from Ishmaelia to a "lush place" fraught with subtle peril. It is not until *Brideshead Revisited* and the novels that follow it that Waugh's personae begin to find their purposes in life. Their discoveries parallel Waugh's own realization that he had been a failure as a man of action and reflect his decision to devote himself to the more withdrawn calling of the Christian artist. Like Waugh, Charles Ryder rejects the army and secular art in favour of representing "man in relation to God."[24] After a long and uneventful life Helena learns that the one deed which she and no one else can perform is the discovery of the Cross. And the saga of Guy Crouchback depicts his retreat from the romantic role of modern crusader into the more modest calling of pious paterfamilias.

From his earliest years Waugh had a firm if unfocused sense of his personal importance. He kept a diary from his seventh year on. He entitled

the early pages, "My History," and in them he recorded his childish ac-
complishments in a satisfied tone and with a strong sense of things to
come. In his second entry he announced an early aspiration: "I have made
up my mind that I am going to be a 'Merry Jack tar,' if my eyes will pass
Mother dous [*sic*] not think they will. If they do not I shall go board a
'Merchantman' for I must go to sea."[25] After many wrong starts in life
Waugh actually became a Marine, but like the others that too proved to
be a false vocation and failed to fulfil its early promise.

In his childhood Evelyn Waugh was high-spirited and "lyrically
happy";[26] he enjoyed a first age of "privacy and love" (p. 87). According
to the vivid, nostalgic account which Waugh gives in his autobiography,
the Hampstead in which he grew up "still bore plain marks of the character given it in the late eighteenth century"; it was "a pleasure garden"
(p. 41). There is little in Waugh's sunny childish activities to presage the
shadows which engulfed him later. In *A Little Learning* Waugh recalls
Hampstead Fair, with its "pentecostal exuberance," Sunday mornings at
"the Rooms" with Miss Hoare at the harmonium, and shopping expedi-
tions to the Finchley Road with Lucy Hodges, his beloved nanny. Among
the many inventions of a happy childhood there was the "Pistol Troop,"
formed in 1912 for "the defence of the kingdom" against the Prussian
Guard. The Pistol Troop had a fort, a Union Jack, a stringent code of
honour, an editor for its own magazine in the person of Evelyn Waugh,
and (prudent invention) a paymaster. In addition to his soldierly activities, Waugh liked to draw—his first love—and to write: "I was not
particularly talented in drawing, but I drew and painted a great deal,
never attempting to portray objects or landscapes, but making graphic
decorations and slap-dash battle scenes in a manner derived from the
study of printed books and magazines. . . . I wrote a great deal: intermit-
tent diaries and illustrated stories. These were all imitative of the worst of
my reading" (pp. 60, 62). When he was seven Waugh attended Heath
Mount School, an institution of "good tone" and "some antiquity"
which was "by general consent the best school in the neighbourhood"
(p. 80). He was brave, clever, and "happy enough" there, although he admits to a certain discontinuity in his self-image, having become "a quite
different and rather nastier boy who had no share in the real life of the
third of the year he spent at home" (p. 62). He began to emerge as a
leader and a bully. His gang tormented Cecil Beaton because he enjoyed
his music lessons, and stuck pins into him. Beaton recalls a typical
encounter:

> Their leader was a boy half the size of the others, wearing Barrie-
> esque green tweed knickerbockers. Recognizing from a distance

that I was the most obvious lamb for the slaughter, the leader, having darted silently towards me at great speed, halted a few inches in front of me with a menacing wild stare, while the bigger boys circled me and growled louder. He then stood on his toes and slowly thrust his face with a diabolical stare, closer and closer to mine, ever closer until the eyes converged into one enormous Cyclops nightmare. It was a clever inauguration to the terrors that followed, and my introduction to Evelyn Waugh.[27]

Few of those who met Waugh ever forgot his bulging, wrathful eyes. "They might have been on stalks," the novelist Henry Green (Henry Yorke in private life) later remarked.[28]

At Heath Mount Waugh edited a magazine entitled *The Cynic*, and during the war, which broke out during his fourth year at school, he drew gory pictures of German cavalry plunging among English infantry. At the same time he raised funds for the Red Cross by collecting jam jars, cut linoleum for soldiers' slippers, raised a patrol of Boy Scouts, and for a time became a messenger at the War Office. According to his father, in *One Man's Road*, Evelyn was also "an irrepressible advocate of Female Suffrage" and "displayed a precocious capacity for organizing his friends."[29] As a child, then, Waugh was both artistic and pugnacious; he treasured his privacy but was also eager to excel as a leader. As a founding member of the Pistol Troop he repelled gangs of boyish marauders, but he also wrote stories, kept diaries, edited magazines, and drew pictures. Already evident is the tension between worldly action and (not yet other-worldly) art which was to shape his life and work.

Three figures dominate Waugh's childhood: his mother, his father, and his nurse, Lucy Hodges. The five years which separated him from his brother "made, in childhood, a complete barrier" between them; thus Alec was not, at least to Evelyn's conscious awareness, a significant influence. Lucy was more important. She was young and, in Waugh's eyes, very beautiful. She was "Chapel," disapproved of his mother's bridge and his father's wine, and read her Bible straight through every six months. Together with his mother, Lucy received Waugh's devoted love: "my mother and Lucy," he says, "were the sole objects of love in the lustrum between pram and prep school" (p. 33).

Waugh says little about his mother, except that she was small, neat, reticent, active, disliked cities, and enjoyed working in her garden. In Waugh's childhood she was one of his "two adored deities" (p. 29), and in his Lancing diary he praises her; but in later years he referred to her as "Mrs. Waugh" and was capable of extremely unfeeling remarks about her. After one especially trying visit, Waugh guiltily recorded in his diary,

"I found her company wholly disagreeable and left with shame that I had not treated her more gently."[30] Gilbert Pinfold leaves his mother after a duty-call, with similar feelings: "Damn. Damn. Damn. . . . Why does everyone except me find it so easy to be nice?"[31]

Waugh's attitude toward his father was much more complicated. According to the affectionate memoir in *A Little Learning*, his father was genial, sociable, unambitious, generous, free from envy and debt, and deeply emotional. Arthur Waugh was a Tory in politics and intermittently Anglo-Catholic in religion. An "incorrigible Victorian" and paterfamilias, he loved to declaim the works of Shakespeare and the great Victorians, or to read them quietly to his assembled family from his armchair. He took a "perennial delight in amateur theatricals" (p. 38), and loved to act. An old-fashioned man of letters in the tradition of Edmund Gosse, whom he feared (and whom Evelyn scorned as insufficiently heroic), Arthur Waugh dismissed the Georgian poets and D. H. Lawrence and T. S. Eliot in favour of Milton, Dryden, and Arnold. He preferred "the poetry of ideas" to that of mood. He was the editor of the Nonesuch Dickens. He was unabashedly domestic, and prized his house in the North End Road as a rural refuge secure from the "murk" of London. Too sentimentally for his son's taste, he wrote, "It encloses a hearth of homely comfort, a hearth that cherishes green thoughts in a green shade" (p. 35). Like John Plant's father in *Work Suspended*, Arthur Waugh deplored the invasion of his pastoral retreat by shops, cinemas, and the underground railway. Literature was a sanctuary too; perhaps even contributing to his son's hostility to secular refuges, Arthur Waugh wrote, "The function of literature is to make for every man a home of the soul, a citadel of the mind, where he may find protection against the assaults of time and fortune, and a sanctuary against adversities."[32]

Arthur Waugh's warm-heartedness is readily apparent in his letters to his old friend, Austin Dobson.[33] In elaborately courteous language, Waugh expresses cordial sentiments concerning Dobson's career as a poet, and he makes earnest observations about his own progress at Chapman and Hall, where by 1902 he was managing director. There are touching moments when Alec Waugh is reported missing in action, and heartfelt moments when he is reported safe. There is virtually no reference to Evelyn. On the occasion of Dobson's seventieth birthday, in 1910, Arthur Waugh canvassed mutual friends and arranged to give Dobson a salver, rosebowl, and candlesticks and "a little cigarette box to complete the gift." He then caused the forty-two ceremoniously worded replies to be bound as a further present to Dobson. The letters, which include responses from Sir Lawrence Alma-Tadema, William Heinemann, Rudyard Kipling, Henry James, and Edmund Gosse, are eloquent testi-

mony to a long-vanished epistolary style and to the popularity of both
Waugh and Dobson.

There can be little doubt that Arthur Waugh was an amiable and estimable man, and that Evelyn's tribute in *A Little Learning* justly reflects
what most people thought of him. But the tribute gives a less than candid
picture of Waugh's personal opinion of his father. Over against his flattering account must be set the fact that until late in his career, no father in
Waugh's fiction is in the least estimable; with the exception of Guy
Crouchback, the typical Waugh character has an irresponsible father or
no father at all. Waugh's animus against fathers, it is certain, stems from
his dislike of Arthur Waugh. The elder Waugh was not an authoritarian;
indeed, his son remembered him most for his absence: "For my first seven
years my father was a figure of minor importance and interest. . . . I think
he paid a visit to the nursery every evening and often made brief efforts to
entertain, but I never particularly welcomed him; in fact, I regarded his
appearance as an interruption and, in what I suppose is an entirely normal fashion, grudged his usurpation of my mother's attention" (p. 33).
Waugh wished that his father had been less sedentary and more heroic;
the cosiness of his somewhat restricted imagination offended him. Despite dutiful comments in his Lancing diary that he thought his father's
autobiography "awfully good," he was acutely embarrassed by its sentimentality, as he must have been by similarly cloying aspects of Arthur
Waugh's other works.[34] When Francis Crease pointed out that the elder
Waugh was "charming, entirely charming, and acting all the time"
(p. 69), Evelyn was surprised. But soon he was able to "see through" his
father and "became critical of him." Waugh did not fail to appreciate his
father's good qualities. But he chose to dwell on his shortcomings, which
he generalized into the failings typical of the entire older generation and
eventually made the central targets of his satire.

At Heath Mount School Waugh was both aggressive and artistic. The
same divided temperament is apparent in Waugh at Lancing College,
which he first attended on 17 May 1917. Waugh's diaries for the period
(they do not begin until 1919) are the product of a public self concerned
with advancement and prestige, but there is at the same time a persistent
preoccupation with art and the need for privacy. In the "tale of success"
(p. 209) which the Lancing diaries record, they present a picture of a supercilious and disagreeable little boy. Waugh later described the self
which is delineated there as "conceited, heartless and cautiously malev-
olent," and found "page after page of consistent caddishness." He says,
"I should like to believe that even in this private journal I was dissembling
a more generous nature. . . . I feel no identity with the boy who wrote it. I
believe I was a warm-hearted child" (p. 127). Waugh is undoubtedly right

in suspecting himself of having "dissembled." The ambitious voice which speaks from the pages of the Lancing diary is the voice of Waugh's first mask. In time he discarded it in favour of another, as he would do with the entire succession of poses which he adopted in the course of his life.

Despite the fact that the cold, acquisitive mask of the Lancing diaries conceals Waugh's insecure and retiring self, it represents a reality, for it indicates what he wanted to be: a man of the world. In keeping with his desire for public success, he intensified his pursuit of leadership, and became arrogant and calculating. He and his friends were known as "Bolshies," he says, and "hunted as a small pack to bring down [their] equals and immediate superiors" (p. 130). He loved rags, hoaxes, and other anti-authoritarian acts which might enhance his prestige. He submitted his science notes in blank verse and concealed cream in the desk of a school-fellow named Grimes "to stink him out." He admits in *A Little Learning* that he was ambitious and self-seeking, and the evidence is everywhere in the diaries. Remarks like the following are common: "I like to have my show working before everyone else gets going. . . . I do want to be a house-captain, chiefly because I know Father wants it very much and because I want other distinctions like editor of the magazine and president of the literary society for which one has to be one. . . . As I expected I have won the Scarlyn. . . . I should really like to pull off the Essay and Poem too."[35] Yet once he had his honours he affected to despise them: "This morning the locker list was posted and I am junior man on the demi-Settle. I did not expect it at all, but am not as elated as I should have expected. . . . I have won the English Verse but it causes me no interest."[36] Short, plump, bespectacled, tone-deaf, his gait an "ungainly trudge,"[37] Waugh did not yet have the grace attributed to him in his Oxford years. But he was a highly successful schoolboy. He won almost every honour open to him: Settle, house captain, Scarlyn, English Verse Prize, Art Exhibition Prize, Horace Prize, president of the Debating Society, editor of the *Lancing College Magazine*. He helped found the Dilettanti Club and won a scholarship to Oxford. He was not an excellent athlete, but he competed at boxing, swimming, cross-country, rugger, squash, and football, at which he experienced some discouraging moments as a goal-keeper. Eager to acquire the social graces, he became an enthusiastic dancer: "I at last mastered the hesitation and learned more foxtrot steps," he writes on one occasion; "I was pleasantly conscious of being the best-dressed man in the room."[38]

Another example of Waugh's flair for leadership was his brain-child, the "Corpse Club." A contemporary recalls it: "[It was] a short-lived society that caused a great stir, since its avowed object was to discourage any form of enthusiasm, its uniform a black tie and a black tassel, its ritual funereal and its attitude provocative. There were thirteen members, eleven corporeal ones and two 'spiritual presences'—the second grave digger in *Hamlet* and 'poor little Jehoiachim! Pathetic little prince!' the opening words of a sermon by the Senior History Master." [39] Members included Evelyn Waugh, "the Undertaker," and Evelyn Newman, "the Chief Mourner." Others were Hugh Molson, Tom Driberg, Dudley Carew, and Roger Fulford: "The Corpses believed that they were being modern and provocative. . . . nothing could show more clearly that 'the English take their pleasure sadly' than the notice received by a newly-elected Corpse: 'the Undertaker finds a mournful pleasure in announcing the interment of the late Mr. C. L. Chamberlin'."

Even while the siren-song of worldly achievement lured him on, Waugh was being drawn towards the domain of art. He loved manuscript illumination, but he also drew caricatures and Beardsleyesque line-drawings, wrote poems, maintained an active interest in theatre and cinema, and wrote a play entitled "Conversion" which was performed at Lancing with great success. Waugh's letters of the period to his friend Dudley Carew contain much criticism and advice on artistic matters: how to write sonnets, *vers libre*, novels. The manuscript of "The Twilight of Language," a speech delivered to the Dilettanti, shows that Waugh knew about contemporary fiction even if he disapproved of Katherine Mansfield. Waugh's desire for artistic expression was still unfocused: "I think I shall either write journalese or *Spectator* essays," he notes on one occasion; on another, "I see I must forswear script and take to caricature"; and on still another, "I feel that I must write prose or burst." [40] The sense of great things to come pervades Waugh's Lancing diaries, issuing in self-important musings on his own possibilities and on those of youth in general: "I know I have something in me but I am desperately afraid it may never come to anything." And again, "I wonder if we are really going to produce any great men or if we will fizzle into mediocrity?" [41] Waugh's youthful concern about his life-work was to reverberate through novel after novel. But at Lancing, rather than choosing a single avenue for self-expression, Waugh chose a dozen: the Dilettanti was facetiously named to honour the practice of doing everything half-heartedly. When his illuminated script received adverse criticism, he wrote, "Apparently if one is ever going to do good work one has to give one's whole life to it. I suppose this is really true of everything. There is no place for the dilettanti." [42] He did not yet act on his own advice.

"Two mentors" who were "equal and opposite influences" helped focus Waugh's exuberance. They were the mysterious Francis Crease, "a neuter, evasive, hypochondriacal recluse" (p. 149), who tutored him as a scribe and provided a tangible example of the aesthetic life, and the elegant J. F. Roxburgh, Waugh's housemaster, who set him a standard of worldliness. In Crease Waugh found a focus for his diffuse interests in drawing and writing and also for that reclusive part of him which was already embarked on a life-long quest for privacy. Needless to say, the secretive Crease was very unlike the genial Arthur Waugh: "I . . . caused some offence to my father by suggesting that until I met Mr. Crease I had lived among philistines" (p. 153). Crease's example swayed Waugh. Not long after meeting him, he wrote, "I see the only way to get any pleasure out of life here is to cut oneself off as much as possible from the tide of events. I have tried plunging in and trying to enjoy the cold water but it was no good. Crease's life is about the best after all." [43] Waugh later rejected Crease, noting, "The spell is broken. His influence is quite gone. I just see a rather silly perhaps casually interesting little man." [44] But Waugh continued to visit Crease in his Oxford years and after; Crease exerted a life-long influence on him.

The more forceful and flamboyant J. F. Roxburgh was Crease's antithesis. Tall, showy, physically impressive, and just back from the war, he was a dandy. His examination papers were elegantly printed and his private letters to parents were inscribed on personally embossed writing paper. He was a stoic and a sceptic who, like an eighteenth-century Anglican bishop, Waugh says, raised doubts without suggesting answers. He was much concerned with appearance, and was an impressive orator and a stickler for precision of grammar and the avoidance of cliché. Roxburgh provided a model for Waugh's incipient dandyism and love of elegance, and showed him the value of a public "manner."

The artist and the man of the world who were incubating within Waugh found their embodiments in Crease and Roxburgh. They coexisted as separate aspects of his personality, and sometimes he emulated the one, sometimes the other. Behind the many other masks which Waugh later adopted, the tension between artist and man of action remains constant. His sense of his own duality was highly developed by the time he reached Lancing. In his diary entry for 19 October 1920 Waugh notes that he has found the "scheme" for his first novel (never to be finished). It is to be "the study of a man with two characters, by his brother."

In his fiction Waugh rings the changes on the possible interactions of his "two characters," and throughout his life he was aware of a related phenomenon: the lack of continuity between the self of one period and the self of a later time. Thus, as well as thinking of himself as a divided personality Waugh began to feel that he lived his life in discrete consecutive sections. "Climacteric" is a word he often used. The opening lines of the Lancing diaries read: "Alec once said that he kept his life in 'water-tight' compartments. It is very true; here I am flung suddenly into an entirely different world, different friends, and different mode of life."[45] In the Lancing diaries and afterwards, Waugh speaks in disparaging terms of Bergson and his integrating *durée*. In Waugh's view, personality had continuity only if its possessor affiliated himself with enduring institutions. All of his early stories, notably *Decline and Fall*, concern themselves with the "change and decay" of personality as opposed to its "duration."

The idea of outgrowing the clutches of a pernicious other self, with a view to penetrating closer to a self which is somehow more real, is central to Waugh's fiction. Often he creates a protagonist who represents a state of mind which he has just escaped, or wishes to escape, then he kills him or sends him packing to some remote place. It is like a sophisticated form of voodoo, a channelling of the primal powers of satire against a part of the self which is to be disowned. Through the systematic destruction of personae such as Paul Pennyfeather, Adam Symes, and Tony Last, Waugh the artist morally evolves; he sheds former selves like a snake shedding its skins. Waugh read Plato's *Republic* in 1925, and the similes of the sun, the divided line, and the cave seem to have influenced his view of maturation as a gradual approach, through the shadows of the visible and intelligible realms, to the light of absolute reality. In *Brideshead Revisited* Waugh compares human maturation to the ripening of a good wine; but perhaps a better analogy is the laborious climb up a long ladder from shadows to light. In Waugh's view, the maturing process—that is, the gradual realization of one's vocation—consists of a perpetual escape from a series of insufficiently enlightened selves. So it is that Paul Pennyfeather and Adam Fenwick-Symes "mysteriously disappear," and Waugh the author of *A Little Learning* feels "no identity" with the caddish little boy of the Lancing diaries. But that same little boy already had the self-castigating frame of mind which was to produce the savage comedy of *Decline and Fall* and *A Handful of Dust*. All he needed was experience and the time to realize his talent.

Waugh says that he abandoned his diary on the day he left Lancing and resumed it on the day he went down from Oxford; in an unpublished portion of the manuscript of *A Little Learning* he observes, "In times of change and high excitement, such as my years at the university. . . . I was too active and dissipated to pause and make a note."[46] But in a letter to Dudley Carew ("Carey"), written while he was at Oxford, Waugh says, "For the last fortnight I have been nearly insane. . . . My diary for the period is destroyed."[47] Subsequently, it appears, he destroyed all the diaries for the eventful Oxford period, and for other stressful times such as his separation from Evelyn Gardner in 1929 and his "Pinfold" hallucinations in 1954.

Despite the paucity of documentation on the Oxford years, three phases may be distinguished in Waugh's life there: shyness, extravagance, and withdrawal. For his first two terms Waugh lived "unobtrusively" in rooms over the Hertford College Junior Common Room. He dined in hall in subfusc clothes, drank beer, smoked a pipe, and cycled through the countryside. In short, he lived like Paul Pennyfeather, or like Charles Ryder before he met Sebastian. In another letter to Carew, Waugh remarks that he is very shy and a little lonely, but is settling down and feels that he is going to be very happy. He says that he hopes to find congenial friends, having so far found only a gloomy scholar, some aristocratic New College men who talked of winter sports and cars, and a Carthusian scholar who talked filth.[48] Then comes a dramatic change, which seems to have stemmed from Waugh's introduction to the wildly unconventional Hypocrites' Club by the eccentric Terence Greenidge. From this period date Waugh's friendships with Richard Pares (his "first homosexual love"),[49] Alastair Graham, and also with Harold Acton, who remembers him as "a prancing faun thinly disguised by conventional apparel."[50] The brilliant friendships Waugh now made mark his entry into what he calls "quintessential Oxford" (p. 167). For Waugh, Oxford was a "Kingdom of Cokayne," a fountain of youth. At Oxford, he says, he was "reborn in full youth," more naive and less cynical than he was at Lancing (pp. 169–70). From now until the end of his "indiscriminate bonhomie" in 1924 he gave four or five luncheon parties a term, and kept open house for a noisy, beer-drinking crowd which met daily for "offal." Waugh's Dionysiac period now began: he developed an interest in Silenus and made wood-cuts of Pan and Bacchus.[51] He wrote to Tom Driberg, then a younger Lancing contemporary, "Do let me most seriously advise you to take to drink. There is nothing like the aesthetic pleasure of being drunk and if you do it in the right way you can avoid being ill next day. That is the greatest thing Oxford has to teach."[52]

Harold Acton exerted the most important intellectual influence on Waugh during this period. Acton, who is in large part the original of Anthony Blanche in *Brideshead Revisited*, had declared war on the traditional aestheticism of the Nineties and on its contemporary representatives. He also disliked the "yokelish" hearties who succeeded the Georgians. An admirer of Rimbaud, Verlaine, the Russian ballet, the Sitwells, and Eliot, Acton led Waugh "far away from Francis Crease to the baroque and the rococo and to *The Waste Land*" (p. 197). In *Memoirs of an Aesthete* he gave expression to his aims: "We should combat ugliness; we should create clarity where there was confusion; we should overcome mass indifference; we should exterminate false prophets." [53] Acton favoured dawns rather than twilights and preferred the early Victorian period to the Nineties, affecting bowler, stock, side-whiskers, and the broad trousers which, he says, eventually led to "Oxford bags." He stressed that the intangible fantasy he loved "did not necessarily mean to turn one's back on actuality." [54] "Actuality" formed the keystone of Acton's views. Even while admitting a certain indebtedness to Acton, Waugh is careful to point out that although Acton was always the leader, he, Waugh, was "not always" the follower. He says in *A Little Learning*, "What, I think, we had in common was *gusto*, in the English use of the word; a zest for the variety and absurdity of the life opening to us; a veneration for (not always the same) artists, a scorn for the bogus" (p. 197). Their scorn for "the bogus" is important—but Acton's scorn stems from a love of actuality while Waugh's is firmly grounded in religion. Waugh's careful phrasing makes it plain that he does not consider himself Acton's disciple, and there is confirmation for his aloofness in Charles Ryder's coolness towards Anthony Blanche in *Brideshead Revisited*.

Throughout Waugh's Oxford years shortage of money was a constant problem. He wildly overspent the by no means meagre allowance which his father gave him, and by early 1924 he was forced to auction off his finely bound and as yet unpaid-for books to alleviate his financial distress. According to Peter Quennell, it was this auction which inaugurated a new phase in Waugh's Oxford life. [55] Abandoning his expensive friends and tastes, Waugh now drank beer and, almost penniless, frequented the dives of South Oxford. In a letter to Carew he glumly remarked that he was "highly depressed" and was "quite broke and rather stupid and quite incredibly depraved morally." [56] He said, "I am keeping my balance but I may crash [?] any moment." [57] Fits of depression and despair now became frequent.

During Waugh's Oxford period the man of the world is not much in evidence; the artist and the (sometimes) happy pagan are in the ascendant. At Oxford he contributed cartoons, articles, and stories to *The Isis*, *The Cherwell*, and *The Oxford Fortnightly Review*. One remarkable story, "Antony, Who Sought Things That Were Lost," appeared in Harold Acton's *The Oxford Broom* (June 1923). In it, Lady Elizabeth begs to be imprisoned with Count Antony "in a cell cut deeply in the grey stone" because "there would be no captivity where Antony was and no freedom where he was not" (p. 16). But their immature love withers in their picturesque prison; Lady Elizabeth makes love to the jailer, and Antony kills her. In another story, "Portrait of a Young Man with Career" (*The Isis*, 30 May 1923), a languid protagonist named "Evelyn" dreams of crushing the skull of a worldly bore who detains him from his bath. Less ambitious than at Lancing, Waugh appears to have made little attempt at Oxford to become a leader. In a February 1922 letter to Carew he writes, "I am not yet the centre of any group but on the fringes of many." [58]

After obtaining a disappointing third in his final schools, Waugh left Oxford one term short of the degree requirements. He had planned to stay with Hugh Lygon in Merton Street. Instead, he went to live with Alastair Graham in a caravan in a field near Beckley; from there they went to Ireland for a vacation. Waugh had known Graham since Christmas 1923, or slightly before, and he later drew upon his character when he created the brilliant Lord Sebastian Flyte of *Brideshead Revisited*. In *A Little Learning* Waugh speaks of him as "the friend of my heart."

Lack of success characterizes the years 1924–28. Waugh calls his diary for the period "a record of continuous failure" (p. 209). Nevertheless, from a chaos of drink and indebtedness his career slowly emerged and took shape. Immediately after leaving Oxford, Waugh began "The Temple at Thatch," a never-to-be-published short novel about "an undergraduate who inherited . . . an eighteenth-century classical folly where he set up house and . . . practised black magic" (p. 223). The young black magician's "Temple" appears to be the first of Waugh's lush places—unless we choose to award that distinction to the cell in "Antony" or to the river scene in "The Balance," which we shall consider in a moment. In September 1924 Waugh wrote and directed *The Scarlet Woman*,[59] a short comic film about the farcical attempts of the Dean of Balliol to convert the Prince of Wales to Roman Catholicism; Arthur Waugh was a delighted onlooker at the filming and screening. Naughty and irreverent, the film hilariously lampoons the Establishment for its indifference to religion and mocks the Catholics for their ineptitude. Beatrice, a poverty-stricken cabaret singer (excellently played by Elsa Lanchester in her first role), resembles the naifs of the early stories, torn between inadequate options. The action ends with a close-up of children's faces in an orphanage, prompting the viewer to wonder where these fatherless innocents will find reliable guidance in the future. Waugh played two roles himself: the decadent Dean of Balliol and the penniless peer, Lord Borrowington. Later in the autumn Waugh enrolled at the Heatherley School of Fine Art in London. His drawings survive, but they are only competent. He later told Julian Jebb that he "didn't have the moral qualities" [60] to be a painter.

Feeling "neglected by Oxford," [61] he began to return on weekends, "still dressed as an undergraduate" in the "new fashion that term—high-necked jumpers and broad trousers" (p. 213). The diaries record hangovers, orgies, flying lavatory-seats, and fires. Waugh says of these bacchanalian weekends, "They . . . rendered me . . . increasingly listless in the drudgery of the life-class. When we closed for Christmas vacation I signed off at Heatherley's" (p. 214). Revolted by his dissipation, he noted in his diary, "I have decided that a gay life is not to be borne and have asked James Guthrie to take me as a pupil in the country." [62] But Guthrie, director of the Pear Tree Press near Bognor Regis, "proved to be entirely dependent upon photography" (p. 214) for his beautiful designs, and Waugh abandoned the idea of becoming his apprentice. After agreeing to forgo his allowance if his father would pay off his debts, he took a fateful step. He accepted a position at Arnold House, in Denbighshire, thereby entering the "heterogeneous and undefinable underworld" of private education (p. 84).

Alastair, who had just returned from Africa, "accepted without reproach [Waugh's] temporary defection from the arts" (p. 216). But Olivia Plunket-Greene, with whom he was falling ever more deeply in love, objected: "She told me that I was a great artist and must not be a schoolmaster." [63] Waugh went anyway, and was intensely unhappy. When not stunning himself with drink to forget his nauseating new profession, he made wood-cuts for Olivia and thought of new books to write, including one about Silenus. [64] During the Easter vacation he went with the Plunket-Greenes and other friends to Lundy Island, where he was surprised to witness "an amazing orgy" [65] and saddened that he could not cure himself of being in love with Olivia.

As the summer term began he wrote, "I think that my finances have never been so desperate or my spirits so depressed." [66] In despair over Acton's lukewarm response to "The Temple at Thatch," and over his failure to become C. K. Scott-Moncrieff's secretary in Pisa, Waugh left a suicide note and swam out to sea under a full moon. But a chance encounter with a school of jelly-fish shocked him into a better mood and he returned safely to shore, to finish his term at Arnold House "with a heart of lead and nerves of fire." [67]

The failure of Waugh's attempt on his life through such a fortuitous change of mood fired his imagination, which was already engaged with a story about the need to outgrow his anarchic Oxford self. The result was a remarkable short novel which gives a foretaste of themes and achievements to come. On 5 May 1925 Waugh notes that he is working out the plan for a new book. On 28 May he writes, "I have quite suddenly received inspiration about my book. I am making the first chapter a cinema

film and have been writing furiously ever since." There can be little doubt
that Waugh's suicide attempt on 2 July influenced the events of his story,
which was finished by 26 August: "It is odd but, I think, quite good," he
observed.

The story is "The Balance: A Yarn of the Good Old Days of Broad
Trousers and High-Necked Jumpers."[68] It is the tale of Adam Doure, a
divided personality whose barbarous nature is on the verge of overcom-
ing his artistic nature. He is in love with Imogen Quest, just as Waugh
was in love with Olivia Plunket-Greene. When Imogen's mother pro-
hibits them from marrying, Adam sinks into suicidal despair. Three sce-
narios flit through his mind in ascending order of preference: suicide at
home, which he rejects as unspeakably vulgar; the suicide of an African
native dragging himself away to a solitary death in the jungle; the suicide
of a decadent Petronian voluptuary among sybaritic delights. Opting for
the last, Adam resolves to have a final, epicurean binge in Oxford before
killing himself. But at Oxford all of Adam's "civilized" friends are busy;
only the demonic Ernest Vaughan, his least-liked friend, is free to accom-
pany him. Ernest lives, as Waugh did, in "one of the uglier and less re-
nowned colleges"; his rooms are a chaos of caricatures, graffiti, and galley
proofs, and a dog-eared drawing of Beelzebub droops upon the wall. His
fellow students recoil from him as from "a black magician." Ernest
proves to be a happy guest, and his spirits soar as Adam's plummet
(Vaughan's love of "rackets" marks him out as a precursor of Basil Seal).
No amount of drink can cheer the suicidal Adam, but the anarchic Ernest
leaps into a car and drives it into a shop-front.[69] Policemen converge and
carry Ernest from the wreck. Now "Adam is alone." The point of all this
is that Ernest Vaughan is an externalization of Adam's suicidal nature,
which has been threatening to upset the precarious balance between life
and death. Ernest must die so that Adam may live. If the story is seen in a
biographical perspective, then "E. V." is the dark half of "E. W." which
so nearly gained the upper hand that moonlit night in July 1925.

At his hotel Adam falls asleep, and in the morning he has become more
rational. He escapes from the "macabre dance of shadows" which he
thinks is all that remains of his desire for death, and, speaking to his reflection in the river, repudiates his self of yesterday as insubstantial. He
identifies "the balance of life and death" with "the balance of appetite
and reason," and adds, "the reason remains constant—the appetite varies." In the end, he says, "circumstance" decides whether the appetite for
life gets the upper hand over the appetite for death. Adam's reflection is
sceptical of his highly naturalistic account, however, and the reader
should be sceptical too. For in attributing "the balance" to mere circumstance, or fortune, Adam has failed to consider his providential escape

from the poison he drank after his binge, and he completely ignores "the Grace of God" which has allowed him to fall asleep. In an interesting assertion, Adam tells his reflection that art is an attempt to "preserve in the shapes of things the personality whose dissolution you foresee inevitably," but this too is of dubious validity. While Waugh probably shared Adam's opinion when he was at Oxford, he soon rejected the notion that art could provide real permanence, and he found a stay in religion instead.

Eighteen months after Waugh wrote this fascinating little tale, and after a long series of rejections, including one by Leonard Woolf, "The Balance" was published in a collection edited by Alec Waugh. Evelyn received £2.5.6. for it and had a good dinner at Thame on the proceeds.

From September 1925 until February 1927, when his headmaster sacked him for drunkenness and for trying to seduce a matron, Waugh taught at Aston Clinton in Buckinghamshire, in "a school for backward peers." His personal life was still a shambles, but he was cheered by the presence of Richard Plunket-Greene and his wife Elizabeth, and by his cousin Claud Cockburn, who lived at nearby Tring. On weekends Waugh visited friends in London and Oxford, travelling by means of a dilapidated motorcycle named "Queensbury." He developed attachments to several of his pupils, whom he soon ceased to call "lunatics" and "poor mad boys."[70] He invited them to tea in his rooms, went swimming and played tennis with them; to one of them he read *The Wind in the Willows*. At Christmas Waugh went to Paris and a homosexual brothel, which he left "in chastity" and without regret.[71] In the spring there were visits from the "monotonously pederastic" Young, who was to figure so spectacularly as Grimes in *Decline and Fall*. On one of his visits Young "seduced a garage boy in the hedge."[72] During the General Strike Waugh became a member of the Civil Constabulary Reserve, an event later incorporated into *Brideshead Revisited*. In August he went to Scotland with Alastair Graham and his mother. Mrs. Graham, Waugh says, "raged a good deal at first." Upon his return, he went to France with Alastair and the Richard Plunket-Greenes, visiting Luna Park, Tours, and Chambord Cathedral. At this time Alastair Graham privately printed Waugh's essay, "The Pre-Raphaelite Brotherhood." Waugh had researched it while recovering from a sprained ankle, an injury which he sustained after jumping from the window of the Clarendon bar to elude friends bearing a dinner invitation.

In the autumn of 1926 Waugh continued to be a part-time Bright Young Person. He attended a party given by "a whole lot of perverse young women with eyeglasses and whisky" and another at which "Sir Francis Laking, dressed first as a girl and then, stark naked, attempted a

Charleston."[73] He resolved on "a life of sobriety, chastity and obedience,"[74] and discharged his debts with £150 given him by his mother.
At Christmas he went to Athens to visit Alastair, who was there on consular service. On the way he read *The Varieties of Religious Experience*
and attempted drawings "for a book . . . to be called the 'Annals of Con-
stitutional Monarchy'."[75] In Athens "the talk . . . [was] only of male
prostitutes." Upon his return he learned that Kegan Paul had rejected his
"mannered and 'literary'" piece called "Noah: or the Future of Intoxication," which he never mentions again. In the middle of February he was
sacked. Penniless, he wrote, "It seems to me the time has arrived to set
about being a man of letters."[76]

Only a few days before, Hugh Chesterman had offered Waugh ten
guineas to contribute to the *New Decameron*. Accordingly, he "spent
two days writing a story about a duke." The story is "The Tutor's Tale,"[77]
and, strongly autobiographical once again, it owes much to Waugh's interest in the "backward peers" at Aston Clinton. Ernest Vaughan reappears. Not dead after all, he has been sent down from Oxford and becomes the tutor of George Verney, the "noticeably underdeveloped"
Duke of Stayle. George has no parents, and his relatives think that he is
mad; but the truth is that they have "kept the boy shut away" because
they do not wish to spend money on him. He has had "no regular education," his clothes are too small, he has never been to London, and he
knows nothing of geography. His aunt speaks to him as if he were a
child of six, and the only thing he has been taught is how to smoke.[78]
George Verney is the first of Waugh's naifs, and his arrested development
stems from the negligence of his elders. He lives behind the "interminable
and dilapidated walls" of Stayle, a quietly decaying sanctuary where time
stands still.[79] Significantly, the gates of Stayle are padlocked: it is the first
example in Waugh of a refuge which proves to be a prison. George and
Ernest set out for London and the Continent; George develops rapidly
and demonstrates "a fresh and acute critical faculty and a natural fastidiousness" which have been stunted but not yet ruined by Stayle. In the end
George's parsimonious relatives change their mind about his European
tour and he is reincarcerated behind the "ironwork" of Stayle. They, not
George, are mad.

The story is only partly about Ernest Vaughan; we notice that once
again "E. V." is one-half of "E. double-you" and that Waugh continues
to think of himself as a split personality and to externalize that split in his
fiction. One of the most interesting aspects of the story is an apparently
innocuous remark of Ernest's: "I am not at all in the habit of moving in
these exalted circles, but I have a rather grand godmother who shows a
sporadic interest in my affairs." One suspects that this "rather grand god-

mother" is the precursor of Margot Best-Chetwynde and Mrs. Rattery—
that is, she is Fortuna herself, the figure who in a variety of guises dominates Waugh's early fiction.

After a miserable month as an usher in a school in Notting Hill Gate,
where the masters "spit in the fire and scratch their genitals," [80] Waugh
joined the staff of the *Daily Express*. Although the editor sacked him
after six weeks, Waugh's short appointment paved the way for later and
more lucrative associations with the press—as correspondent for *The
Times* at Haile Selassie's coronation and for the *Daily Mail* during the
Italian invasion of Ethiopia. Spring brought his first meeting with "such a
nice girl called Evelyn Gardner." [81] He now displayed an increasing interest in fashions and nightlife, wrote his first review articles for the *Bookman*, and on 3 September began *Decline and Fall*. Applications for other
teaching positions and for "a fantastic job about toothbrushes" [82] fell
through. In October he enrolled in the Academy of Carpentry in South-
ampton Row. As Evelyn Gardner and *Decline and Fall* occupied more
and more of his time, Waugh ceased to make diary entries. By the time he
began again, six months later, he had published *Rossetti*, [83] completed
*Decline and Fall*, and was contemplating a (never-to-be-completed) biography of Charles Wesley.

Less than three years before, Waugh's "Julian apathy" had brought
him to the brink of suicide; now Fortune was again smiling on him. He
had two books to his credit, and soon Evelyn Gardner was to become his
bride. We must now pause to consider the disastrous relationship which
barely a year later left Waugh embittered and disillusioned.

Waugh's diary entries for this turbulent period are irregular and somewhat guarded, and some portions (December 1927–June 1928, November 1928–May 1930) appear to have been destroyed. Christopher
Sykes's biography sheds a little light on Waugh's activities at this time, as
do Waugh's *Letters*, but I have chosen to rely upon the recollections of
Lady Pansy Lamb (then Pansy Pakenham, who "played . . . the confidante throughout" this period ). [84] Pansy Lamb and Evelyn Gardner were
girl friends and débutantes in the Twenties, and at the time when Waugh
first met them, the two young women were sharing rooms in an Ebury
Street bed and breakfast hotel. Although it was perhaps not usual for former débutantes to live in such circumstances, their unconventional arrangements had the blessing of Evelyn Gardner's mother. Lady Burghclere regarded Pansy as a "steady" girl, and saw her as a guardian angel
for her sometimes wayward daughter, who had already demonstrated an
unfortunate predilection for "cads and bounders." [85]

As Lady Pansy Lamb remembers her, Evelyn Gardner was a generous
and often extravagant young woman of "enormous charm." At twenty-

four, she was small, with a round face, round dark eyes, small nose
and mouth, and "beautiful long slender hands." She lacked her sisters'
beauty, but was nevertheless "delightful," "full of attractions," and animated by an "attractive spontaneity." She liked to tease, but "was never a
heartless flirt"; on the contrary, she was warm and kind. One of her most
remarkable gifts was her ability to establish a rapport immediately with
anyone she met—shop-people and servants "adored her" and "would do
anything for her" because she drew out their tales of misfortune and listened to them with great sympathy. But the spontaneity that could be attractive also made her restless: admirer after fascinated admirer expressed his devotion only to find that she had "flitted off" with someone
new. Pansy Lamb recalls that Evelyn Gardner did not want to make com-
mitments, and could not sustain relationships under unfavourable conditions. "At that time she was not prepared to take the rough with the
smooth." Although she was generous, she was also "light," for she somehow "couldn't feel how her actions affected other people." She "wanted a
lot of attention to keep her going," and "was not a person to be patient."
Yet she did not brood: after their marriage failed, Waugh showed that he
was "a person of deep resentments and long-standing feelings," but his
former wife was "utterly without spleen of any kind."

Evelyn Gardner's first engagement was to "an impecunious member of
the *beau monde* in the Guards," a "principled person who took marriage
seriously." [86] The relationship might have succeeded if Lady Burghclere
had not disapproved of the young man's poverty. Perhaps this frustrated
early love affair was damaging to Evelyn Gardner, for after it she "was
always getting engaged to unsuitable people." When her mother took her
to Australia to break off her relationship with the guardsman, she became engaged to the ship's purser. Pansy, confidante in the matter of the
guardsman, was "shocked" at Evelyn Gardner's behaviour; she was even
more upset when, not long afterwards, Evelyn became engaged to "a
frightful bounder" named Barry Gifford, the secretary of Mrs. Brooke, "a
vulgar little woman" who was married to one of the "White Rajahs" and
bore the title of "Ranee of Sarawak." Evelyn's engagement to the illegitimate Gifford soon broke down, and in the meantime she met Evelyn
Waugh. Dudley Carew says that the two Evelyns met in his flat, [87] but
Pansy Lamb recalls that Waugh had come in the Ranee's train to Ebury
Street. "No particular impression was made at first," and "it was only
gradually that [Waugh] began to court Evelyn Gardner seriously." Pansy
fostered the relationship, for here at last, despite his defects, was an acceptable suitor. As she later remarked, "Evelyn was not a very suitable
*parti*, but at least he was not middle-aged." She wrote, "I saw Evelyn W.
chiefly as a possible husband for Evelyn G. and my energies were directed

to coping with the difficulties, parental, financial, temperamental with which they were surrounded." [88]

During the next six months Waugh saw "a certain amount" of Olivia Plunket-Greene, his most serious previous attachment, and "a lot" of Evelyn Gardner.[89] A deceptively casual diary entry in early December indicates that Waugh planned to spend Christmas with Charles Sutro "unless engaged to be married before then."[90] Four days later he was. He proposed at the Ritz and was supported in his suit by Pansy who spoke in his favour to Evelyn Gardner's elder sister Alathea Fry. (Pansy, meanwhile, had become secretly engaged to the painter Henry Lamb, whom she had met while studying architecture.) Early in the winter of 1927–28 Pansy and Evelyn Gardner moved from Ebury Street to Sloane Square, and from there they went to a boarding house in Wimborne, Dorset, where they remained until May. There they had visitors: Henry Lamb, who had a house in nearby Poole, and Evelyn Waugh, who came to stay in a pub called the Barley Mow a few miles away.

By Easter the two Evelyns decided to break the news of their engagement to their parents. The Waughs took it well enough, but Lady Burghclere was angry; she did not want an unemployed carpenter with a £2-a-week allowance as her son-in-law, and she made the audacious pair pledge that they would not be secretly married. Upon returning to London, Waugh went home to North End Road, while Pansy and Evelyn Gardner went to new lodgings in Montague Place; and there, for a time, the matter rested.

Although she was impatient by nature, Evelyn Gardner was not anxious to marry. She was far more experienced in such matters than her fiancé, for her many adventures had greatly changed her from "the old-fashioned thing" she had been when Pansy Pakenham first knew her. As before, she was finding it hard to make a commitment. And there is even the possibility, as Lady Pansy later remarked, that Evelyn Gardner was sensually cold and cared more about the emotional excitement of the *affaire* than about the stability and love it offered. In any event, she was not eager to marry, but Evelyn Waugh was; "the ardour was all on his side." And so she agreed. She later told a shocked Nancy Mitford that she had never loved Waugh, and had only married him in order to escape her domineering mother.[91]

Evelyn Waugh and Evelyn Gardner (or "he-Evelyn" and "she-Evelyn," as their friends now called them) were married in St. Paul's Portman Square at noon on 27 June 1928. They had bought their wedding licence a few days earlier, according to Waugh, after having "got bored waiting for the right bus" to the motion pictures.[92] It was "a dreary low church," Lady Pansy recalls, "not the sort that our relations would go to, with

posters outside asking, 'are you saved?'" After champagne cocktails at
the 500 Club and a luncheon at Boulestin's (provided by Harold Acton, who witnessed the ceremony with Pansy, Alec Waugh, and Robert
Byron), the two Evelyns entrained for Oxford and Beckley, where in earlier years Waugh had stayed with Alastair Graham. A week later Waugh
wrote to his parents and to Lady Burghclere, announcing the marriage.
The elder Waughs feared that she-Evelyn's mother would think they had
been in collusion, but "made the best of a bad job." However, Lady
Burghclere was enraged ("quite inexpressibly pained" was how she put
it)[93] at seeing her daughter escape into matrimony.

Nine days later the Waughs were back in London, and he-Evelyn was
"hard at work on proofs of Decline and Fall," accepted by Ralph Strauss
at Chapman and Hall after Tom Balston at Duckworth's had found it too
risqué. After living for a short time with Waugh's parents at Golders
Green, the two Evelyns took up residence in a small flat in Canonbury
Square, "a remote, unfashionable and dilapidated part of London in
those days," and for some months lived there in happy domesticity.
Waugh varnished newspapers onto chests and contentedly monitored the
sales of Decline and Fall. In early October she-Evelyn fell ill with a nervous disorder and convalesced for a month. "She was always rather delicate," Lady Pansy Lamb recalls; "her parents were quite old—her father
was in his sixties and her mother in her forties when she was born." Then
early in the winter of 1928–29 the newly-weds embarked on the ill-
starred Mediterranean cruise which later formed the basis of Labels
(1930). In Labels they appear under the pseudonyms of "Geoffrey" and
"Juliet" and their activities are reported in the third person by a bachelor
narrator. Certain painful circumstances explain Waugh's oblique narrative method. "Juliet" nearly died of pneumonia in Port Said, and by the
time Waugh sat down to write about their travels, his wife had fallen in
love with another man. During this period, possibly, she-Evelyn experienced what Pansy Lamb has termed "the hardness in Waugh's nature"
and "his intolerance of feminine caprices"; possibly, as Christopher Sykes
speculates, her sickness destroyed her love for her husband.[94] In any
event, when she returned she was not the same young woman who had
embarked a few short months before. The collapse of Waugh's marriage
several months later came as a complete surprise to him. In July, when he
was away in the country working on his second novel, his wife wrote to
tell him that she had fallen in love with John Heygate. Waugh was "utterly astonished"; it was "a nasty jar," preceded, as he wrote to his parents, "by no kind of quarrel or estrangement."[95] She-Evelyn wrote also to
Pansy Lamb and told her, "I have decided to go off with John." Pansy did
not even know who "John" was. He turned out to be a writer at the BBC

who "was considered good-looking and had curly hair, like Millais. He was also very selfish." Waugh initiated proceedings with the aid of the eccentric lawyer E. S. P. Haynes, and by June 1930 the divorce was formally granted. Lady Pansy was "pained and shocked and distressed" at the turn of events, and later wrote, "The breakup of their marriage . . . came as a great shock to me, and I always felt slightly guilty for having promoted it. However Evelyn Waugh never seemed to blame me." [96] For his part, Waugh wrote to Harold Acton, "I did not know it was possible to be so miserable and live, but I am told that this is a common experience." [97]

Waugh concluded Labels with a wry tribute to the goddess Fortuna, "the least capricious of deities," who "arranges things on the just and rigid system that no one shall be very happy for very long." [98] Three months after his divorce was granted, Waugh repudiated the world of Fortuna—"the world of wild aberration without theological significance," [99] as he later called it—by entering the Roman Catholic Church. Waugh's transition from pagan to Christian appears abrupt. But although his choice seems incompatible with his previous way of life, we shall see that it was by no means sudden or unpremeditated.

## CHAPTER 2

# God and Taste

Waugh was religious from his earliest years. His family tree "burgeoned on every twig" with Anglican churchmen, and his own youthful "ecclesiological interests" were Anglo-Catholic. When Waugh was nine his father gave him Mary MacGregor's *The Story of Rome*, having inscribed it:

> *All roads, they tell us, lead to Rome;*
> *Yet, Evelyn, stay awhile at home!* [1]

As a child Waugh attended Sunday services with Lucy, his nonconformist nanny. But in 1915 his parents began to take him to the Anglo-Catholic services of Basil Bourchier, a "highly flamboyant" and "totally preposterous parson" (pp. 91–92) who preached at St. Jude's Hampstead Garden Suburb. Anglo-Catholicism was not new to Arthur Waugh. At the time of his son's birth "he had a brief Anglo-Catholic phase and frequented St. Augustine's Kilburn . . . but he never took very seriously the doctrines taught there" (p. 68). Even though the elder Waugh took "the doctrines" lightly, they deeply affected his son, who later held his father responsible for leading him into a heretical belief.

Until 1915 Waugh's drawings had dealt with the usual exotica of childhood: slaves, Hindus, natives, war. After that time, they began to feature "saints and angels inspired by mediaeval illuminations" (p. 93). One of these, remarkably well done, shows St. Augustine disembarking in England. [2] Waugh now went about the countryside investigating "church decorations and the degrees of Anglicanism—'Prot, Mod, High, Spikey'—which they represented" (p. 93). Waugh preferred the "Spikey." A representative diary entry from Waugh's eleventh year reads: "In the evening we went to church. We struck a horrible low one. I was the only person who crossed myself and bowed to the altar." Another reads: "It is a beautiful old [church] and is very spikey. It has got some very Roman candles on sort of rings standing on the ground but without the image in the centre. The Blessed Sacrament is reserved in the Lady Chapel."³ Waugh made a little shrine bearing frontals and statues of saints, before which he burned incense; chasubles and Erastianism were now considerations of major importance. He expressed the desire to become a clergyman, but his mother was not sympathetic. In emulation of Newman's "Dream of Gerontius" he composed "The World to Come," a "poem about Purgatory in the metre of *Hiawatha*."⁴ Speaking in the first person, the young poet describes his own death and introduction to the other world under the tutelage of the angel Michael. He sees look-alike armies of warlike Christians wielding crosses and Madonnas, and these are contrasted with a Moslem "with a kind and gentle bearing."⁵ The narrator's downward gaze typifies the *sub specie aeternitatis* point of view which Waugh later brought to bear on life and used in his novels.

Waugh's interest in Anglo-Catholicism persisted well into his years at Lancing College where, in his second term, he "defied convention by kneeling at the *incarnatus* in the creed at Holy Communion." He suffered no recriminations for his piety, for "if there was no great devotion at Lancing there was a respect for religion" (p. 109). Church-going was of central importance at Lancing, where the chapel was considered the most "spectacular post-Reformation ecclesiastical building in the kingdom" (p. 98). Waugh did not find it excessive to attend chapel twice a day and three times on Sundays. Indeed, he found "refuge from the surrounding loneliness" in the morning and evening services (p. 112), and he read *The Bible in Art*, *The Divine Comedy*, and *The Child's Book of Saints*.

By the end of Waugh's stay at Lancing, his "phase of churchiness" (p. 94) was over. Chapel began to bore him, and he "lightheartedly" shed his inherited faith under the influence of Pope, Leibnitz, and the Oxford theologian, Rawlinson.⁶ In his diary for 13 June 1921 Waugh notes, "In the last few weeks I have ceased to be a Christian (sensation off!) . . . I am sure it is only a phase." Tom Driberg remembers that when they were sacristans at Lancing Waugh once prepared the communion table and walked away, saying, "If it's good enough for me, it's good enough for God." Yet he denies that Waugh ever completely lost his faith.⁷ What Waugh certainly *did* lose at this time, however, was his respect for the authenticity of Anglicanism. As he later said to John Freeman, "Well, I think I'd always—that is to say always from the age of 16 or so—realised that Catholicism was Christianity, that all the other forms of Christianity were only good so far as they chipped little bits off the main block."⁸ Moreover, Waugh characteristically exaggerated when he told Freeman that "from sixteen to twenty-eight I didn't go to church at all."

In later life Waugh rejected his "precocious religiosity" as an "absurd" hobby, based on merely aesthetic attractions. Yet he declined to "dismiss as pure fancy these intimations of truths which I was more soberly, but still most imperfectly to grasp in later years" (p. 94). Even through the "rollicking joke" of Basil Bourchier Waugh had "some glimpse of higher mysteries" (p. 92). The position he reached well before the time of his conversion was that Anglicanism and Anglo-Catholicism lacked validity as real forms of Christianity. Since they imitated Roman Catholicism and were derived from it, they were parodies and heresies. As Waugh wrote years later in letters to John Betjeman, "Many things have puzzled me from time to time about the Christian religion but one thing has always been self evident—the bogosity of the Church of England . . . The nearer these people ape the ways of Catholics the nearer they approach flat blasphemy." "Catholics and Anglo-Catholics . . . may look alike to you," he wrote to Betjeman, adding that they were as different as "Trust House timbering and a genuine Tudor building." [9] Delusively beautiful as they were, however, Anglicanism and Anglo-Catholicism were not altogether worthless, for they could act as routes to the true faith, just as Charles Ryder's love of profane art foreshadows his love of God in *Brideshead Revisited*.

Waugh claims that he never attended chapel at Oxford. His life there seems to have been as pagan as the wood-cuts of Pan and Dionysus which he liked to make. One of his Oxford short stories centres on a black mass. [10] And in his letters to Dudley Carew he is often sarcastic about religion. In an early letter he complains that the university has too much religion and too few brains in it; in another he recounts how he has steeled his heart like Pharaoh to escape conversion by an American revivalist. [11] But in a letter of slightly later date he confesses, "Chesterton beckons like a star." [12]

Despite the dissipation of his post-Oxford years, Waugh did not altogether forget religion. He still went to church; [13] furthermore, he was now talking about Roman Catholicism: "Claud and I took Audrey to supper," he notes on 22 December 1925, "and sat up until 7 in the morning arguing about the Roman Church." On 20 January 1926 he notes that Olivia's mother "has lent [him] von Hügel's letters to her to read." (These were letters of spiritual counsel from the Roman Catholic theologian, Baron von Hügel; the pious Gwen Plunket-Greene, later a Roman Catholic convert, exerted a strong influence on Waugh at this time. In *Decline and Fall* Paul Pennyfeather offers a copy of von Hügel to his friend Stubbs.) On 31 July 1926 he "got drunk in the evening and argued about foreigners and absolution." And on 20 February 1927 he records, "Next Thursday I am to visit a Father Underhill about being a parson. Last night I was drunk. How odd those two sentences seem together."

Father Underhill, alas, "spoke respectfully of the Duke of Westminster and disrespectfully of my vocation to the church." It would seem, then, that even during the riotous Twenties, and well before *Decline and Fall* and *Vile Bodies*, Waugh was still interested in religion. And this evidence comes from diaries which are especially reticent about spiritual matters.

From 23 November 1928 to 19 May 1930, Waugh's diaries are blank, probably destroyed in an attempt to expunge all trace of Evelyn Gardner. But profound changes were taking place, because only a month and a half after the diaries resume, Waugh notes, "To tea at Alexander Square with Olivia. I said would she please find a Jesuit to instruct me." Olivia Plunket-Greene succeeded, and six days later on 8 July Waugh noted that he had been to see Father Martin D'Arcy: "blue chin and fine, slippery mind." To John Freeman Waugh later said, "I was under instruction—literally under instruction—for about three months, but of course I'd interested myself in it before, reading books independently and so on." [14] On 29 September 1930 Waugh entered the Roman Catholic Church. Characteristically, Waugh's decision was rational rather than sentimental: "and so on firm intellectual conviction but with little emotion I was admitted into the Church." [15]

Waugh was surprisingly open about this dramatic and highly personal development, and on several occasions attempted to explain what he had done. In a 1930 *Daily Express* article he drew a characteristic distinction, claiming that the present choice in Western civilization was not between Protestantism and Catholicism, but between (Catholic) Christianity and chaos; civilization "came into being through Christianity, and without it has no significance or power to command allegiance." [16] He argued that it was "no longer possible, as it was in the time of Gibbon, to accept the benefits of civilization, and at the same time deny the supernatural order upon which it rests." In "Come Inside" (1949) he argued, "England was Catholic for nine hundred years, then Protestant for three hundred, then agnostic for a century. The Catholic structure still lies lightly buried beneath every phase of English life; history, topography, law, archaeology everywhere reveal Catholic origins." [17] Logic showed him, he said, that "no heresy or schism could be right and the Church wrong": "It was possible that all were wrong, that the whole Christian revelation was an imposture or a misconception. But if the Christian revelation was true, then the Church was the society founded by Christ and all other bodies were only good so far as they had salvaged something from the wrecks of the Great Schism and the Reformation. This proposition seemed so plain to me that it admitted of no discussion." In 1953 he reverted to the same question when he said to Stephen Black, "I never in my life doubted that Roman Catholicism—never in my reasoning life—

was the genuine form of Christianity. But for a long time I didn't believe in the truth of it." [18]

It is evident, then, that religion fascinated Waugh throughout his life, except perhaps in his Oxford years; thus his religious life by no means began with his conversion. From about his sixteenth year he believed that Roman Catholicism was the only true form of Christianity, that Protestantism was a heresy and Anglicanism only a pale copy. He never wholly repudiated them, however, because even through their mists of error they provided a glimpse of "higher mysteries." He believed that there has been a steady decline, through identifiable stages, away from the Catholic continuum in England so that at present Catholicism has returned, figuratively, to the catacombs. Finally, he was convinced that unless civilization is animated by correct religious values, it turns into a shadowy, insubstantial fraud. Since in the English Establishment only a "trickle of divine power survived the reformation & . . . petered out," [19] Waugh depicts modern England as a fake society with less authenticity than the image on a film or the voice from a phonograph record. It is a society which recalls the echoing, distorted, and value-free world of Forster's Marabar Caves. The hollowness of civilization without grace is one of Waugh's major themes.

From the beginning of his career Waugh believed that the hollowness of modern British culture stemmed from a crucial failure of taste, although it was some time before he explicitly connected that failure with the absence of religious values. In Waugh's journalism right after *Decline and Fall* there is a preoccupation with what he liked to call the "bogus." Setting himself up as a spokesman for youth, he also became one of its harshest critics. He claimed that young people lacked "qualitative standards" and that they even preferred the second-rate: "People no longer speak of 'pearls' and 'artificial pearls' but of 'pearls' and 'real pearls'. . . . There is more or less of anything: a bottle of champagne or two bottles, but no idea that between one bottle and another differences of date and brand should suggest a preference." [20]

Waugh pointed to two main reasons for the rise of the "bogus" quantitative world: the "substitutes" of wartime and the failure of fathers to educate their offspring. No "imposition by rigid discipline . . . of the standards of civilization" ever took place, and so the younger generation became "the ineffectual and undiscriminating people we lament today." [21]

Waugh's early novels and travel books do not at first glance appear to be animated by a religious impulse; indeed, they seem to reflect the more dandified ideal of taste represented by Harold Acton. Acton and Waugh both scorned the fraudulent and the derivative, but Waugh's "disgusto," as one reviewer called it, sprang from deeper convictions than Acton's. We get fleeting glimpses of these when the dandy's mask slips from place. In *Rossetti*, for example, Waugh implies that Rossetti's lack of "essential rectitude"[22]—Waugh's prerequisite for great art—stems from the fact that he had religiosity but not religion. Lacking valid taste, he could not produce valid art. Religion is important in *Decline and Fall*, too: Paul Pennyfeather studies Anglican theology and approves of the suppression of heretics; Prendergast, the lapsed Anglican rector who becomes a "Modern Churchman," is decapitated by a lunatic Calvinist. In *Labels* Waugh briefly remarks that Ruskin would have led a more valuable life if he had been a Catholic. And in *Vile Bodies* Waugh lampoons evangelism, theosophy, and Methodism while dealing out ambiguous treatment to the enigmatic Father Rothschild, s.j. Of course, these fleeting allusions to religion do not in themselves establish the Christian basis of Waugh's early novels, but taken together with "The Balance" they encourage us to admit it as a possibiity. Waugh's early work manifestly concerns bad taste—the glass and aluminium King's Thursday, the barbarous Bright Young People. If it can be shown that this bad taste springs from bad faith, then these apparently superficial little books may take on fuller significance as Christian, perhaps even Roman Catholic satires.

What is, after all, the basis of good taste? Disregarding the maxim which says that the question cannot be solved, Waugh believed that good taste was the force which could vanquish the bogus ("the whole of thought and taste consists in distinguishing between similars")[23] and that it was rooted in a recognition of God's reasonable design for the universe. Good taste, he was convinced, was the special insight which came from the exercise of "right reason"—man's reason assisted by grace. Waugh believed that taste was a question of God, and dissented from the more fashionable view that God was a question of taste. In his view, art was not valid unless it was thematically concerned with God and formally incorporated decorum, clarity, and order. As a young man Waugh wisely avoided doctrinaire pronouncements on the subject, and before *Brideshead Revisited* he treated it only obliquely.

As Waugh's career advanced, he became more explicit about his vision of history. He believed that the Reformation had crucially deflected British history from its proper course. Britain, in his view, was cut off from the vital springs of faith by that fatal sundering of the ways, and its culture was eviscerated as time compounded the initial folly. In *Edmund Campion* Waugh describes the long aftermath of schism:

> In these circumstances the Tudor dynasty came to an end, which in three generations had changed the aspect and temper of England.

They left a new aristocracy, a new religion, a new system of government; the generation was already in its childhood that was to
send King Charles to the scaffold; the new, rich families who were
to introduce the House of Hanover, were already in the second
stage of their metamorphosis from the freebooters of Edward VI's
reign to the conspirators of 1688 and the sceptical, cultured
oligarchs of the eighteenth century. The vast exuberance of the Renaissance had been canalised. England was secure, independent, insular; the course of her history lay plain ahead; competitive
nationalism, competitive industrialism, competitive imperialism,
the looms and coal mines and counting houses, the joint-stock
companies and the cantonments; the power and the weakness of
great possessions.[24]

Waugh believed that England had been culturally maimed by the actions
of Henry VIII, and needed a successful counter-Reformation to correct
matters. As he wrote in 1955, "The determining events of our history are,
two of them, conquests and one betrayal. It may seem to us now that for
the fullest development of our national genius we required a third conquest, by Philip of Spain."[25] The zany events of Waugh's satires have
much to do with the fact that no such conquest ever took place, and his
"serious" novels all look forward to it. It is interesting to observe, finally,
that Waugh talks about Catholicism in terms of freedom and amplitude.
In *Edmund Campion* he observes that "the spacious, luminous world of
Catholic humanism . . . ended with Henry's break with the Pope."[26] And
in "Come Inside" he describes his own life within the Church as "an endless delighted tour of discovery in the huge territory of which I was made
free."[27] Catholic life is ample, authentic, and free; existence apart from
the Church is shrunken, false, and servile. This is why the hollow and
culturally deprived England of *Decline and Fall* and *Vile Bodies* is so
often depicted as tasteless, derivative, and confining: a spiritual prison.
Although readers sometimes find it hard to believe that a moral vision
animates Waugh's early books, it can be argued that they are images of a
debased world ruled by bad faith, bad taste, and mere Fortune. Waugh
does not endorse the chaos he so fascinatedly describes; instead, he uses
irony and allusion to make disorder imply order and fraud imply truth.
No moral judgment is expressed, but one is suggested everywhere.

## CHAPTER 3

# The Artist

After outgrowing his early attraction to aestheticism, Evelyn Waugh soon developed markedly classical tastes and wrote feelingly of the monuments of the Augustan age of English architecture. "They stand on all sides of us," he said, "rebuking, in their measured Johnsonian diction, their degenerate posterity." [1] Waugh delighted in eighteenth-century ornamentation because "every piece of it has been designed for a specific purpose in accordance with a system of artistic law." That "system" was encapsulated in the Vitruvian or Palladian orders, a set of proportions so correct that while the classical architects often made Gothic or Oriental "jokes," they never made classical jokes: "It was a style based on exact measurement and proportion; the relation of height to thickness in a column, the degree of its taper, the relation of capital to architrave, the particular ranges of ornament that were grouped together by convention." After a designer had mastered the orders—Tuscan, Doric, Ionic, Corinthian, Composite—and after his mind had been "conditioned to move automatically in the golden proportions," he was free to "indulge the most exuberant fancies." The acceptance of order liberated the designer's creativity: Palladian decorum became a "diction" and a "grammar" which allowed the artist to speak. Waugh never became a painter or an architect, but his affinity with the Augustans is reflected in the way his own creative temperament had been liberated by a sense of classical decorum and "specific purpose." Fantasy based on order is the essence of his fiction.

As an artist, Waugh found his spiritual home in the eighteenth century and always remained profoundly at odds with his own time. He often stated that he was less concerned with ideology or psychology than with style, technique, and language. "A work of art," he crustily informed the editor of the *Spectator*, "is not a matter of thinking beautiful thoughts or experiencing tender emotions (though those are its raw materials), but of intelligence, skill, taste, proportion, knowledge, discipline and industry; especially discipline." [2] He valued the "authority and sanctity" of the English language, and numbered himself among the "thin line of devotees who made its refinement and adornment their life's work." In the "disintegrated society of today," he said, the artist's only service was "to create little independent systems of order of his own" like a monk "after the first barbarian victories." [3] In so doing, the artist must have the "essential rectitude" that Rossetti lacked; it was wrong to suppose, as did "the muddled Victorian mind," that "the artist should be melancholy, morbid, uncontrolled, and generally slightly deranged." The artist should not be surrounded by a "romance of decay" and a "spiritual inadequacy," for art was an intensely moral activity.[4] There could be heresy in art just as in religion: Picasso and Gertrude Stein were "aesthetically in the same position as, theologically, a mortal-sinner who has put himself outside the world order of God's mercy." [5]

In Waugh's view, the working artist was necessarily a solitary and unsociable figure. He wrote to his wife in 1944, "I long for your company at all times except one. When I am working I must be alone. I should never be able to maintain the fervent preoccupation which is absolutely necessary to composition, if you were at close quarters with me." A little later he proposed buying "a secret house to which no guests would come," and after the war seriously thought about retiring to "a castle in Ireland," where he proposed to "immure" his family. Except for Laura, he wrote, he "would go further afield to Africa." [6]

Sometimes, like Dennis Barlow in *The Loved One*, the artist is a frontiersman who travels to exotic places for inspiration. At other times, the artist is a scribe, a monk, "in the dark age opening." [7] As he aged, Waugh changed from pioneer to monk, from explorer to recluse. In a 1963 diary entry he noted: "It was fun thirty-five years ago to travel far and in great discomfort to meet people whose entire conception of life and manner of expression were alien. Now one has only to leave one's gates." [8] Frontiersman or monk, the artist is a repository of traditional values, and is therefore a reactionary: "An artist must be reactionary. He has to stand out against the tenor of the age and not go flopping along; he must offer some little opposition." [9] Often Waugh's opposition seems to have stemmed from sheer contrariness; as he said in *Remote People*, the artist is just a man out of sympathy with his own age.[10] And in *A Tourist in Africa* he remarked that the artist is "crabbed and assiduous and touchy and jealous and generally unclubbable." [11]

As a young man, Waugh composed his novels rapidly. He told Julian Jebb that he was able to hold the whole of a novel in his head and complete it within six weeks (an exaggeration, as it turns out). But he came to disagree with theories of inspiration, feeling, as he said in *Ninety-Two Days* (1934), more affinity with Trollope's deliberateness than with the effusiveness of the Romantics. He remained a very careful writer and in his later years he was even subject to writer's block. He told Stephen Black in 1953 that writing got harder as he grew older, and was "disagreeable work": "I write everything about twice, I suppose. . . . I tear up the bad effort and start again. And there are a great many changes all the time. If I'm at work on a book, the words are running in my head all the time, and I'll get up in the middle of a meal to run off to change a word." [12]

Waugh parried all attempts to link his work with his personality: "Whatever interior changes there were," he wrote after returning from British Guiana in 1933, ". . . are the writer's own property, and not a marketable commodity." [13] When the editors of *Life* "blithely proposed to publish a series of photographic illustrations of [his] books based on the originals from which the characters were drawn," Waugh "answered threatening them with imprisonment." [14] He returned a too-inquisitive letter from "a female American Catholic" to her husband, urging him to restrain his wife "from writing impertinent letters to men she does not know." [15] And when he received a questionnaire from an American schoolgirl, he wrote to her headmistress urging her to "mete out condign punishment to this unhappy child." [16] He castigated American readers who thought that his friendship was included in the price of his book, and he deplored the tendency of modern reviewers to "write about the author rather than the book." [17] He repeatedly denied that there was any connection between his life and his art. "I think that any work of art is something exterior to oneself," he asserted; "it's the making of something whether it's a bed-table or a book." [18] And on another occasion he said, "I'm not interested in myself, it is these works I make that interest me." [19] Waugh's persona, Gilbert Pinfold, compared himself with the artists and craftsmen of the late eighteenth century, and claimed that he belonged to "a generation notable for elegance and variety of contrivance." His books were only "objects which he had made, things quite external to himself." [20]

While Waugh's intense love of privacy makes his pose as an impersonal artist understandable, the reader must be allowed to reject it. Waugh's work is not at all "external to himself"; in fact, his novels are all firmly rooted in his own experience. The germs of most of his books are plainly evident in his diaries, and many diary passages are transposed almost verbatim into his fiction. Waugh's use of personal experience in his fiction extended even to dramatizing and working out the dilemmas which beset him in real life. Often the characters who confront one another in his books are the conflicting selves who battle for supremacy in his own psyche. Writing was Waugh's means of coming to terms with the world. He used his fiction as a means of exorcising states of mind which had to be outgrown, and as the forum for the central debate of his life: the artist versus the man of action.

As early as his Lancing days Waugh felt torn between the demands of art and action, as exemplified by his mentors Crease and Roxburgh. He told an interviewer many years later, "My early dream was to be a man of action. . . . Like exploring or being a carpenter or making objects; adventurer of any kind." [21] On 25 June 1930 Waugh paid homage to Carl van Vechten in a sly autograph: "To Carl v. V. the playboy of the western world, who shares with the present Lord Rosslyn the distinction of being the one man of letters who is also a man of the world, in sincere admiration from E. W." [22] Although Waugh became an artist, he always remained vulnerable to the allure of the public life, and his work dramatizes the split.

Writing with a certain self-reference in *Rossetti*, Waugh claimed that there were "two main attitudes towards the rest of the universe." [23] On the one hand there was "the breezy, common-sense attitude to life," and on the other there was "the solemn perception of process"; most people, he said, lived their lives according to both attitudes at once, romantics and mystics simultaneously. In *Remote People* Waugh evoked the contrast between the man of action and the man of taste but confessed, "I shall never in actual fact become a 'hardboiled man of the world'." [24] Commenting on World War II, he wrote, "It is only in war that successful men and artists come into contact." [25] Although he continued to contrast the artistic and active lives as late as *A Tourist in Africa* (1960), it was the war which largely—but not entirely—cured him of the desire for action. In a revealing diary entry of 29 August 1943, he confesses: "I wrote to Frank [Pakenham] very early in the war to say that its chief use would be to cure artists of the illusion that they were men of action. It has worked its cure with me. . . . I don't want to be of service to anyone or anything. I simply want to do my work as an artist." [26] In 1945 he wrote, "I thank God to find myself still a writer," [27] and from this time on the diaries record a steady withdrawal from the world. He was not old, but he began to live the life of an elderly recluse. As he himself admitted, it was all partly an act: "Though I make-believe to be detached from the world I find a day without post or newspapers strangely flat." [28] Still, there was much truth in the pretence, and Waugh's bleak diary account of his postwar years makes sombre entertainment.

Essentially, Waugh's love of the artistic life was a love of solitude, for in solitude he could be unique, unencumbered by the look-alike throngs of "multuplets" who persecuted him. After the war Waugh refused to communicate by telephone and posted a sign which read, "No Admittance on Business." To undesirable invitations he replied by postcard, "Mr. Evelyn Waugh deeply regrets that he is unable to do what is so kindly proposed," and he considered composing form letters in varying degrees of bluntness to be determined by the occupation of his correspondent and the nature of the enquiry. He won a celebrated law suit against Nancy Spain of the *Daily Express*, who had appeared uninvited at his door. His motto became "Liberty, Diversity, Privacy."[29] And in 1960 he said to John Freeman, "I lead a life of absolute solitude; the country is a place where I can be silent."[30] He also told Freeman, "I'm still a pure aesthete."

To what degree and in what sense was Waugh an "aesthete"? When he was only fourteen he published an article "In Defence of Cubism," and although he soon turned into the most anti-modern of modernists, he never ceased to write about art and architecture. In his preface to *The Decorative Designs of Francis Crease* he paid homage to his old mentor, and in *Rossetti* and *Labels* he laid the groundwork for the idiosyncratic neoclassicism which shapes his fiction. In his middle years he collected furnishings and paintings by (sometimes obscure) Victorian masters, and he stocked his extensive library with eighteenth- and nineteenth-century volumes on art and architecture. In his frequent book reviews he paid meticulous attention to layout and design as well as to content. He ridiculed functionalism in architecture and propaganda in art. Like Gilbert Pinfold, he abhorred public tastes like "plastic, Picasso, sunbathing, and jazz—everything, in fact, that had happened in his own lifetime." He sought (but always within the classical canons of harmony and proportion) the unusual and the singular.

From the beginning Waugh wanted to be different and yet the same, unique and yet orthodox. At Lancing he deeply desired to be accepted by his fellows, yet held aloof from them. Recalling his "inconsistent" impulses, he wrote, "I did not admire the other boys. I did not want to be like them. But, in contradiction, I wanted to be one of them. . . . I simply longed to remain myself and yet be accepted as one of this distasteful mob. I cannot explain it, but I think that was what I felt."[31] Waugh's ambivalent desire helped shape that most personal of all his possessions, his self-image. Much like a Regency beau or Nineties dandy, Waugh sought a style that would be both unique and traditional; he found it, of course, in the past, and he used it to set himself apart from what his character Ambrose Silk uncharitably calls "the herd."

There can be no doubt that Waugh had much in common with the dandy tradition. He prized the ideals of grace, elegance, wit, and composure; he inclined toward tradition in religion, conservatism in politics, and form in art. He expressed contempt for the ordinary, the routine, and the sentimental.[32] At Oxford he rejected the haunts of the scholar and the "hearty" in order to enjoy the company of aesthetes. In 1929 he praised that most rarefied of all aesthetes, Ronald Firbank, and he dedicated his first novel to Harold Acton "in homage and affection."

Yet Waugh was not a dandy at heart, for his conviction of the need for unique personal style sprang from far remoter sources than the Regency and the 1890s. Despite his interest in new suits and silver-topped canes at Oxford, Waugh was not a "perfect flower of outward elegance,"[33] as Beerbohm defined the dandy. Nor did he fully answer to Ellen Moers's description of a dandy as "a creature perfect in all externals and careless of anything below the surface, a man dedicated solely to his own perfection through a ritual of taste."[34] Indeed, Waugh often affected grotesquely unstylish attire. Mark Gerson's photographs[35] show him clad in outrageously vivid checks, and at Edith Sitwell's reception into the Catholic Church he presented himself in "a loud check suit, red tie and boater with ribbons."[36] Christopher Sykes describes a suit made at Waugh's instance from Household Cavalry cloth: "Never in history had this cloth been used for the making of a suit. On a light reddish-brown background it has a bright red check about three inches square. . . . The result surpassed the wildest extravagances of an old-fashioned music-hall comedian. A weird touch of obscenity was added, as the tailor cut the cloth in such a way that a bright red line from the checks ran down the fly-buttons."[37] Neither in his clothing nor in his behaviour, which was sometimes too rowdy, sometimes too morose, but seldom moderate, was Waugh that perfect social creature, the dandy. It would be idle to argue that Waugh was not mesmerized for a time by the brilliant young aesthetes he met at Oxford. But he outgrew his infatuation. Even though all the evidence points to a torrid flirtation with aestheticism, Waugh never completely succumbed, for his inflexible moral sense exerted a constant brake on any impulse he may have felt to lose himself in the enchanted world of art for art's sake.

Waugh's brief romance with Oxford aestheticism confirmed rather than established his conviction of the need for personal style. He had long believed that each man was unique, but that belief was derived from neither Brummell, Wilde, Beerbohm, Crease, Firbank, nor Acton. Rather, it stemmed from his interest in the concept of vocation. In the end it was Roman Catholicism rather than dandyism which offered him a way of being unique and orthodox at one and the same time.

Because of his naturally religious temperament, Waugh developed into an aesthete of a highly distinctive kind. As a Roman Catholic aesthete, he sharply criticized central figures in the aesthetic tradition. He dismissed Rossetti for lacking moral rectitude, he parodied Pater for glorifying the new paganism, and he rejected that ultimate aesthete, Oscar Wilde. In the novels of his middle years he attacked aestheticism as an immature and dangerous error, and he tried to exorcise the early influence of Crease, Acton, and Alastair Graham. The rejection of his early aestheticism is a dominant theme in Waugh's fiction, for he was Augustine's heir, not Wilde's. The intelligence behind Waugh's quizzing-glass was always Christian.

Yet despite Waugh's profound distrust of aestheticism, he remained its legatee in one important respect: his perception of himself as a split personality. Just like his persona, Gilbert Pinfold, "When he ceased to be alone, when he swung into his club or stumped up the nursery stairs, he left half of himself behind, and the other half swelled to fill its place."[38] Pinfold's cleft self sounds distinctly Ninetyish, and reminds us of the generation that produced *Dr. Jekyll and Mr. Hyde* (1885), *The Picture of Dorian Gray* (1890), and *The Happy Hypocrite* (1896). As Richard Ellmann points out, "the last decade of the century is thronged by extravagant poseurs"[39] such as the early Yeats, Lionel Johnson, Aubrey Beardsley, the young James Joyce, Walter Pater, Oscar Wilde, George Russell, Mallarmé, Valéry, and the remarkable William Sharp.[40] It is evident that Waugh imbibed either directly or at second hand through Harold Acton the Wildean preference for the "beautiful unreal world of art" over the "imperfect world of coarse uncompleted passion."[41] And along with the *fin de siècle*'s half-resentful, half-frightened attitude toward real life, Waugh also absorbed its solution: the creation of a brilliantly artificial second self to outface the contingencies of real life.

In his discussion of W. B. Yeats's formative years, Richard Ellmann draws attention to "the verbal distinction that becomes common towards the end of the nineteenth century between personality and character, the former as in some way the conscious product of the latter."[42] "Character," he says, refers to "the insignificant man who is *given*," while "personality" refers to "the significant man who is *made* by the first."

As a youth, Waugh must have absorbed as a matter of course from the spirit of the times the distinction between "character" and "personality," the one animalistic, the other civilized. The reader of Waugh's diaries can watch him assiduously developing a personality which was, by the time he joined the Hypocrites' Club at Oxford, that of a young aesthete. Waugh invented a new, fabricated self which, after many permutations, became Pinfold's "front of pomposity mitigated by indiscretion, that was as hard, bright and antiquated as a cuirass."[43] The insignificant "given" man was unworked clay, the earthly son of an earthly father with sadly conventional tastes. But the artificial man was his own son; he stood outside the realm of change, a work of art creating other works of art. In attempting to root out the barbarous and transient "given" man in favour of an artificial self, Waugh repudiated everything which reminded him of his undistinguished background. In particular, he rejected Arthur Waugh and his self-indulgent sentimentality, his unstylish optimism, his bourgeois cosiness, his Anglo-Catholic religion, and his obsolescent literary opinions. ("Terrible man my father," he remarked at age eleven; "he likes Kipling.") [44] Waugh eventually thought the better of aestheticism but he never ceased to regard himself as a battleground between savagery and civilization; although he cast aside the mask of aesthete, he adopted others, and he continued to do so until he died. Yeats might have said of Waugh, as he did of Wilde, "it was the duty of everybody to have a conception of themselves, and he intended to conceive of himself." [45]

There was perpetual strife in Waugh between the man who was "given" and the man who was "made." He was a man of extremes, capable of delicately recoiling from Stephen Spender's prose with "the horror of seeing a Sèvres vase in the hands of a chimpanzee," [46] while sharing with his character Scott-King "a peculiar relish in contemplating the victories of barbarism." [47] Waugh's novels and travel books about "remote places" betray the extent to which savagery fascinated him, and the truth is that the jungles of Africa and South America mirrored his own thinly veiled barbarism. "Barbarism is never finally defeated," Waugh announced in 1939; "we are all potential recruits for anarchy. . . . Once the prisons of the mind have been opened, the orgy is on." [48] He was referring to events in Mexico, but he might as well have been speaking of himself.

Even though Waugh tried to suppress the "given" man, he soon came to distrust the dandy, the first of the men who were "made." A long sequence of poses followed: journalist, globe-trotter and explorer, officer and gentleman, aging scholar, pious and secluded paterfamilias. The rift between character and personality grew at last so great that Waugh was able to write about his last pose as "eccentric don and testy colonel" in the third person, writing of Pinfold as of someone else, and frankly admitting that he was "neither a scholar nor a regular soldier" and that the whole thing was a "burlesque." [49] In his declining years he drifted into a painful dilemma: he loathed his "natural" self (as Sykes says, he was a victim of self-hatred), [50] but he was not able to accept, finally, any artificial persona. He vacillated to the end between art and action, mask and "given" man. He came to exemplify what Maurice Beebe has noted about the heroes of artist-novels: "the Divided Self of the artist-man [wavers] between the Ivory Tower and the Sacred Fount, between the 'holy' or aesthetic demands of his mission as artist and his natural desire as a human being to participate in the life around him." [51]

Which is more real, mask or man? Oscar Wilde supplies one possible answer: "I treated art as the supreme reality and life as a mere mode of fiction." [52] When he was twenty, Waugh might have concurred, but he was too much of a puritan to persist for long in an aesthete's view of art. Harsh experience in "the world of wild aberration" [53] finally showed him that despite what Wilde believed, art by itself could be no "shield from the sordid perils of actual existence." Moreover, while the fabricated man and his art might be in some sense immortal, they were not genuine. Here Waugh's insistence on the "real" led him into a predicament for which there could be but one solution; having found that the posed self was false because it was only art, and that the given self was false because it was only natural, he came to believe in the end that the real self was the religious self, and that true art was the art that served faith. From his late twenties, Waugh waged war on two fronts: against the animalism of the "given" man and against the merely human art of the manufactured man. In his novels Waugh repeatedly juxtaposes animalism and humanism and shows that in the absence of grace, there is little to choose between them.

Far from becoming a "latter-day decadent," as one early reviewer implied he would, [54] Waugh relentlessly destroyed the lush places of secular art with the zeal of a Roundhead crusading against idolatry. The "Composed Hermitage," Ambrose's minaret, Whispering Glades, Mountjoy, and the Castello Crouchback—all these are sacked and ruined. To the end of Waugh's days, the demands both of faith and real life made him suspicious of Ambrose Silk's Ivory Tower of "pure art." Despite his claim to John Freeman in 1960 that he was still "a pure aesthete," Waugh never wholly accepted his role as an artist because as a man of action he craved public experience and as a man of faith he condemned "pure art" as unwholesome.

Waugh never completely overcame the allure of aestheticism's immature lush places. *Basil Seal Rides Again* (1963) is charged with the desire to recover the "manner of . . . youth," but even here Waugh is ambivalent about immaturity: his persona Basil Seal laments the loss of his own anarchic youth but defeats the young bohemian, Albright, by claiming his paternity. To the end, the lush places at once attracted and repelled Waugh, and in consequence he was never able to arrive at any truly charitable love for the world. The world was merely preliminary, and to love it for itself was to pervert one's destiny and imprison one's soul.

There is a recurrent situation in Waugh's fiction, in which the protagonist is pursued and parodied by a mimicking shadow; this is one of the worst fates that can befall a Waugh character, for it reduces him to the condition of a caricature. To have a shadow is to lose one's authenticity and uniqueness; it is to lose one's soul. Worst of all, perhaps, it is to lose one's style. In *Put Out More Flags*, for example, Ambrose Silk finds himself surrounded by figures who are "gross reflections and caricatures of himself";[55] shortly after, he disappears to featureless Ireland. In *Men at Arms* Guy Crouchback finds himself "diminished and caricatured by duplication"[56] and with difficulty survives his training period. In a diary passage which finds its way almost verbatim into *Put Out More Flags* and *Officers and Gentlemen*, Waugh notes, "It was always exhilarating as soon as one was alone: despondent troops were a dead weight on one's spirit and usefulness."[57] Each of Waugh's novels is characterized by the basic gesture of leaving someone behind. Sometimes one character leaves another behind—as Adam Doure leaves Ernest Vaughan, or as Guy Crouchback leaves Apthorpe. At other times the author leaves his own protagonist behind, as in *Decline and Fall*. In each case the gesture means that the author wins uniqueness and maturity through his escape from a shadowy other self whose presence has parodied and impeded him. The clearest statement of the attempt to escape from a shadow occurs in *Brideshead Revisited*:

> The human soul enjoys . . . rare, classic periods, but, apart from them, we are seldom single or unique; we keep company in this world with a hoard of abstractions and reflexions and counterfeits of ourselves—the sensual man, the economic man, the man of reason, the beast, the machine and the sleep-walker, and heaven knows what besides, all in our own image, indistinguishable from ourselves to the outward eye. We get borne along, out of sight in the press, unresisting, till we get the chance to drop behind unnoticed, or to dodge down a side street, pause, breathe freely and take our bearings, or to push ahead, out-distance our shadows, lead them a dance, so that when at length they catch up with us, they look at one another askance, knowing we have a secret we shall never share.[58]

Possibly because it smacked too much of his "p.m.," or persecution mania, Waugh later deleted the passage; nevertheless it describes a recurrent moment in his fiction. The attempt to "outdistance" a shadow takes place in novel after novel, on the part either of the protagonist or of the author himself. Heroism and moral insight are essential. If the protagonist "dodges" or "pushes ahead" through a decisive or heroic act (like Guy Crouchback or Gilbert Pinfold), then the leech-like shadow drops away. But if like Tony Last the protagonist attempts to elude his shadow without taking significant moral action, then his incubus only tightens its grip. Whether or not the protagonist succeeds, the author always matures through the protagonist's example.

A character turns into a caricature when he is in spiritual bad taste, and that happens when he disregards his "right properties" and distinctive purpose. In *Brideshead Revisited* Julia Flyte escapes from the "shadows" when she realizes that she has been made for "some other purpose" than "living in sin" with Charles Ryder. The related motifs of solitude and uniqueness are expressions of Waugh's profound desire to live in touch with a genuine reality; their opposites, shadows and bad taste, are what he hoped to avoid by choosing the secluded vocation of the religious artist. Like "Edward" in his Oxford short story of that name, Waugh always wished to be a man "of unique achievement."

## CHAPTER 4

*I am by nature a bully and a scold. . . . I am beastly.*

*Letters of Evelyn Waugh*

# The Man and the Critics

Moody as a youth and crusty in middle age, Waugh was less responsible as a man than as a satirist. His behaviour was often extreme; moreover, his striking appearance intensified his impact on a public ever ready to be shocked. Harold Acton says that in his early twenties Waugh resembled a "prancing faun" with "hyacinthine locks";[1] Pansy Lamb says that in his late twenties he was "small, golden-haired and pink-complexioned, but this was counteracted by fierce, rather glaring eyes and pouting lips."[2] Sir Henry ("Chips") Channon remembers him at thirty as "a ventriloquist's doll, with his shiny nose,"[3] and by his late forties he resembled an ironic cherub, his nearly expressionless face "a little like a boyish Winston Churchill's."[4] Leo Rosten recalls, "He was pudgy, moon-faced, pink-cheeked, his skin very clear and shiny, a roly-poly figure in a countryman's heavy tweed suit and waistcoat. It was his eyes that arrested me: small, set far apart in that fair, moony globe, intensely blue; and they glittered. . . . [He was] a florid Humpty-Dumpty . . . his pixie eyebrows executing a silent dialogue—not with me, but with whatever satirical selves were bubbling within him."[5]

Waugh revelled in courting opprobrium. As Lady Pansy Lamb wrote, "He was of a strong character and mentally active, intolerant and apt to take an extreme line about people and places. Sometimes this seemed merely capricious—a reaction from a previous enthusiasm—but it was partly the romantic temperament—like Disraeli he wanted the aristocracy to be more colourful, eccentrics to be more eccentric, politicians to be more wicked, scandals to be more scandalous. I never knew how much he believed in the stories he told."[6] To the newspapers he sent outrageous opinions couched in supercilious language. He announced that he would never vote in a parliamentary election because he did not presume to advise his sovereign in her choice of servants.[7] For a time he pretended to admire Hitler, and in *Waugh in Abyssinia* he rhapsodized over the order

Italy was imposing on the most heretical corner of the dark continent. Rose Macaulay dismissed the book as the work of a Fascist,[8] but Waugh preferred to think of himself as a Christian. When asked whether he was "for, or against Franco and Fascism," he expressed sympathy for Franco but characterized Fascism and Communism as twin evils: "I'm not a Fascist nor shall I become one unless it were the only alternative to Marxism." He found it "mischievous to suggest that such an option [was] imminent," but impishly omitted to say that the choice which overrode both the others was his faith.[9] Waugh had a long history of pretending to revere the forbidden: in his teens he "intermittently pretended to be a socialist" and "at other times . . . advocated the restoration of the Stuarts, anarchism, and the rule of a hereditary caste."[10] In the debating room at Lancing, "it was the fad to speak against our convictions. Anyone, we argued, can plead a cause in which he sympathizes; it took a clever fellow to find arguments for the enemy."[11] Like Gilbert Pinfold's, Waugh's outrageous views were often "half-facetious"[12]—as Nancy Mitford wrote, "One of the clues to Evelyn's strange nature is his love of teasing"[13]—but they earned him the reputation of a curmudgeon and a crank.

Waugh loved to make scenes. At a Foyle's book luncheon he caused discomfiture by ostentatiously lowering his ear-trumpet when Malcolm Muggeridge rose to speak. When the head waiter at the Ritz began to make a fuss over Waugh by offering him a central table where he might be on view, Waugh, who "disliked being patronized," presented his ear-trumpet and made the waiter speak at top volume, to the amusement of all present. Then he innocently requested a secluded table in the corner. Once there, he said loudly, "I'm very interested in one subject." "What's that?" asked his host. "Buggery," replied Waugh, with a gratifying effect upon their smart auditors.[14] Waugh loved witty, allusive conversation and would engage in endless (but stylish) gossip. Howard E. Hugo recalls him in top form at Harvard in 1948 with his friend Maurice Bowra: "When we entered, Bowra and Waugh were discussing 'Lady Something-or-Other.' 'She has now taken to absinthe, drugs and small black boys,' Waugh was saying with solemnity. This occasioned antiphonal exchanges between them: 'How too, too depraved, how sick-making, how utterly too much, now really'."[15]

Some twenty years later Bowra looked back on his friendship with Waugh.[16] According to Bowra, Waugh "passed and condemned on no small scale." He had arrived at Oxford as an innocent but had turned into "a vicious boy." Although he was "extremely generous," he was also "very envious"; "if you praised anyone, he would derogate them." He was "a marvellous gossip" and, despite the fact that Cyril Connolly found him "a most disloyal man," he was always "extremely faithful" to

Bowra. His sense of humour was often very whimsical, often very dark. He claimed to have greatly enjoyed a party at which Father Ronald Knox fell on the floor and one of the Lygon sisters got locked in the lavatory. It was like him to remark, of someone who had been crushed by a truck, "He was accident-prone," or to say in a voice of total gloom, "Randolph's impotent," or to announce that he liked Salem because that was where the witches were burned. Bowra said, "It was characteristic of him that if you told him some lurid piece of news he would say, 'Horrible, horrible. You couldn't please me more.'"[17] Waugh was "a very bad fellow" and he had "no moral beauty at all," Bowra remarked. "But you mustn't think I didn't love him; when he turned up my life was enhanced." Moreover, "he was the best writer of his generation."

The novelist Henry Green first met Waugh while still an undergraduate and became a close friend. Although he was "an absolutely brilliant creature" and "very able," he "seemed unpopular," Green said.[18] He was belligerent, and "a fighter." He "couldn't control his tongue—he was savage. Most people were frightened of him." According to Green, he "had the complex of a small man," and as he aged, "his temper grew worse and worse." Green was best man at Waugh's wedding to Laura Herbert in 1937, but they fell out soon afterwards, when Green and his wife unwisely smoked between courses. They never met again.

Green perceived Waugh as "a terrific social climber" who "was determined to make it; he was a snob . . . titles made a great difference to him." "He never voted," Green said, because "he was utterly against the democratic principle; yet he was not in the least a fascist." Green recalled that before meeting him Lady Diana Cooper "absolutely trembled at what Waugh would be like," but they got along well, and with Lady Diana and Hazel Lavery behind him, "he rose quickly." For her part, Diana Cooper admitted that Waugh's prejudices often "reduced her to tears."[19] Waugh was "absolutely a convert," Green said, yet he "couldn't make peace with the Catholic Church"; increasingly he began to question his faith and was "utterly miserable" most of the time. According to Green, Waugh went on one occasion "to see the Pope and was said to have lectured him for half an hour. 'But Mr. Waugh, I am a Catholic too,' the Pope is said to have replied."[20]

Waugh's correspondence with his literary agent, A. D. Peters, affords a fascinating glimpse into the professional life of a shrewd and hard-nosed man of letters. This remarkable collection, now at the University of Texas, is composed of eighteen filing boxes containing some forty folders, and spans the years 1929–63. While most of the letters concern routine matters, others revealingly demonstrate that Waugh's attitude to agents, editors, and publishers (especially Americans) varied from impatience to extremes of ungovernable rage.

"I'm afraid I shall never get to understand literary people," Waugh wrote to Peters in 1934 in a characteristic understatement. "Whenever I deal with them direct I seem to put their silly backs up." [21] Waugh was right, and indirect dealing was seldom any better. When John Farrar asked Peters when *Black Mischief* would be finished, Waugh fumed about "troublesome Yanks" and told Peters, "Old Farrar mustn't get in a fuss" . . . "Farrar's letter is all balls to me. How the Americans do gas." [22] When Richard Sherman of *Vanity Fair* refused to pay for a "hastily put-together" article, and Carl Brandt failed to force Sherman to pay for it, Waugh immediately transferred his business to a different American agent, telling Peters, "You can't tell me a thing I don't know about the low quality of my journalism." [23] After Mark Goulden of the *Sunday Referee* described another article as "uninteresting and uninspired," Waugh wrote to Peters, "Mr. Goulden must be off his rocker. Any article I write is worth exactly what I have been offered for it." [24] To Carol Hill, who took over as Waugh's American agent after Waugh fired Brandt, John Farrar wrote that Waugh would never be contented anywhere.[25] Carol Hill warned Peters about Waugh's "uneven production" and bad sales record,[26] but Waugh replied to Peters, "Will you tell the Yanks that their job is to buy paper and ink and not to criticize books. . . . God rot them." [27] Annoyed at being made "whipping boy," [28] Carol Hill faded from the scene along with Farrar and Rinehart, and the more stable but not uneventful era of Harold Matson and Little, Brown began. Waugh started off in good form, tartly telling Peters that the "new Yank agent" was never to cable except in an emergency and should use "the customary journalistic jargon to save me money." [29] In 1944, apparently unaware of his own role in such matters, Waugh glumly observed to Peters, "I have not been happy in my relations with American editors." [30]

Now there followed threats of a writ against Alexander Korda, the possibility of suing the War Office for plagiarism, and a squabble with Penguin over *Work Suspended*. Waugh also began to feud with Chapman and Hall, and instructed Peters, "Will you please explain to them in terms of one syllable" that they "get paid by the reader roughly in proportion to the work they do and the risks they run." [31] Explaining to Peters that "Fan-Fare" was "written expressly for the American lower-middle classes," he told him to take out a warrant for debt against *Life* magazine: "Luce must cough-up." [32] In Hollywood for the abortive filming of *Brideshead Revisited*, Waugh was "so constantly arrogant . . . as to have left a trail of bloody but unbowed heads behind him." [33] Sir Laurence

Olivier, he said a little later, "must be insane" for wanting to film *The Loved One*. Bob Hope was "a king among bores." [34] When an unlucky BBC announcer quoted prematurely from *Helena*, Waugh urged Peters, "Let us pursue him with fire and sword." [35] Soon he was threatening to fire his American agent, Harold Matson, for not sending him enough cigars: "The provision of cigars by the Americans is an essential service. . . . The unexplained failure of the Americans to send cigars drives me from the country." [36] Throughout all this, Waugh's acrimony seldom extended to the prudent Peters, who with unflagging tact steered his obstreperous client to success. Behaving with extreme circumspection, "Pete" became a lifelong and indispensable friend, deftly and patiently translating Waugh's thunderous outbursts about "obscene Yanks" and "American baboons" into polite and soothing business letters.

Stories about Waugh's fits of rudeness are by now almost legendary. Lady Mary Lygon remembers "a very nice American lady" who at dinner said to Waugh, "Oh Mr. Waugh, I did so enjoy *Brideshead Revisited*. I thought it such a good book." "Oh did you?" said Evelyn. "I thought it was a good book but if a common, boring American woman like you says it's good, it must be very bad." [37] Harold Acton recalls outbursts of "rudeness . . . so extreme as to be fascinating," as in Waugh's exchange with a British consul who tried to make small talk: "I've a map of Mount Ararat which might interest you," said the consul. "Why should it?" parried Evelyn. "Has the Ark been found?" [38] In the war "he bullied [his men] in a way they were unused to. He bewildered them." [39] He told a superior officer who objected to his drinking that he could not change the habits of a lifetime for a whim of his. [40] He loved to snub the media. When an eager American journalist asked Waugh to comment on Will Rogers's statement that the purpose of art is not to make a man think but to make him happy, Waugh icily inquired, "Mr. Rogers is dead, I understand?" The obliging journalist replied, "That's right, sir, guess he passed over some years back." Said Waugh, "Then he knows better now, good morning." [41] When Nancy Mitford invited Waugh to meet "a young French intellectual," he "behaved with such atrocious incivility and unkindness that the admirer was reduced to tears." Afterwards Miss Mitford demanded to know how he could behave so brutally while claiming to be a Christian. He responded, "You have no idea how much nastier I would be if I was not a Catholic. Without supernatural aid I would hardly be a human being." [42] Annoyed beyond endurance by Waugh's use of his ear-trumpet during dinner, his friend Ann Fleming gave it a tremendous blow with a spoon, nearly deafening him.

The American critic Edmund Wilson was one of Waugh's most enthusiastic admirers, but all that ended at a 1945 dinner party given by Cyril

Connolly. The guests were warned not to ask Wilson about his latest novel, which his English publisher had just rejected as pornographic. Immediately Waugh began to cross-examine him at length upon the forbidden subject.[43] Waugh's calculated indiscretion, together with his decision to "chuck appointment to show London to insignificant Yank named Edmund Wilson, critic," may help to explain Wilson's sour response to Waugh's later fiction: *Brideshead*, published only two months after the events just related, was "a bitter blow" to Wilson. The Wilson confrontation was evidently malicious, and Waugh may have undertaken it with a view to keeping his reputation fresh. But while the important financial benefits which accrued from such outrageous performances cannot be ignored, there can be little doubt that Waugh's astounding misbehaviour was often completely involuntary.

Perhaps because of Waugh's chronic persecution-complex, his reaction to novelty was instinctively hostile. Of a new wartime acquaintance he noted, "I began my relationship with my customary loathing."[44] But acquaintances did not necessarily improve upon longer association. In an essay on the genial creator of Mr. Pickwick, Waugh says, "The more we know of Dickens, the less we like him"[45]—and Waugh's attitude was similar towards the people he met in real life. He told an interviewer, "One quarrels, I suppose, twice a year, and one makes a new friend about once every two years."[46]

Waugh's acerbity intimidated his acquaintances. Lady Pansy Lamb says that his letters are full of "scandal and frightful language,"[47] and Christopher Sykes admits he feared what might appear in the second, unfinished, volume of Waugh's autobiography. Others were alarmed when they learned that the *Observer* planned to publish excerpts from his diaries.[48] Their apprehensions proved well grounded, and for a time the columns of the *Observer* rang with howls of outrage and denial; meanwhile other old friends cowered in silence behind the flimsy camouflage afforded by dashes and asterisks.

Waugh's diaries say many uncomplimentary things about others, but very little about his own inward life. In 1930 he defended his radically external approach: "Nobody wants to read other people's reflections on life and religion and politics, but the routine of their day, properly recorded, is always interesting, and will become more so as conditions change with the years."[49] But the reader who disconsolately traces Waugh's routine might well disagree, for diaries as taciturn as these are not to everyone's taste. Reticent though they are, however, the diaries are illuminating. Like his novels, Waugh's diaries spring from a succession of poses, and contrary to what one might expect, they are in many ways fiction. This is not to say that they are fallacious, although there are certainly enough well-documented protests from outraged victims to suggest that such is sometimes the case. Waugh the diarist is writing for effect; he is writing "literature," complete with distancing devices, personae, and comic exaggeration and diminishment. The Evelyn Waugh of the diaries is a product of his own literary art, a series of personae designed to shield the diarist from the world's scrutiny and, it must often seem, from his own. In a *Lancing College Magazine* editorial Waugh forecast that "the youngest generation" would be hard-headed and reticent: "middle-aged observers will find it hard to see the soul in the youngest generation." [50] The young Waugh's prediction is true of himself, for even in his private diaries it is hard to see Waugh's soul. In his diaries, as in public, Waugh assumed "burlesques" of himself. Did he finally, in some "ultimate curlicue" of solitude, put aside his masks and acknowledge his real self? And—tantalizing question—what was that real self like? The diaries do not tell us, but his novels record the fascinating conflict which went on between that self and its many poses.

In Waugh's case it is often hard to disengage the masks from the face behind them, but one thing is plain: he seldom chose a flattering burlesque. He appeared to take a perverse pleasure in projecting the image of a man who was deficient in courtesy, patience, tolerance, humility, and—most grievous lack of all—charity. He flaunted his boredom and his dislike of change. He cultivated bad habits and paraded his addiction to them: chloral and bromide taken in crème de menthe, massive doses of paraldehyde which made visitors think the gas had been left on, painkillers, cigars, and frequent infusions of favourite liquors. He enjoyed suing people for libel, and he baited interviewers by luring them from one indiscretion into another.

Waugh's unpleasant characteristics may well be the defences, as his brother has argued, of a shy and sentimental man. [51] But Waugh was more complicated than that: deeply insecure yet lured on by intimations of success, he sought fulfilment in some small niche of an impossible world. He longed for security, but found it threatening and—worse still—boring; accordingly, the heart-breaking sameness of the life of material security is central to all his novels. Wyndham Lewis once asserted that Waugh was a child of time and a time-writer, [52] but in fact he was profoundly frightened by time; he feared change and dreaded the future, which in his view could harbour only disaster. He was deeply moved by the spectacle of aimless transience and waste which the modern world presented, and he bent his energies toward finding substance amid the shadows. Waugh found stays against confusion in faith, in the art which served faith, and, after an unhappy first attempt, in marriage. But these solutions never wholly satisfied him.

One of Waugh's most pronounced characteristics was his tendency towards the death-wish that tempts both Dennis Barlow and Guy Crouchback. Father Martin D'Arcy notes that Waugh's self-portrait in *Pinfold* conceals his "better qualities and the momentum of his faith" and reveals "misanthropy and despair."[53] And Christopher Sykes traces Waugh's despair to "self-hatred"; speaking of Waugh's relentlessly unflattering depiction of himself in his diaries, he says:

> When he came to portray himself, he . . . inevitably presented a self-caricature. But he had added incentive, a continuing and distressing psychological abnormality which took the form of a lifelong tendency towards self-hatred. In later years he saw this as a "sense of sin." He was almost morbidly aware of his faults. Harold Acton hit a nail on the head when he said in his memoirs that Evelyn's "lovable qualities . . . could only be described by others." Evelyn, not only by ordinary modesty, but abnormally by his disposition, was quite incapable not only of that task but of any ordinary implication of good qualities. He needed to fight against so much self-reproach that he was constantly confronted by temptations to despair.[54]

Nor, despite the injunctions of his faith, did Waugh resist those temptations to despair. He was a perfectionist who could never live up to his own expectations; in his public behaviour as in his private diaries and in *Pinfold*, he punished himself for falling short of his ideals. As a reporter he found the Abyssinian conflict a "disappointing war," but that was wholly typical of him: he lived in almost constant exasperation and perpetual disappointment.

Is Waugh a "responsible" satirist? Sooner or later anyone who thinks seriously about Waugh will find it necessary to ask whether he is a serious moralist, what his values are, and how those values are embodied in his work. In general, such questions have been raised with reluctance and answered in haste, for most critics reject the idea that Waugh writes satire from any consistent moral position, and they are even less prepared to admit that his touchstone is faith. They treat him in various ways: as an amoral Oxford wit, a dandy, an incurable romantic in love with an idealized lost past, a testy critic of all that is modern, or as a comic technician whose stylish prose bears no intellectual scrutiny. Waugh himself fostered such opinions by denying that he was a satirist at all. "Are your books meant to be satirical?" a reader inquired. "No," Waugh replied,

> Satire is a matter of period. It flourishes in a stable society and presupposes homogeneous moral standards—the early Roman Empire and 18th Century Europe. It is aimed at inconsistency and hypocrisy. It exposes polite cruelty and folly by exaggerating them. It seeks to produce shame. All this has no place in the Century of the Common Man where vice no longer pays lip service to virtue. The artist's only service to the disintegrated society of today is to create little independent systems of order of his own. I foresee in the dark age opening that the scribes may play the part of the monks after the first barbarian victories. They were not satirists.[55]

We must pause over this deftly worded statement because, while it confirms that Waugh regarded himself as a moralist (he compares himself to a monkish preserver of values), it denies that he saw himself as a militant moralist, or satirist. Waugh's denial rests upon a very particular understanding of satire. In his opinion the audience must share the satirist's values so that the satirist may produce shame by exaggerating inconsistency, hypocrisy, polite cruelty, and folly. But, Waugh argues, satiric exaggeration is impossible today because there are no shared standards—and here we may confidently infer that some of the standards Waugh has in mind are Christian virtues. In his eyes, modern life is already exaggerated, already a gross caricature of what it should be, so the monk-like novelist in his catacomb simply chronicles aberrant behaviour, like a scribe.

The inhabitants of the distorted modern world resemble the characters of that immature novelist, John Plant, who "takes the whole man and reduces him to a manageable abstraction."[56] Waugh attacks such abstractions in "Fan-Fare," where he charges that modern novelists pay no attention to their characters' souls: "The failure of modern novelists since and including James Joyce is one of presumption and exorbitance. They are not content with the artificial figures which hitherto passed so gracefully as men and women. They try to represent the whole human mind and soul and yet omit its determining character—that of being God's creature with a defined purpose."[57] Waugh argues that characters who stand in no affirmative relation to God are merely wooden parodies of whole men; they are denizens of a world which has distorted itself by turning away from sustaining values. Since the secular City is already a travesty and recognizes no shame, Waugh can argue that there can be no satire in the modern world, and that he is not a satirist but a scribe.

Waugh's assertions raise many questions. In the first place, the view that the satirist corrects vices by inducing shame is unsound; there can be few intelligent satirists who have seriously believed that their work would change society. Second, while it is theoretically true that there can be no communication and therefore no satire without shared values, it is surely false to claim that there are no shared values *at all* in today's world. Won't our common humanity always make communication—and satire—possible? Third, is it not rather melodramatic of Waugh to imply that there is no audience which shares his views? The Roman Catholic Church contains millions of members, and the standards of the British upper classes are not yet extinct. Indeed, although Waugh does not say so in "Fan-Fare," he often intimated that his novels address an audience of like-minded readers in a private language charged with innuendo and allusion. Fourth, readers more tolerant and objective than Waugh may well maintain that in chronicling modern life, Waugh also exaggerates it. However realistic Waugh may have thought he was being, characters like Grimes, Fagan, and Prendergast are surely caricatures. Certainly it would be rash to argue that Agatha Runcible does not represent a distortion of ordinary reality.

Although Waugh denies it in "Fan-Fare," then, there can be little doubt that even if they are not absolutely homogeneous, the shared values required for satire still exist. And not only do they still exist, but Waugh exploits them for satiric effect. In summary, Waugh's "little independent systems of order" are neither as independent nor as unexaggerated as he claims. His novels are all rooted in Augustinian Catholicism and the values of the English upper classes; and there are many other readers who can appreciate Waugh's satire perfectly well without agreeing, chapter and verse, with his world-view.

It is easy to understand why Waugh disavowed any satiric intent. When he made his celebrated "Fan-Fare" statement in 1946, he had failed as a "man of the world" and had resolved to become indifferent to it. "I am not impatient of its manifest follies," he wrote in August 1943, "and don't want to influence opinions or events, or expose humbug or anything of that kind." Plainly, any admission that he thought of himself as a satirist would have contradicted his pose of indifference (and it *was* a pose; in private he fulminated about the world's failings). Moreover, Waugh was becoming more and more reactionary, especially in matters of religion, and he found that his voice was now often raised alone. Accordingly, he yielded to the urge to see himself as a scribe in the catacombs and melodramatically exaggerated the distance between himself and his audience. Finally, Waugh's satire (if once again it can be called that) depends upon reticence and obliquity; had Waugh confessed to being a satirist, he might have had to explain his indirect method—a consequence surely repugnant to him.

Other factors have contributed to the widespread notion that Waugh is an irresponsible satirist, and it will be well to examine them now.

Waugh's critics often deny that his fiction has a moral basis because it is cruel. Frederick J. Stopp observes, "There have always been those who have felt repulsion at some incident in the novels which seemed to them to speak of childish and perverse delight in crudeness and cruelty for its own sake." [58] But like Swift, who was also cruel, Waugh seldom uses cruelty for its own sake. The harshness he displays in his fiction is almost always a sign of a profoundly agitated moral indignation; it is not irresponsible. And it might be added that those who like their satire purged of cruelty mistake the nature of the genre.

Waugh's apparent inconsistency is another obstacle in the way of establishing a moral dimension in his fiction. Stopp complained long ago that he could find no pattern in Waugh's random attacks,[59] and George Mikes, Conor Cruise O'Brien, and Graham Martin have all echoed his claim that there is "no stable and settled conviction" in Waugh's work.[60] Malcolm Bradbury argues that Waugh offers "no secure centres of value" in his early work: Waugh writes "at once social chronicle and fantasy in a spirit of comic delight that absolves him from consistent moral presentation." [61] James F. Carens, in a more recent analysis, inclines towards Bradbury's view: "Throughout the first stage of his career, [Waugh] offers only the most fleeting glimpses into a positive and affirmative standard. . . . Not until *Brideshead Revisited*, in which his Catholicism is revealed for the first time, does a positive force significantly emerge to oppose everything that the novelist rejects. . . . The early novels remain generally negative and destructive; and, consequently, Waugh is criticized for lacking a high moral purpose and writing satire without a moral centre." [62] In the latest significant attempt to come to terms with Waugh's comic vision, Martin Green resorts like Bradbury to a theory of "delight" and maintains that Waugh "writes from no ultimate moral position, wholly delighted"; he is "both for and against everyone, or rather no one. . . . The best in Waugh is . . . not satirical, if by satire we mean making a thing funny by holding it up against some standard the writer fairly consistently recommends, as Amis and John Wain and Shaw and Swift and Pope do." [63] But to argue that Waugh is "wholly delighted" at the idiocies he records is to be deaf to a constant undertone of censure; surely the truth is that Waugh disapproves of what delights him, and is fascinated by what he deplores. It is this ambivalence which provides the very germ and matrix of his art. Waugh is not outside the satiric tradition of Jonathan Swift; on the contrary, he is firmly within it.

As if recalling the Lancing editorial in which he proclaimed that the "youngest generation" would be reticent, Waugh conforms (unintentionally, of course) to his father's conviction that the artist should avoid the methods of "the pulpit and the hustings" and should work through "suggestion" and "implication." [64] He is not "absent" from novels like *Decline and Fall* and *Vile Bodies*. Like many another "impersonal" author, he is present through his style. As Wayne Booth has so exhaustively demonstrated, "We must never forget that though the author can to some extent choose his disguises, he can never choose to disappear." [65] Titles, epigraphs, settings, symbols, literary allusions, the arrangement of episodes: these are all signs of the author's ordering hand and moral nature, and they can affect readers in ways they hardly suspect. As Waugh said, "All literature implies moral standards and criticisms—the less explicit the better." [66] Like many modern novelists who have left their novels by way of the front door and have slipped back in through the skylight, Waugh is far more present in his early work than he appears to be—and so are his values.

By means of charged language Waugh manipulates his reader's response through a form of "subliminal seduction." It is a method which has not gone unnoticed. Peter Green observes that Waugh "would appeal to what we are learning to call the Hidden Persuaders." [67] And in a perceptive piece on Waugh's prose style, George Greene remarks on "its notable range of epithet, its richness of implication." [68] He says, "Waugh is constantly prodding at the frontier of our verbal memories as well as our sensibility," and he notices that Waugh avoids the appearance of ideological persuasion. But despite Greene's reservations, persuasion does stand at the base of Waugh's method. Like any other traditional satirist, he wishes to substitute his own convictions for the "wrong" values which he attacks. Even in *Brideshead* and after, where the moralist advances with scourge in hand, there is a high degree of indirection.

Waugh's private meaning is so well concealed that the uninitiated reader might question its presence. Present it is, however, as Waugh himself many times implied. "Much can be done by innuendo," he declared in a 1959 review of *The Dictionary of National Biography*. [69] As early as 1932 he approvingly wrote, "Humour, particularly of the allusive kind which appeals to a common standard of culture, is present in everything that Mr. Pryce-Jones writes." [70] In commending Malcolm Muggeridge's *In a Valley of This Restless Mind* in 1939 he observed, "There is an abundance of literary allusion and concealed quotation to flatter the reader's knowledge." [71] Of his own novel, *Helena*, he said, "There's lots of hidden humour in it," [72] and he praised the poems of Ronald Knox as "allusive, ingenious, dandified, esoteric." [73] In a 1942 letter to Lady Dorothy Lygon he wrote, "Could you not get into Combined Operations? Then we could write one another official letters full of deep double meanings." [74] "Every family and set develops its private vocabulary and syntax," Waugh wrote in an open letter to Nancy Mitford; "What can their critics hope to make of the undertones and innuendoes, the evocative, reminiscent epithets of, say, Tony Powell or Leslie Hartley?" [75] In an illuminating review of Graham Greene's *British Dramatists* he wrote, "There seem to me only two ways in which you can properly write a very small book about a big subject. You may either take your readers on an equality, credit them with the same education and tastes as yourself, trust them to recognize your allusions and, in the main, to desire the same effects, and so throw out for their entertainment and subsequent discussion a number of personal opinions and theories; or, alternatively, you can play the schoolmaster and attempt to compress your own superior learning into a convenient and acceptable form." [76] In his early fiction Waugh avoids "playing the schoolmaster" by muting and dramatizing the moral point he wants to make. Like Ronald Firbank, whom he briefly admired, he conveys his meaning indirectly through innuendo and through the calculated arrangement of scenes and characters.

A lingering suspicion of style itself has proved to be another factor inhibiting readers from treating Waugh as a serious satirist. A. E. Dyson, for example, treats Waugh as a stylist who has no "right to satirize": "Take away the verbal precision, and you crash down too heavily on the meaning." [77] Dyson's separation of style and content reflects the notion that style is a mere jacket for meaning: there is something to say, and style is a way of saying it. But style is not a way of *saying* something, it is a way of *seeing* it. Style itself has meaning. As Richard M. Ohmann remarks, style is "not merely embellishment" and consists of the "hidden" and "highly general" meanings implicit in a writer's usual way of expressing himself. [78] In most writers style is intimately related to content because it is part of content. Surely this is the case with Waugh too; surely there *is* a "vital union of form and moral content" in his work.

Waugh repeatedly discredited merely ornamental styles as "bogus," and it would be odd to find that he had failed to practise what he preached. He often claimed that style should not be merely superficial but should irradiate all parts of a work. While he frequently deplored the "flight from magnificence" in modern writing, he did not mean to imply that he thought of style as a carpenter might think of lacquer. For him, style must be "structural": "properly understood style is not a seductive decoration added to a functional structure; it is of the essence of a work of art." [79] That is why (to turn for a moment from style to wit) Waugh was able at the outset of his career to approve so strongly of Ronald Firbank. Even though Firbank's comedy is fanciful in the extreme, it emanates from the very deepest levels of his work; it is not merely superficial. In comparing Firbank with Oscar Wilde, Waugh finds that Wilde's wit "is ornamental; Firbank's is structural. Wilde is rococo; Firbank is baroque."[80]

When Waugh travelled to Barcelona in 1929 he discovered another whimsical artist whose style was integral to his work. The artist was Gaudi, creator of the bizarre Church of the Holy Family and other architectural marvels in the Parc Güell. Even though Gaudi was not to Waugh's emergent Augustan tastes, Waugh liked him because, like Firbank, he was thoroughly rather than superficially fantastic. And behind everything he did, however surreal, there was a firm sense of principle and method. (It did not matter that Waugh did not share Gaudi's artistic principles; what did matter was that he found Gaudi's fantasies responsibly and uniformly rooted in method: without the constraints of his method there could never have been any successful liberation of his fancy.) Gaudi was thoroughly original because his style was "essential." In Waugh's opinion, good style is neither derivative nor superficial; rather, it is original and integral. But how does an artist develop a style which is not bogus?

According to Waugh, an "essential" style is achieved only through discipline. The artist who wishes to have a truly original style must verse himself so thoroughly in the traditional shaping principles of his craft that he will involuntarily manifest those principles in whatever he creates, however fanciful it may be. However idiosyncratic, personal, or "new" his work appears to be, it will bear the imprint of a tradition larger than himself.[81] Waugh's favourite tradition was neo-classicism, which seemed to him to reflect the Christian view of a universe governed by intelligent design. In a discussion of the benefits of mastering the Palladian orders Waugh remarks, "By studying 'the Orders' you can produce Chippendale Chinese; by studying Chippendale Chinese you will produce nothing but magazine covers."[82] According to Waugh, correct aesthetic discipline liberates the artist from the second-rate (the merely personal or the merely derivative), just as correct moral discipline frees him from the prison of selfhood or dead convention. Discipline is liberation; or, to reverse this, "freedom produces sterility."[83]

In Waugh's view, a lasting style possesses the qualities of lucidity, elegance, and individuality, and only the artist who has disciplined both his aesthetic and moral principles can achieve it. From the first Waugh knew that the great artist needed "a high moral purpose." Looking back on his anarchic post-Oxford days at the Heatherley School of Art in Bloomsbury, Waugh declared that he gave up his ambition to become a painter because he "didn't have the moral qualities."[84] Like Gaudi's Church of the Holy Family, then, Waugh's comic world may appear shapeless and fantasticated; but even in evoking disorder, his measured prose implies discipline as the cure. Like the neo-classical designers who were free "to indulge the most exuberant fancies" because they had mastered the Palladian orders, Waugh was able to create his fantastic comic world because his inventiveness had been liberated by religious constraint.

## CHAPTER 5

*The book was frequently and rightly praised for its originality, and it is probably true to say that it is the most original of all his books. He denied this. He insisted that it was excessively derivative. "But from what?" I once asked him. "Oh, a great many books, I'm afraid," he replied laughing, but he never particularized.*

Christopher Sykes, *Evelyn Waugh*

# *Decline and Fall*

Exhilaratingly fresh and funny, yet implicitly serious, *Decline and Fall* is the work of two Waughs. One is the subversive and immature Waugh who rejoices in the anarchic self-indulgence of Captain Grimes and his naughty world—and this is the inventive and delightful early Waugh most readers know and relish. But there is another Waugh, detectable only as a tonal effect here or as an allusion, a significant juxtaposition there. This is Waugh the heresimach, the guardian of civilized values; full of unspoken disparagement, this Waugh is a powerful reality who cannot be ignored, for he silently orders the events of the novel and shapes its outcome. If Waugh had merely loved or merely hated what he wrote about, he would have been a lesser writer.[1] But *Decline and Fall* is the child of his love and hate and as such, like King's Thursday, one of its central images, it is "much more elaborate than it looks from outside."[2]

When on 23 January 1925 Waugh left London to become an instructor at Arnold House, Denbighshire, he took with him his "drawing things," his "abortive notes for 'The Temple'," *Alice in Wonderland*, and *The Golden Bough*.[3] His new career in pedagogy proved to be far from agreeable, and his attention soon gravitated towards more creative matters. In February he wrote to Harold Acton, "I want to write a story about Silenus—very English & sentimental—a Falstaff forever babbling o' green fields—but shall never have time."[4] He did not pursue the subject, turning instead to "The Balance," which preoccupied him throughout the desperately unhappy spring and summer of 1925. But at Aston Clinton, a year after first mentioning Silenus, he had a new idea: "I thought of a novel to write—but doubtless I shall do nothing of the sort."[5] Yet a book was incubating, for on 30 October he noted, "Some days ago I wrote to the publishers of the *Today and Tomorrow* series sug-

gesting that I should write them a book on 'Noah: or the Future of Intoxication.' To my surprise and pleasure they welcome the idea enthusiastically."⁶ Waugh never described the contents of "Noah," but its title
suggests that it was a study of the abuse of wine from the beginning of
time to the present day. Noah, of course, was recorded history's first
oenophile and it seems that the thought of one of the first fathers of the
human race behaving in an inebriated manner in the sight of his children
struck a responsive chord in Waugh's imagination. The book was finished
within two months, "though badly," and Waugh went to spend the
Christmas vacation with his friend Alastair Graham, who was now a
consular attaché in Athens. Upon his return from that dissipated odyssey,
Waugh found that Kegan Paul had rejected "Noah"; "It is rather a blow
as I was counting on the money for it but perhaps it is a good thing. I was
not pleased with it."⁷

There can be little doubt that Waugh's "book about Silenus" (the bibulous tutor of the infant god Dionysus) represented an early conception of
"Noah." Although Waugh mentions neither book again, he did not forget them, for the motif of intoxicated and irresponsible authority recurs
in *Decline and Fall* (1928) where it forms the novel's central theme. *Decline and Fall* is a concise universal history of drunkenness, and it demonstrates that "the future of intoxication"—or Dionysiac disorder—among
the old means spiritual incarceration for the young.

Although Waugh was on the side of order, he was fascinated by its opposite, for it was older than Noah, and had never been stamped out despite constant suppression. In 1939 Waugh wrote, "barbarism is never
finally defeated,"⁸ but he had demonstrated that truth much earlier in the
memorable figure of Captain Grimes, who dominates *Decline and Fall*.
Modelled on "the lecher from Denbighshire," the "monotonously pederastic" usher named Young who on a visit to Aston Clinton "seduced a
garage boy in the hedge,"⁹ Grimes is a resilient survival figure. He is in
harmony with the promptings of primitive humanity and self-indulgently
believes that happiness consists in doing exactly what he wants.¹⁰ Grimes
pretends to be a gentleman and a representative of civilization but with
his uncanny ability to "land on his feet," he is really an emblem of the
anarchy which is "never finally defeated." In a wonderful paraphrase of
the passage in *The Renaissance* in which Pater claims that the Mona Lisa
exemplifies neo-paganism and represents the "modern idea," Waugh describes Grimes's background (pp. 264–65):

> Paul knew that Grimes was not dead. . . . He was a life force. Sen-
> tenced to death in Flanders, he popped up in Wales; drowned in
> Wales, he emerged in South America; engulfed in the dark mystery

of Egdon Mire, he would rise again somewhere at some time, shaking from his limbs the musty integuments of the tomb. Surely he had followed in the Bacchic train of distant Arcady, and played on the reeds of myth by forgotten streams, and taught the childish satyrs the art of love? Had he not suffered unscathed the fearful dooms of all the offended gods of all the histories, fire, brimstone, and yawning earthquakes, plague, and pestilence? Had he not stood, like the Pompeian sentry, while the Citadels of the Plain fell to ruin about his ears? Had he not, like some grease-caked Channel-swimmer, breasted the waves of the Deluge? Had he not moved unseen when the darkness covered the waters?[11]

Grimes's history is a caricature of the history of barbarism. Despite a long sequence of mock-deaths, he always survives because he personifies an immortal vitality which is completely at home in the chaotic and chance-governed natural world. Order by contrast is artificial and alien to the fallen world, and although discipline has held barbarism at bay throughout history, Waugh's novel shows that it is now beginning to fail in its task. Waugh habitually viewed history as an unending contest between order and disorder, a battle "that can never be lost and may never be won until the Last Trump."[12] But in *Decline and Fall* the victory of anarchy seems imminent, for puny authority-figures like Prendergast, Sniggs, and Maltravers cannot stem the rising tide of savagery for long.

Why, if he later believed that order could never lose, does Waugh show it near eclipse here? The answer implicit in the novel's action is that modern authority is enfeebled because it is no longer animated by the *right kind* of discipline. It would be idle to argue that Waugh's verdict carries much objective truth, for the Roman Catholic Church in Britain was vigorous enough in the 1920s. However, his diagnosis carries psychological truth, for the British Establishment, with its state schools and state church, provided him with no stability in the face of disorder.

The fantastic plot of *Decline and Fall* shuttles Paul in a dizzying whirl from Oxford to Llannabba School to Mayfair to Blackstone and Egdon prisons and back to Oxford where, disguised as his own cousin, he resumes his studies as an Anglican ordinand. Following Paul in his travels, Waugh astringently satirizes what Paul encounters: the Establishment's education system, the state church, high society, the legal system, politics and politicians, the penal system and the nineteenth-century idea of the gentleman, the "whole code of ready-made honour that is the still small voice, trained to command, of the Englishman all the world over" (p. 247). The result of Waugh's sharp-eyed tour is outrageously hilarious satire, and the critics have been unstinting in their praise of his surreal, self-contained, and riotously funny fictional universe. For example, in a very apt observation, Nigel Dennis has remarked upon Waugh's comic dexterity—his ability to hold "five characters in each hand"—and has praised his fiction for "its fantastic gravity in the face of the ridiculous, its levity over accepted forms of seriousness, its high narrative flash-point accompanied by one sleight of hand after another."[13] Dennis admirably captures the effervescent surface-texture of Waugh's early novels, and he goes farther than most recent critics in seeing (although imperfectly)[14] that beneath their superficial glitter there lies a serious moral dimension.

In the case of *Decline and Fall*, Waugh scrutinizes the deficiencies of irresponsible authority-figures, their drinking glasses raised on high, their voices raised in bibulous contention. Waugh strikes the keynote in his brilliantly understated first scene, in which two officials of Scone College conceal themselves while the Bollinger (in real life the Bullingdon) Club riots unchecked all around them. In their bottle-green evening coats, the Bollinger members are aristocrats and captains of society, yet they perpetrate acts of unspeakable barbarism. "Three years ago," the narrator says enthusiastically in the insouciant and ostensibly approving tones that will become his trademark, "a fox had been brought in in a cage and stoned to death with champagne bottles. What an evening that had been!" (p. 1).

Watching the turmoil in the quadrangle from a safe distance, Mr. Sniggs and Mr. Postlethwaite secretly share the Bollinger's taste for savagery, for "there is some very particular port in the senior common-room cellars that is only brought up when the College fines have reached £50" (p. 2). They do not intervene, therefore, praying instead: "Oh, please God, make them attack the Chapel" (p. 3). As for the other senior members of Scone College, they "were all scattered over Boar's Hill and North Oxford at gay, contentious little parties, or at other senior common-rooms, or at the meetings of learned societies, for the annual Bollinger dinner is a difficult time for those in authority" (p. 1). In the absence of authority, the atavistic aristocrats attack a typical modern man. Their victim is polite Paul Pennyfeather, an abstemious and overwhelmingly dull theology student who is "consumedly shy of drunkards" (p. 5). By chance, it seems, Paul strays into the undiscriminating clutches of the barbarous Lumsden of Strathdrummond, who drunkenly mistakes Paul's tie for the "Boller" tie. Paul is not literally torn apart and eaten, as he would have been at a real bacchanalia, but he is ruined nonetheless: "debagged," he runs the length of the quadrangle in his shorts and because of this orgiastic behaviour he is expelled from his humanistic haven amid a barrage of empty platitudes. As "some one of no importance" (p. 6) who in any case couldn't pay his fine, Paul becomes a *pharmakos* upon whom the authorities can vent their indignation with impunity. Not for the last time in the novel, irresponsible and hypocritical authority feathers its own nest by encouraging the disorder it should be suppressing.

After a brief and brilliant scene in which fatherless Paul's self-seeking guardian profitably disinherits him to the music of Gilbert and Sullivan, Paul applies, at random in a random world, to Church and Gargoyle, scholastic agents, where he is again exploited. His misfortunes lead him to an underpaid job at Llannabba School, under the dubious direction of that Dickensian old fraud, Augustus Fagan. Like Grimes, Fagan is another survival-figure and has been around for a long time. Waugh deftly characterizes him in a few evocative lines: "He was very tall and very old and very well dressed; he had sunken eyes and rather long white hair over jet black eyebrows. His head was very long, and swayed lightly as he spoke; his voice had a thousand modulations, as though at some remote time he had taken lessons in elocution; the backs of his hands were hairy, and his fingers were crooked like claws" (p. 13). With his penchant for style and "vision" over substance (his horrid school is "built upon an ideal"), Fagan is flamboyant and opportunistic hypocrisy itself, a bad actor who resembles a *"jeune premier."*[15] His mock-feudal college is as two-faced as he is, presenting "two quite different aspects, according as you approach it from the Bangor or the coast road" (p. 16). In immortal lines Fagan suavely counsels pretense: "We schoolmasters must temper discretion with deceit. . . . Utility, economy and apparent durability are the qualities to be sought for" (pp. 22, 59).

In the prison-like confines of Llannabba, Paul meets two strange colleagues: Captain Grimes, who makes it a rule to do exactly what he pleases, and Mr. Prendergast, who maintains the reverse: "It doesn't do to rely on one's own feelings, does it, not in anything?" (p. 50). Each character is wrong in his own way. As a natural force, Grimes disregards order, while Prendergast represents the perversion of the only order that can stop him. Prendergast was once an Anglican rector blessed with a lucrative living ("it was such an attractive church, not old, but *very* beautiful"), but he lost it all because suddenly he had "Doubts" for "no apparent reason." Waugh does not say so of course, but Prendergast had his doubts because he had the wrong faith. Instead of Providence he had only Fortune and circumstance to guide him, and his grievous lack has precipitated his decay. Eventually he becomes "a species of person called a 'Modern Churchman' who . . . need not commit himself to any religious belief" (p. 185).

As the narrative advances, the characters arrange themselves in the ranks either of disorder or wrong order. Fagan, Margot, and Silenus are all spiritually related to Grimes, and so is Philbrick, the universal impostor. Like Grimes, he survives all bad fortune; masquerading as a butler, a burglar, a gambler, a novelist, and a cinema magnate, he has no real identity and represents the featureless interchangeability of an age devoid of distinct moral values. On the other hand, little Lord Tangent resembles Mr. Prendergast as a figure of fading power. The inebriated Prendergast wounds him slightly in the heel with Philbrick's revolver, and the maltreated little boy declines from scene to scene. Using a trick he learned from Ronald Firbank, Waugh tells us at intervals that Tangent's foot has turned black, that it has been amputated, and eventually, apropos of something else, that Tangent has died. Tangent's problem is parental neglect: like the entire younger generation, he has been improperly raised. His mother, Lady Circumference, is modelled on Alastair Graham's tyrannical mother. As we learn in *Vile Bodies*, she represents the "fine phalanx of the passing order," an order which Waugh admires to some extent; nevertheless he criticizes it sharply and attributes its "passing" to its faulty values and to the erratic discipline it exerts over its offspring. Lady Circumference advises Paul to "knock about" her "dunderhead" of a son, while diffident Lord Circumference emerges from "the shadows" to converse about war, the inevitable result of his own ineffectuality.

Paul wavers between Grimes and Prendergast, disorder and wrong order; he never glimpses the right order which the novel's moral dialectic implies. He is spiritually akin to dim Mr. Prendergast, but in his bizarre new surroundings and under the subversive influence of Grimes, he inclines steadily towards anarchy and the world of Chance: he sets his unruly pupils an essay topic on "Self-indulgence" ("there will be a prize of half a crown for the longest essay, irrespective of any possible merit"), and he rules his classroom with "no punishments, no reprisals, no exertion" (pp. 43, 47). When the enlightened Potts writes to notify Paul that Trumpington has offered him twenty pounds for damages, Paul momentarily agrees that he is honour-bound to reject it. His respectable identity depends upon it; moreover, "It is a test-case of the durability of [his] ideals" (p. 51). Anticipating Paul's response the resourceful Grimes accepts the money, and "a great wave of satisfaction" surges up in Paul. "To the durability of ideals," he says ironically, drinking the first of many toasts and slipping further into the orbit of Captain Grimes. At the Hotel Metropole he drinks a champagne toast to his good luck and draws still further away from Potts and his "enlightened" views about gentility and discipline.

As Paul abandons his flimsy Victorian ethics, events begin to move more swiftly. The uproariously funny school sports come next, and the little boys scamper aimlessly around the track like contestants in Lewis Carroll's caucus-race.[16] Here, amid images of the sham and the circular,

Paul meets the fabulously rich and cosmopolitan South American heiress, Margot Beste-Chetwynde ("Beste," one supposes, as in "beast"). She owns two houses in England, one Tudor and the other dating from the reign of William and Mary. It is to the former, now hideously remodelled, that Margot invites Paul as tutor to her son Peter.

Enigmatically the narrator says that the great house is a "new-born monster to whose birth ageless and forgotten cultures had been in travail" (p. 180). He means that it is an inevitable consequence of its own increasingly secular past; it is the house of false order. Before its "renovation" it "stood on the place which since the reign of Bloody Mary had been the seat of the Earls of Pastmaster. For three centuries the poverty and inertia of this noble family had preserved its home unmodified by any of the succeeding fashions that fell upon domestic architecture. No wing had been added, no window filled in; no portico, façade, terrace, orangery, tower, or battlement marred its timbered front" (p. 148). The Earls of Pastmaster are very probably the new Tudor aristocracy of whom Waugh speaks in *Edmund Campion* (p. 3), and King's Thursday is a material representation of the "new religion, . . . new system of government" which came into being after 1558.

Like King's Thursday, the new church and state lingered on unchanged only by virtue of "poverty and inertia"; but by the twentieth century the last Earl of Pastmaster has become weary of inhabiting a museum-piece. He sells the house to his widowed sister-in-law, but instead of maintaining it like all the Pastmasters before her, she levels it in favour of something "clean and square." Just as Prendergast the lapsed Anglican is decapitated, so the house of Anglican England gradually becomes wholly secularized, to be replaced by a tasteless and dehumanized structure more suitable to the profane spirit of the age. Neighbours rescue bits of carved stone for their gardens, and its archaic panelling goes to South Kensington, where foreign students admire it.

King's Thursday is the house of perverted doctrine, and perpetual "renovation" is its inevitable destiny. Its misfortunes shadow forth what Waugh later describes as "the heresies of the sixteenth and seventeenth century, the agnosticism of the eighteenth century, the atheism of the nineteenth and twentieth centuries."[17] Scone College and Llannabba are part of its history (temporal periods exist spatially, side by side, in this novel), and Silenus's "surprising creation of ferro-concrete and aluminium" is its current manifestation. Before the novel is over, the house is remodelled again. As Paul approaches this ruined ark past "the housekeeper's wife, white-aproned as Mrs. Noah," he expects to find "something enduring and serene in a world that had lost its reason and would so stand when the chaos and confusion were forgotten" (p. 162). Instead, he finds a dreadful structure of vita-glass, furnished with pneumatic rubber furniture, leather-hung walls, sunken malachite bathtubs, and porcelain ceilings. India-rubber fungi decorate the recessed conservatory; a tank of octopuses dominates another room.

Margot's new mansion has been brought into being by Professor Otto Silenus, a robot-like genius who loathes individuality. "What an immature, self-destructive, antiquated mischief is man," he says, lapsing into a parody of Hamlet:

> How obscure and gross his prancing and chattering on his little stage of evolution! How loathsome and beyond words boring all the thoughts and self-approval of this biological by-product! this half-formed, ill-conditioned body! this erratic, maladjusted mechanism of his soul: on one side the harmonious instincts and balanced responses of the animal, on the other the inflexible purpose of the engine, and between them man, equally alien from the *being* of Nature and the *doing* of the machine, the vile *becoming*! (pp. 157–58)

"The vile *becoming*": if Grimes embodies man's ungoverned bestial drives, Silenus speaks for those who would replace faulty but striving humanity with the antiseptic perfection of the automaton.

When Paul leaves Llannabba for King's Thursday, he steps forth into the value-free modern world. His pupil is the new Lord Pastmaster, a precocious and amoral youth who admires both Havelock Ellis and *The Wind in the Willows*. He is a creature of appetite, always eating peaches and, notably, gull's eggs: "I've eaten your eggs," said Peter. "I just couldn't help it" (p. 207). Adept at using a cocktail shaker, Peter is a new pagan, perhaps a new Dionysus, and when his mother retires for the weekend doped with veronal, he hosts a modern bacchanalia attended by Martin Gaythorne-Brodie, David Lennox, Pamela Popham, and Kevin Saunderson.[18] The advent of these bright young bacchantes at King's Thursday is inevitable, for their neo-paganism has long been implicit in the chequered history of the house. Paul, all unaware of Waugh's irony, reads himself to sleep each night with *The Golden Bough*.

If Peter is another incarnation of Dionysus, who is Margot? In one sense she too is a bacchante, for she tells Chokey, "I could eat you up every bit" (p. 101); but she has an even greater significance. As the guiding principle behind Paul's misadventures, Margot is an embodiment of Fortuna herself, the spirit of the wheel at Luna Park, and the force which takes over when the world denies God and Providence. With her lack of proportion, she recalls Huxley's Mrs. Viveash. Events in her realm are chaotic and unpredictable: "it's just something that's going to happen," she tells Paul when she decides to marry Lord Maltravers and legitimize herself. But "Fortune's a strumpet" who seduces Paul in a chapter named after the "Pervigilium Veneris," a late Latin poem written for the eve of the festival of Venus. With its repeated refrain "Tomorrow shall the loveless love, the lover love tomorrow," the poem suits Paul. But it also suits Margot, for she is Venus herself, perhaps even Venus Erucina, whose places of worship were associated with harlots and ritual prostitution. Margot jokingly offers Paul a job protecting her from swans, thereby obliquely invoking a line from the "Pervigilium Veneris": "Now hoarsely trumpeting the swans plunge over the pools." Then she offers him marriage and a post as helper in her "entertainment" chain. Naively watching Margot interview prospective candidates, Paul remarks:

> "Margot, you're wonderful. You ought to have been an empress."
> "Don't say that you were a Christian slave, dearest."
> "It never occurred to me," said Paul. (p. 191)

Restored to its context, the allusion seems to indicate that Margot is nothing less than the Whore of Babylon.[19]

Just when the wedding preparations are nearly complete, Margot sends Paul to Marseilles to sort out certain difficulties with her "entertainers" who are en route to Rio. Proud of his increasing *savoir faire*, Paul arrives in Marseilles with a great sense of freedom. But worldly as Paul thinks he is, he is so naive that he fails to recognize the true nature of his mission even when he stands amid the fleshpots of rue Ventomargy, which in his diaries Waugh describes as the "toughest" street in Europe.[20] In contrast to St. Paul, Paul Pennyfeather experiences no epiphany and no growth; because of his inadequate cultural heritage he lacks insight, and dull-wittedly reflects that Margot is right in wishing to "rescue her protégés from this place of temptation and danger" (p. 199). Paul pays off the immigration officials and departs, still gloriously ignorant of what he has really done, but hard on his heels comes his constraining "shadow" Potts, who gets closer with every step Paul takes into "the world."

Back in England after his successful mission into the vortex of the flesh trade, Paul fills his glass with brandy and drinks a toast with Alastair: "To Fortune," he says, "a much-maligned Lady" (p. 185). His fortunes are at their apogee and, revelling in his freedom, Paul has now escaped his narrow existence at Scone. He has abandoned his feeble ideals and has taken Fortune as his guide; he has exchanged wrong order for complete disorder. Instantly the door opens and Paul is arrested, tried as a white-slaver, and sent to jail. There seems to be no logic or justice in the

swift turn of events. But could there in fact be a connection between
Paul's new freedom and his incarceration?

A multitude of gentle hints within the novel suggests that licence and
imprisonment are related, but it may be useful to look outside the novel
for a moment. When Waugh chastised "the younger generation" in 1929,
he wrote, "When they should have been whipped and taught Greek para-
digms, they were set arguing about birth control and nationalization. . . .
It is hardly surprising that they were Bolshevik at eighteen and bored at
twenty." [21] Waugh's message here is that unrestrained freedom is itself a
form of imprisonment, and that the cure is discipline. When we turn to
*Decline and Fall*, we find Waugh dramatizing the same conviction. For
example, he pokes fun at the "enlightened" views on discipline held by
Paul and Potts. And when the prison schoolmaster asks Paul what his
standard was when he left school, Paul replies, "Well, I don't quite know.
I don't think we had standards" (p. 217). Waugh mercilessly lampoons
Sir Wilfred Lucas-Dockery who, in his enlightened refusal to frustrate the
creative urge, tolerantly equips a crazed carpenter with a saw. It is wholly
appropriate that Mr. Prendergast, who can't keep discipline, is assassi-
nated by a man who hasn't been disciplined (moreover, as a Calvinist, the
lunatic is a product of Prendergast's schismatic Anglicanism: like many
other Waugh characters, Prendergast is killed by what he has created).

Waugh's conviction that the woes of the modern world stem from lack
of discipline may not seem altogether original. But what may appear
ordinary when baldly stated can be effective when dramatized, as it is
throughout *Decline and Fall*. Waugh's novel images forth a paradox well
known to theologians: licence is imprisonment and conformity to God's
will is freedom. [22] So it is that Paul's movement towards worldly freedom
proves to be a movement towards jail. In a spiritual sense, Paul does not
really move at all, for Scone, Llannabba, and King's Thursday are already
prisons. Thus there is more than meets the eye in Prendergast's contention, "Criminals are just as bad as boys, I find" (p. 218). The same is true
of the narrator's cheeky observation that anyone who has been to an English public school will always feel completely at home in prison. Amus-
ingly, it is Lucas-Dockery's aim to minimize the difference between prison
and normal life by having the prisoners "carry on with their avocations
in civilized life" (p. 220)—but since "civilized life" is already a prison, his
plan is hardly necessary.

How did modern life become a prison of the spirit? Waugh traces the
problem to patriarchal irresponsibility: instead of suppressing disorder,
fathers encouraged it through tacit consent or active participation. But
the prison of modern life was not built in a day and so Waugh examines it
*sub specie aeternitatis* in order to trace its origins right back to the begin-

ning of time. Through veiled symbolism and fleeting allusion, he presents in *Decline and Fall* an oblique history of savagery and Dionysiac disorder; as with E. M. Forster's novelists in the British Library, time here assumes spatial form.

Through allusions to Noah, Silenus,[23] Augustus, and Edward Gibbon (the novel's title links ancient and modern barbarians), Waugh extends his survey of irresponsible authority past Biblical times and Greek and Roman history to Britain itself. First there is Lumsden of Strathdrummond—a "druidical rocking stone"—and then there are the mistletoe-draped musicians of Llannabba. Revolted by this ape-like band, Dr. Fagan gives voice to a suavely cruel synopsis of Wales which directs Waugh's mock-history of Britain ever closer to modern times:[24] "I often think . . . that we can trace almost all the disasters of English history to the influence of Wales. Think of Edward of Carnarvon, the first Prince of Wales, a perverse life, Pennyfeather, and an unseemly death, then the Tudors and the dissolution of the Church, then Lloyd George, the temperance movement, Nonconformity and lust stalking hand in hand through the country, wasting and ravaging. But perhaps you think I exaggerate? I have a certain rhetorical tendency, I admit" (p. 81). Paul replies, "No, no," but Waugh privately considers that bad teachers like Fagan (whose original in Dickens taught orphans to pick pockets) have far more to do with "the disasters of English history" than Wales does.

By virtue of its reference to the Tudors and the dissolution of the Church, Fagan's merciless lampoon of the Welsh takes us into the age of post-Reformation England. Silenus's parody of Hamlet's "What a piece of work is a man" and Chokey's parody of Shylock's "Hath not a Jew eyes?" implicate the age of Shakespeare. Margot's London home, which was built just after the Glorious Revolution in 1688, incriminates the seventeenth century. Allusions to Pope and Dr. Johnson (and to Swift—Grimes on horseback suggests the Yahoos and the Houyhnhnms) extend Waugh's allusive history to the eighteenth century. But in Waugh's eyes the merely ethical and secular nineteenth century is the worst offender, hence the allusions to Browning, Arnold, Butler, Morris, Thackeray, Dickens, Frazer, Longfellow, Smiles's *Self-Help*, Dean Stanley's *The Eastern Church*, Hardy, and the nineteenth-century radicals.

At Blackstone Gaol (named, perhaps, for the confining effect of Sir William Blackstone's Puritan jurisprudence) the environment is threadbare Church of England: Paul's meagre reading-matter includes a mid-Victorian book of Anglican prayers; on Sundays the "very broad-minded" Prendergast blasphemes against "the beauties of sixteenth-century diction" (p. 225), and the warders are all Church of England. Presiding over the undisciplined prison of Anglican England is the too-tolerant

Sir Wilfred Lucas-Dockery, for whom justice is the disregard of precedent.

Egdon Heath Penal Settlement is a later chapter in Waugh's anthology of barbarism. Waugh borrows its name from an appropriate source: Hardy's *Return of the Native*.[25] It is another prison governed by chance, and Grimes escapes from it because it is turning him into "a giddy machine" (p. 259). But regardless of whether Paul is at Blackstone, Egdon, Scone, Llannabba, or King's Thursday, he is always in jail, for all of modern England is a prison of the soul. As Prendergast says wearily, "Oh, well, it's all much the same really" (p. 44).

Irresponsible fathers like Maltravers,[26] Lord Pastmaster, Lord Circumference, and indulgent Mr. Clutterbuck (brewer of beer for the new bacchantes) have turned England into a spiritual dungeon. Like Lord Utteridge, who says that the dearest wish of his life has been gratified when his son is kidnapped, all the fathers in *Decline and Fall* are "unnatural" fathers (p. 67). They have no discipline, and (even though he has avoided fatherhood), Grimes speaks for them all when he advocates self-indulgence: "I don't believe one can ever be unhappy for long provided one does just exactly what one wants to and when one wants to" (p. 38). Because they have no restraint, they are all in a prison without bars, a prison which is more confining than Blackstone or Egdon; after all (to borrow two chapter headings), "Stone Walls do not a Prison Make," "Nor Iron Bars a Cage."

Who has lured these fathers astray? In one sense they are the victims of original sin (as Waugh says elsewhere, "the consequences of every human act for good or ill are an endless progression")[27] but in another sense they have been seduced by the wrong love. Augustine says that two loves produced two cities: the City of God and the City of Man. In *Decline and Fall*, which is an allusive history of the City of Man, Waugh depicts a perverted world in which the love of God has been ousted by the love of the senses. Rather than worshipping God, Waugh's characters prefer Dionysiac intoxication and lust. Throughout the rollicking, fast-paced narrative, inebriated characters hold their glasses aloft amid a babble of voices. There is the champagne-glutted Bollinger Club; Grimes swilling beer at "Mrs. Roberts'"; Prendergast with his wig awry hotly debating the late development of the rood-screen; the young revellers at King's Thursday; the intoxicated surgeon who signs Paul's death-certificate; the repeated toasts to that much-maligned lady, Fortune. Paul himself joins this rabble-rout, and his arrest occurs just as he raises his brimming glass for yet another toast. But the presiding deity of wrong love is Margot Beste-Chetwynde. As a combination of Fortune, Venus, and the Whore of Babylon, she has intoxicated and misled the world of fathers in age after age, and in post-Reformation England she marries into the decaying house of Pastmaster. When Margot supersedes doddering Lord Pastmaster, England's last vestiges of right love and justice yield finally to a new kind of infidel who is so far outside the sphere of right and wrong that she thinks nothing of poisoning a husband or using a fiancé as a pimp. She belongs to one species, and Paul, her vassal, belongs to another. In jail Paul soon sees that there is "one law for her and another for himself" (p. 248): he has made a mistake in trying to join her and so he retreats to his former world of outdated precept and leaves her to live by the law of Nature.

In jail Paul meets many old friends, for licence has led them all to the same place. He enjoys prison; in particular, he likes his newfound solitude: "It was so exhilarating . . . to have no anxiety ever about what kind of impression he was making; in fact to be free" (p. 224). If too much freedom can be a prison for the spirit, constraint, paradoxically, can be liberating. At Egdon there are brilliantly funny moments as new novels, sherry, winter roses, pâté de foie gras, and pigeon pie mysteriously appear in Paul's cell. "An aged burglar" righteously objects when inadvertently given Paul's caviar instead of his ration of bacon. Grimes escapes into the mist on horseback, "passing" once again, and Paul takes a leaf from Grimes's book as he too "expires" in a nursing home run by Augustus Fagan, "M.D." Paul's "death" is an important moment for, having been reduced to a mere shadow by his entry into Fortune's domain, he is now finally rent in pieces by her savage devotees. (At this point in the novel we are not far removed from the cannibal feast at the end of *Black Mischief*.) Like Prudence Courteney, Paul Pennyfeather is the last vestige of an old but inadequate régime which is now giving way to a new order of mere chance and contingency. Like King Arthur in parody, "Paul got into the boat and was rowed away. Sir Alastair, like Sir Bedivere, watched him out of sight" (p. 240). The "mysterious disappearance of Paul Pennyfeather" is not so mysterious after all: it reflects the death of a civilization whose only options have been wrong order or disorder. Waugh reaches out of the book to implicate all modern bacchantes in Paul's fate: "After supper Dr. Fagan made a little speech. 'I think this an important evening for most of us,' he said, 'most of all for my dear friend and sometime colleague Paul Pennyfeather, in whose death to-night we are all to some extent participants'" (p. 271). Once again the revellers raise their glasses to Fortune, whose "amazing cohesiveness" governs their riotous world in the absence of Providence.

After recovering awhile in Corfu (where Waugh himself had gone in 1927) Paul returns to Oxford, where, since there is no farther to fall, he enters a world of mere repetition. He disguises himself as his own cousin and pursues the same studies as before; his new friend Stubbs is just another Potts, and as the novel closes, Peter Pastmaster hosts the Bollinger Club just as Alastair did at the outset. Paul's fate is Waugh's comment on Britain's infinite regress into a world of moral impotence from which it is now powerless to be reborn. Paul, the new Arthur, will never rescue Britain, for he is a fraud lost in a wilderness of mirrors.

Before Paul leaves Corfu for England, Professor Silenus gives him a lengthy piece of advice about life, which he compares to "the big wheel at Luna Park" (p. 277). Critics have had difficulty in understanding Silenus's remarks, but incongruous as it may seem, Silenus speaks for Waugh at this point, and for once Waugh is being sincere. Like Silenus, Waugh believes that people fall into two types: the static and the dynamic, the Apollonian and the Dionysiac—or, to phrase it differently, men of taste and men of the world. Waugh speaks autobiographically here, and sees himself as a retiring Paul Pennyfeather who somehow has tumbled into a world of savages and has been badly mauled.[28] Like Paul, he is "clearly meant to stay in the seats" because he is of a "different species spiritually" from the barbarous world around him; like Paul he is static, not dynamic. While it is apparent that Silenus's speech represents Waugh's realization that he need not commit himself to Fortune's wheel after all, one further distinction needs to be made.

At the end of the novel Paul steps off the wheel of Fortune and returns to the bleachers. Does this mean that the novel's conclusion is affirmative and that Waugh approves of Paul in the end? Although it may seem that he approves, he is in fact deeply critical: after all, while the world may be a dreadful place, Waugh intimates that not just any refuge from it will do, for some are false. At Scone Paul returns to his "enlightened" life and to his theology studies. Having experienced the dangers of the aberrant and orgiastic world, he now thinks he has become a staunch disciplinarian and righteously condemns an errant Bishop of Bithynia and some wayward Ebionites: "Quite right to suppress them" (p. 288). Paul thinks that he is now highly orthodox, but what Waugh impishly avoids saying is that as an *Anglican* ordinand, Paul is as heretical as the deviants he so curtly dismisses.

In the Epilogue Peter Pastmaster, now hosting the Bollinger, stumbles drunkenly into Paul's rooms and announces that Paul's intention to become a clergyman is "damned funny" (p. 287). It *is* "damned funny," because Paul's new refuge will prove to be no less of a prison than King's Thursday or Egdon. If Peter is stuck in self-indulgence, Paul is caught in false worship. At Egdon Heath Penal Settlement there are two new stained-glass windows in the chapel. "Lovely they are, St. Peter and St. Paul in prison being released by an angel" (p. 245). Peter Pastmaster and

Paul Pennyfeather are also in prison, but there is no liberating angel in sight; no Lady Philosophy consoles these captives of Fortune.

The characteristic dream-like effect of *Decline and Fall* stems from its combination of explosively funny farce qualified by moral seriousness. The latter is everywhere felt but nowhere expressed, for Waugh is too accomplished a satirist to allow any character to articulate his values explicitly. Indeed, it is contrary to his satiric strategy to allow any figure within his satire even to have such insight, though sometimes he mischievously places his most deeply cherished views in the mouth of some wholly inappropriate character. How then is Waugh to convey his beliefs if he eschews authorial commentary and declines to use any character consistently as a mouthpiece? He solves this problem, a familiar one in modern fiction, by resorting to indirection, innuendo, and meaningfully juxtaposed events to implant his attitudes in the reader subliminally.[29] Examples are obvious enough when they are pointed out, but thanks to Waugh's cheeky sleight of hand, they are seldom noticed. When Paul departs from Scone, for example, he leaves behind Dean Stanley's *Eastern Church*, a study of ancient heretics being appropriate reading for their modern counterparts. Grimes grotesquely quotes, "God's in his Heaven; all's right with the world" (p. 38); Dr. Fagan leads prayers by reading from the Bible at random; the boys repeat the Lord's prayer in a "quiet chatter" (p. 39); drunken Mr. Prendergast quarrels with the Vicar over the Apostolic claims of the heretical Church of Abyssinia. Chokey, "divine" and "an angel," would "give all the jazz in the world for just one little stone from one of your cathedrals" (p. 101). Philbrick, the archimpostor, claims to be a Roman Catholic; and a similar fraud "thought 'e was Bishop of Bath and Wells, and confirmed a whole lot of kids—very reverent, too" (p. 145). The coincidental meeting of Bill, a former pimp, with Grimes, a prospective pimp, is a "pure act of God" (p. 184). The prison staff at Blackstone Gaol are all Church of England, and the ambivalent "thought for the day" is "Sense of Sin is Sense of Waste" (p. 223). Criminals converse about Prendergast's murder by singing, "O God our help in ages past, / Where's Prendergast today?" (p. 243). And at the marriage of Flossie and Grimes the Vicar ambiguously says, "Our experience of life has taught us that *one* is not enough" (p. 136).

If *Decline and Fall* possesses only parodic examples of good faith, it is no less devoid of good taste; this is because right reason, upon which taste and faith are founded, has been overcome by mere appetite. Waugh repeatedly uses examples of bad taste as hallmarks of moral corruption and irrationality: Fagan is pretentiously overdressed; Prendergast wears a ratty old blazer and a disgraceful tie; Philbrick wears a ghastly mustard-

coloured suit of plus-fours and a diamond tie-pin. Flossie and Dingy, excess and defect, are dressed as befits their natures. Note also the revolting
décor of the office in which Margot interviews young ladies for "Latin-
American Entertainments": "Two stuffed buffaloes stood one on each
side of the door. The carpet was grass-green marked out with white lines,
and the walls were hung with netting. The lights were in glass footballs,
and the furniture was ingeniously designed of bats and polo-sticks and
golf-clubs. Athletic groups of the early 'nineties and a painting of a prize
ram hung on the walls. . . . The bell . . . was in the eye of a salmon trout"
(pp. 189–90). Often Waugh gives his badly dressed and morally shabby
characters an appropriately infernal position in front of the fire. Here is
Paul's first glimpse of Flossie: "Sitting before the fire, with a glass bottle of
sweets in her lap, was a brightly dressed woman in early middle age" (p.
20). Dr. Fagan is there too: "He stood at the end of a long room with his
back to a rococo marble chimney piece: he wore a velvet dinner-jacket."
And at prayers Grimes sits "beside the baronial chimney piece" (p. 38).
    But Waugh's most effective silent touchstone is his own style. The out-
rageous events of the novel seem even more atrocious because they are
narrated in a suave and urbane prose of technical perfection. This prose is
impeccable, modulated, nuanced, dandified, and it never flags or falters,
thereby providing in itself a lucid and continuous model of good taste
against which the events it describes are measured and found wanting.
"Mildly censorious detachment" is how Waugh described his tone.[30]
When the discrepancy between the nonchalant style and gruesome subject matter becomes extreme, we have Waugh's characteristic mode, the
comic macabre. Take, for example, the narrator's smooth remark on Tangent's failure to win the race: "Clearly Tangent was not going to win; he
was sitting on the grass crying because he had been wounded in the foot
by Mr. Prendergast's bullet" (p. 87). Or his judicious comment on the
latter's death: "From all points of view it was lucky that the madman had
chosen Mr. Prendergast for attack" (p. 243). Or Margot's conversational
sang-froid:

> "Who's that dear, dim, drunk little man?"
> "That is the person who shot my son."
> "My dear, how too shattering for you. Not dead, I hope?" (p. 104)

Waugh makes the outrageous sound normal because to him the normal
was outrageous.
    No one within Waugh's novel is reasonable, or has good faith or good
taste (or for that matter, good literary style—note Philbrick's melodramatic tall tales). Only the majestically insouciant voice of the narrator

shows that there can be a stay against confusion in the formally elegant art born of right reason. In his pose as dandified narrator, Waugh conquers the chaos he writes about by making it the stuff of his fastidious art; such an art confers individuality and identity upon its creator.

We may conclude, then, that a set of moral values stands behind the crazy caperings of Captain Grimes and the comic impudence with which his fantastic world is described. To be sure, all the characters are spiritually too underprivileged to recognize these values and to profit from them. But unlike the characters, neither the reader nor the author remains locked inside the narrative and they may profit even if the characters do not. The insistent recurrence of the theme of identity in *Decline and Fall* and, before it, "The Balance," allows us to conclude that Paul's problems were to a large extent Waugh's. Because of his lack of discernment Paul remains stuck in the bogus "newspaper-world" of boring repetition and he abandons his quest for a coherent identity. Waugh on the other hand profits by Paul's sad example and exchanges the fragmented sham world for an enduring institution which, in his view, enshrines continuity and right order.

CHAPTER 6

# *Vile Bodies*

In the summer of 1929 Waugh retired to a country hotel to begin writing his second novel, and after three days he telegraphed, "Novel moving fast all characters seasick."[1] He described it to Harold Acton as "a welter of sex and snobbery . . . about bright young people."[2] Three weeks later he returned to London following his wife's admission that she was in love with John Heygate. He remained in London long enough to start legal proceedings against Evelyn Gardner; back in the country "he worked fast; and the novel was finished by December."[3] His brother Alec "read it in proof at Christmas" and it was published in January 1930, the month of Waugh's divorce.

Looking back on *Vile Bodies* some thirty years later, Waugh spoke slightingly of it, influenced perhaps by unhappy memories: "It was a bad book, I think, not so carefully constructed as the first. Separate scenes tended to go on for too long. . . . It was second-hand too. I cribbed much of the scene at the customs from Firbank. I popularized a fashionable language, like the Beatnik writers today, and the book caught on."[4] Sales soon exceeded those of the already popular *Decline and Fall*; modish people instantly adopted Waugh's "shy-making" language; a stage version appeared; the London press clamoured for articles. Aware that he was now valuable property, Waugh announced to his literary agent A. D. Peters, "I will only do *feature* articles . . . with photographs of me and [a] general air of importance."[5]

Like *Decline and Fall*, *Vile Bodies* is a scintillatingly funny attack on irresponsible authority born of cultural decay, but a rising note of bitterness now qualifies Waugh's comic exuberance. Heralding his later disgust with the world, the new sourness is felt in the "cumulative futility"[6] of the latter part of the novel, the part he wrote after he discovered his wife's infidelity. Upon hearing the bad news he told his brother that there was not enough religion in the world: "There's nothing to stop young people doing whatever they feel like doing at the moment."[7] While Waugh ridicules certain incidental victims who stray into his line of fire, such as publishers, politicians, socialites, and the news and motion-picture industries, his major target is aberrant religion. In the Firbankian opening chapter a motley collection of the faithless return through stormy waters from France to England: "to avert the terrors of sea-sickness they had indulged in every kind of civilised witch-craft, but they were lacking in faith."[8] In the absence of faith, these voyagers are all hostages of Fortune and, as in *Decline and Fall*, their irreligion has led to aimless dissipation. In *Decline and Fall* the vicissitudes of Paul Penny-feather provide an excuse for Waugh's survey of irresponsible authority; in *Vile Bodies* Waugh's pretext for his survey of heresy is Adam Fenwick-Symes's typically modern conviction that he can achieve marital stability by committing himself to the pursuit of Fortune.

Although he is surrounded by people who find London "just exactly heaven" and "divine," Adam never considers religion; instead, sheer chance governs his quest for identity and vocation and reduces it to a game of snakes-and-ladders. After an ignorant customs official thwarts his attempt to make his fortune through art, Adam wins £1,000 by the flip of a coin, but he promptly loses his money to a "drunk Major" who promises to bet it on a dark horse at the "November Handicap." Coincidence brings Adam and the Major together from time to time, and on each occasion Adam thinks that he'll be able to marry Nina Blount; but bad luck always intervenes, leaving him in his original bankrupt condition. At last Adam and the Major meet on an apocalyptic battlefield and, after reading a letter from the suggestively named Nina, Adam receives his fortune, now worth "about nothing."

"Nothing" is the reward of all those who devote themselves to Fortune in this novel. Mr. Outrage, "last week's Prime Minister" and the creature of chance, is typical of those who govern Adam's world. Prufrockian in his attempts at secular love, Mr. Outrage is even more indecisive in matters of divine love: "Was Mr. Outrage an immortal soul, thought Mr. Outrage; had he wings, was he free and unconfined, was he born for eternity? He sipped his champagne, fingered his ribbon of the Order of Merit, and resigned himself to the dust" (p. 141).

Agatha Runcible is another "vile body" who opts for the here and now and whose ultimate prize is "dust." When she goes to watch the "Speed Kings" race, "beneficent . . . Providence" preserves her as she throws a lighted cigarette towards an open drum of gasoline. But nothing can save her when as "spare driver" she slips behind the wheel of car number 13 and drunkenly speeds around the racetrack—one of this novel's images for Fortune's wheel. As the driver of a racing-car, Agatha becomes the plaything of chance: in the narrator's words, such cars lack "essential identity" and are the "masters of men. . . . [They] are in perpetual flux; a vortex of combining and disintegrating units; like the confluence of traffic at some spot where many roads meet, streams of mechanism come together, mingle and separate again" (p. 178). Unable to control this fortuitous assemblage of parts, Agatha collides with an "Omega," turns "left instead of right at Church Corner" (p. 195), and crashes into a market cross. After a party at her fashionable Wimpole Street nursing home, she hallucinates and dies despite being told that "there's nothing to worry about. *Nothing at all*" (p. 224). Before her death she cries, "How people are *disappearing*, Adam" (p. 209). But she shouldn't have been surprised, for oblivion is the inevitable fate of Fortune's many devotees.

In *Labels* Waugh describes Monte Carlo as a "pavilion in an exposition arranged in time instead of in space—the Palace of Habitable Europe in the early twentieth century."[9] A similar vision informs *Vile Bodies*. Here Waugh disregards chronological sequence in order to make all eras co-present, and he confronts his readers with an array of dwellings, each one a "pavilion in an exposition" of spiritual decay. As the plot moves forward, Adam's search for equilibrium speeds him from "pavilion" to "pavilion," and through Adam's encounters Waugh examines the origins of England's spiritual bankruptcy.

In January 1926, after an excursion to Paris, Waugh wrote, "The journey was disgusting, and I think that I am so unlikely to forget it that I will not write about it at all."[10] *Vile Bodies* opens in the middle of a similarly "disgusting" journey with a representative selection of English society all at sea in a Channel ferry. Their captain does a crossword puzzle amid the gale, their former prime minister lies drugged in an erotic sleep, and the prurient older generation tipsily wonder where they have mislaid the sal volatile. Also on board this storm-tossed ark are the Bright Young People, "the undiscriminating and ineffectual people we lament today," as Waugh said in a 1929 article.[11] They include Agatha Runcible, Miles Malpractice, Archie Schwert ("the *most* bogus man"), and Adam, who in his perception that marriage ought to endure, and in his distaste for the Bright Young People's parties, is minimally more perceptive than the others. Together they represent the debased legacy of all that has happened in English history, and therefore all that is yet to happen in the novel. There too is Mrs. Hoop, devotee of yoga and fad religions: "I'm through with theosophy after this journey. Reckon I'll give the Catholics the once over" (p. 15). The charismatic and perverted woman evangelist, Mrs. Ape, is on board with her shabby "Angels," who personify all the virtues the modern world has forgotten. Transparently modelled on Aimée Semple McPherson, Mrs. Ape treats religion as a money-maker: "Hope's what you want and Hope's what I got," she tells the sea-sick cardplayers (p. 14), and turns a tidy profit on her hymn-session. Present too is Father Rothschild, s.j., who is sharply criticized even though he is a Catholic priest and articulates Waugh's own diagnosis of modern wantonness by finding it "all in some way historical" (p. 143).

Readers have often had difficulty with Rothschild, not knowing whether Waugh approves of him or not. While Waugh unquestionably endorses Rothschild's religion, he disapproves thoroughly of the weak way he implements it. Waugh's symbolic shorthand comes to our assistance in the matter: even though as an ostensible representative of the universal Church Rothschild carries a world atlas and six books in six different languages, he carries them, along with a false beard, in a borrowed suitcase of imitation crocodile. Waugh reinforces these intimations of fraudulence by telling us that Rothschild resembles a plaster reproduction of a Notre Dame gargoyle. He and his faith are in danger: "High above his head swung Mrs. Melrose Ape's travel-worn Packard car, bearing the dirt of three continents" (p. 2). With his love of conspiracies and his uncanny omniscience—he predicts that Mr. Outrage will once again become prime minister—Father Rothschild is more like an agent of Fortune than a priest of God.

After the customs agent confiscates his "life" and his *Purgatorio*, Adam travels up to London where, from a booth in the Eliot-like Underground, he telephones his fiancée, Nina Blount. They have become engaged by mail, and their special problem from now on will be to find a material basis for their marriage. Adam's first stop, and his first move into the past is Shepheard's Hotel (in reality Rosa Lewis's Cavendish Hotel, from which Waugh was forever banished after the publication of *Vile Bodies*). Ponderous Edwardian bric-à-brac chokes its gloomy chambers, and a hilarious crowd of aging misfits swills champagne in the overdecorated parlour: "One can go to 'Shepheard's' parched with modernity any day, if Lottie likes one's face, and still draw up, cool and uncontaminated, great healing draughts from the well of Edwardian certainty" (p. 32). In this bulwark of Philistia, where no actors or artists are allowed, Adam lets the ubiquitous and Firbankian Major put his newfound wealth on the wheel of Fortune by betting it on "quite the worst sort of horse" (p. 43). When he reappears on "the biggest battlefield in the history of the world" at the end of the novel (p. 247), the Major has grown far more powerful. Now a General, with "pretty" decorations, he seduces Chastity, whose monotonous life of fleshly delights bears the "one thing after another" stamp of life in Fortune's realm.[12] The gross perversion of Chastity by Fortune perhaps reflects Waugh's belief that his marriage to Evelyn Gardner had failed because the young couple had let themselves become Fortune's hostages. Ironically, it is Ginger Littlejohn (modelled on "the basement boy," John Heygate),[13] who says, "After all, damn it, what does being in love mean if you can't trust a person?" (p. 219). Adam knows that a marriage is "bogus" if it doesn't "*go on*—for quite a long time" (p. 132), but he never finds "something different" from Fortune to base it on.

"One thing after another": Archie Schwert's party comes next, and here poor Miss Mouse is too timid to "dance like a Bacchante before them all" (p. 52). But disorder will out, and so the hilarious episode ends with Miss Runcible dressed as a Hottentot in the prime minister's study; her civilized savagery topples the government. On the one hand Waugh sympathizes with Miss Mouse and her primitive desires, and he relishes the eruption of barbarism in the heart of authority. But there is another side of Waugh which loathes anarchy as a force preventing self-fulfilment rather than permitting it. The more Waugh loved savagery the more he hated it, for he came to see that self-indulgence turned people into mere victims of contingency.

After Archie Schwert's party, Adam takes his second step into the past: he goes to Colonel Blount's decaying mock-Gothic manor, Doubting 'All. Here innuendo says it all: a stupid sheep precedes the taxi up the drive, the Colonel mistakes Adam for a vacuum-cleaner salesman, talks about films, and reads an old volume of *Punch*, which he shuts "with a broad sweep of the arm rather as the headmaster of Adam's private school used to shut the Bible after evening prayers" (p. 72). A "fire burning in a fine rococo fireplace" (p. 70) intimates that this fusty Victorian world is hell.[14] A cabinet containing relics shows that it is as defunct as a museum-piece, and its motley furnishings reflect its spiritual fragmentation. While the reader cannot ignore Waugh's wonderfully realistic portrait of the old Colonel, he should realize that, as so often in Waugh's fiction, he has one foot in fantasy and the other in parable. The Colonel's repeated failures to recognize Adam reflect a lack of discernment born of spiritual dullness, and the fact that he is driven daily to the cinema by the Anglican Rector suggests the source of his dullness. Blount gives Adam a cheque for £1,000, signed "Charlie Chaplin," and back in London, Adam capers with it in front of a mirror before Nina points out the fraud: "Well, I'm damned," says Adam. "The old devil" (p. 86). Waugh's allusive language creates a vague sense of malaise stemming from no apparent cause, but it also implies the cure.

Before moving further into the past, Waugh counterpoints past and present. Lady Metroland's party is a nodal point and a splendid tour de force; for the first time since the Channel crossing, most of the characters are reunited. The operative principle here is the misrepresentation of distortion—that is, gossip about evangelism—and the catalyst is Lord Simon Balcairn. Balcairn, almost certainly a composite of columnists Patrick Balfour and Tom Driberg, represents a long and noble lineage now so debased that it sells gossip. The disgraced columnist enters Margot's party in disguise, but is detected and expelled by Rothschild who, although often incognito himself, is "endowed with a penetrating acumen in the detection of falsehood and exaggeration" (p. 33). Balcairn kills himself, thereby preparing the way for Adam as his successor; but he does not die before writing his extremely funny and wholly fallacious account of Mrs. Ape's conversion of the English upper classes. Balcairn's story is a fine example of the way Waugh's satire can cut two ways. On the one hand, Mrs. Ape's evangelism is even more disreputable than the Rector's Anglicanism and Lady Circumference is right to reject it. On the other hand Waugh satirizes her and everyone else for taking the *Excess* to court: in modern England, he implies, salvation is only a nasty rumour and to be accused of penitence is grounds for libel.

The novel's most marvellously preposterous pages now ensue as Adam, having found a temporary vocation as Mr. Chatterbox, invents a host of "Notable Invalids" and "Titled Eccentrics." Adam celebrates "popular deaf peeresses" and "chub fuddlers" with abnormally large ears; he becomes an arbiter of taste, inventing the fashionable sculptor Provna, the accomplished Count Cincinnati, and the brilliant Mrs. Imogen Quest. Devoid of any taste of their own, fashionable readers imitate Adam's fraudulent taste, wearing "the ultra-fashionable black suede shoes" and "the new bottle-green bowler" and rushing to the allegedly trendy buffet at the Sloane Square tube station, where "Mr. Benfleet . . . saw no one but Mrs. Hoop and Lord Vanburgh and a plebeian toper with a celluloid collar" (p. 125).

Waugh juxtaposes the younger generation's party in a captive dirigible with the older generation's party in Anchorage House, Lady Circumference's town mansion. Anchorage House is Waugh's third step into the past. A "picturesque bit" of "dominating and august dimensions" (pp. 125–26), it provokes "a confused but very glorious dream of eighteenth century elegance" in Mrs. Hoop. It is here that Father Rothschild gives his important diagnosis of the roots of the Bright Young People's wantonness:

> "Don't you think," said Father Rothschild gently, "that perhaps it is all in some way historical? I don't think people ever *want* to lose their faith either in religion or in anything else. I know very few young people, but it seems to me that they are all possessed with an almost fatal hunger for permanence. I think all these divorces

show that. People aren't content just to muddle along nowadays. . . . And this word 'bogus' they all use. . . . They won't make the best of a bad job nowadays. My private schoolmaster used to say, 'If a thing's worth doing at all, it's worth doing well.' My Church has taught that in different words for several centuries. But these young people have got hold of another end of the stick, and for all we know it may be the right one. They say, 'If a thing's not worth doing well, it's not worth doing at all.' It makes everything very difficult for them." (p. 143)

Rothschild sees that as the result of an "historical" accident, the modern world has inverted the Church's teachings. But while he knows the cause of the problem, he does nothing about it. As early as the first chapter Waugh says that he adopts an attitude of "Asiatic resignation" (p. 1) and that to him "no passage was worse than any other" (p. 8); he simply turns "his face to the wall" (p. 14). His lack of discrimination and lack of effective leadership qualify him as a target for Waugh's satire. After Lady Circumference's party, Rothschild rides out of the novel on his motorcycle, dressed in overalls; he never reappears, leaving England and his faith as the pawns of chance.

Still in search of his fortune, Adam returns to Colonel Blount's nineteenth-century house, where Mr. Isaacs of the Wonderfilm Company of Great Britain directs the "film-life of John Wesley." Currents of phoniness cross and recross in this craftily executed episode, which begins when a cigar-smoking actor dressed as Bishop Philpotts demands, "Here, what in hell do *you* want?" (p. 154). Adam's failure to realize that the Anglican Bishop is only an actor adds zest to the Bishop's funny account of the shooting and cutting up into little bits of Effie La Touche, Countess of Huntingdon. This misunderstanding resolved, Adam sees a group dressed in eighteenth-century costume singing hymns before a camera, under the direction of a wigged cleric; not far away stand scene-shifters "with the transept of Exeter Cathedral in sections of canvas and matchboarding" (p. 155). At the centre of all this pretence stands that dubious director, Mr. Isaacs, who wants to sell his film to Adam before he has even finished it. His sales pitch to Adam is charged with double entendres, and illuminates Rothschild's comments about "historical" decay:

"Now this film," he said in what seemed a well-practised little speech, "of which you have just witnessed a mere fragment, marks a stepping-stone in the development of the British Film Industry. It is the most important All-Talkie super-religious film to be produced solely in this country by British artists and management and by British capital. It has been directed throughout regardless of difficulty and expense, and supervised by a staff of expert historians and theologians. Nothing has been omitted that would contribute to the meticulous accuracy of every detail." (p. 158)

Owned and directed by Mr. Isaacs, the Wonderfilm Company of Great Britain and its productions are entirely British and give a very good *impression* of authenticity. In other words, the Wonderfilm Company is Britain itself, and the events in British history have been "films" ever since the company was founded, an event which no doubt took place in Tudor times: "Have a card. That's the name of the company in the corner. Not the one that's scratched out. The one written above" (p. 157). A hand-me-down firm, the Wonderfilm Company chronicles the empty extravaganza which ensued when the Elizabethan settlement inverted the course of British history and turned it into a "film." The "film-life of John Wesley" is but one episode in a continuing story of compounded fraud. An earlier film, says Colonel Blount, uncomprehending medium for Waugh's irony, was "quite a revolution in Film Art" (p. 163); that film, one suspects, was the Reformation. Waugh insinuates that England repudiated Catholicism but succeeded only in feebly imitating it. As a result, post-Reformation British history has become an insubstantial shadow-play, and in it, as in Mr. Isaacs's film, frantically fast passages alternate with unendurably prolonged scenes—that is, impermanence alternates with boredom. In *Decline and Fall* Prendergast, the lapsed Anglican, shoots the eighteenth century in the person of little Lord Tangent and is later decapitated by a lunatic Calvinist. In *Vile Bodies* Wesley's Methodism is another grotesque child of schism and so Mr. Isaacs's slipshod film is an imitation of a distortion. Evangelical Mrs. Ape, with her tweeds and magnetic smile, is another distant successor of schism, both inverted and perverted.

Mr. Isaacs is an archetypal exploiter of religion, perhaps an early version of the Wandering Jew whom Helena meets in her novel. But postReformation history is no longer profitable, and so Mr. Isaacs sells out, presumably taking with him the extra "hundred feet or so of galloping horses" which he will fit in "somewhere else" (p. 162). As an enthusiastic actor in the film and an emblem of the consequences of the Reformation, Colonel Blount loses his money by purchasing a film about the causes of his own ruin. He is modelled on Arthur Waugh, Waugh's theatrical father. Colonel Blount tries to sell his film to Adam, the younger generation, but Adam is bankrupt, precisely because of the spiritual insolvency of people like Blount. Just as Paul, in *Decline and Fall*, is too blind to see what has made him blind, so Adam is too poor to buy more of what has made him poor.

The John Wesley episode marks the end of the novel's movement into the past, and from here on it rushes forward to its inevitable catastrophe. Fired by Lord Monomark for creating fraudulent gossip, Adam goes with Agatha Runcible and Miles Malpractice to the motor races, spending the night in a flea-pit named the Royal George, "by the edge of a canal" (p. 170) reminiscent of the one in *The Waste Land*. Protruding from its stagnant waters "rose little islands of scrap-iron and bottles; a derelict perambulator lay partially submerged under the opposite bank" (p. 172). The outing is not a complete success: Adam fails once again to catch the drunk Major, and Agatha crashes into a market cross and later expires. Adam sells Nina to his rival for the price of his hotel bill and the happy couple fly off to their honeymoon in Monte Carlo, where Waugh and Evelyn Gardner had gone in 1929. Culturally bankrupt, Ginger peers down at England and tries to quote from *Richard II* about "This scepter'd isle, this earth of majesty, this something or other Eden" (p. 222), but confuses it with *The Merchant of Venice*. Nina gazes down upon a sickening panorama of canals and suburbs where "men and women were indistinguishable except as tiny spots" (p. 223). The scene is Waugh's version of Eliot's "birth and copulation and death" in "Fragment of an Agon."

Adam and Nina are reunited in the thirteenth chapter, Ginger having been called up by "a direct act of fate" to serve in the war which has been quietly brewing all along. Adam impersonates Ginger and spends a good old-fashioned Christmas with Nina at Doubting 'All, his imposture detected by everyone but Nina's dull-witted father. The adulterous couple pass a cosy evening at the Rector's house, watching "A Brand from the Burning" (Waugh loves to make characters watch the causes of their own disaster), and the projector triggers a short-circuit which plunges the whole house into darkness for the entire Christmas weekend. In eloquently unstated contrast to the "good news" of the first Christmas stands the "very terrible news" of war, which the Rector hears while listening to a carol-service on the wireless. The cataclysm takes the characters by surprise, but not Waugh; even at the age of twenty-six, "it was never later than Mr. Pinfold thought." [15]

As he does in *Decline and Fall*, Waugh once again implants the touchstones of faith and taste through charged language. We don't need the "Author's Note" to tell us that Waugh is writing from a Christian perspective,[16] for faith is invoked by its absence, as is taste: Agatha Runcible, modelled on the Hon. Elizabeth Ponsonby, leader of the Bright Young

People, is a paragon of gross taste, clad in men's trousers, constantly "working hard with lipstick and compact" (p. 25), and often being mistaken for a tart. As in *Decline and Fall*, the worse a character's taste, the worse his morals. Again the dandified voice of the narrator provides a norm of order and restrained good taste, but it is not quite the same voice as before. This dandy is older and more self-conscious in the way he derides content through tone. Not only is he more knowingly droll, but he is also far less detached from the action than is the narrator of *Decline and Fall*. Almost one of the Bright Young People himself, but not really approving of them, the *Vile Bodies* narrator grants himself revealing editorial privileges: "Oh, Bright Young People!" he murmurs in a parenthesis (p. 24); in another he tells his reader that the Censorship Bill is "a statesmanlike and much-needed measure which empower[s] a committee of five atheists to destroy all books" (p. 136); on another occasion he complains about "all that succession and repetition of massed humanity" (p. 133). He lectures the reader on the distinction between "being" and "becoming" as exemplified by motor cars (pp. 177–78). He is altogether a more loquacious and distinctive narrator than the coolly outrageous one of *Decline and Fall*, and he is rather more compassionate.

In "Happy Ending" Adam finds himself sitting on a splintered tree stump on the world's biggest battlefield. There are no landmarks in this waste land, for everything is "burnt or broken." The catastrophe is the inevitable result of spiritual drunkenness, but people's bad behaviour only gets worse: Vanburgh gets a "divine" job inventing the war news; Doubting 'All becomes a hospital where the soldiers "adore" Blount's film, which dramatizes a cause of their own pain, and Nina is about to bear Adam's illegitimate child. Archie Schwert, "the *most* bogus man," is paradoxically imprisoned as an alien. The "drunk Major" seduces Chastity while Adam, an uncomprehending witness, falls asleep. His £1,000 is now worth "a couple of drinks and a newspaper" (p. 249), for apocalypse is near. As the name "Fenwick" suggests, Adam is a glimmering light in a dark swamp. He has enjoyed more insight than his friends: he knows that "things simply can't go on much longer" (p. 214) and "would give anything in the world for something different" (p. 215). His desire for "something different," something unique, links him with Tony Last and his "fear in a handful of dust"; but his moral blindness prevents him from seeing that what he seeks cannot be found "in the world." The novel's title, from Philippians 3:21, suggests where Adam should look for significant change:

For our conversation is in heaven; from whence also we look for the Saviour, the Lord Jesus Christ:

Who shall change our vile body, that it may be fashioned like
unto his glorious body, according to the working whereby
he is able even to subdue all things unto himself.

But because culturally undernourished Adam doesn't know where to
look, he remains, as the epigraphs suggest, on an Alice-in-Wonderland
treadmill, crying unreal tears. Like Agatha and Miles, and like Paul Pennyfeather before them, Adam will "mysteriously disappear," obliterated
by a random and haphazard universe.

## CHAPTER 7

# *Black Mischief*

*Decline and Fall* and *Vile Bodies* are comic accounts of the aftermath of schism in the heart of civilization, but in *Black Mischief* (1932) Waugh changes ground to examine the bizarre effects of revolution among "remote people." *Black Mischief* stems from Waugh's trip to Abyssinia in 1930 to cover the coronation of Haile Selassie for *The Times*. Waugh's friend Alastair Graham, then an attaché in the British high commissioner's office in Cairo, had been fascinated by the bizarre deportment of two Abyssinian crown princes who wore their bowler hats during luncheon: "It was this—his only—experience of Abyssinian politics that caused Graham to urge Waugh, whose tastes he knew, to attend as a spectator the coronation of the Lion of Judah."[1] Waugh went, and was spellbound by what he saw: "In this rich African setting were jumbled together, for a few days, people of every race and temper, all involved in one way or another with that complex of hysteria and apathy, majesty and farce; a company shot through with every degree of animosity and suspicion."[2] New surroundings always roused Waugh's sense of the absurd, and the result of his tonic visit to the African "distorting mirror" was a "first-rate" and "genuinely exciting" novel even more exuberant than its predecessors.[3] Almost all the characters and events can be found in the *Diaries* or in Abyssinian history: "Amurath" is Menelik, "Seth" is Ras Tafari, and "Achon" is Lej Yasu, rumoured to be "the real heir to the throne . . . hidden in the mountains, fettered with chains of solid gold."[4] Ngumo's journey to the heretical "Monastery of St. Mark" stems from Waugh's own expedition with the irrepressible Professor Whittemore to Debra Lebanos Monastery. Dame Mildred Porch and Miss Sarah Tin find their originals in "two formidable ladies" on a crusade against prostitution and drug trafficking. "Boaz" was Waugh's own nickname.[5] Waugh's intensely imaginative involvement with the scene utterly transmutes the facts, of course; even *Remote People* (1931), the travel book based on the

journey, is well on the way to fantasy. There Waugh describes "the gal-
vanized and translated reality of the preposterous Alice in Wonderland
fortnight,"[6] and several phrases recur almost verbatim in *Black Mischief*.

*Black Mischief* displays Waugh's fascination with anarchy more vividly than his first two novels, but below the surface extravagance powerful motifs and structural patterns indicate that he had not exhausted
what he had to say about the reciprocal relationship between civilization
and barbarism. Waugh liked to draw morals from experience: Mexico,
for example, provided an "object lesson," and so did Abyssinia. Abyssinia seemed very different from England but Waugh perceived that beneath its outlandish customs it was all too similar. "Why go abroad?"
Waugh asks sardonically in *Remote People*. "See England first. Just
watch London knock spots off the Dark Continent."[7]

In order to dramatize his conviction that polite cruelty can "knock
spots off" savagery, Waugh invents the absurd island empire of Azania,
which at first glance seems to stand in contrast to England but upon
closer inspection proves to be a looking-glass distortion of it. First there
were the cannibals; then came the Christian Portuguese, the Arabs, and a
sequence of "enlightened" native rulers. The first of these was the mighty
Amurath, who became the revolutionary and progressive Emperor of
Azania. Amurath's daughter immediately perverted the true line of succession by kidnapping the legal heir, Achon, so that the crown might descend to her son, Seyid. As the novel opens, Seyid loses his crown to his
son, Seth, and his life to Seth's men, who eat him: a forcible reminder
that Azania's long history of supersession has not erased its true, barbaric
nature. As progress gains a foothold in the island, it superficially defeats
the original savagery: "instincts of the swamp and desert and forest
mingled with the austere tradition of the desert."[8] Debra Dowa, the capital, "gradually lost all evidence of national character" (p. 19). But progress never wholly absorbs barbarism, which from time to time bursts
forth from its "sunless, forbidden places" to reassert itself.

Naively disregarding the lessons of the past, Seth euphorically announces to the victorious General Connolly, "We are Progress and the
New Age. . . . We are Light and Speed and Strength, Steel and Steam,
Youth, To-day and To-morrow" (p. 52). Getting up on "a high horse
about Progress" in his headquarters in the old Portuguese fort, which
serves by turns as a refuge and as a prison, he forces advanced measures
upon his subjects, thereby provoking a coup d'état. The rebellion issues
in an attempt to restore the "true" line of succession in the figure of
Achon, who has been imprisoned in a monastery all his life. But Achon
perishes under the weight of his new crown, and anarchy reigns. As a
result of its long history of "progress," Azania becomes a featureless joint

protectorate, ruled by insufferable foreign service agents guzzling sundowners: anarchy reduced to order. But the error of the French and English, as of the Portuguese, Arabs, Amurath, Seyid, and Seth before them, is to suppose that no further change will take place. As Waugh wrote in *Remote People* (pp. 180–81), "The process will go on, because it is an organic process in human life."

And indeed, as the novel ends, the waves lap ominously against the shores of the tranquil new protectorate—a hint that change will continue. For within the orderly new Azania, as within the "little inside" of the tom-tit in *The Mikado*, there is "a rather tough worm": the barbarians in the interior, who remain untouched by the declensions of civilized power on the coast. "Black, naked, anthropophagous," the Wanda[9] and the Sakuyu live untamed except when, from time to time, European armies press them into service. Their assistance is always decisive, for barbarism is far mightier than superficial progress. Precariously held in check and largely ignored except when it unexpectedly bubbles to the surface, barbarism outlasts the feeble inroads of European civilization. At all times, somewhere in the world, "the balance" between order and barbarism is shifting; and this is because there is an insidious savagery at the heart of civilization and in the core of each "modern man." Waugh personifies civilized savagery in a remarkable protagonist, an exploitive and unruly figure who barbarously cleans his pipe with gold manicure scissors and escapes from the bonds of society into refreshing four-day "rackets." This important figure is Basil Seal, who in one sense embodies change itself. But before we examine Basil, let us turn again to the wayward society which awakens his interest.

Far away from the warring factions on the coast, far beyond the terminus of that farcical flower of progress, the Grand Chemin de Fer Impérial d'Azanie, there lies the Monastery of St. Mark. This bizarre sanctuary is the "centre of Azanian spiritual life" (p. 220). With its superstitious monks promenading under yellow sunshades near the tumbled coffins of the faithful, the Monastery of St. Mark (the least of the Evangelists) is only a slight caricature of what Waugh said he saw at Debra Lebanos, where "all the monks had mistresses and children."[10] The evidence supplied by other writers suggests that Waugh did not exaggerate. Dean Stanley in *The Eastern Church* (that compendium of heresy which Paul Pennyfeather likes to read) regards the "Nestorians" as the worst of all heretics. In a passage that Waugh almost certainly knew, Stanley writes:

> But there is a daughter of the Coptic Church, yet further south, which is the extremest type of what may be called Oriental ultramontanism. The Church of Abyssinia, founded in the fourth cen-

tury by the Church of Alexandria, furnishes the one example of a nation savage yet Christian; showing us, on the one hand, the force of the Christian faith in maintaining its superiority at all against such immense disadvantages, and, on the other hand, the utmost amount of superstition with which a Christian Church can be overlaid without perishing altogether. . . . The endless controversies respecting the natures of Christ, which have expired elsewhere, still rage in that barbarous country.[11]

Stanley goes on to quote from "Harris's Ethiopia": "Abyssinia, as she now is, presents the most singular compound of vanity, meekness, and ferocity; of devotion, superstition and ignorance. . . . There is, perhaps, no portion of the whole continent to which European civilization might be applied with better ultimate results." In his delighted outrage at the Abyssinian Church, with its ridiculous heresies and specious relics, Waugh names it after Nestorius, an heretical fifth-century patriarch of Constantinople, who denied the hypostatic union and maintained the existence of two distinct persons in Christ.

Right next to the Wanda jungle and therefore literally bordering on barbarism, the Monastery of St. Mark enshrines the natural tendency to heresy which grows, Waugh maintains, in direct proportion to man's distance from the heart of his faith. Since, as we have already noticed, heterodoxy is slavery, the Nestorians' remote refuge from orthodoxy is really a prison which prevents them from maturing in their faith. Their chief prize, and the novel's best example of the retarding effects of heresy, is the unfortunate Prince Achon. His sire, the mighty Amurath, "had received education of a kind from Nestorian monks" (p. 12), and Achon reaps the gruesome reward. Stooped, blind, toothless and infirm, Achon represents the moral frailty which results when authority is guided by heretical religion. Locked in the prison of heresy, the legal heir has become an impotent slave; and in the absence of rightful authority his nation strives toward the condition of a utopia but reverts to a moral jungle. Waugh's view of English history since the Tudors was not dissimilar (note, by the way, that Seth orders a "Tudor model" wireless set).

Waugh has a certain amount of fun at the expense of the Wanda and the Sakuyu, but the real objects of his ridicule are the so-called "progressives" who try to improve the human condition while ignoring the essential barbarism and waywardness of human nature. As Waugh remarks in *Robbery Under Law*, "We are all potential recruits for anarchy. Unremitting effort is needed to keep men living together at peace. . . . Once the prisons of the mind have been opened, the orgy is on."[12] At its deepest level of meaning, *Black Mischief* could be set in England as easily as in

Azania; the exotic setting merely permits a more fanciful elaboration of the theme. In England as in Azania, civilization is under the same "constant assault" and the source of this assault is every man's Wanda jungle and Monastery of St. Mark.

In such a precarious world it is a dangerous luxury to become preoccupied, as Seth does, with autogyros and *Nacktkultur* while forgetting the cannibals in the interior. The innovations which he proposes amount to changes in name only. Instead of paying his soldiers, Seth simply promotes them all to corporals; "raw beef" is permissible if it is called "steak tartare"; the site of the Anglican Cathedral becomes "Place Marie Stopes." The series of supersessions which constitute Azanian history are merely nominal changes: Youkoumian casually crosses out "Seyid" and substitutes "Seth" on his calling card.

Just as there is a comic gap in Azania between words and what they represent, so there is a discrepancy between theory and reality. Drawing upon his fantastic "scraps of learning" (p. 190), Seth creates and destroys without a thought for the realities in the interior, abolishing the death penalty, marriage, infant mortality, mortgages, and emigration. His chimerical initiatives culminate in the printing of just under three million pounds of counterfeit money. Like his banknotes, the whole of Seth's little empire is counterfeit because he drapes its inward barbarism in the colours of European progress. Waugh dramatizes the emptiness of Seth's liberal pretensions by drawing together the motley population of Debra Dowa in the riotous victory masquerade at the Perroquet. After brooding in silence over his backward subjects ("I trust no one . . . I am alone"), Seth yields the royal box to the uncouth peer, Ngumo, and departs. The savage Ngumo represents the reality behind Seth's ambitions, and he oversees a night of masked revelry in which everything from Sir Samson Courteney's cardboard nose to Mr. Youkoumian's champagne is phoney. Because barbarism presides in the place of authentic authority, everything in Azania is appearance without essence and imitation without substance. A civilization without spiritual values is as insubstantial as a photograph; thus, on the day before Seth's victory, the harbour at Matodi "lay still as a photograph" (p. 20). Later Dame Mildred Porch and Miss Sarah Tin take pictures of the ill-starred birth-control pageant: frauds photograph a fraud.[13]

If it is amusing to watch progressives vainly struggling to redeem barbarism, it is even funnier (in a rather chilling way) to see the effortless manner in which savagery perverts progress. Here it is important to observe that in Waugh's view, a high civilization depends upon a firm sense of hierarchy and design—in short, upon right reason. As long as a civilization conforms to the will of God, it partakes of His well-formed design and can withstand the onslaught of shapeless barbarism; but as soon as it turns away from God's will, its distinctiveness becomes blurred and featureless. Azania is an example of a society which pretends to the name of civilization while replacing right reason by appetite. This civilization will never convert barbarism; barbarism will convert it. Here, identity and purpose undergo constant distortion. Connolly's hungry soldiers dine on their new boots, mistaking them for some rare delicacy; other savages misconstrue the humane exhortations of those intrepid ladies, Dame Mildred Porch and Miss Sarah Tin, and enthusiastically pledge to be modern in their cruelty to animals. Because appetite is natural to them, it never occurs to them that anyone could think that cruelty is wrong. There is no decorum in Azania: the natives use a tank as a punishment cell, rail spikes as spear heads, and telegraph wire as jewellery; Seyid nearly wins the war by claiming that a photograph of Seth in his Oxford gown is really Seth dressed as an English Mohammedan; Connolly successfully retaliates by asserting that Seth is a reincarnation of Amurath. And despite Youkoumian's confident belief that the natives "can't use [contraception] for nothing else but what it's for," instinctive appetite prompts them to assume that it must be an aphrodisiac. Perhaps the most explicit example of the frustration of progress is the derelict motor car which is inhabited by a family of natives and which blocks the route of Seth's parade. The symbol of the primitives in the machine implies that progress of a certain kind carries within it from the first the seeds of its own decay; it demonstrates that merely secular progress is just another kind of barbarism. By extension, Azania is not just another preposterous "remote place"; it is the reality behind modern England.

In weaving his tapestry of corrupt native officials and obscure diplomats, Waugh lingers over the richly comic figure of Sir Samson Courteney, representative of His Britannic Majesty's Government. Sir Samson is an important Waugh character. "A man of singular personal charm," inspired perhaps by Alastair Graham, Sir Samson is a precursor of William Boot and Sebastian. He refuses to grow up and accept his responsibilities, and his gentle decline in diplomatic circles has stemmed from an immature and chronic love of privacy. What he desires amounts to a secular form of monasticism: "Such a useless life," as Dame Mildred rightly says, "and so selfish" (p. 219). Although he has been employed to deal with public events, Sir Samson shuns them. While Seth's rebellion rages, Sir Samson in his isolated legation plays parlour games, tennis, and croquet. He is more upset about the lack of kedgeree and fresh asparagus than he is about protecting British nationals from being massacred. As time passes, he finds "incursions from the outside world increasingly disturbing" (p. 67), and to avoid "official stuff" he disconnects his telephone after dinner. Childish pursuits prevent him from protesting the demolition of the Anglican Cathedral, and he's "far too busy" to attend to the moral welfare of his daughter. A spiritual weakling, as his name ironically suggests, he spends his time knitting, and his irresponsibility infects the entire legation. Anstruther plays chess by telegram, and honorary attaché William Bland decodes official messages in bed, where he loses the cypher-book. Lady Courteney tends her garden, which contains "water-lilies and an immature maze." In "sprawling, schoolroom characters" her daughter Prudence records adolescent *pensées* in her "Panorama of Life": she believes that sex completes man's existence and that man should attune himself to nature's cycles. When they play bridge, all these moral infants forget "what a no trump call means," and therefore will "have to pass." They act according to their appetites, not their reason, and this practice will lead them to disaster.

The legation compound is already isolated, but Sir Samson withdraws even further from reality into his favourite retreat, his bathtub. Here, playing with an india-rubber sea-serpent, he achieves a dream of absolute and infantile freedom in an archetypal lush place: "Soon he was rapt in day-dream about the pleistocene age, where among mists and vast, unpeopled crags schools of deep-sea monsters splashed and sported; oh happy fifth day of creation, thought the Envoy Extraordinary, oh radiant infant sun, newly weaned from the breast of darkness, oh rich steam of the soggy continents, oh jolly whales and sea-serpents frisking in new brine" (p. 79). But soon there is a knock at the door and "crude disillusionment" as he abruptly returns to reality. It is an interesting moment, and a very familiar one in Waugh's fiction. It is the recurrent moment of disappointment. Like Sir Samson, other characters such as Paul Pennyfeather, Adam Symes, Tony Last, William Boot, Charles Ryder, and Guy Crouchback are expelled from their lush places into a dull and sordid world. Their loss of security is the archetypal event in Waugh's world: whether it is William Boot's airplane flight or Guy Crouchback's parachute jump, the euphoria is brief and the disillusionment is lasting.

Sir Samson's attempt to hide from the world is doomed to failure. When Seth is deposed and anarchy rules once more, a motley group of British nationals barricade themselves in the envoy's house, which is now cut off from the coast. "*One thing after another*," cries the petulant Sir Samson, caught in the grip of time and change.[14] Not for the first time or the last in Waugh's fiction, a refuge turns into a prison, and immaturity proves to be its own jail.

Into this amorphous empire of frauds, barbarians, and infants there strides Basil Seal, a colossus among Waugh's comic characters. If Paul Pennyfeather and Adam Fenwick-Symes were the naive victims of civilization's decay, Basil is a worldling who exploits civilization and causes decay. On the moral level of *Black Mischief* he represents civilized barbarism, and on the psychological level he is an aspect of Waugh himself: the man of the world.

From the start, Waugh is at pains to show that Basil is no longer at home in an England which has become too boringly stable for comfort. To everyone he meets he laments, "Isn't London hell?" The antipathy is mutual: he is expelled by the jaded, civilized barbarians in whose flat he awakens; a stuffy old codger at his club reprimands him; his sister no longer idolizes him; and Margot Metroland, once the epitome of polite savagery, is through with him. Basil's once-riotous cronies Alastair and Sonia are slowing down. Bankrupt now, they never go out, and the "masked parties, savage parties" of the Bright Young People are things of the past. Despite England's increasing seriousness, Basil, who has "no self control" and is "no longer a child, twenty-eight this year" (Waugh's own age), refuses to grow up. Unkempt, insolent, with pouchy, contemptuous eyes, proud "childish mouth," and whiskey-glass in hand, Basil remains resolutely selfish and unconventional, very much like Ernest Vaughan in "The Balance." Despite (or perhaps because of) their sophistication, women love him, especially the super-civilized Mrs. Angela Lyne. Basil frustrates his mother's plan to settle him in a sensible law office and follows his barbaric inclinations to remote Azania. Like Seth, he is alone.

Like Waugh's other early novels, *Black Mischief* has a pronounced figurative dimension. As the story advances, it becomes apparent that Basil Seal is Waugh's personification of an historical force. That force is instability, or change itself. Bored and "fed up with London and English politics," he tells his mother, "Every year or so there's *one* place in the globe worth going to where things are happening. The secret is to find out where and be on the spot in time. . . . History doesn't happen everywhere at once. Azania is going to be terrific" (p. 108). Like a cannibal, Basil the civilized savage is versatile, exploiting everyone and everything. In *Put Out More Flags*, Waugh tells us that he was used to "a system of push, appeasement, agitation and blackmail," and that he "played pirates alone." [15] Basil Seal flourishes in periods of incipient disorder, and he goes to every trouble-spot on the globe. He cannot tolerate too much order. He epitomizes Waugh's view that nothing is more agreeable than being a dissident. In his own person he encapsulates the force which tips the delicate balance between reason and appetite; to use Adam Doure's word from "The Balance," Basil is "circumstance." As his name suggests, he is a king of disruption, a "balancing seal" who makes sure that order never prevails too long in any one place. The personification of a demonic secular providence, he is a male counterpart of the goddess, Fortune. We have seen his likes before in the person of Margot Metroland. Mrs. Rattery of *A Handful of Dust* is a similar character, as is the portly Mr. Baldwin, who floats out of the sky to change the course of events in *Scoop*. It should be observed that Waugh's figures of Fortune often appear together with characters of the unaided reason, whom they usually exploit and destroy: Margot ruins Paul, Basil consumes Prudence, and Mrs. Rattery presides over the collapse of Tony Last's mock-feudal paradise. *Scoop* is different, because the worldly Baldwin assists William Boot rather than destroying him. In *Basil Seal Rides Again* the hungry Basil goes on a diet—but that is a joke that we can't appreciate unless we perceive that he was once civilized appetency incarnate.

The novel's structure confirms Basil and Seth as similar opposites. They have an affinity for one another, for they are both "Emperors," and they are both solitary and unpopular; they have been moving towards a conjunction for a long time. Basil's four-day racket at the Conservative ball coincides in time with Seth's battle against Seyid at Ukaka pass. When Waugh picks up the narrative, the revolutionary Seth has been "dictating since dawn" and, as if by telepathy, the subversive Basil awakens "late in the afternoon" amid the bad taste of civilized barbarism. A lady who has been "eating sardines from the tin with a shoe horn" says, "Quite thought you were dead" (p. 85). But Basil is not dead. Although excessive stability has rendered him moribund, the news from Azania revives him. Dropping in at three different parties (and thereby giving Waugh a chance to survey the eating habits of civilized savages), Basil collects an emerald bracelet from his mother and a large cheque from Angela Lyne; soon he is en route to Azania.

The paths of Basil and Seth cross at the railway station in Debra Dowa, and again at the Victory Ball at the Perroquet. On both occasions Basil is in the company of Connolly, the white man who understands barbarism. At the Perroquet Seth recognizes Basil but misunderstands his nature, wrongly believing him to be "the personification of all that glittering, intangible Western culture to which he aspired" (p. 142). At last he thinks he has found the one man he can trust, and Basil enters his service as Minister of Modernization. Once again Basil is ready to preside over a rite of change and supersession.

The first tremor occurs when General Connolly objects to Seth's ludicrous edict that his army should wear boots. Connolly offers to solve the problem (p. 169) but Basil "hesitated in a decision of greater importance than either of them realized. . . . Was it some atavistic sense of a caste, an instinct of superiority, that held him aloof? Or was it vexed megalomania . . . ?" Although Waugh does not say so, the answer is that Basil is innately devoted to disorder and uses the break with Connolly to promote it. The pace of the narrative accelerates as Connolly, Ballon, and the Patriarch plan a coup d'état while Seth goes berserk over modern ideas; the prison of Seth's mind having been opened, "the orgy is on." Basil grows increasingly fatigued as his subversive influence makes itself felt; then, after Seth produces a fortune in counterfeit banknotes, he returns to his office feeling "very tired." A shift in "balance" is now imminent. Only a racket will refresh the tired king of disorder; accordingly the tempo increases again and civil war threatens. Dame Mildred and Miss Tin are welcomed at the hilarious "Cruelty to Animals" banquet; Ngumo retrieves Achon from his long imprisonment; and Seth, alone once more, tries to demolish the Anglican Cathedral single-handedly. "Things seem breaking up here," Basil says as war-fever mounts (p. 230). The politic Youkoumian and other sensible people flee to the coast, but not Basil. Even though "the work of the Ministry seemed suddenly over," he wants "to stay and see the racket" (pp. 234,233). Finally, as Seth's birth control pageant winds through the streets, the coup takes place, Achon is crowned, and Basil's "ministry" is nearly done.

In order to sanctify the new monarch, an Office and a Mass "of enormous length" and complexity take place in "an octagonal, domed building, consisting of a concentric ambulatory round an inner sanctuary" (p. 258). This concealed sanctuary is the very heart of heresy and is another of Waugh's spiritual prisons.[16] The abortive coronation of Achon is an emblematic moment: when authority is imprisoned by heresy it becomes blind and impotent, and the sudden resumption of responsibility proves lethal to it.

Now there is no authority at all in Azania, and the British seek refuge in their legation, where they meet Basil. In keeping with the novel's principle of cultural transvestism, Basil now disguises himself as a Sakuyu merchant, and frightens his countrymen into turning their retreat into a fortress. Basil takes command of the transition from peace to war, then as the diplomats and their families prepare to fly away he is "reduced to unimportance, . . . a solitary figure in his white Sakuyu robes leaning over his rifle like a sentinel" (p. 273). Like a guardian, a force of history, Basil presides over the withdrawal of civilization. When Prudence says that she's worried about him, he replies, "Don't you do that, Prudence. It's one of the things there's no sense in at all" (p. 268). His cryptic language recalls the way Margot Beste-Chetwynde tells Paul Pennyfeather, "That's just the way it's going to happen." Like Margot, Basil is a personification of history without grace—he is mere linear consecutiveness, Sir Samson's "one thing after another."

Basil completes his ministry deep in the heart of cannibal country where, like some high priest of barbarism, he praises the dead Seth as a mighty Emperor whose progeny is beyond number. Basil is right, for Seth personifies that other powerful aberration, progress without grace. At the bacchanalia following Seth's cremation, Basil discovers that he has inadvertently consumed Prudence. In considering whether Prudence's macabre fate is merely gratuitous and disgusting, as Ernest Oldmeadow of the *Tablet* charged, or whether Waugh is justified in punishing her so severely, we must remember that we are dealing with another Waughian parable.

The appropriateness of Prudence's grisly end becomes more apparent when we realize that she is this novel's Paul Pennyfeather, her civilization's sacrificial lamb. She is a typical modern English girl, immature, lacking in experience, and therefore a natural victim of the civilized savagery which has produced her. She naively treats life as a sequence of games and records her second-hand emotions in her "Panorama of Life." She lives according to her appetites, and despite her name, she demonstrates little prudence. Her feather-brained sire has ill-prepared her for life, and she inherits and intensifies his weaknesses. Like many other children in Waugh's novels, Prudence inherits lax ethics without spiritual substance. She flees to London and the heart of civilization, but her plane crashes and the cannibals put her into a stew. Her failure to reach England is of no consequence, for what happens to Prudence in the Wanda jungle is only a literal version of what would have happened to her in England, where civilized barbarians like Sonia Digby-Vane-Trumpington (Wanda Holden) would have made short work of her. In being eaten, Prudence achieves the "natural heritage" of the typical English girl, though in a different manner than she has expected. But Prudence is not merely an immature English girl. In her wish that the soul of man should attune itself to nature alone, she is also an immature artist, and her "mysterious disappearance" is repeated by other bad artists in later novels.

Many aspects of Waugh's novel, including the image of Prudence stewed in a pot, proved offensive to certain devout readers, and a spirited exchange took place in the *Tablet*. The editor, Ernest Oldmeadow, called *Black Mischief* a "foul invention" and "a disgrace to anybody professing the Catholic name." Particulars about Waugh's "outrageous lapses" followed, and then came a letter of protest signed by "twelve prominent English Catholics." Other readers sprang to Waugh's defence, but neither his supporters nor his detractors remotely understood what Waugh was saying in his novel. During the controversy, which raged for some weeks in the columns of the *Tablet*, Waugh was travelling in British Guiana and Brazil, and when he returned he responded to the charges of atheism, immorality, and cruelty in "An Open Letter to His Eminence the Cardinal Archbishop of Westminster." [17] In a powerful and persuasive argument,

Waugh rejected Oldmeadow's charges as "grossly scurrilous" and accused him of "a literal-mindedness that is scarcely sane." While finding it
"painful to have to explain my jokes" and resenting being forced into
"the slightly ludicrous position of reviewing my own book," he coun-
tered Oldmeadow's allegations one by one, and concluded with an account of Prudence and the cannibal banquet:

> The story deals with the conflict of civilization, with all its atten-
> dant and deplorable ills, and barbarism. The plan of my book
> throughout was to keep the darker aspects of barbarism con-
> tinually and unobtrusively present, a black and mischievous back-
> ground against which the civilized and semi-civilized characters
> performed their parts: I wished it to be like the continuous, remote
> throbbing of those handdrums, constantly audible, never visible,
> which every traveller in Africa will remember as one of his most
> haunting impressions. I introduced the cannibal theme in the first
> chapter and repeated it in another key in the incident of the sol-
> diers eating their boots, thus hoping to prepare the reader for the
> sudden tragedy when barbarism at last emerges from the shadows
> and usurps the stage. It is not unlikely that I failed in this; that the
> transition was too rapid, the catastrophe too large.[18]

Justifiably indignant as he was, Waugh must also have been amused
by the spectacle of eminent ecclesiastics quibbling over a book about
cannibalism. Yet he responded with remarkable restraint, so that even
though his argument is full enough to exonerate him, there is a certain
reticence about it. Waugh could have argued that *Black Mischief* was a
very Christian book in its demonstration that the civilized savages of England should take stock of their condition. And to refute Oldmeadow's
slurs on his piety, he could have pointed to the novel's attack on immaturity, perversion, and heresy. But Waugh was never much given to apolo-
gizing, and felt disinclined to explain; and so he contented himself with
denying the accusations. He did not wholly "explain his joke." Indeed,
his "Open Letter" was not made public, Ronald Knox having persuaded
Waugh that it was not the sort of thing to bring before the Cardinal
Archbishop of Westminster.[19]
    Like its two predecessors, *Black Mischief* contains pronounced figura-
tive and moral dimensions behind its surface fantasy, but Waugh diverges
in certain respects from the method of *Decline and Fall* and *Vile Bodies*.
His new style is more discursive, rhetorical, and experimental; his narrative voice is more mature and far less distanced and precious; there is not
as much use of innuendo to implant a moral dimension. With its richness

of detail and local colour, *Black Mischief* is a more explicit novel than *Vile Bodies*. There are interesting technical innovations—the telegraphic, staccato lines which describe Basil's voyage to Azania; the characterization of poor Mr. Raith, who consists of nothing but his dialogue, and the use of the seasons to emphasize the cyclical return of barbarism. Whether or not Waugh had his eye on *The Waste Land* and its admonitory thunder, it is noticeable that the Azanian landscape remains bone-dry until Seth is deposed and Sir Samson flies away. Barbarism reasserts itself with the inevitability of the returning rains. Structurally the novel is more complicated than earlier ones because of its double focus on England and Azania, and because of its superabundance of character and event. Its major flaw, perhaps, is that its exuberance is insufficiently controlled: the young Evelyn Waugh advised Dudley Carew to "MAKE THINGS HAPPEN" in his novels,[20] but here almost too much happens.

*Black Mischief* is a two-pronged satire which strikes simultaneously at the savages of the jungle and the modern city; a powerful protagonist, Basil Seal, soldier of Fortune, bridges the gap between them. Basil's barbarism fascinated Waugh, who longed for change and disorder even though he couldn't tolerate it. Waugh was never able to sustain the "elusive ideal" of action, and so he chose the gentler ideal of art—art which served God, not man, and which promoted the values of good faith and good taste. In *Black Mischief*, as in the earlier novels, these saving values are systematically implied rather than explicitly articulated.

## CHAPTER 8

# *A Handful of Dust*

In *Black Mischief* Waugh satirizes a barbarous native chieftain who tries to behave like a civilized man, but in the more sombre *A Handful of Dust* (1932) he studies "other sorts of savage at home and the civilized man's helpless plight among them."[1] Waugh's target changes from barbarism in general to a specific aspect of polite barbarism: the collapse of marital relations in the house of England. Here, perhaps more than anywhere else in his fiction, Waugh displays his bitterness at Evelyn Gardner's infidelity, and in the person of Anthony Last he criticizes himself for his own naiveté and excessive tolerance. Here the dandified innocence of the earlier books gives place to an astringently unsentimental narrative voice, and in the reiterated asides about Tony's habit of trusting Brenda there is a rising note of sardonic rage behind the grim hilarity. Waugh's new tone is less neutral and more blackly ironic, his manner is more realistic, and his subject—a broken marriage, the death of a child, and the horrible fate of an indulgent father—gives his novel a poignant, almost tragic quality. In its devastating attack on the mind-boggling infidelity of Brenda and her "gang of gossips,"[2] *A Handful of Dust* is a cautionary tale about the dangers which lie in store for those whose negligent fathers fail to prepare them to handle civilized—and mainly female—barbarism. Jock Grant-Menzies complacently asserts, "The whole world is civilized now" (p. 270); be that as it may, savages surround Tony in the chambers of Hetton as in the forests of South America. "The Amazon stuff had to be there," Waugh wrote in 1934. "The scheme was a Gothic man in the hands of savages—first Mrs. Beaver etc., then the real ones, finally the silver foxes at Hetton."[3]

In *A Handful of Dust* Waugh once again attacks the debased modern world of frauds and shadows, and readers are often at a loss to find any countervailing centre of positive values in the novel. Some look to Tony Last, while others look to Hetton Abbey itself; but since Waugh is not yet at the stage where he enshrines affirmative values in character or symbol, his readers must seek them instead in his language and structure. Waugh's novel can be puzzling. Malcolm Bradbury, for example, notes Waugh's assertion that *A Handful of Dust* contains all he has to say about humanism, and wonders, "What has Waugh to say about humanism? It is hard to know."[4] But the novel's language and its "two-world" structure provide an answer. What Waugh has to say about humanism is that without faith it is no better than barbarism and is a cause of England's present state of decay. Tony Last's mock-Gothic Hetton Abbey is neither the embodiment of a "desirable" set of values nor a "centre of incorruptibility" as Bradbury says; it is just the reverse. The structural lines of force in the novel show that the reality behind the humanism of Tony Last and Hetton Abbey is barbaric Mr. Todd in his hut. The charged language of the novel shows that despite superficial differences Todd and Tony have an underlying affinity: both are death-loving fathers who withdraw from reality and from responsibility.

*A Handful of Dust* opens in the gloomy Edwardian living room of the interior decorator Mrs. Beaver, who rapaciously gobbles her yoghourt and speaks with ghoulish satisfaction of a fire which has just gutted the house of a prospective client. Like Fagan and other rogues, she stands with her back to the fire; a little later Tony announces, "She's hell" (p. 44). We know that her morals are indifferent because she has undiscriminating taste; her house is "crowded with the unsaleable furniture of two larger houses, without pretension to any period, least of all to the present" (p. 14). Mrs. Beaver has inherited the miscellaneous taste of the past, but lacking faith she also lacks good taste; nevertheless, as the arbitress of modern fashion, she covers fine old rooms in chromium plating and sheepskin carpets. A shadowy and featureless figure, she likes to "disregard [structure] altogether"; she splits up houses, and at her urging, her layabout son John splits up Tony Last's home. The first of many dangerous females who prey on Tony, she even sells Tony's successors a monument to mark his passing.

Like his mother, John Beaver has fallen heir to centuries of degenerating taste. On his dressing table stands the motley "collection of sombre and bulky objects that had stood in his father's dressing room" (p. 14). Despite its solid, reassuring appearance, all this motley Edwardian deadwood is only an attempt to compensate materially for a spiritual void. With such an empty inheritance, modern John Beaver is well equipped to become one of the many parasites who feast on Tony, the reluctant host. Beaver is a professional guest whose main desire in life is to avoid being responsible for anyone else. A grotesquely funny sponger, he is as morally bankrupt as he is impecunious. With his watery associations (he is "cold as a fish"), Beaver belongs to the submerged, fallen world which we shall see again in *Scoop*. As if in anticipation of Arthur Atwater's acceptance of John Plant's invitation in *Work Suspended*, London's "only spare man" accepts Tony's wholly insincere invitation to spend a weekend at Hetton, and Tony's elaborate Victorian refuge soon collapses under the onslaught of Beaver's featureless barbarism.

With its gasoliers, galleries, gargoyles, turrets, and its bedrooms named for Tennysonian versions of Arthur's knights, Hetton is the moribund house of England in the nineteenth century. There was a time when as "one of the notable houses of the country" it had actuality, but having been rebuilt "in the Gothic style," the former abbey is now cold, empty, and "devoid of interest" (p. 27). A drawbridge separates it from the world; lancet windows of "armorial stained glass" pervert the light and produce an "ecclesiastical gloom"; the noisy clock overhead erratically counts the hours; visitors photograph it as a curiosity. Dilapidated, impractical, its chill punctuated by "blasts of hot air" (p. 28), Hetton is driving Tony bankrupt; he plans improvements but "death duties" keep him in debt to the past. The country house tradition is good if it has actuality, but Tony perpetuates a vanishing practice out of mere duty and sense of precedent.

Waugh shares Tony's nostalgia for the cloistered, vanished life which Hetton represents, but unlike Tony he realizes that this debilitating nostalgia must be outgrown. He realizes that "things of tender memory and proud possession" (p. 28) are mutually exclusive for the mature man. But Tony is immature, and his love for the past holds him back, turning his refuge into a jail: "I can't possibly get away," he tells Brenda; "always here," he assures Jock Grant-Menzies (pp. 31,124). Ever since his nursery days he has slept in Morgan le Fay—apart from Brenda, in Guinevere—surrounded as if enchanted by "a gallery representative of every phase of his adolescence" (p. 30). A childish Arthur who fails to see that the old order passes, Tony belongs to Brat's Club, a club of spurious antiquity and "recent origin . . . intended for young men" (p. 19) and their immature elders. Tony chastises John Andrew for crying, but when they drink, Tony and Jock behave "like infants." Brenda is childish too, and she and Tony daily enact "scenes of domestic playfulness" of which the narrator pretends to approve but in fact is deeply critical.

Like other Waugh naifs, Tony Last is intent on his privacy. Named possibly for St. Anthony, the Egyptian hermit and founder of Christian monasticism, Tony is always delighted when he has a free weekend, for visitors interrupt his routine as a retired country gentleman. "When someone's awful you just run away and hide," says Brenda with the cheeky prefiguring typical of the novel (p. 58). But Brenda is starved for company and despite herself she enjoys the horrible Beaver's visit. Soon her affinities draw her to London, where there is no lack of company, and she leaves her husband alone in the country. Inevitably, the man who has loved solitude begs for visitors, but it is too late: excessive retirement and other ills have ruined his marriage.

Despite Waugh's apparent sympathy for Tony, and despite the pity which Tony's adversities frequently generate in the reader, Waugh criticizes him sharply for his pose "as an upright God-fearing gentleman of the old school," whose "simple, mildly ceremonious . . . Sunday morning . . . had evolved, more or less spontaneously, from the more severe practices of his parents" (p. 51). As far as Tony is concerned, religion is only a toy, a slightly onerous part of his "madly feudal" Sunday morning charade. He dissuades Beaver from coming to church because he "wouldn't enjoy" it, and he contemplates "the question of bathrooms and lavatories" while going through "the familiar motions of sitting, standing and leaning forward" (p. 53), a pale copy of his sterner grandfather in his "large pitch pine pew." (In Tony's absence Brenda symbolically descends "the great staircase step by step through alternations of dusk and rainbow" to join Beaver, who "emerges from the shadows below.")[5] When the minister calls after John Andrew's death, Tony is more explicit about his attitude to faith: he complains, "It was very painful . . . after all the last thing one wants to talk about at a time like this is religion" (p. 182). The spires of six churches are visible from Brenda's bedroom, which has a fireplace "like a tomb of the thirteenth century" (p. 28). Yet no real sense of religion penetrates Hetton's ornate Victorian walls, for Tony Last has impeccable manners but no faith. Prayers have not been said there since the war, that Armageddon which in Waugh's view unleashed the "intolerable tolerance" which now vitiates England.

Good conduct—the conduct befitting a Victorian patriarch—is more important to Tony than religion: he lamely lectures Brenda on her feudal duties, and admonishes John Andrew for using ungentlemanly language. But Waugh makes it clear that Tony is only acting a role: as Brenda says, "You're so much better at being serious than I am" (p. 39). Other sly nudges show that while Tony plays the role of Victorian paterfamilias, Brenda plays the role of châtelaine and Beaver plays the well-tried role of guest: they are all engaged in bogus behaviour.

Brenda's "very fair, under-water look," which makes her resemble "a nereid emerging from fathomless depths of clear water" (pp. 17,31) links her with the fishy Beaver;[6] accordingly, they play "analogies" about one another. Tony rejects Brenda's claim that Beaver is "quite like us in some ways" (p. 58), but the reader should not accept his denial too quickly; Tony is closer to the cat-like Brenda and the animalistic Beaver than he thinks. When, in a horrible and hilarious parody of his life with Brenda, Tony takes Milly and Winnie to the seaside to qualify for his divorce, onlookers criticize him as an "*unnatural beast*" for wanting to let Winnie bathe. Others are "curious to see what new enormity this mad father might attempt" (p. 226). The passage sounds facetious, but Waugh agrees: Tony *is* a beastly father because he is still-a faithless child.

But Tony is not the only false teacher in the novel. Brenda is another: she abandons John Andrew as if he were Oliver Twist and focuses her ruinous pedagogy upon John Beaver. Faced with Beaver's gaucherie, she says, "You've got to *learn* to be nicer" (p. 77), and with frank enthusiasm she instructs him in illicit love. The novel abounds with bad teaching: Brenda takes fictitious classes in economics and goes to fortune-tellers; obese Reggie St. Cloud, "the Head of the Family," gives bad advice; Mr. Todd learns from Dickens and from his bigamous father, allegedly "a man of education." Because of all this false instruction, there is ever-deepening delusion with no hope of enlightenment: like other Waugh novels, *A Handful of Dust* parodies the *Bildungsroman* genre.[7] Reggie St. Cloud advises Tony to sell Hetton for a school, but Hetton is already an academy for immaturity and irresponsibility. Tony's Aunt Frances thinks that the plans of Hetton resemble a Pecksniffian orphanage, and she is very nearly right, for John Andrew *is* "a poor little bastard" whose parents have neglected his well-being and development. They both "laugh . . . a great deal" about John Andrew's bad language and his fall from Thunderclap.

Coupled with Tony's unhealthy tendency to retreat is his excessive tolerance, a fault which Waugh had deplored as early as 1929 when he traced the younger generation's lack of discrimination to their elders' "jolly tolerance."[8] In 1932 Waugh inveighed against lenity again, remarking, "It is better to be narrow-minded than to have no mind, to hold limited and rigid principles than none at all."[9] Two years later, in *A Handful of Dust*, Waugh embodied dangerous tolerance in the person of Tony Last. Tony agrees to write Brenda's speech for her and reverses his decision not to go to Angela's for the New Year. He forbids John Andrew to ride Thunderclap and then relents; he postpones his duties in order to go to the movies; he refuses Brenda her flat and then gives in; he lets Mrs. Beaver redecorate the morning room in chrome and sheepskin; against his better judgment he allows John Andrew to ride in the hunt. Continuing to be tolerant even after tolerance has cost him his marriage, he allows Milly to bring the horrible Winnie to Brighton and buys drinks for the detectives who take evidence against him. The melodramatic Princess Jenny Abdul Akbar says, "Life teaches one to be tolerant" (p. 139), but Waugh believes just the reverse: had Tony been less tolerant, "circumstances" would not have led him to Mr. Todd.

What accounts for Tony's debilitating tolerance? Waugh blames the war, but more specifically he blames Tony's merely formal attachment to the sapless faith represented by that marvellous comic creation, the Reverend Mr. Tendril. Mindlessly repeating the sermons he has used years ago in India, Tendril intones, "How difficult it is for us . . . to realize that this is indeed Christmas. . . . Instead of the placid ox and ass of Bethlehem, . . . we have for companions the ravening tiger and the exotic camel, the furtive jackal and the ponderous elephant" (p. 96)[10]—farce on one level but truth on another, for as we have seen in *Black Mischief*, Waugh regards England as a moral jungle. Tendril's words lack actuality for his congregation, who "crouched silently for a few seconds and made for the door. There was no sign of recognition until they were outside among the graves" (p. 55). The moribund counterpart in this novel of Prendergast and the Rector of *Vile Bodies*, Tendril is the heir of schism and one of the sources of Tony's blighting tolerance.

Because Tony pays mere lip-service to religion (a religion, moreover, which Waugh regards as heretical), he is utterly unable to come to terms with "polite cruelty." Not surprisingly perhaps, in view of Waugh's unhappy experience with Evelyn Gardner, most of the civilized savages in this book are female. These odious women are all associated with animals. The cat-like Brenda enjoys "bitching" Beaver; her sister Marjorie has a dog named Djinn[11] who lacks any "spark of human feeling" (p. 65); the musky Jenny Abdul Akbar tells of the horses that belonged to her husband, a descendant of the Prophet. Not least, there is Mrs. Rattery, with whom Tony plays animal snap, and the rapacious Mrs. Beaver. Some of Waugh's women are oddly mannish: Joyce handles crates like a man in Mrs. Beaver's basement, and the accomplished Mrs. Rattery talks and rides like a man. Brenda and her "gossips" go to fortune-tellers and chiropractors, drink Sedobrol, and pervert language[12] in a species of "thieves' slang, by which the syllables of each word [are] transposed" (p. 129). They encourage Brenda to abandon her son and her child-like husband.

The abandoned child is one of the novel's central images: in ironic contrast to Mrs. Beaver, who stands by John Beaver, and Milly the whore, who won't abandon Winnie, and Mr. Todd, who takes care of Tony, respectable Brenda Last turns her son into an orphan. In a repetition of the abandonment motif, Rosa the Indian leaves Tony and his false guide in the jungle, and Tony feverishly conflates her with Brenda: "She will say nothing cruel. . . . there will be no hard words. She hopes you will be great friends afterwards as before. But she will leave you" (p. 325). Most of the women in the book behave treacherously, and at Brat's Club Tony becomes one of the solitary men in low spirits eating dinner: "They are those who have been abandoned at the last minute by their women" (p. 105). In connection with the motif of the abandoned child, one remembers that Waugh's film, *The Scarlet Woman*, ends in an orphanage.

When, under the influence of Beaver's stories about broken marriages, Brenda unexpectedly enters into a liaison with him, her friends are delighted. And in ceasing to be "the imprisoned princess of fairy story," Brenda feels no guilt, managing instead to make Tony feel ashamed when he tries to breach the privacy of her *pied-à-terre*: "He'll be tortured with guilt for weeks to come," says Brenda, with unwitting accuracy (p. 122). Feeling uneasy about her absence, she tries to "get him interested in a girl" and there ensues the brutal episode in which the theatrical Jenny Abdul Akbar tries to seduce Tony. She fails, and in a chilling scene, Tony feels "touched" by his wife's disappointment that he has not proved unfaithful. Privately she agrees that she has "done far more than most wives would to cheer the old boy up" (p. 148), and self-righteously perseveres in her affair. When she comes to Hetton on a rare visit, she turns Tony away from her bed with excuses about beauty-cream and sedatives. There is fury behind all this (as always, Waugh is careful to preserve a tone of neutrality or apparent approval), and it is no coincidence that Jock Grant-Menzies is made to speak of "women and pigs" in the same breath. Waugh's irony reaches an incomparably sardonic level when in arranging Tony's infidelity his divorce lawyer proudly tells about a wife who has impersonated a wife: "Lately we had a particularly delicate case involving a man of very rigid morality and a certain diffidence. In the end his own wife consented to go with him and supply the evidence. She wore a red wig. It was quite successful" (p. 204). Needless to say, Tony's sojourn with Milly at Brighton is a truthful parody of his life with Brenda at Hetton. The episode is another example of how the figurative leads to the literal in Waugh: Tony's untrustworthy wife has "poise" and because of it he goes to Brighton with a whore who can be trusted "to behave anywhere" (p. 221). Tony's "reasonable and decent" life collapses, yet despite the "all-encompassing chaos that shrieked about his ears" (p. 216), he only intensifies his chivalrous behaviour.

In ostensibly approving tones, the narrator attributes the Lasts' successful marriage to "Brenda's pretty ways and Tony's good sense" (p. 43). But this is tongue-in-cheek, for what he really means is that Brenda uses her charm to enchant her husband, whose unaided reason cannot withstand her duplicity. Tony educates his son to be a gentleman, but Waugh intimates that such a lax education will render the pupil vulnerable to the dangers of life. John Andrew possesses an inborn candour (he speaks with "a firm voice" as he repeats Ben Hackett's coarse stories, tells John Beaver that he should go to work, and denounces the Moulay's horsemanship), but his saving bluntness is destroyed by Hetton's hollowly polite atmosphere.

Implicit in Waugh's treatment of Tony's courtesy is an attack on empty chivalry, which rules that men should protect and idealize their ladies regardless of danger to themselves. Waugh implies that chivalry without grace is in the end suicidal, and that in educating John Andrew in courtesy, Tony is really instructing him not to defend himself, especially against women. Dwelling as he does in a stately house where the bedrooms are named for members of the Round Table, John Andrew can hardly resist such teaching. When seductive Jenny Abdul Akbar arrives with her tales of galloping horses, John Andrew is "fascinated"—just as his father is enchanted by Brenda. Although John Andrew swears that he can't have enough of horses, he dies of chivalry, a little Hippolytus destroyed by a woman's horse. After his death one of Jenny's handkerchiefs is found in his drawer—she has given her little knight a deadly "favour." [13]

It is evident that in being educated as a gentleman, John Andrew is actually being prepared as a sacrifice. Day after day he rides the ominously named Thunderclap as (amid echoes of Siegfried Sassoon) he is schooled in the long and noble tradition of English horsemanship. Unfortunately, that tradition has now degenerated into the spectacle of the fox hunt, an emblem of the disorder and dislocation of upper-class England: "They were a somewhat ill-tempered lot, contemptuous of each other's performance, hostile to strangers, torn by internal rancour, united only in their dislike of the Master" (pp. 157–58). Decadent as the hunt may be, it enthralls John Andrew, who wants to be "in at the death" (p. 159). Waugh is at his best here as he prepares the ground for the inevitable catastrophe. He paints a detailed picture of the hunt: unobtrusively he lets us know that Thunderclap is nervous and once pulls John Andrew "out of his balance"; [14] Miss Tendril, clad in a mackintosh, [15] arrives on her motorbike; Miss Ripon's horse is skittish. Much to John Andrew's disappointment, the hunt is soon over, for there is no fox to be found. "Then this happened": Miss Tendril's motorcycle frightens Miss Ripon's horse, which kicks John Andrew in the head. He lies in the ditch, "bent double." [16] He had hoped that Colonel Inch would "blood" him if he were "in at the death," and ironically he gets his wish. The irony intensifies when the Colonel asks whether Tony "would care to have the huntsman blow 'Gone to Ground' at the funeral" (p. 171). "Atrocious" as the suggestion sounds, it is very apt, for by removing all his defences, Tony has reduced his son to the state of a sacrificial victim, a fox in a fox-hunt ritually hunted down by his elders. Ben Hacket promises him, "You'll get a hunt right enough," and he does (p. 160).

We turn our attention now to the important figure who visits Hetton at the time of John Andrew's death. She is a very rich cosmopolitan divorcée, tall, erect, deft, impersonal. She loves "big bridge" and morphine, and she travels by air. She is austere, serene, and remote, plays "a very elaborate patience," and in the hunt she rides an "absurd horse." Who is this sinister and suggestive figure? There seems little doubt that she is Fortune, the goddess who rules the faithless modern world. The "five vast trunks" into which her possessions are packed are the five continents themselves. It is she who presides over the rapid and apparently inexplicable shift from weal to woe which ruins Tony's idyllic life. A force of nature, she "never [notices] houses much" (p. 156)—that is, pays no attention to the transient works of man. We get a foretaste of her love of change when she dons overalls and helps the workmen strip the morning room. She offers no consolation when disaster strikes, for she embodies the mindless chance which has caused it. When Jock asks her "what on earth" they can tell Tony about John Andrew's death, she aptly responds, "I'm the last person to have about on an occasion like this" (p. 166). "You can't ever tell what's going to hurt people," she warns cryptically when Tony speculates on how Brenda will take the news (p. 172). Tony asserts that the accident "just happened" and the coroner agrees that "nobody was in any way to blame for the misadventure" (p. 190); but Waugh knows that chance is to blame, and he blames Tony for placing himself so wholly in the grip of circumstance.[17] Chivalrous to a fault, Tony has prepared the way for his own catastrophe, and in the midst of sudden chaos he continues to practise the courtesy which has ruined him: how awful it must be for Miss Tendril, Miss Ripon, and Brenda, he says.

Brenda must be told, and in a scene of savage irony, Mrs. Rattery, the goddess of Fortune, keeps Tony company while they wait for Brenda's return from London. Something in Tony's anxiety about how to pass the time prompts her to stay and watch over him. Repeatedly Tony wonders aloud at how swiftly things have changed: "It's almost incredible, isn't it, everything becoming absolutely different, suddenly like that?" Mrs. Rattery replies, "It's always that way" (p. 172). She knows, for she is change itself ("I'll go and change now," she says). Tony wants to ease the strain of waiting, but there is nothing to be done: "It's a pity you don't play patience," says Mrs. Rattery, sitting "intent over her game" (p. 174). The narrator says that she establishes order, sequence, and precedence, but in fact, she has as much trouble with her cards as T. S. Eliot's Madame Sosostris; her game "nearly [comes] to a solution" and then bogs down: "Mrs. Rattery brooded over her chequer of cards and then drew them towards her into a heap, haphazard once more and without meaning. . . 'It's a heart-breaking game,' she said." Waugh agrees: the life governed by mere chance *is* a heart-breaking game, and one must have patience to get through it. "What can we do about it?" Tony asks. "There isn't anything we can do," Mrs. Rattery replies. "We've just got to wait" (p. 176).

Waugh's own chronic boredom invests this oblique exchange with sardonic overtones, and the reader with an ear for irony will see that the portrait of Tony waiting with Mrs. Rattery forms a powerful statement about the excruciating aimlessness of the merely secular existence. Well before Beckett's two tramps began their futile waiting for Godot, Waugh (who in 1956 missed the first act and professed not to have understood the play) dramatized the tedium of mundane life in Tony Last's game of animal snap with Fortune. Since this is a book of non-recognition scenes, Tony fails to profit from his experience, and as the novel ends he continues to wait as an unwilling guest in Mr. Todd's house. There is only ironic development in *A Handful of Dust*: Tony changes from reluctant host to reluctant guest, and from a weak father to a weak son. His hopeless waiting completes the symmetry of the novel, which has begun with John Beaver, the all-too-willing guest, waiting with "despair" for an invitation. In the jungle as in the city, Waugh implies, life is empty and boring, and secular man plays games to pass the time, "distracted" as T. S. Eliot says, "from distraction by distraction."

Jock Grant-Menzies carries the news of John Andrew's death to Brenda's flat in a large "featureless" house remodelled by Mrs. Beaver. An anonymous rabbit-warren of single rooms suitable for "base love," this shadowy dwelling with its "pretty" furnishings resembles a Spenserian or Chaucerian palace—a house of unfaithful women, perhaps. It is like the crystallization of an anxiety dream, for Tony never succeeds in reaching the flat except by telephone, and even then his rival John Beaver is there before him.[18] Brenda's secret hideaway reflects her own selfish withdrawal (at Hetton she wants "a small sitting room more or less to myself") and it epitomizes the savagery of London, the tag-end of the historical spiral, and the pit of the inferno. Here people "kill in the gentlest manner" (p. 325), for they are civilized barbarians. Appetite governs their behaviour: a drop of butter glitters on the Princess Abdul Akbar's chin as she tries to seduce Tony, and Reggie St. Cloud, oafishly comic "head of the family," ravenously consumes "things that others usually left on their plates, the heads and tails of whiting, whole mouthfuls of chicken bone, peach stones and apple cores, cheese rinds and the fibrous parts of the artichoke" (p. 231).

When Jock arrives, Brenda is away having her fortune told from the soles of her feet, but her neighbour, Jenny Abdul Akbar, invites him in. Her bad taste tells us all we need to know about the morals which prevail in her household:

> The Princess's single room was furnished promiscuously and with truly Eastern disregard of the right properties of things; swords meant to adorn the state robes of a moorish caid were swung from the picture rail; mats made for prayer were strewn on the divan; the carpet on the floor had been made in Bokhara as a wall covering; while over the dressing table was draped a shawl made in Yokohama for sale to cruise-passengers; an octagonal table from Port Said held a Thibetan Buddha of pale soapstone; six ivory elephants from Bombay stood along the top of the radiator. Other cultures, too, were represented . . ." (p. 180)

When Brenda receives the bad news she thinks Jock means John Beaver, and is desolate; when she learns that he means her son John Andrew, she blurts out, "Oh thank God," and collapses into a "gilt" chair. Her marriage is at an end, and she writes to Tony, "If John Andrew had not died things might not have happened like this" (p. 190). But Waugh knows that Brenda's reasoning is inverted, like everything else in her world. The truth is that John Andrew dies because his parents have based their marriage on nothing more stable than charm.

In the divorce proceedings, "it was thought convenient that Brenda should appear as plaintiff" (p. 202). The arrangement is not as unjust as it appears, for as a too-indulgent husband and father, Tony is in part responsible for what has happened. Even on the hilarious divorce outing at Brighton, Tony perseveres in his tolerant chivalry, but his courtesy reaches a limit when Brenda unexpectedly demands too much alimony. Tony won't give up Hetton and all that it means to him (he is even more attached to retirement than he is to good manners), and so he withdraws from the rigged divorce case, leaving Brenda in the hands of the ironically named solicitor, Mr. Graceful; gradually the Beavers lose interest in her and make their own westward journey. Tony's charade as the secluded patriarch of Hetton is over: "a whole Gothic world had come to grief" (p. 236).

Acting according to "the conduct expected of a husband in his circumstances" (p. 180), and with a "feeling of evasion dominant in his mind,"

Tony sails for South America "in search of a City" with the false guide, Dr. Messinger. Implicitly, Waugh criticizes Tony for not facing up to things: his "evasion" drives him ever more deeply into prison. Like the pigeon he had won as a youth when he was a "cyclist" at Tours, Tony is set free only to be recaptured, and in the grotesque and terrifying conclusion, his search for a secluded City leads him straight into the clutches of Mr. Todd.[19]

The City is significant in several ways. On the most immediate level, it is the fabulous Eldorado, which Raleigh and others sought, "sometimes down in Matto Grosso, sometimes on the upper Orinoco in what is now Venezuela" (p. 250). In 1932 Waugh himself sought a town in northern Brazil. It is called Boa Vista, and in *Ninety-Two Days* he recounts the adversities he experienced while trying to reach this remote settlement. As he struggled toward it, the nondescript collection of huts gradually presented itself to his fancy as the gorgeous Eldorado of legend. When at last he arrived, the reality profoundly disappointed him: "Already, in the few hours of my sojourn there, the Boa Vista of my imagination had come to grief. Gone; engulfed in an earthquake, uprooted by a tornado and tossed sky-high like chaff in the wind, scorched up like Jericho, ploughed like Carthage, bought, demolished and transported brick by brick to another continent as though it had taken the fancy of Mr. Hearst; tall Troy was down."[20]

Tony's City is the wretched Boa Vista of fact which lurks behind the gorgeous Eldorado of myth. But there is more to it than that. For Tony the City is an imaginative intensification of Hetton: "It was Gothic in character, all vanes and pinnacles, gargoyles, battlements, groining and tracery, pavilions and terraces, a transfigured Hetton, . . . a coral citadel . . . a tapestry landscape filled with heraldic and fabulous animals and symmetrical, disproportionate blossom" (p. 253). But instead of finding a transfigured Hetton or Camelot, Tony stumbles upon Todd's squalid little settlement. The conjunction is appropriate, however, for Mr. Todd's dirt-floored hut is the reality behind the decayed humanistic value-system of Hetton itself.

Even before Waugh had left England, his friend Peter Fleming had fired his imagination with the idea of Eldorado. Fleming had gone to South America as a special correspondent for *The Times* in search of the mysterious Colonel Fawcett, who had disappeared while in search of "amazing ruins of ancient cities . . . incomparably older than those in Egypt," ruins which were said to exist "in the far interior of Matto Grosso." Like others before him, Fleming failed to find Fawcett, and concluded, "Everything points to the whole expedition having perished in the summer of 1925, probably at the hands of Indians."[21] Fleming's return coincided with Waugh's departure; in his diary entry for 4 December 1932, Waugh notes, "Tea with Peter Fleming to talk of equipment for forests." Even though there is no reference to Fawcett in the diary or in Waugh's 1933 review of Fleming's *Brazilian Adventure*, there can be no doubt that the two men talked about Fawcett and about whether he was dead or stricken by amnesia or—as one of the most persuasive rumours had it— held captive. Waugh apparently preferred the last-named possibility, and when he reached Boa Vista his own disappointment fused with the notion of a captive Colonel Fawcett to produce "The Man Who Liked Dickens," a short story from which chapters five and six of *A Handful of Dust* were later derived.[22] An additional ingredient in this bizarre medley of fact and hearsay was the profound impression made on Waugh by the mad "mulatto evangelist," Mr. Christie, who claimed to enjoy visionary contact with "the total assembly of the elect in heaven"[23] and who said he had foreknowledge of Waugh's arrival. It was Christie, Waugh later wrote, who easily could have held him captive. Although Christie was Todd's original, it was not he who "liked Dickens": the priests at the mission of St. Ignatius were the ones who gave Waugh *Dombey and Son* and *Martin Chuzzlewit* to while away the hours.

The fate of Tony (or Henty, as he is called in the short story), derives in part from Waugh's chronic dread of boredom. His first three travel books show how intensely he suffered from *tedium vitae*, and in later years he feared it so profoundly that it gave him bad dreams. As he wrote in his diary some time later, "A night disturbed by a sort of nightmare that is becoming more frequent with me and I am inclined to believe is peculiar to myself. Dreams of unendurable boredom—of reading page after page of dullness, of being told endless, pointless jokes, of sitting through cinema films devoid of interest."[24] Waugh says that he experienced "four days of degrading boredom" at Boa Vista, and by the time of his next diary entry he had "thought of a plot for a short story." The theme of that story was waiting; and in *A Handful of Dust* Waugh amplifies that theme to demonstrate that hopeless waiting is the essence of the merely secular life.

Tony's City, then, is the unendurably boring City of Man which Waugh regards as a gross material parody of the City of God. According to St. Augustine, the two cities—one devoted to the flesh, the other to the spirit—were formed originally by the separation of the good and bad angels.[25] This makes an interesting comparison with Dr. Messinger's account of his City: "It was the result of a migration from Peru at the beginning of the fifteenth century when the Incas were at the height of their power. It is mentioned in all the early Spanish documents as a popular legend. One of the younger princes rebelled and led his people off into the forest" (p. 251). Waugh regarded the secular city as a place where "younger" people could hide from maturity and purpose, and Dr. Messinger's City epitomizes the idea of the world as a refuge. Established by the rebellion of a "younger prince," the City is a "radiant sanctuary" (p. 185) which Tony elaborates into a gorgeous palace of childish make-believe. Indeed, as he approaches it he regresses into childhood: in his fever he needs "constant nursing" and lies "awake in the darkness crying" (pp. 305, 311); in his ears there is the same muffled roar he heard in sea-shells as a child. Moreover, the "phantoms" which perplex him bear a surprising similarity to those which flooded John Andrew's mind at Hetton. But the City is not just any childish refuge; cut off from the world by "five hundred years of isolation," it sounds remarkably like Anglican England itself, an immature and heretical retreat from God's design: Tony imagines how he and the methodical Messinger "would arrive under the walls of the City like the Vikings at Byzantium" (p. 258). Tony's secular city is ruled by appetite; accordingly, Ambrose offers it to him to eat: "The City is served" (p. 317).

En route to his false refuge, Tony has a brief shipboard romance with a young woman named Thérèse de Vitré, who is returning to her true refuge and her strong father in Catholic, hierarchical Trinidad. (According to his "Open Letter to the Cardinal Archbishop of Westminster," Waugh made his first Easter retreat there.) Thérèse knows that she must choose a husband, and for a time it seems that she has found one in Tony. But when she learns that Tony is already married, she rejects him. There can be little doubt that Thérèse de Vitré is drawn to some extent from Teresa ("Baby") Jungman, a daughter of Mrs. Richard Guinness. Waugh proposed marriage to her, but they were both Roman Catholics and his previous marriage interfered: "Popped question . . . and got raspberry. So that is that, eh. Stiff upper lip and dropped cock." [26] Away he went, therefore, with a "heart of lead" [27] on a distinctly penitential journey to South America which was designed to end their relationship. Waugh told Henry Yorke that the sentimental interlude with Thérèse was "probably a mistake," [28] but it makes a useful point: having forfeited his chance to be guided by the faith of a good woman, Tony advances with Messinger, or mere rationalism, to the South American coast. But, as Waugh had perceived as early as "The Balance," the man guided by reason alone risks losing his balance. Bald-headed Dr. Messinger comes to grief when his canoe tips over, [29] and Tony also loses his equilibrium and enters a realm of nightmarish hallucination governed by Mr. Todd (or as he was originally named, Mr. McMaster).

Who, then, is Mr. Todd? To begin with his deepest level of significance, Todd (or *Tod*) is what his name implies. He is death, or (to quote from

"The Balance") he is "the appetite for death" which results when circumstance alters the delicate balance between appetite and reason in the man who has no faith. Thus, when Messinger overbalances, Tony has no rationality to support him and tumbles into the clutches of brutal appetency, or spiritual death.

But there is more to say about Mr. Todd. First, he is a bad father. His own father was a missionary who abandoned his wife (and presumably his mission) to look for gold in Guiana, where he found Todd's Indian mother. Todd emulates his neglectful father by running away—in Todd's case, to a remote savannah watered by a stream which is "not marked on any map": "Although Mr. Todd had lived in Amazonas for nearly sixty years, no one except a few families of Pie-wie Indians was aware of his existence" (p. 321). So insular are the Indians (many of whom are Todd's natural children) that they have never heard of Brazil or Dutch Guiana. Tony is the first stranger Todd has seen "for a very long time," and he does not expect to see any others. As he tells Tony, "Our life here is so retired . . . no pleasures except reading . . . I do not suppose we shall ever have visitors again" (p. 340). Because of his seclusion, everything about Todd is painfully limited. He cannot read, has not the Word, and even the material of his simple hut is "local" and "indigenous." The only books he has ever known are by his beloved Dickens, from whom he learns a few picturesque and wrong-headed notions about a tender-hearted God (the cross commemorating the arrival of Tony and the death of his black predecessor is only a "pretty idea"). The aimless personification of the sort of deviant provincialism that Waugh castigates at the end of *Labels*, Todd lives a repetitive and insular existence. We might well regard him as boredom itself—the boredom that springs from man's flight from vocation in the profane world. Although Tony calls him his "jailer," Todd's tyranny is based less on law than on lethargy. Interestingly, his way of imprisoning Tony is to give him absolute freedom but no guidance: "But my friend, what is keeping you? You are under no restraint. Go when you like" (p. 335).

The offspring of irresponsibility and apostasy (his father abandons his mission to hunt for gold), Todd resembles the vitiated spirit of post-Reformation England itself—his hut is only Hetton in a different key.[30] The downward spiral of history begins with "Todd's" ascendancy: generations of fathers have emulated his abdication from responsibility. Just as young John Andrew learns the wrong things from Tony, so Tony goes right back to the well-head of error to sit at the feet of Mr. Todd, the man who liked Dickens. Waugh later attacked Charles Dickens for his insular smugness and called him an "unhappy hypocrite";[31] thus in reading the works of the sentimental and tolerant Dickens, Tony learns all about the causes of his own disaster. Todd is the archetypal wrong-headed sire, an Archimago who has led his own sons into error, and his pernicious influence goes unchecked until, in an apparently dissimilar context, Lord Marchmain returns to his faith on his deathbed. Is there any connection between Mr. Todd and Waugh's own amiable father? Interestingly enough, Arthur Waugh edited the Nonesuch Dickens and treasured his Hampstead house as a rural retreat.

So far we have thought of Mr. Todd as death, and as an archetypal father of irresponsibility. But from a different point of view, Todd is an aspect of Tony himself: he is the blunt truth behind Tony's elaborate charade, the irresponsibility and death-loving barbarism within that Tony has never acknowledged. Tony looks like a "God-fearing gentleman of the old school," but behind his pretense he is as unregenerate and excommunicate as Todd. The more Tony tries to disown his real nature by veiling it in polite behaviour, the more certain he is to encounter it half a world away in the dark "interior." Tony gravitates toward Todd because they have a secret affinity, but Tony never perceives their kinship, rather like a man who fails to recognize his reflection in a mirror. As so often in Waugh, the figurative becomes literal: in England Tony was a polite barbarian, leading a life that was death, and in South America he lives with "Mr. Death" among real barbarians. In England he had nightmares; in South America he inhabits one. In England Brenda found it "torture" when Tony read to her and John Andrew; in Brazil Tony finds it torture to read to Mr. Todd. As before, Tony lives in servitude to his own savagery, and as before, he follows a deadly routine, waiting for a release that will never happen.

Because Tony fails to see and accept his unregeneracy, he can't do anything about it. Waugh's implicit view is that Tony must take personal responsibility for what has happened to him. In *Robbery Under Law* Waugh makes an observation which may be useful here: "Man is by nature an exile, haunted, even at the height of his prosperity, by nostalgia for Eden; individually and collectively he is always in search of an oppressor who will take responsibility for his ills. . . . anything will do so long as he can focus on it his sense of grievance and convince himself that his own inadequacy is due to some exterior cause."[32] In finding Mr. Todd, Tony paradoxically reaches his land of heart's desire, a paradise where he is never at a loss for someone other than himself to blame. And Todd accepts the blame readily, for the more Tony disowns his shortcomings, the more powerful Mr. Todd becomes. Tony's relationship with Todd resembles that of Marlow and Kurtz in *Heart of Darkness*.[33] But unlike Tony, Marlow escapes from that deadly symbiosis when he realizes that he too is capable of Kurtz's crimes.

One of the epigraphs to *The Waste Land* concerns the Cumaean Sibyl who has asked Apollo for as many days of life as there are grains of sand, but has forgotten to ask for perpetual youth. As a result, she grows older and frailer, waiting without hope for a death that will not come. Tony, who waits hopelessly for deliverance, is similar, but he bears an even greater resemblance to the questor of Eliot's poem. In the grail legends, as exemplified by *Parsifal*, the king suffers a sexual injury and is immured in his castle; a blight descends upon his country, which turns into a waste land controlled by a dragon. When some pure knight, or questor, fights his way to the "chapel perilous" and asks certain questions about the sacraments, he is able to kill the dragon, free the "Fisher King," and restore the king's land. Like the questing knight, Tony Last, "explorer," struggles through a waste land. His is composed of indistinguishable rivers, stony ground, red pebbles, and grass that rustles like newspapers. There is "no sign" of the City, and the map begins to take on a "mythical" appearance. Unlike the pure knight of legend, who is guided by faith, Tony does not seek the right goal, and he does not know the right questions. Rather than freeing the maimed king, he becomes one of the denizens of the waste land, waiting for a release that never comes. Tony is bored, but not quite to death. Like Paul Pennyfeather and Adam Symes, he does not die, for that would be too heroic an achievement for this stultifying world. A search party carries away his watch and a photograph of his grave (appropriate evidence), but Tony lives on; nothing will avail him except Mrs. Rattery's "patience"[34] as day follows indistinguishable day like the grains that fall from a handful of dust.

Waugh implies that only by rising above the level of Mr. Todd's merely natural existence can Tony and England escape from the tyranny of time, which of course is one of the novel's major themes. But this they cannot do, for their bankrupt culture has blinded them to any spiritual alternative. Tony continues to hide from the City of God, the "house" from which all the others in the novel have diverged, and the Richard Lasts who inherit Hetton, the house of England, intensify rather than correct his errors. Over their heads the great clock irregularly counts the hours; Richard's son Teddy is twenty-two but still lives at home; Molly Last rides a motorcycle; Richard and Teddy hunt with the Pigstanton. Like Tony, the new Lasts are tolerant: Richard speaks "tolerantly" (p. 345) and tolerantly defends Brenda's right to marry Jock Grant-Menzies. Like Tony, they withdraw: even more rooms are "kept locked and shuttered" (p. 344); a "skeleton staff" operates the house. Moreover, where Tony had raised but one fox—his son John Andrew—Richard Last raises hundreds of the young savages: "It was by means of them that he hoped one day to restore Hetton to the glory that it had enjoyed in the days of his cousin Tony" (p. 348). This is restoration by the wrong means, and the novel closes on a deceptive note of optimism which veils Waugh's bitter despair: the "blameless" citizens of England fail again to realize that they are raising young barbarians in order to hunt them down and kill them—a variation on the cannibalism of *Black Mischief*. Their civilized savagery differs from actual savagery only in the sense that it is more hypocritical. "*Du côté de chez Beaver*" and "*du côté de chez Todd*"[35] are the same: barbarous realms where games of patience are the pastime. Tony's monument of "local" stone—the one Mrs. Beaver sells to the Lasts—is the tombstone of a narrow and time-bound culture which practises manners without grace.

Although many readers consider *A Handful of Dust* its author's masterpiece, Waugh gradually altered the technique he employed to describe the adventures of Tony Last. Indeed, for some years he turned away from novel-writing altogether. He wrote the Hawthornden prize-winning *Edmund Campion* (1935), in which he is explicit about the values and historical vision behind his early novels; he journeyed two more times to Abyssinia, and he wrote the controversial *Waugh in Abyssinia* (1936). He published *Mr. Loveday's Little Outing and Other Sad Stories* (1936), an uneven collection. In September 1933 he met Laura Herbert (a cousin of Evelyn Gardner's), had his first marriage annulled after much delay, married Laura in April 1937, and settled in Piers Court, Stinchcombe, near Dursley, Gloucestershire. "Stinkers," as the Waughs affectionately called it, was to be their home until 1956, when they retreated even further from the world to Combe Florey House, near Taunton. During the Thirties, thanks to his shrewd literary agent, A. D. Peters, Waugh was in demand as a contributor to *Harper's Bazaar*, *Cosmopolitan*, *The Passing Show*, *Vogue*, *Town and Country*, *Nash's Pall Mall Magazine*, the *Graphic*, the *Fortnightly Review*, and several large dailies. He reviewed books regularly for the *Spectator*, the *Tablet*, and for the short-lived *Night and Day*. For Alexander Korda he wrote the scenario of a never-to-be produced and "vulgar" film called "Lovelies from America." In all, three and a half years elapsed before he published *Scoop*, which differs in important respects from his first four satires. Before we consider *Scoop* and the other middle novels (*Work Suspended*, *Put Out More Flags*, and *Brideshead Revisited*), it will be useful to recall the characteristics of the early style.

Waugh's early novels are surreal, fantasticated, and ostensibly amoral, but on the figurative level they are parables about freedom, servitude, and vocation. In most morality plays the protagonist profits from, or at least perceives, his error in a climactic recognition-scene. Waugh's special con-

tribution is the non-recognition scene, in which the spiritually blind protagonist comes face to face with the cause of his ruin and fails to perceive
it. In *Vile Bodies*, for example, Adam Symes, the universal victim,
watches as gross materialism in the shape of a drunk Major completes
the ruin of Chastity. And in *A Handful of Dust* Tony Last fails to recognize his own moral nature in the person of Mr. Todd, and so he spends
the rest of his life reading the works of Dickens. Up until *Scoop*, Waugh's
naifs always "mysteriously disappear"; and although they disappear in
various ways, their macabre fates are all attributable to culturally induced lack of insight.

In his four early satires the absence from British history of faith and
taste preoccupies Waugh. He implies that the absence of these values has
reduced England to the condition of a cartoon, and his primary targets
are the irresponsible fathers who have negligently allowed the dry rot
to set in. Distrust of the older generation is evident throughout all of
Waugh's early fiction, and it results in his idiosyncratic vision of an England populated by culturally disinherited waifs and orphans, exploited
and oppressed by their senile elders. The emblematic scenes which
Waugh presents to his naifs' uncomprehending eyes often take place in
houses which represent various periods of the past, and one of Waugh's
favourite devices is to make different temporal periods coexist side by
side. The more Waugh's witless *ingénus* travel, the more their novels take
the form of surveys of cultural decay. Sometimes, not content with the
examples of figurative barbarism which England provides, Waugh con-
signs his protagonists to the actual barbarism of "remote places."

Waugh's dislike of corrupt authority imparts a serious dimension to his
apparently frivolous satires. The discrepancy between the levels of action
and parable creates an ambivalent tone of condemnation and compassion; as a result of this deceptive tone Waugh is able to ambush readers
who mistakenly sympathize with characters whom he in fact deplores.
The same discrepancy generates an inverted chain of causation in which
the parable-level supplies the real explanation for what happens on the
level of action. Thus John Andrew's death is the result, not the cause, of
his parents' separation.

The most familiar moment in Waugh's fiction is the rapid shift from
elation to despondency, as in Paul Pennyfeather's delight at his projected
marriage to Margot and his immediate incarceration for white slavery.
This recurrent moment is usually presided over by a figure representing
Fortune and is associated with the reader's awareness that what the protagonist thought was a sanctuary is in fact a prison: unlimited secular
freedom is a spiritual dungeon. Waugh's vision is tragi-comic; his characters always miss the heavenly security they desire because they are be-

trayed by their animal appetites—a situation which is also familiar in Aldous Huxley's novels.

Waugh's narrative voice modulates from novel to novel; it describes his protagonist's adventures in a pungent and decorous style which becomes a major touchstone of taste and values in each novel. Other hints about Waugh's value-system enter his work through charged language and significantly juxtaposed scenes. The early novels are full of coincidences but the reader does not find them incongruous in Waugh's internally coherent fictional universe where the fantastic is normal. Waugh's plots are circular and bring the reader, but not the protagonist, to the point where (to use Northrop Frye's phrase), he can "escape from an incorrect procedure."[36] Waugh advances his narratives through repetition with variation; in his conservative comedies, *plus ça change, plus c'est la même chose.*[37] So it is that Azania is really England, and the worlds of Beaver and Todd are the same. In *Decline and Fall* Paul's limited experience leads him to prison and mock-death, but in a variation on this, Prendergast's lack of experience issues in his actual death as Paul's prison chaplain. In 1929 Waugh preferred Firbank to Wilde because Firbank was baroque and Wilde only rococo. Waugh's plots are baroque too—in novel after novel even the most minor details unexpectedly imitate the underlying shape. Eventually we shall see that Waugh's entire canon is baroque in this sense: each novel constitutes a set of unique variations on an underlying structure of recurrent themes and lifelong preoccupations.

Waugh's early characters are "flat" and he treats them strictly from the outside, but because Waugh is a moralist, their emblematic values give them a compensating luminousness. Considered from a biographical standpoint, the major characters often represent aspects of their creator's psyche, and their emblematic interactions reflect the working-out of Waugh's personal conflicts. Waugh's settings are almost always symbolic, and the décor of his houses is a sure guide to their owners' morals. A related device is symbolic recapitulation: Silenus's parable of the wheel sums up Paul's misadventures, while the history of the Wonderfilm company obliquely recapitulates the history of England.

The dense tissue of allusion, innuendo, symbolism, allegory, irony, theology, and externalized personal conflict which Waugh uses in *A Handful of Dust* typifies his early method, and there are readers who believe that he never wrote as well again. In *Scoop* he begins to turn away from his rigorous objectivity, and vague hints of affirmation and subjectivity sound a distant prelude to *Brideshead Revisited.*

CHAPTER 9

*Happiness . . . is not a goddess but a gift of God.*

Saint Augustine, *The City of God*

# *Scoop*

*Scoop* is a mellower and more affirmative book than its predecessors, and there can be little doubt that its sunniness stems from the newfound contentment that marked Waugh's middle thirties. Since 1930 he had been constantly on the move, his possessions so meagre that they could fit in a porter's barrow. Insular by nature, he had nevertheless become a globe-trotter. He knew the Mediterranean and remote places in Africa; he had been to Palestine, South America, the Caribbean, Morocco, and the Arctic.[1] He had travelled three times to Abyssinia. But by 1937 he was finally on the verge of stability as he prepared to marry Laura Herbert and settle in the English West Country. Below its surface insouciance, *Scoop* accordingly betrays Waugh's desire for a more mature way of life and style of writing. It is an unprecedentedly serene book, and although it is based on Waugh's Abyssinian experiences, its effervescent good humour shows little of the rancour which is all too evident in *Waugh in Abyssinia*.

Waugh went to Abyssinia in 1934 to cover the war for the *Daily Mail*, and he returned in August 1936 for additional material for *Waugh in Abyssinia*. A reading of the latter shows that many of the most outrageously comic parts of *Scoop* have a solid basis in fact: Ishmaelia is Abyssinia (with overtones of civil war Spain and America); Jacksonville is Addis Ababa; the Young Ishmaelites are the *Jeunesse d'Ethiopie*; and Gabriel Benito is Dr. Lorenzo Taesus, "a suave, beady-eyed little Tigrean."[2] Like President Jackson, Ras Tafari liked to play both ends against the middle with investors; and, like the Ishmaelian government, the Ethiopian authorities first confined the journalists to Addis Ababa and then sent them to Dessye to get them "out of harm's way."[3] Kätchen and her husband probably owe something to "the remarkable Haroun al-Raschid, . . . who had shaved his head, had an attractive blonde wife, a manservant called Fritz, and a fine custom-built car. He and his entourage disappeared in the last stages of the war, and afterwards the Abyssinians claimed that he was really a Wehrmacht colonel, his wife a coding clerk, and Fritz a German navy radio operator."[4] The cosmopolitan Mr. Baldwin was inspired in part by F. W. Rickett, the British agent for American financial interests, and the news of the oil concession he nearly won forms the original for the "scoop" of the novel's title.

In real life Waugh was the one who was scooped. Absent on a trip to Jijiga with his friend Patrick Balfour of the *Evening Standard*, Waugh missed the Rickett story and was "badly left oil concession." The reporter who got the scoop was the veteran Sir Perceval Phillips of the *Daily Telegraph* who appears in *Scoop* as Sir Jocelyn Hitchcock, the creator of totally fraudulent news. (Accomplishing in fiction what he failed to do in fact, Waugh lets William scoop Sir Jocelyn.) Following the Rickett episode, Waugh obtained a remarkable scoop from the Italian minister, Count Vinci, who told him that Italian functionaries were shortly to leave the country. Vinci's tip was tantamount to an admission that war was about to begin, and its parallel in *Scoop* is attaché Bannister's story about the Russian agent Smerdyakev (a brief tribute, perhaps, to *The Brothers Karamazov*). In *Scoop* William can't use Bannister's news because the unethical Shumble has ruined it. In actual fact, Waugh, aware of the thriving black market in pirated news at the telegraph office, tried to preserve his scoop by sending it in Latin. His editor thought the message was a joke and put it in the waste-basket.

Since the combat took place in remote areas of the country, no one got to see much war in Addis Ababa. As Waugh wrote to Laura, "No one is allowed to leave Addis so all those adventures I came for will not happen. Sad. Still all this will make a funny novel so it isn't wasted. The only trouble is there is no chance of making a serious war book as I hoped."[5] In the novel, the Fascists are German, not Italian, and the coup comes from the Left, not from the Right. It takes place right in town, and not only does William get the scoop Waugh had missed, but Baldwin composes and sends it for him. Thus the piece of news which disgraced Waugh the globe-trotting reporter marks the moment when timid William Boot begins to make good; the downfall of Waugh, the man of the world, is transformed into the ascendancy of Boot, the retiring man.

Waugh returned from his final visit to Abyssinia on 12 September 1936. Within three weeks he had finished *Waugh in Abyssinia*, and a month later he began *Scoop*. He told A. D. Peters, "It is light and excellent,"[6] but his progress was slow, partly because he was house-hunting in the West Country, and partly because his imagination does not seem to have been fully engaged with his subject. It was, after all, his fourth book about Ethiopia. In January 1937 he and Laura bought secluded Piers Court in Gloucestershire, and during February and March Waugh worked in his favourite retreat, the Easton Court Hotel, in Chagford, Devon. He noted, "the novel . . . has good material but shaky structure."[7] On 17 April he married Laura Herbert; a month later the novel was still dragging on: "Wrote novel very badly all week."[8] He seems to have finished *Scoop* by November; after three more months of revisions it was finally published in May 1938. Meanwhile portions of the novel had previously appeared as short stories in *Town and Country* and other magazines.

In a 1957 "Memorandum for Messrs. Endfield and Fisz," who for a time planned to film *Scoop*, Waugh wrote, "This novel is a light satire on modern journalism, not a schoolboy's adventure story of plot, counterplot, capture and escape. Such incidents as provoke this misconception are extraneous to the main theme which is to expose the pretensions of foreign correspondents, popularized in countless novels, plays, autobiographies and films, to be heroes, statesmen and diplomats . . . [In *Scoop*] a potentially serious situation is being treated frivolously, sensationally and dishonestly by the assembled Press."[9] Although Waugh's memorandum oversimplifies his novel, there is no question that *Scoop* is, ostensibly at least, "a novel about journalists." Its protagonist is twenty-three year-old William Boot, who writes a "bi-weekly half-column devoted to Nature";[10] like other Waugh naifs before him, he is torn loose from his peaceful obscurity and catapulted into an alien world where he becomes the victim of forces beyond his control. Reluctantly, William becomes a foreign correspondent for *The Beast*, and by adopting a point of view not far removed from William's innocent perspective, Waugh is able to subject the already bizarre world of journalism to even greater ridicule.

On that fateful (or at least chanceful) day when as the victim of a case of mistaken identity William reports to *Beast* headquarters in London, he enters a zany comic world governed by incompetence, misrepresentation, and outright fraud. Girls with "Punch-and-Judy" accents guide the lifts, a trick cyclist edits the sporting page, the foreign editor can't find Reykjavik on the map, and domineering Lord Copper has to look up the date of the Battle of Hastings. The debased world of Copper, and of his rival, Zinc of *The Brute*, is a fishy, submarine place:[11] the concierge sits in his enclosure "like a fish in an aquarium" (p. 35); deep in the bowels of the massive building leagues of newsprint are defiled "in grotto-blue light" (p. 249). One of the greatest of all Fleet Street stories concerns the Nobel Peace Prize winner, Wenlock Jakes, who from the wrong capital boldly reported a war he had never seen, thereby causing a revolution.[12] In Jacksonville there is cut-throat competition for news: because of mutual distrust, the journalists all squeeze into the same ramshackle hotel; whoever gets the daily bundle of telegrams opens and reads them all;

huge sums are paid to servants to steal information. The odious Shumble composes a free fantasy on the political connections of a train conductor, while in their frenzy to catch up, the other journalists spend a fortune wiring distorted information back home. When these "sheaves of misinformation" reach London, sub-editors complete the farce by reducing them to "blank nonsense" (p. 249). Yet, inaccurate as they are, news reports are seldom "absolutely, point blank wrong." As Mr. Baldwin says, "Those who are in the know can usually discern an embryo truth, a little grit of fact, like the core of a pearl, round which has been deposited the delicate layers of ornament" (p. 233). News reports are ornamental caricatures of the truth; thus journalism is to fact what heresy is to true religion. The obnoxious Corker, who takes William under his wing, sums it all up when he says, "News is what a chap who doesn't care much about anything wants to read" (p. 87).

In Waugh's view, journalism debases language and parodies the truth. As original founts of error, therefore, *The Beast* and its influential rivals are in part responsible for the gross bad taste which has ruined the modern world. Algernon Stitch carries a newspaper in his mouth, and Mrs. Stitch has picturesque ruins painted on the bedroom ceilings of her elegant Hawksmoor house;[13] she urges her decorator to copy a lion's head from a photograph taken at "Twisbury" Manor. She eats pâté de foie gras with a shoe horn, and her glossy little black car is always where it shouldn't be: on the sidewalk, bowling through Hyde Park, and in the "Gentlemen's Lavatory Sloane Street." "Coarse particles" fall from "a once-decent Nash façade" which is being demolished in central London (p. 9), but the decay of taste is evident at Boot Magna too, with its dying trees and defunct fountain. *The Beast* is the very oracle of barbarism, so the closer William gets to the world of journalism, the more bad taste he finds. On board the suggestively named *Francmaçon*, the passengers sprawl on crimson settees beneath bogus heraldic ceilngs, and light emanates from "imitation windows of stained, armorial glass" (p. 77). Corker, whom William now meets, appears as if conjured "by a djinn who had imperfectly understood his instructions" (p. 84). He is "not dressed for this climate," sits uninvited in the wrong chair, has bad fish and fake Scotch, and collects a roomful of Oriental curios made of synthetic ivory. He has just broken the news of a man's suicide to the wrong widow, and his telegraphic name is "Unnatural."

*Scoop*'s comical survey of bad taste focuses on literary style. John Courteney Boot's style is "a very nice little style," according to Lord Copper; Lady Cockpurse finds it "divine," but candid little Josephine finds it "banal." William Boot carefully models his lush phrasing on that of his predecessor, the Rector—one of several links in the novel between bad taste and bad faith.[14] But the worst style of all belongs to the journalists, who transmit their fallacious stories in hideous "cablese" to be further distorted by their editors. Phillip Knightley gives a useful account of these cables:

> Filing facilities were not only primitive, but laughable as well. To begin with, the cable rate was . . . about half a crown in British currency, one of the dearest rates in the world at that time. This led the correspondents to invent the most complicated "cablese" in a desperate attempt to cram as much as possible into a message—for instance, SLONGS for "as long as." Since the cable clerk, tapping away at his Morse key, did not understand half the languages in which he was so laboriously transmitting the correspondents' messages, the cablese served further to bewilder him. Cables arrived in London and New York so garbled as to be nearly unintelligible.
> . . . Before censorship was officially imposed, a story went around among the correspondents that the garbling of their cables was deliberate, and intended instead of censorship because it was cheaper and less likely to cause protests.[15]

Waugh himself practised "cablese." When the *Daily Mail* inquired about a Red Cross nurse said to be killed in a bombing raid, Waugh replied, "Nurse unupblown." [16]

The presiding genius of bad journalistic style is Lord Copper, pinnacled high in the intense inane of Copper House, his head "empty of thought" (p. 279) as he sketches a little cow. Copper is bad taste incarnate: he has a "ghastly library," a "frightful mansion," an "execrable country seat," and serves dreadful food and treacly brandy. Copper House boasts a Sassanian lounge and a Byzantine vestibule. (As usual in Waugh, Eastern art is a sign of perverted taste and morals.) In the vestibule stands "a chryselephantine effigy of Lord Copper in coronation robes . . . on a polygonal malachite pedestal" (p. 30). Rosewood doors of great "depravity of design" (p. 52) sequester him from the world, and beside them is installed "a little bell of synthetic ivory." His banquets, "like everything that was to Lord Copper's taste, . . . were unduly large and unduly long" (p. 299). Stupid and ponderous, the king of the Philistines, tyrannous Copper disseminates misinformation into "two million apathetic homes" (p. 214). His employees are the servants of his bad taste: "definitely," and "up to a point, Lord Copper," are their timid replies.[17] At his banquets, even those who were "normally the slaves of other masters were, Lord Copper felt, his for the evening" (p. 300).

Set against the atrocious taste of Copper's restrictive world is Waugh's own impeccable style, which is pungent, polished, crisp.[18] The reader will remember many examples of Waugh's urbane language: Mrs. Stitch's tiny black car, which resembles "a midget's funeral hearse" (p. 8) "dexterously swerving between the lovers" in Hyde Park (p. 62); purple-haired Mr. Baldwin, whose hands "rose and spread configuring the swell and climax of his argument" (p. 71); the "elderly princesses [who] sat in little pools of deportment" at the Duchess of Stayle's ball (p. 96); and William Boot defying "the doctrinaire zoology of Fleet Street" (p. 27). Best of all, perhaps, is Waugh's deadpan description of the colonization of Ishmaelia (pp. 101–2):

> Various courageous Europeans, in the 'seventies of the last century, came to Ishmaelia, or near it, furnished with suitable equipment of cuckoo clocks, phonographs, opera hats, draft-treaties and flags of the nations which they had been obliged to leave. They came as missionaries, ambassadors, tradesmen, prospectors, natural scientists. None returned. They were eaten, every one of them; some raw, others stewed and seasoned—according to local usage and the calendar (for the better sort of Ishmaelites have been Christian for many centuries and will not publicly eat human flesh, uncooked, in Lent, without special and costly dispensation from their bishop).

What, one wonders, could be farther removed from William's native Boot Magna?

Let us examine Boot Magna more closely. We notice right away that William's tasteful eighteenth-century home is decrepit; nothing has changed since the house was built, but it is now on the verge of collapse. Its ancient trees are about to fall, and "strange tides" move its lake, which irregularly alternates between flood and dryness. The secret of the "ornamental cascade" on the terrace is now in the grave with the gardener. Boot Magna's ample roof shelters a multitude of widowed and single Boots (none of them parents) and their many servants, including Troutbeck, the "aged boy," and Nurse Granger, playfully named for Maimie Lygon's pet dog.[19] The Boots are excessively self-concerned: Uncle Bernard has devoted his life to the study of his own pedigree, there is always a scramble for the morning newspapers, and the family's eating habits are selfish too:[20] "In course of time each member of the Boot family had evolved an individual style of eating; before each plate was ranged a little store of seasonings and delicacies, all marked with their owner's initials—onion salt, Bombay duck, gherkins, garlic vinegar, Dijon mustard, pea-nut butter, icing sugar, varieties of biscuit from Bath and Tunbridge Wells, Parmesan cheese, and a dozen other jars and bottles and tins mingled incongruously with the heavy, Georgian silver" (p. 287).

Old as the Boots are, none of them have matured: in a playful mood William's sister alters his manuscript from "badger" to "great crested grebe" throughout; and aging Uncle Theodore hankers after late-adolescent noctambulations in London. William himself is slow to grow up: his greatest ambition is "to keep [his] job in *Lush Places* and go on living at home" (p. 41). Like Prudence Courteney, William loves the cycles of nature and celebrates them in art. He has neither good faith nor good taste. A young pagan, his song is Herrick's "Nay not so much as out of bed? / When all the birds have Matins said" (p. 25). Sacred music is not unknown at Boot Magna, but it is Protestant music sung in "irregular snatches" by adolescent Uncle Theodore, who likes to repeat the same line over and over again. He swears "by Jove," not by God. None of the Boots are interested in the authentic permanence implicit in Uncle Theodore's rendition of "In Thy courts no more are needed, sun by day nor moon by night" (p. 279); with its "cluttered" hall and "double" staircase, Boot Magna is infected by the false permanence of grotesquely prolonged childhood. Poor Mr. Salter, as incongruous in the country as William is in the city, stays in Priscilla's room with its motley collection of china animals, trophies, and "prettily flowered" basin. The butler shuts Salter's door in "pantomime," a word which sums up the hollow innocence of this atrophied world.

Hidden in the remote West Country (it makes Salter feel "like a Roman legionary . . . tramping through forests beyond the Roman pale"), concealed at the end of a long driveway, and miles from train, telegraph, and telephone service, Boot Magna is the quintessential lush place. Though it is better than Lord Copper's twisted world, it is still dangerous, and Waugh implies that it is time for William to abandon his refuge before it becomes his prison, as it has become for Uncle Theodore. With its wonderful collection of single and unmatched Boots, all pursuing their own idiosyncratic courses, Boot Magna is a funny yet sinister Never-neverland, modelled in part on Pixton Park, the Herbert family home near Dulverton, Somerset. In depicting it, Waugh also takes a facetious glance ahead at the rural life he himself was soon to adopt.

When we compare Boot Magna with Ishmaelia, that "hitherto happy commonwealth" toward which "Boot of *The Beast*" unenthusiastically makes his way, we discover that they are surprisingly similar. Like Boot Magna Ishmaelia is isolated from the rest of the world—not by hedgerows but by "desert, forest and swamp"; neglected and forgotten, Ishmaelia has been "ruled off the maps and its immunity guaranteed" (p. 102). As its name suggests, it is a nation of outcasts. Its large ruling family—one is never sure just how many there are—are the dusky counterparts of the Boots, and as Paul Farr points out, they are all named for progressives and liberals: Smiles, Rathbone, Pankhurst, Garnett, Mander, Athol, Huxley, Earl Russell, Gollancz.[21] Like the Boots, the Jacksons are regressive isolationists: they have kept their nation out of the Great War, and the current President Jackson wants to retire. Like Boot Magna, then, Ishmaelia is a refuge, and like all refuges in Waugh's early fiction, this one turns into a prison when the Communists lock up the Jacksons.

Ishmaelia is of course Abyssinia, about whose unfair isolation Waugh bitterly complained in *Waugh in Abyssinia*: "Abyssinia could not claim recognition on equal terms by the civilized nations and at the same time maintain her barbarous isolation; she must put her natural resources at the disposal of the world."[22] In recording reclusive William Boot's visit to civil war Ishmaelia, Waugh examines the dangers inherent in personal and political isolationism.

If at Boot Magna William spent his days contemplating nature, he intensifies that activity in Jacksonville: he lives at the Pension Dressler, surrounded by a pig, a milch-goat, and "baboons, gorillas, cheetahs."[23] Inconspicuous as it may seem, beastliness becomes the constant backdrop against which William's adventures unfold: his nickname is "Beastly," he works for *The Beast*, and Kätchen, with whom he falls in love, lives in a "beastly" attic.

At Boot Magna strange tides move the lake unpredictably, but in Ishmaelia flood and fair weather alternate regularly. William's sojourn in Ishmaelia bridges the transition from winter to summer, and Waugh carefully charts the change: "The granite sky wept. . . . So the rain fell and the afternoon and evening were succeeded by another night and another morning" (pp. 112,130). When the rains suddenly end and the skies clear, the natives celebrate "summer holiday" and the turn of the season by dancing and drinking and "trumpeting against the defeated devils of winter" (p. 203). Even the milch-goat casts off "the doubts of winter" and responds to "the newborn sun" (p. 210). In Ishmaelia William is firmly lodged in the world of cyclical return and natural sequence; he had feared that Ishmaelia would not be lush, but contrary to his fears, it is even lusher than Boot Magna.

If Boot Magna is a dying lush place, Ishmaelia is robust, new, just-born. When the rains end, a huge rainbow stands in the heavens, reminiscent of God's covenant with Noah: "It was a morning of ethereal splendour—such a morning as Noah knew as he gazed from his pitchy bulwarks over limitless, sunlit waters while the dove circled and mounted and became lost in the shining heavens; such a morning as only the angels saw on the first day" (p. 202). In the passage just quoted, we notice a stylistic trick of Waugh's: although the rain has stopped, the "limitless, sunlit waters" have not yet receded; thus, figuratively speaking, Ishmaelia is so new that it is still under water.[24] It might be the infantile submarine world that Sir Samson day-dreams about in *Black Mischief*.

In this rain-sodden new world naive William Boot, unaccustomed to such overpowering lushness, becomes infatuated. The object of his adolescent affection is Kätchen, who, as the "wife" of a bigamous German prospector, is adept at navigating the perilous waters of the fallen world. She dresses for her element in "red gum boots, shiny and wet, spattered with the mud of the streets. Her mackintosh dripped on the linoleum and she carried a half open, dripping umbrella, held away from her side" (p. 142). When William sees her a second time, she is dressed in the same way and "seem[s] to be just as wet" (p. 153). By her own admission, Kätchen can "swim *very* well" (p. 156). Soon William is intoxicated with this pale young woman with the damp golden hair and enters the drunken, underwater world of profane love and Prufrockian erotic fantasy: "He was in love. It was the first time in twenty-three years; he was suffused and inflated and tipsy with love. . . . For twenty-three years he had remained celibate and heart-whole; landbound. Now for the first time he was far from shore, submerged among deep waters, below wind and tide, where huge trees raised their spongy flowers and monstrous things without fur or feather, wing or foot, passed silently, in submarine twilight. A lush place" (p. 172). Kätchen, an opportunist, strategically delays but soon gives in; and next morning innocent William awakens "in a new world" (p. 197)—the world of experience.

In characteristic Waugh fashion, William's euphoric happiness leads to disappointment, for fatherless Kätchen is a phoney (she thinks she resembles a film-star and admires her reflection in the mirror). When her "husband" returns, she escapes with him across the flood in a scene rich with the hallmarks we have come to associate with fraudulence. In William's canoe, they sit "as though embarking upon the ornamental waters of a fair-ground; lovers for the day's outing, who had stood close in a queue, and now waited half reluctant to launch into the closer intimacy of the grottoes and transparencies" (p. 224).

Kätchen may appear to be a new kind of Waugh character, but we have seen her kind before. A creature of the world of experience, she is a survivor like Grimes, who "breasted the waves of the Deluge" and moved when darkness covered the face of the waters on the first day of Creation.

A traitorous and abandoning female whose husband's once-shaven head resembles "a clipped yew in a neglected garden" (p. 215), she is an Eve and a Delilah, one with the pariahs and hyenas who constantly howl in the "new," fallen world. At ease in the water, she is akin to Brenda Last, Lord St. Cloud's daughter, whom Waugh compares to "a nereid emerging from fathomless depths of clear water." Christopher Sykes observes that Waugh had a taste for women with an "underwater look," and says, "Lady Brenda [Last] was a type that always captivated Evelyn. Miss Edna Best [was] . . . a perfect example of the kind of beauty he most enjoyed. His first wife was another; so was [Teresa Jungman,] whom he hoped to marry at this time." [25] While there is something of Teresa Jungman in Kätchen, the configuration of the characters suggests that the blonde *femme fatale* of *Scoop* owes more to Evelyn Gardner, who introduced Waugh into the painful world of experience and profane love.

Another of Waugh's attachments in the early Thirties was to Lady Diana Cooper, wife of the Conservative MP and future cabinet minister, Duff Cooper. In 1932 Lady Diana was acting in the Max Reinhardt production of Karl Volmöller's *The Miracle*, in which she played the part of the Virgin Mary, "an exacting piece of acting as she was required to stand as a statue for long periods." [26] When she was on tour, Waugh visited her on weekends, when they "would drive about visiting country houses." [27] Waugh was devoted to her, and before he left for British Guiana, he spent a "strained hour in Diana's dressing-room." [28] Lady Diana is the Mrs. Stitch of *Scoop*, the War Trilogy, and *A Tourist in Africa*. In *Scoop* Waugh establishes her as a more benevolent version of Margot Beste-Chetwynde, his earlier Fortuna. The opening scene (Waugh admits in his diary that it describes "Diana's early morning") [29] is like a comic version of an allegorical episode from Chaucer or Spenser. It shows that Mrs. Stitch is one of the forces which govern the fallen, sublunary world. Punctual, knowledgeable, versatile, she signs cheques, dictates into the telephone, and listens to her daughter Josephine (in reality young Lord Norwich) misconstrue a suggestive passage from Virgil. She gives instructions to an elegant young man who is painting picturesque castles on the ceiling, tells him to copy a lion's head and urges him to make the owl show up clearly because she is "particularly attached" to it (p. 6). Her interest in crossword puzzles recalls Mrs. Rattery's elaborate game of patience and her "absurd" little car reminds us of the latter's "absurd" horse. Friends resort to her for help, for she wields vast influence. (Indeed, in a passage which Waugh wisely expunged, she remarks to John Counteney Boot, "If only you'd take Holy Orders, John. I could fix you up nicely. I'm particularly fond of the Archbishop.") [30] Influential though she is, Julia Stitch is even more unreliable than Mrs. Rattery or Margot; with her "face of clay" and her tendency to mistake people's identities, she is a distinctly fallible Fortuna. Associated with the moon (she is a Diana, with "piercing shafts of charm"), she is change itself; she controls the various tides of the novel, including the "tropic tide" of Lord Copper's boring oratory. She is lovely but scatter-brained, and her well-intentioned but erratic activities result in William's sudden removal to Ishmaelia. Since the confusion of the two different Boots results from an error in discernment (one recalls the similar misfortunes of Paul Penny-feather and Adam Symes), Waugh may be implying that the fallen world cannot by itself generate any truly discriminating taste.

*Decline and Fall*, *Black Mischief*, and *A Handful of Dust* each have one Fortuna-figure, but *Scoop* has two. The first half of the novel is governed by Mrs. Stitch, and the second by that sinister-comic creation, Mr. Baldwin, named for Stanley Baldwin, the former prime minister. Waugh is at the top of his puckish form in his innuendo-charged description of Baldwin, who is a force of requital, a modern Nemesis. William inadvertently does Baldwin a favour when, his heart about to glory, "lark-like, in the high places" (p. 70), he allows the distinguished traveller to fly with him. Baldwin never forgets kindnesses—nor, one supposes, injuries—so, when William is at the end of his tether in the Ishmaelian conflict, Baldwin repays the favour. The enigmatic Baldwin is tastelessly bejewelled, and his conical, auburn-fringed pate reflects the sunlight; he is cosmopolitan and infinitely experienced. Slightly Eastern in appearance (Waugh's cue for the profane), he carries a coroneted *crêpe de chine* handkerchief and he resembles a Turk or a prize Pekingese. He claims to be British and holds a Costa Rican passport, but he is polyglot and could be from everywhere (as of course he is). He is fabulously rich and moves in the highest circles. He owns a vineyard in Bordeaux which produces better wine than Château Mouton-Rothschild, and a "little house at Antibes" with the "largest octopus in captivity" and a chef who is expert in preparing seafood. He represents "his own" interests. His "particularly delicate stomach" and digestive pills confirm that he is a figure of appetite.

Ubiquitous, versatile, and ambidextrous, Baldwin is a force of secular causation—the "one thing after another" that distresses Sir Samson Courteney—and so his dinner, "undeviating as the train itself," follows its linear and "changeless course from consommé to bombe" (p. 74). His "snake-skin toes" recall Margot Beste-Chetwynde's "lizard-skin feet" and the serpent of experience in the Garden of Eden. When William in his adversity prays for a *deus ex machina* (he prays not to God but to the offended great crested grebe of nature), Baldwin floats from the skies to "requite" William's earlier favour. Baldwin parachutes into the morally submerged world we have already noticed: "The little domed tent paused and gently sank, as though immersed in depths of limpid water" (p. 227). Just as Basil descends into the King's Road down a staircase covered in linoleum,[31] so Baldwin descends into Ishmaelia and the world of experience, "rung by rung." He is a profane god of fallen nature, and the milchgoat "reverently" makes way for him.

It is Mr. Baldwin (a pseudonym, of course, for he has many names in the "high places" where he dwells) who rescues William from the Communist coup and from certain imprisonment. After preparing an exotic luncheon in slightly bad taste, Baldwin's servant sends the first of the dispatches that are to make William famous (the wireless mast, as befits such versatility, is disguised as a eucalyptus tree). Baldwin himself clarifies the Ishmaelian situation for the still-innocent William. He explains that there has been a competition for the mineral rights of Ishmaelia, which he himself now owns, as he has been "fortunately" enough placed to buy out President Jackson. To prevent the sale, his rivals the Russians and the Germans have decided to overthrow Jackson, and at the time of Baldwin's intercession, the Russians are "momentarily in the ascendant" (p. 236). In a hilarious scene which unfolds "with the happy inconsequence of an early comedy film," Baldwin incites a drunken Swedish evangelist to liberate the Jacksons. Fraud expels fraud. After the successful "counter-revolution," he composes and types William's next dispatch "with immense speed" and retires early, for he has "had an unusually active day" (p. 245).

We have noticed that Waugh often externalizes his own conflicts in the persons of his protagonists. Paul Pennyfeather's search for a vocation and Adam Symes's quest for stability through marriage are examples. In *Scoop* Waugh splits himself into two personae, as he had done previously in "The Balance" and "The Tutor's Tale." In *Scoop* John Courteney Boot, with his life of Rimbaud and his travel book about life among the Patagonian Indians, is the worldly Waugh: Boot goes to Patagonia and the Antarctic while Waugh went to British Guiana and Spitzbergen. Waugh's globe-trotting self is a haunter of coteries, a friend of people in high places, and is pursued by an amorous "American girl." It is not possible to identify with certainty the girl who hounds John Boot out of London, but she may derive from Teresa Jungman, from whom Waugh in a sense ran away when he went to South America. The "American girl" gives Boot "a lucky pig to wear round [his] neck . . . made of bog-oak from Tipperary" (p. 87). Teresa Jungman gave Waugh a St. Christopher medal.

Waugh externalizes his unworldly side in his other Boot: "William Boot, countryman," author of *Lush Places*. It is William, younger than John, who falls in love with Kätchen, or Evelyn Gardner. Thus, by means of his two personae, his two Boots,[32] Waugh fictionally scrutinizes his two most important previous affairs of the heart on the eve of his marriage to Laura Herbert. And over both relationships there presides the luminous figure of Mrs. Stitch (Lady Diana), Waugh's confidante and guide in matters of love. "Boot," it should be added, was a racehorse in Waugh's "Captain Hance Saga," the rambling and never-published chronicle to which Lady Diana loved to listen, and "Pride of Boot" appears in her autobiography.

Why did Waugh visualize the gentler side of his person as a naive nature-writer dwelling in a remote West Country manor? An answer may be found in the pages of the *Daily Mail*. Throughout the Thirties, there appeared regularly on its variety page a short, lyrical column entitled "A Countryman's Diary," signed "P.W.D.I." and later, "Percy W. D. Izzard." Many of Waugh's witty contributions on manners and morals appeared on the same page. The contrast between Izzard's bucolic musings and his own worldly banter (and later his war reports) must have struck a chord in Waugh's imagination. When he sought a persona for his adventures as a war correspondent, he simply selected the wrong writer from the variety page, much as Salter chooses the wrong Boot. Waugh must have relished the absurdity of sending Izzard to Abyssinia where the "undiscriminating" nature columnist does a better job than the hardened veteran reporters. The other reason Waugh chose a rural character as a persona was that by the time of writing *Scoop* he had become far more sympathetic to the secluded life of the country than ever before.

*Scoop* marks the beginning of a turning-point in Waugh's career that is not complete until *Brideshead*. If we compare *Scoop* with *Black Mischief*, we find that in several ways *Scoop* reverses the earlier novel. In *Black Mischief* we saw the action over the shoulder of Basil, who is a soldier of Fortune and a representative of change. But in *Scoop* we adopt the perspective of innocent William, who is the victim of change and experience. In *Black Mischief* the action moves toward disaster and the reassertion of barbarism as the rains begin; but in *Scoop* the rains end and the action moves toward a happier resolution. Both novels conclude with banquets (bacchanalias are by now established Waugh motifs), but instead of being eaten, William is not even present: Uncle Theodore replaces him as proxy and savours the prospect of shady activities in London financed by a lucrative lifetime contract. However, the most important reversal is that for the first time ever, Fortune helps a Waugh *in-*

*génu* rather than harming him; through the benevolent action of Mr. Baldwin, William returns safely to Boot Magna and to "the green places of [his] heart" (p. 227). In *Scoop* Fortune is nearly as benignant as the Providence which governs the later fiction. There can be no doubt that the unprecedentedly happy course of *Scoop*'s plot is influenced by Waugh's sunny good temper during what was certainly the happiest period of his post-Oxford life. As he wrote in his diary the day after his marriage on 17 April 1937, "lovely day, lovely house, lovely wife, great happiness."[33]

But not everything is sunny in *Scoop*. Although the narrative begins in the morning with the aged servants at their "elevenses" and William quoting from Herrick, it ends under the baleful, changing, and reflected light of the moon. William has by now returned in safety to his ramshackle lush place, but his security is precarious. Waugh obliquely tells us that William's refuge is old, sterile, and vulnerable:

> The harvest moon hung, brilliant and immense, over the elm trees. In the lanes around Boot Magna motor-cycles or decrepit cars travelled noisily home from the village whist drive; Mr. Atwater, the bad character, packed his pockets for the night's sport; the smell of petrol hung about the hedges but inside the park everything was sweet and still. For a few feet ahead the lights of the car shed a feeble, yellow glow; beyond, the warm land lay white as frost[34] and, as they emerged from the black tunnel of evergreen around the gates into the open pasture, the drive with its sharply defined ruts and hollows might have been a strip of the moon itself, a volcanic field cold since the creation. (p. 263)

The curious double note of security and infertility suggests that William's peacefulness will be purchased at too high a price if long continued.

At the end of the novel (which was carefully reworked in manuscript), Waugh reiterates William's danger. We have already noticed that Mrs. Stitch, the moon goddess, is "particularly attached to the owl." William, for his part, is "particularly attached" to rodents (p. 25). The instalment of "Lush Places" which William writes as the novel ends is a daylight scene in which "maternal rodents pilot their furry brood through the stubble" of "golden" hay. But when William puts down his pen and draws the curtains, "moonlight streamed into the room" while "outside the owls hunted maternal rodents and their furry brood" (p. 308). So it is that even here, in the bosom of William's sanctuary, change and decay (the moon) and appetite (the predatory owl) are operative. Unless William can grow up, he will not long avoid them. Waugh sharply criticizes

William and all the childish Boots for their failure to mature—which for Waugh means trading "change and decay" for "Thou who changest not."

Because William is an artist of sorts, we may say that the conclusion of *Scoop* adumbrates Waugh's condemnation of the immature (that is, not explicitly religious) art which he himself has produced until now. William is the immature artist, who finds protection from owls and moonlight in the falsely reassuring glow of his unrealistic fictional world. As soon as he puts down his pen, the cold lunar light shines in, and his vulnerability is clear. In its implied criticism of William Boot, as of John Courteney Boot, who is dispatched to the Antarctic, *Scoop* is a veiled farewell to Waugh's earlier mode, and to his lost childish innocence. *Scoop* prefigures *Work Suspended*, *Put Out More Flags*, and *Brideshead Revisited*, which in their concern with maturity all stand in sharp contrast to the rebellious early novels. Waugh's second marriage was undoubtedly responsible for his new maturity; now, instead of criticizing fathers, he will be one.

## CHAPTER 10

# *Work Suspended*

*Work Suspended* is so different from Waugh's earlier books that at first glance it might be the work of some other novelist. It marks a complete about-face in Waugh's fictional method, towards subjectivity, realism, rounded characterization, first-person discursive narration, and a highly metaphorical and interpretive style. Moreover, it is a serious love-story, something altogether new in Waugh. Through the remarkable new persona of the maturing man, it dramatizes Waugh's revised view of himself as a serious artist in a serious world. Waugh was very pleased with his book, for (to use the words of his artist-hero, John Plant) it enabled him to avoid becoming "a purely technical expert" and offered him "new worlds to conquer."[1] Surrounded by the peaceful domesticity of Piers Court, Waugh wrote tranquilly while the war-clouds gathered, and three months after the outbreak of hostilities, he was still hard at work on his novel. He wrote to A. N. Roughead, "Am writing A 1 novel and filling in 6 forms daily in the hope of getting a commission in the marines."[2] In his diary he noted, "I take the MS of my novel up to my bedroom for fear it should be burned in the night. It has in fact got to interest me so much that for the first time since the war began I have ceased to fret about not being on active service."[3] But he lost interest in completing his novel, and abandoned it after joining the Royal Marines in December 1939. It now exists in two versions: the original, published in 1942 (by itself, against the advice of A. D. Peters), and a revised but equally incomplete version published in 1948 together with "other stories written before the Second World War." Waugh dedicated the 1942 edition to Alexander Woollcott, with the words, "It is now clear to me that even if I were again to have the leisure and will to finish it, the work would be vain, for the world in which and for which it was designed, has ceased to exist. So far as it went, this was my best writing."

Since the novel is only one-quarter complete it is difficult to assess, but

as it stands it records the vicissitudes of Waugh's persona, John Plant, a
successful thirty-three-year-old novelist who, following his father's death,
tries to burn the bridges which link him with his irresponsible youth.[4]
The novel is highly autobiographical. While Plant's experiences do not
always correspond in detail with the facts of Waugh's life (Waugh's own
father, for example, did not die until 1943), they reflect Waugh's belief
that his literary style should keep pace with his growth as an individual.
He had recently assumed the responsibilities of a house-owner, husband,
and father;[5] therefore he had to jettison the style of *Vile Bodies* and
*Scoop* in favour of a more mature manner. In *Work Suspended* it is evident that Waugh intended to make John Plant shake off the incubus
which retarded his development, but he abandoned his work before the
new pattern of Plant's life was clearly established. Waugh's attempt at a
mature style does not fully succeed here, and in a "Postscript" which
Waugh added to the 1948 edition, John Plant writes, "Neither book—
the last of my old life, the first of my new—was ever finished."[6]

Although *Work Suspended* is stylistically different from Waugh's early
work, it amplifies familiar themes and situations. We have seen that
*Scoop* is an artist-novel about a city Boot and a country Boot, the public
man and the private man. At the end of *Scoop* the public Boot goes to
Antarctica and the private Boot returns to Boot Magna, there to compose
his next contribution to "Lush Places." The menacing imagery insinuates
that his security will be short-lived. In *Work Suspended* the public and
private Waughs are externalized in two old university friends who are
now highly successful writers: Roger Simmonds and John Plant. Their
diametrically opposed artistic modes encapsulate two aesthetic currents
which dominated prewar England. Simmonds, the public artist (his history of "funny novels" and "jobs with newspapers and film companies"
resembles Waugh's), has perverted his art by subordinating it to his political interests. Having become a Marxist, he writes a play called "Internal
Combustion" in which "all the characters [are] parts of a motor-car"
(p. 44) and he has "cut human beings out altogether" because individuality spoils political theatre. John Plant, the retiring side of Waugh, demonstrates the dangers inherent in the other extreme: because of excessive
withdrawal his art has become mere art for art's sake, technically perfect
but essentially bloodless.

John Plant is a disagreeable character. Selfish, immature, untrusting,
atheistical, he is a reclusive figure who has "tried a dozen or more retreats
in England or abroad—country inns, furnished cottages, seaside hotels
out of the season" (p. 6). Yet because he has never faced reality, he has
never truly left home, as he himself admits. When we first meet him he

has sought and found seclusion in Fez, where Waugh himself went to write *A Handful of Dust*. There he has adopted a mode of life which is carefully calculated to absolve him from any sort of commitment. He practises economy and austerity, dislikes "profusion," eliminates money as much as possible from his life, inhabits a simple hotel, and scrupulously avoids any personal contact which might interfere with his prolonged adolescence. He exposes "the bare minimum" of himself in conversation with the British consul, with whom he enjoys a "serenely remote" relationship; when visiting Fatima in the *quartier toléré*, he leaves his cash and identification papers at his hotel, revelling in "privacy and anonymity, the hide-and-seek with one's own personality which redeems vice of its tedium" (p. 20). He tells Fatima that he is a fruiterer with a wife and six children in England. In his awareness of the pleasures of anonymity, Plant makes a typically adolescent evasion: he shirks the basic adult responsibility of having characteristics, and in attempting to remain a man with no qualities he resembles Waugh's most immature protagonist, Paul Pennyfeather, who is a mere "shadow." Not surprisingly, his greatest admirer is Julia, an infatuated adolescent.

John Plant's fictional method is what one would expect of a reclusive writer. His procedure is exact but mechanical, and he has reduced the artist's life to rule. In segments which Waugh cut from the 1948 edition because he may have thought the irony too obvious, Plant proudly maintains that his thrillers are "bloodless" and abound in "adornment and concealment" (pp. 1–2). All unaware of his creator's contempt for the fraudulent, he asserts, "I relish the masked buttresses, false domes, superfluous columns, all the subterfuges of literary architecture and the plaster and gilt of its decoration" (p. 2). Later he condemns "live" figures out of hand and endorses abstract, stylized characters. In a remarkable passage which was cut from the 1948 edition and which a few readers still sometimes mistake for Waugh's own artistic manifesto,[6] Plant describes his method: "The algebra of fiction must reduce its problems to symbols if they are to be soluble at all. . . . There is no place in literature for a live man, solid and active. At best the author may maintain a kind of Dickensian menagerie, where his characters live behind bars, in darkness, to be liberated twice nightly for a brief gambol under the arc lamps; . . . The alternative, classical expedient is to take the whole man and reduce him to a manageable abstraction. . . . It is, anyway, in the classical way that I have striven to write" (pp. 82–83). At first glance, Plant's method sounds all right, but in fact his "manageable abstractions" are precisely what Waugh attacks in "Fan-Fare," where he argues that characters who are "pure abstractions" are incomplete and insufficient. Those who protest that Waugh's own novels are filled with abstractions must remember that Waugh does not endorse them, as Plant does, but bitterly criticizes them: they are what result when "you . . . leave God out."[7]

It is in Plant's inability to come to terms with love that he is most objectionable. Calling it "this hooded stranger" (p. 82), he avoids it in his own life, and his fictional treatment of love is woefully inadequate. Plant says that love is "a problem beyond the proper scope of letters" (p. 81). But Waugh does not agree with Plant here. Waugh believes that love is only "beyond the proper scope of letters" to the novelist who, like Plant, is content to use "manageable abstractions," the "artificial figures which hitherto passed so gracefully as men and women."[8] To write convincingly of love, the novelist must cease to employ abstract characters and begin "to represent man more fully." To Waugh, that meant "only one thing, man in his relation to God." If "you . . . leave God out" you also leave out love and compassion; and to change your writing style you must change your life style. Plant says that he has always written in the "classical way" and that he will now write in the same manner of Lucy. But the classical way is inadequate: before the stunted Plant can write of Lucy he must truly love someone, and he must exchange his brittle classical style for something more substantial—for the style, in short, of *Work Suspended* itself.

As the novel begins, Plant is very far indeed from love: he and his friends routinely pass girls along; he treats love as "a parlour game" and sees sexual relationships "in terms of ownership and use"; he admits, "There was little love and no trust at all between any of my friends" (p. 113). In the Moulay Abdullah he makes noncommmittal love to the "ornamented" Fatima and then anonymously retires to his obscure hotel, where he cares for no one. As always in Waugh, lack of precise identity proves dangerous: Plant's failure to bring his papers to the Moulay Abdullah results in his arrest as, once again, a refuge becomes a prison. The Consul vouches for Plant, but the mishap ruins his seclusion. Once again he takes flight (one recalls Lord Jim's long series of retreats toward the wish-fulfilment land of Patusan), this time to England, where he seeks a refuge which will not prove to be a prison. He voices his fear of invasion in this all-important remark: "It lay at the root of the problem of privacy; the choice which torments to the verge of mania, between perpetual flight and perpetual siege; and the unresolved universal paradox of losing things in order to find them" (p. 49).

In his constant retreat from responsibility, Plant is only the latest in a long line of Waugh protagonists who are imprisoned by their immaturity—immaturity which has fallen to them from the lax hands of their fathers. It is suitable, therefore, that the event which initiates his recovery is the death of his father. A dotty old fraud, Plant's father comes from the same mould as Colonel Blount of *Vile Bodies*. He is "a dogmatic atheist of the old-fashioned cast" (p. 10), a theatrical Royal Academician who has a taste for huge, old-fashioned decorative canvasses. Despite his leniency as a father, he likes the discipline and severity afforded by Old Testament topics; one of his early successes (p. 19) was "Agag Before Samuel"—a notably bloody canvas (filled, interestingly, with a whole Noah's Ark of animals). Because he can paint in any style, he turns a tidy profit on the side through art forgery. He treats his annual exhibition as a "bluff" and a "private joke." His unfashionable house with its "masculine smell" contains room after room furnished in conflicting tastes; menacingly, ramshackle flats encroach upon its now tangled garden. He himself articulates the long historical decline which has made him "a Dodo," once caricatured by Beerbohm, and his son "a petrified egg" (p. 12). Father and son are very much alike: both are aloof and atheistical; both are austerely parsimonious in life yet highly decorative in their art; and both have classical or Johnsonian views about art. Plainly (or perhaps not so plainly, since Waugh veils the connection), an irresponsible father has engendered an even more irresponsible son.

Despite the elder Plant's kinship with the loathed parents of earlier novels, there is an unexpected development in the way Waugh treats him. While Plant senior embodies everything that he once despised, Waugh is almost sympathetic to him. More importantly, he allows the son to be reconciled with him. His father's death liberates Plant from what his father represents, and it is noteworthy that their reconciliation is one of taste. As John Plant stands before his father's last painting, he suddenly feels a new respect for it, and sees that the artist "had an historic position, for he completed a period of English painting that through other circumstances had never, until him, come to maturity . . . my esteem for my father took form and my sense of loss became tangible and permanent" (p. 40).

Plant's reconciliation with his father's taste is essential, for it gives him something to build on.[9] In the early novels there could be no regeneration for young "petrified eggs" because they felt no kinship with their fathers' values and tastes. The elder Plant's death liberates his son from fatherly laxness, but paradoxically puts him in touch with sustaining tradition. Waugh invests the event with a maximum of significance, for Plant's recognition of his father's merit marks the start of Waugh's own belated truce with the world of fathers. It signals the end of his tendency to respond to the world by blaming fathers, and it marks the start of his own personal responsibility, as a husband and father, for his own life. This is not to say that John Plant reverts to his father's style—after all, he does consign his father's house to the wreckers, who tear it to pieces, exposing its rooms, "three-sided like stage settings" (p. 66).

John Plant's attitude towards his father deserves careful scrutiny, for it has sometimes been misunderstood. In an important early statement on *Work Suspended*, Nigel Dennis draws attention to what he regards as "the sharp line that had emerged to divide the intellectuals of the Left from such as Evelyn Waugh," and he argues that "there was at issue a literal walking out from the paternal halls."[10] The Leftists, he says, "walked out," but Waugh remained behind, rejecting the pleas of Spender, Auden, and Day Lewis to "advance to rebuild." Yet if we examine Waugh's fiction up to and including *Scoop*, it is apparent that Waugh habitually regarded "paternal halls" as prisons from which he ardently wished to escape. Waugh's failure to depart from his father's house is emphatically not the result of an uncritical idolatry of the past; on the contrary, he detested much of it and was only prevented from leaving by a debilitating nostalgia which he recognized as immature and repeatedly tried to overcome in novel after novel. Even in *Work Suspended*, where John Plant accepts his father's style, he does not conform to it but merely recognizes its separate merit. In so doing he frees himself from the shackles of rebellion and sets himself at liberty to establish an identity of his own. Now he can reject his immature style, which "had absolutely nothing of himself in it" (p. 5), and he can seek a permanent home and a mature love relationship.

If there is an underlying similarity between John Plant and his father, there is an even more unexpected likeness between Plant and the strange man who kills his father. Arthur Atwater carries all the hallmarks of Waugh's modern barbarians: he has a "savage grip," a concave forehead, and a lop-sided hat; he is always on time, and his pedigree allegedly stretches back to Henry VII. With his raincoat, Atwater (alias Thurston) belongs to the murky submarine world which we have already noticed in *Scoop*; many of his "associates" have "lately disappeared"—just like Paul Pennyfeather. No two characters could seem more different than Plant and Atwater, but Waugh deftly hints at their affinity. Both characters love seclusion: Plant has "tried a dozen or more retreats in England and abroad," while Atwater longs to "get away" (p. 135) to "somewhere else" (p. 56), such as Rhodesia or Bolivia, where there is "no one to worry you" (p. 136). Just as Atwater has an adolescent view of frontier life (he thinks it consists of orchids, parrots, butterflies, hammocks, fish, and fruit), so Plant visits a glamorous *quartier toléré* which recalls the East "as adolescents imagine it" (p. 27). In gaining access to Plant, Atwater acts "under false pretences" by using one of his many pseudonyms;

but this is not very different from Plant, who loves anonymity and lies about himself to Fatima. Both characters are resentfully class-conscious, though in different ways, and both love privacy: they meet in a "nondescript" private room which Atwater finds very "snug." Plant is a traveller and Atwater is a travelling salesman.

It is in the area of art that the two figures are most alike. Plant is an artist, but because of his father's frivolous view of art (he ridicules those who buy his work, considers his annual sale a joke, and practises art-forgery), Plant has never risen above the level of a proficient entertainer. Similarly, Atwater "should have liked to be an artist . . . only the family went broke." His father took him "away from school young" (p. 56). Nevertheless, he is so good at spinning "yarns" that when Plant needs distraction from his immature dread of child-birth, he gives him a pound and urges him to go on chattering. Atwater responds, "I see. You're paying me for my entertainment value. You think I'm a kind of monkey" (p. 140). The truth is, of course, that they are both "monkeys"; as they stand side by side gazing at "Humboldt's Gibbon" at the Zoo, only a railing separates them both from what they regard. Metaphorically these two immature figures (Plant unmarried and Atwater an associate of the Bachelors' Club) are in the cage they are looking at. Both have been arrested (Plant in Morocco and Atwater in England), and although both have been discharged, they are still imprisoned by their prolonged adolescence. In their grotesquely arrested development, they are both as frightful as the ape that scares the passersby. Being frightful is important to them both: Plant frightens the readers of his Gothic thrillers and Atwater, in running down Plant's father, "thought [he'd] give him a fright" (p. 55).

With his impudence, vulgar diction, and immature bad taste (he gets a refund for his funeral wreath from the son of the man he has killed), Arthur Atwater is bad style incarnate. In essence, he is a parody of the state of John Plant's soul, a caricature-double, and he represents what Plant must overcome in himself before he can successfully change his style and grow up. Although we cannot know for sure, it seems evident that the plot called for Atwater to be violently expelled from the action, like Ambrose Silk in *Put Out More Flags*, or to die, like Apthorpe in *Men at Arms*. After having "separated, for the time" (p. 146) at the door of the Wimpole Club, with its trumpery décor, Plant and Atwater were apparently scheduled to meet again at Plant's newly acquired country house. There, very likely, there would have ensued a struggle for supremacy which would have proved fatal to Atwater: "Why don't you come and live with me," Plant drunkenly says as they part; "Stay as long

as you like. Die there" (p. 146). Like Apthorpe, who is Guy Crouchback's parody-double in *Men at Arms*, Atwater has a tendency to get
"spifflicated," and so it is entirely possible that alcohol was to do him in,
as it does Apthorpe. It is interesting to observe that Atwater enters the
narrative only after Plant expresses his desire to mature, just as Apthorpe
appears after Guy takes a crucial step forward. They embody the weight
of illusion and the dead past which Plant and Crouchback must shake off
in order to develop.

After his father's death has made him desire to rise above the level of a
mere technician, Plant takes another step in the right direction by rejecting the regressive lure of the house which his friends want him to buy. It is
called "A Composed Hermitage in the Chinese Taste," the sort of architectural "joke" that Waugh had deplored only a year before in "A Call to
the Orders." [11] The extravagantly motley design of the Hermitage has a
powerfully nostalgic effect upon Plant's friends, but it is no longer an appropriate home for the mature artist:

> Roger's engraving showed a pavilion, still rigidly orthodox in plan,
> but, in elevation decked with ornament conceived in wild igno-
> rance of oriental forms; there were balconies and balustrades of
> geometric patterns; the cornice swerved upwards at the corners in
> the lines of a pagoda; the roof was crowned with an onion cupola
> which might have been Russian, bells hung from the capital of bar-
> ley-sugar columns; the windows were freely derived from the Al-
> hambra; there was a minaret. To complete the atmosphere the
> engraver had added a little group of Turkish military performing
> the bastinado upon a curiously complacent malefactor, an Arabian
> camel and a mandarin carrying a bird in a cage. (pp. 108–9)

Like Atwater, the Composed Hermitage embodies a force which re-
tards Plant's growth. It represents the aestheticism and romanticism
which lurk behind the cynical and conventional poses of John Plant and
his repellent friends. It embodies the frivolity and adolescence at the
heart of the serious Thirties. It epitomizes, to use Plant's own words, "a
kind of nostalgia for the style of living which we emphatically rejected in
practical affairs. The notabilities of Whig society became, for us, what
the Arthurian paladins were in the time of Tennyson" (p. 72). Over-
poweringly seductive, the Composed Hermitage is a perversion and an
illusion, this novel's lush place. In a sense it is Plant's father's house all
over again. It is the beckoning yet inaccessible past, a pitfall and a prison.
In Waugh's own experience it is his youthful period of aestheticism at

Oxford. In urging Plant to buy and inhabit the Hermitage, Roger Simmonds in effect urges him to remain the "petrified egg" which his father has made him. But suddenly a new voice enters the narrative. It is that of Lucy, Roger's pregnant wife, and she says, "I can't think why John should want to have a house like that" (p. 74). Accordingly, Plant turns his back on the immature Hermitage and together he and Lucy begin to seek the right house for the homeless artist: "That quest became the structure of our friendship" (p. 115).

The differences between Lucy and Plant are those which exist "between those who were born before the Great War and those born after it" (p. 91). As Waugh predicted when he was still in his teens, the prewar generation has become tough, cynical, and guarded.[12] Lucy on the other hand belongs to a younger generation and is less cynical; indeed, she is candour itself. When Plant drops in unexpectedly, she is not offended by his rudeness, does not snub him, and even though they have never met before, she uses his first name. Unlike Plant, she is not intent upon privacy: for her, "the question of intrusion did not arise" (p. 88). She is not interested in deception or false casualness; when she invites Plant to dinner, she signs legibly, unpretentiously. She is a generous and unselfish girl who avoids falseness of all kinds. But Lucy's refusal to give him special recognition, to see him as an individual, proves a "highly provocative attitude" to Plant, who resolves to force his friendship upon her: "I sought recognition. I wanted to assert the simple fact of my separate and individual existence" (p. 100).

Because he has "little else to think about," Plant proceeds to gain Lucy's recognition "as in a parlour game"; in short, he uses her for entertainment. Yet imperceptibly entertainment gives way to love, and because of Plant's kindness to her cousin Julia, she admits him to her tiny circle of friends. Plant is dazzled by Lucy's openness in friendship which, significantly, he describes in terms of a large house which is always completely open (p. 112). Plant enters the house of Lucy, a "rich estate" which is far different from the lush Composed Hermitage or the secluded Moroccan hotel. Lucy's friendship is more spacious than the secret nests of childhood friendship, and in her "house" he grows and develops—just like the baby in Lucy's womb. Plant morally evolves just as Lucy's unborn child takes on shape and character within her; he moves from the state of a moral foetus through that of an ape to that of a new-born child with a burgeoning personality. Lucy has hated her unborn "baby," but after its birth she loves it: "I love him. I do really. I never thought I should. He's such a *person*" (p. 149). Waugh adds irony to his parable by causing Sister Kemp to praise the infant as "a fine big man" (p. 150). In fact, the reverse is true: Plant the "fine big man" is a moral nursling and has far to go before he reaches adulthood.

Christopher Sykes points to the possibility that Lucy is modelled on Diana Guinness, later Mosley, whom Waugh loved possessively but platonically after the collapse of his first marriage. In a 1966 letter Waugh admitted to Diana Mosley, "I was infatuated with you. Not of course that I aspired to your bed but I wanted you to myself as especial confidante and comrade. After Jonathan's birth you began to enlarge your circle." [13] But in another letter he denies any connection between Diana Mosley and Lucy: "there is not a single point in common between you and the heroine except pregnancy. Yours was the first pregnancy I observed." Waugh's disclaimer is justified: Plant is not twenty-seven, as Waugh would have been in 1930, but thirty-three. He is no fledgling novelist and love-lorn youth; rather, he is a successful novelist. Like Plant Waugh wished to change his style, but the woman he loved was not Diana Guinness; it was his own fiancée Laura Herbert, who helped Waugh find a house, as Lucy helps Plant. Later, when Waugh was writing *Work Suspended*, Laura, like Lucy, was expecting a child (Auberon, born 18 November 1939; perhaps coincidentally, the last diary reference Waugh makes to *Work Suspended* is on 17 November 1939). On the basis of this evidence, we may conclude that Lucy owes more to Laura Waugh than to Diana Guinness. [14]

Are there other models for Lucy Simmonds? Julia calls her "an angel" and she "recognizes" Plant, so we might be justified in regarding her as a secular Santa Lucia, patron saint of light and vision. In view of the fact that she gives birth to both John Plant and her own baby, she is possibly Waugh's version of the light-bringing goddess Lucina, who was said to bring unborn infants to the light of day. Lucina's name is "an epithet applied to both Diana and Juno but particularly to the latter as protectress of women, especially in childbirth. As a goddess especially of moonlight, and hence controller of the menses, Lucina's functions spread over the entire birth cycle." [15] A pagan and therefore inauthentic goddess, Lucy nevertheless brings the soul of John Plant to light. The connection with the goddess Diana and with moonlight suggests that Lucy owes something to Lady Diana Cooper as well as to Lady Diana Mosley and Laura Waugh.

After the birth of her child, Lucy is no longer interested in Plant, the private Waugh, [16] but she has performed the important function of awakening his ability to love and bringing it to light. Lucy's act is noble if inadvertent, yet there are enough hints to suggest that Waugh does not entirely approve of her. For example, she is a recent convert to Marxism and listens to news of labour strikes on the wireless (a machine Waugh loathed); as a teenager, she wore a mackintosh[17] and impersonated a reporter; she prefers concrete and steel to bourgeois architecture, and one of her best friends lives in the East—always a sure sign of Waugh's disapproval. We may conclude that Lucy is the imperfect means through which the perfect can act: we shall see the same thing in *Brideshead*, where Charles Ryder reaches the authentic through love of the inauthentic.

Christopher Sykes says that *Work Suspended* is "a book in which one not only finds much to admire but, quite literally, nothing to fault."[18] But despite Sykes's praise, and despite the high esteem in which Waugh himself held the novel, the reader may well find Waugh's narrative implausible. For example, with the benefit of hindsight one sees how the parable of Plant-as-foetus leads him into contact with Lucy, but at first reading one is liable to find their relationship unlikely. There are other problems. Too often the serious new style is verbose: for example, the over-extended military metaphors narrowly miss pretentiousness. The comparison of Lucy and Roger to horses is not a success nor is Plant's account of his ecstasies in a Somerset garden; at this stage in his career Waugh cannot write convincingly about love. One notes, too, that there is a disagreeable sententiousness about the theme of successful maturation when it becomes too explicit. In addition, Waugh is not yet in full control of the first-person narrative method. Since Plant is telling his story retrospectively, there should be more evidence of distance between the narrator and the evolving protagonist. But Plant's hostility to his earlier self is far too oblique, and comes out only by implication. One suspects that Waugh's problem in this area stems from more than technical awkwardness, for it seems that he likes immature John Plant more than the solid citizen who was scheduled to replace him. And this, perhaps, is one reason why the novel was suspended.

Waugh's failure to jettison John Plant is interesting for technical reasons, for it places his whole persona-method in clearer perspective. In each novel Waugh creates a persona whom he rejects, like a snake shedding its outworn skin. In the early novels the macabre fate of the protagonist is a stage in the growth of his creator; he is left to suffer in ignorance while the author moves forward, escaping by virtue of his example. In the later fiction the author's criticism of his personae is more explicit, but instead of abandoning them to disaster, Waugh enables them to overcome their failings by granting them the moral insight which he consistently denied his early characters. *Work Suspended* marks the attempted transition. Here, for the first time, Waugh was going to develop a protagonist rather than discard him. But for some reason—one doubts that it was really because of the war—John Plant was left in his unregenerate state. It is possible that Waugh simply liked Plant too much as he was, or saw that in some periods immaturity is an advantage, or, not yet able to write well about love, could not convincingly engineer the change.[19]

Waugh knew where his story was headed, for according to Sykes he explained the rest of the plot to a friend, who explained it to Sykes, who forgot.[20] What would have happened? As things stand, Plant retreats to his house in the country, having forfeited Lucy's interest, and, it appears, having forgotten his drunken invitation to Atwater, who seems certain to accept it. Is it possible that (by analogy with the marriages of Basil Seal and Guy Crouchback) Roger would die, leaving Plant to marry Lucy and adopt the baby, as Guy adopts little Trimmer? Would Atwater's visit be as disastrous to Plant as, say, Beaver's is to Tony? Or, since this is Waugh's first "mature" novel, would Plant defeat the pernicious Atwater in some way, perhaps with Julia's help? Waugh almost certainly envisioned an affirmative conclusion, possibly one in which he would confer maturity and identity upon Plant by having him marry Julia. Waugh may have *The Two Gentlemen of Verona* in mind (there is a striking similarity in names) when he prompts Plant to reflect, "I saw myself and Lucy as characters in the stock intrigue of renaissance comedy, where the heroine follows the hero in male attire and is wooed by him, unknowing, in the terms of rough friendship" (p. 119). Had Waugh been able to finish his novel, in all likelihood he would have caused his public and private selves, his "two gentlemen," to settle down with appropriate brides: Simmonds with Lucy and Plant with Julia.

But by 1942 Waugh had decided not to finish his novel because, as he said in his dedication to Woollcott, "the world . . . for which it was designed [had] ceased to exist." *Put Out More Flags*, which Waugh wrote when he could have been completing *Work Suspended*, seems to support the idea that Plant's rudeness, deceitfulness, and aggression, intolerable in peacetime, were useful in war. We may therefore conclude that in *Work Suspended* Waugh was on the verge of administering the *coup de grâce* to his anarchic self when war suddenly gave it a new lease on life. Three years later, in *Put Out More Flags*, Basil Seal accordingly reappears and flourishes, while artistic Cedric Lyne and Ambrose Silk are consigned to oblivion.

On the whole, the faults of *Work Suspended* stem from Waugh's attempt to change his style and his persona before he was ready. But the shortcomings of his unfinished novel are rectified in *Brideshead Revisited*, towards which *Work Suspended* looks in many ways. In *Brideshead* Waugh's handling of first-person narration, character-motivation, and style show that he profited from his apprenticeship in *Work Suspended*. The quest of the artist for a home continues in *Brideshead*, where it fails again, to be resolved only near the end of Waugh's life in *Unconditional Surrender*. *Work Suspended* fails stylistically and it stops short of providing the artist with a home. But it records his crucial escape from his father's house, and in this it emphatically marks the culmination of Waugh's early period.[21]

## CHAPTER 11

# *Put Out More Flags*

When war was declared on 3 September 1939, Waugh's immediate response was to seek employment at the Ministry of Information, but his attitude quickly became more bellicose. Soon he was casting about for a regiment and seems to have shared with his persona Guy Crouchback a feeling of grim relief about the war; for Waugh, as for Guy, it drew the confused political situation into sharp focus and rekindled the desire for positive action in the public world. Waugh wanted to acquit himself honourably in a just war, but both sides soon resolved themselves into "teams of indistinguishable louts."[1] Waugh's disappointment was profound and lasting. Immediately after being demobilized, he entered into premature old age, bitterly repelling the world from his gates and looking back on the war with rancour. On 1 July 1945 he wrote in his diary, "Back at Pixton after nearly a month in England leading the life of an old man pottering between the Hyde Park Hotel, White's and the Beefsteak."[2] Three months later he complained, "News from the world still horrible."[3] A year later he reflected on the advantages of retreating to Ireland, "of completely retiring from further experience and settling in an upstairs library to garner the forty-three-year harvest." He was certain that "England as a great power is done for," that "it is no country in which to bring up children. But how long will Liberty, Diversity, Privacy survive anywhere?"[4] Before the war he tried to resist the escapist allure of immature aestheticism; after the war he sank with a vengeance into a different kind of solitude. Privacy was always an "unresolved universal paradox"[5] for Waugh, perhaps the central dilemma of his life.

In view of the dejection which engulfed Waugh after he wrote it, *Put Out More Flags* is an interesting document, for it represents the first and last time he ever allowed himself to express enthusiasm in print. It shows the magnitude of his hopes and the intensity of his disillusionment. Its tone is jauntily optimistic and, it may be, just a little too patriotic for today's less ardent tastes. It is, as Waugh admits, a "period piece," a chapter in the history of "that odd, dead period before the Churchillian renaissance."[6] Its subject is the achievement of a warlike mentality in the lethargic early stages of the "Great Bore War," and the sacrifices which are necessary to that end. It concerns the fates of the individualistic artist and the individualistic man of the world in time of war—that is, the fate of privacy in a public era.

In *Work Suspended* Waugh prods the immature artist into growing up. But in *Put Out More Flags* he is less gentle: in the person of Ambrose Silk the uncommitted artist is bundled off into unhappy exile, and in the person of Cedric Lyne the ineffectual aesthete is liquidated. It is Basil Seal, the man of action, who now emerges triumphant. The world of *Put Out More Flags* appears at first glance to be more straightforward than that of the earlier novels—there is a war on, and its demands make duty plain: as Basil says, "There's only one serious occupation for a chap now, that's killing Germans" (p. 255). Yet as we shall see, Waugh's lingering attachment to aestheticism imparts a curious undertone of ambiguity to his first war novel.

*Put Out More Flags* takes its shape from the relationship between Basil Seal and Ambrose Silk.[7] The superannuated rogue and the aging aesthete are similar opposites: each is highly individualistic and neither can find a place in the bureaucratic morass of "total war." They are old friends who have "maintained a shadowy, mutually derisive acquaintance since they were undergraduates" (p. 42)—that is, they are expressions of the artistic and active sides of Waugh's personality, *and* of the split personality which Waugh diagnoses in the national life of England. Ambrose and Basil have drifted apart in recent years, but now, in wartime, Ambrose admits, "I hunger for his company" (p. 71). Ambrose gets his wish sooner than he expects as their paths converge on the steps of the Ministry of Information: once again the artist and the man of action are reunited. In 1953 Waugh remarked on the way war brings "successful men and artists . . . into close contact,"[8] and in *Put Out More Flags* he comments on the same phenomenon: "Socrates marching to the sea with Xenophon, Virgil sanctifying Roman military rule, Horace singing the sweetness of dying for one's country, the troubadours riding to war, Cervantes in the galleys at Lepanto, Milton working himself blind in the public service" (p. 49). But World War II is different: now for the first time there is no place in war for art, which Waugh pictures at the foot of a long historical decline.

Ambrose's fate is predictable. His "primrose path" of decadent art has led from Diaghilev through Lovat Fraser and Cocteau to the world of fashionable photographers and set-designers. Lately he has allowed his artistic tastes to become contaminated by politics; indeed, as a member

of Poppet Green's Communist cell he even expresses approval of her
ghastly jaundice-coloured head of Aphrodite. He further taints his art by
working for the Ministry of Information. Ambrose's story concerns his
loss of individuality. He thinks he is "a single, sane individual" but as the
novel advances, a world of replicas and impostors gradually engulfs his
"singularity." Nostalgically he tells his publisher, Mr. Bentley, "The decline of England . . . dates from the day we abandoned coal fuel. . . . We
used to live in a fog, the splendid, luminous, tawny fogs of our early
childhood. . . . The fog lifts, the world sees us as we are, and worse still
we see ourselves as we are. It was a carnival ball, my dear, which when
the guests unmasked at midnight, was found to be composed entirely of
impostors" (p. 203). This fraudulent world now encompasses Ambrose:
"There were only a few restaurants, now, which he could frequent without fear of ridicule and there he was surrounded, as though by distorting
mirrors, with gross reflections and caricatures of himself" (p. 50). He
lives in "an age which made a type of him, a figure of farce" (p. 54).
Moreover, he notices that he often parodies himself: "Mine is the brazen
voice of Apuleius's Ass, turning its own words to ridicule" (p. 72). Ambrose is losing his actuality and is becoming superfluous.

Ambrose is the lingering representative of the aestheticism of the past,
from Greece and Arabia to its last fine flowering in the Oxford of the
Twenties. But he has outlived his time, and now he represents the softness
which in time of war is a liability. The parable operates on both a personal and a national level: before Waugh, and England, can extricate
themselves from the lethargy of the "phoney war," Ambrose must go.
Waugh's attitude is ambivalent but in the end puritanical: Ambrose represents a way of life which Waugh likes, but which he sacrifices out of a
sense of duty.

Ambrose's desire for privacy comes under attack. He wants to change
Europe's "conventual" society into something resembling the "cenobitic"
society of China.[9] He likes private jokes and innuendo-laden conversation. He has a fantasy of himself in an ivory tower, which is the equiv-
alent in this novel of the "Composed Hermitage in the Chinese Taste"
which John Plant rejects in *Work Suspended*: "He stood on a high, sugary
pinnacle, on a new Tower of Babel; like a muezzin calling his message to
a world of domes and clouds" (p. 133). This kind of privacy is no good in
the modern world, for it is vulnerable, immature, and vaguely heathen.
As an escapist and an infidel, Ambrose is doomed. He wishes for limbo,
not heaven, for in limbo there is "no communal order; but wine and conversation and imperfect, various humanity. Limbo for the unbaptized, for
the pious heathen, the sincere sceptic" (p. 72). In his thirst for privacy
Ambrose resembles William Boot and John Plant (and, plainly, one facet

of his creator), but his sad fate shows that seclusion cannot be tolerated in the public world of war. When his one piece of "pure art" is falsified at Basil's instigation, Ambrose flees from England under suspicion of being a Fascist. Reduced now to an impostor himself, he escapes dressed as a priest; he sits on a crate of fish and reads a racing paper instead of a breviary. He goes to the blurred, neutral land of Ireland where he gets the limbo for which he has so rashly wished:

> In a soft, green valley where a stream ran through close-cropped, spongy pasture and the grass grew down below the stream's edge and merged there with the water-weeds; where a road ran between grass verges and tumbled walls, and the grass merged into moss which spread upwards and over the tumbled stones of the walls; . . . where the prints of ass and pig, goose and calf and horse mingled indifferently with those of barefoot children; . . . where mist and smoke never lifted and the sun never fell direct, and evening came slowly in infinite gradations of shadow; where the priest came seldom . . . there stood an inn which was frequented in bygone days by fishermen. (p. 235)

In this foggy rural prison Ambrose lives out the truth behind his life in England, and here his immature and graceless art dies at last:

> He spread foolscap on the dining-room table and the soft, moist air settled on it and permeated it so that when, on the third day, he sat down to make a start, the ink spread and the lines ran together, leaving what might have been a brush stroke of indigo paint where there should have been a sentence of prose. Ambrose laid down the pen and because the floor sloped where the house had settled, it rolled down the table, and down the floor-boards and under the mahogany sideboard, and lay there among napkin rings and small coins and corks and the sweepings of half a century. (p. 236)

In support of Ambrose, and of Waugh's evident nostalgia for him, it should be noted that he is not presented as disagreeable or dangerous; rather, circumstances have turned him into a luxury that England can no longer afford. Behind Waugh's sardonic account of Ambrose's banishment flow powerful cross-currents of regret, and we may conclude that the exorcism of Ambrose and aestheticism from Waugh's character was no simple matter.

As Ambrose's fortunes wane, Basil's improve, but he too undergoes a loss of individuality. In Basil's case the loss is healthy, for as his mother rightly says, "It's always been Basil's *individuality* that's been wrong" (p. 29). The best example of Basil's individuality is his exploitation of his sister's artsy-craftsy neighbours by means of the awful Connollys. Basil's Nazi-like system "postulate[s] for success a peace-loving, orderly and honourable world in which to operate" (p. 59). But in a public, warlike world, such idiosyncratic acts of spoliation must cease. Basil "the Athenian" must be restrained; he must abandon his dreams of romantic individuality and must "sit at the public tables of Sparta, clipped blue at the neck where before his dark hair had hung untidily to his collar" (p. 35). Moreover, he must outgrow the immaturity so gruesomely embodied by the Connolly children, who shadow him, and must hand them on to his hungry successor, the graceless, one-legged "Mr. Todhunter" on his chair by the fire. But above all he must give up his irregular liaison with Angela Lyne and become more serious about her.

Waugh talks about Angela's "properties," her "personality," her "characteristic" fashions, and says, "her smartness was individual" (p. 31). But her uniqueness is almost a thing of the past: her face is now "mute . . . cool and conventionally removed from the human," and she has taken on the appearance of a "cosmopolitan, passionless, barren, civilized woman" (p. 32). Angela's loss of spontaneity stems from her unhappy passion for Basil; unable to escape from "the ironic Fates," she has become selfish and her appearance has "become a hobby and a distraction, a pursuit entirely self-regarding and self-rewarding." Like Ambrose, "this golden daughter of fortune" is drifting into the condition of a caricature: "She watched herself moving in the mirrors of the civilized world as a prisoner will watch the antics of a rat" (p. 33).

Before Basil and Angela may escape Fortune's domination and join forces, they must shake off their old aesthetic attachments. Basil must drive out Ambrose, and Angela must break away from her effete and ineffectual husband, Cedric. Their new and more serious union will be beneficial to both of them: it will free Angela from her dehumanized "desert island," and it will restrain Basil's excessive individualism. Their new understanding will supersede the immature and debilitating influence of aestheticism, and will epitomize the maturation of England, upon which victory in war depends.

A lover of cloistered beauty (water gardens, dolphins, grottoes, an octopus, a "bridge in the Chinese taste"), Cedric Lyne is marked down for destruction. Like Ambrose's, his kind of solitude is unthinkable in wartime. Like Waugh (see *Diaries*, p. 502), Cedric goes to war and becomes "weary of the weight of dependent soldiery which throughout the operations encumbered him and depressed his spirits" (p. 240). As a result, he undertakes a dangerous mission all alone:

As he walked alone he was exhilarated with the sense of being one man, one pair of legs, one pair of eyes, one brain, sent on a single, intelligible task; one man alone could go freely anywhere on the earth's surface; multiply him, put him in a drove and by each addition of his fellows you subtract something that is of value, make him so much less a man; this was the crazy mathematics of war. . . . No one had anything against the individual; as long as he was alone he was free and safe; there's danger in numbers; divided we stand, united we fall, thought Cedric, striding happily towards the enemy, shaking from his boots all the frustration of corporate life. (p. 241)

Not much later, a bullet kills him, and Basil and Angela are free to marry.

Waugh takes his two epigraphs from Lin Yutang's *The Importance of Living*.[10] In many ways Lin's book is unlikely reading-matter for Waugh, who often uses references to the Orient in a context of disapproval. But since Harold Acton (one of the originals for Ambrose Silk)[11] had returned from China in 1939, it is possible that he prompted Waugh to read it. The maxims which Waugh quotes glorify the military life—but as we might expect, he twists them. Culled out of context, the maxims do not represent Lin's or Waugh's real views about soldiers. Evidence from elsewhere in his book shows that Lin values the life of the solitary over that of the soldiery. In a section entitled "The Scamp as Ideal," Lin says that he values the "scamp" over the "disciplined and regimented soldier."[12] Despite the ostensible approval of military life in the epigraphs, Waugh is very ambivalent about it; thus while Basil, Waugh's scamp, must enter the war, he does not become a "disciplined, obedient, regimented, and uniformed coolie," a "subject for ribaldry." Instead, he becomes a member of a distinguished *corps d'élite*, and avoids the dehumanizing anonymity of the ranks. The modified individualism which Basil finally achieves almost certainly reflects the constraints Waugh had to impose on his own singularity before he could don a uniform.

*Put Out More Flags* is a large canvas, a broad survey of individual responses to the war. Waugh pokes fun at Peter Pastmaster and Alastair Trumpington, who settle down as solid citizens, and he ridicules the foolish optimism of Lady Seal and Sir Joseph Mainwaring. He lampoons Poppet Green and her Communist colleagues, with their tasteless art and their endless harangues about the orthodoxy of Parsnip and Pimpernell (Auden and Isherwood), who departed for the United States when the war began. But his main target—aside from Ambrose, who in any case works there—is the Ministry of Information. As the well-head of government propaganda, censorship, and political art, the ministry excited Waugh's especial disgust and sharpened his sense of the absurd. It was housed in the Senate House of the University of London, with a large information area in the William Beveridge Hall; Ambrose sees its "vast bulk" insulting the autumnal sky as he approaches (p. 73). In Waugh's view, the "great hive" was a house of rumour and misinformation, the very heart of everything which was phoniest about the "phoney war"; hence it forms the setting for much of the novel.

To judge from the accounts of others, it seems that Waugh's sardonic caricature of the ministry is accurate. Malcolm Muggeridge, who worked there, sarcastically recalls how George Orwell broadcast *Areopagitica* and *The Waste Land* to "listeners in Cawnpore, Kuala Lumpur and Rangoon," and how Graham Greene examined "the possibility of throwing stigmata and other miraculous occurrences into the battle for the mind in Latin America." Muggeridge found the religious department virtually as Waugh describes it: "[it] gathered in ever more personnel, including a miscellaneous collection of Roman Catholic lay intellectuals, a Jesuit or two, as well as a representative atheist." [13]

Harold Nicolson was parliamentary secretary to Duff Cooper, who was minister of information in 1940–41. He wrote in his diary that the ministry "has been staffed by duds at the top and all the good people are in the most subordinate positions. The rage and fury of the newspaper men passes all bounds. John Gunther, for instance, told me that he had asked one of the censors for the text of our leaflet which was dropped over Germany. The request was refused. He asked why. The answer was, 'we are not allowed to disclose information which might be of value to the enemy.' Then, when Gunther pointed out that two million of these leaflets had been dropped over Germany, the man blinked and said, 'Yes, something must be wrong there'." [14] Duff Cooper himself refers to his ministry as "a monster . . . so large, so voluminous, so amorphous, that no single man could cope with it." [15]

Restrained to some extent, perhaps, by his friendship with Duff Cooper's wife, "Mrs. Stitch," Waugh does not attack Cooper directly. But he mercilessly lampoons the ministry's "wild make-believe" [16] along with its apathy, inefficiency, lax security, and bureaucratic idiocies. What Waugh hates most about the ministry is the way it prostitutes art to serve war. In the past the sword and the pen had enjoyed a noble relationship; but now the alliance of art and war results in the ideological poetry of Parsnip and Pimpernell, Poppet Green's yellow Aphrodite, and Ambrose's pointless toil as "representative of Atheism in the religious department" (p. 129). The once-honoured craft of letters is now in disrepute: "To Hell with being a man-of-letters," writes the author of "Nazi Destiny," when he discovers that art will not get him to Scapa Flow (p. 82).

Pinnacled high in the labyrinthine ministry is the office of Geoffrey

Bentley, who is probably modelled to some extent on A. D. Peters. Waugh describes Mr. Bentley's office as "an enclave of culture in a barbaric world" (p. 130), but the reader should not accept this verdict without reservation. The motley décor of the office, with its sink, card-table, Empire furniture, ceiling by Angelica Kaufmann, and massive Nollekens busts of George III and Mrs. Siddons, hints at the sorry state of the art which originates there.[17] Ambrose and Mr. Bentley plan the *Ivory Tower*. They intend it to be "a purely artistic paper," but after Basil tampers with the copy, it reads like Fascist propaganda. Accordingly, Ambrose is hounded into solitary exile and "old Rampole" the publisher is sent to jail, where he learns to enjoy reading. Like Ambrose's fate, Rampole's is particularly appropriate. All his life he has deplored books, especially novels, but now he falls prey to the delusive "charm" of one of his own romantic authors. In old age Rampole enters the prison of immature art, the captive of what he himself has helped to create.

From *Decline and Fall* onward, a major subject of Waugh's satire is World War I's debilitating legacy of permissiveness. In novel after novel, Waugh blames the weakness of sons upon the irresponsibility of their fathers. In *Put Out More Flags* Waugh identifies aestheticism as an additional culprit. He dislikes it because he finds it escapist and immature— one more result of paternal irresponsibility. Waugh hoped that the weakness produced by World War I would be corrected by the realities of a second war, and in *Put Out More Flags* he forecasts the belated maturation of England (and himself) through the symbolic repudiation of Ambrose Silk and Cedric Lyne. The novel ends on a note of optimism unique in Waugh's fiction: there is "a new spirit abroad" (p. 256). But one wonders about the accuracy and even the sincerity of this pronouncement, for below Waugh's euphoric public-mindedness there runs a powerful undertone of regret for privacy. Indeed, it may seem to some readers that Waugh's optimism is tinged by irony and that his deepest sympathies are with Ambrose and the golden past. Others may find Waugh's tone self-consciously forced and coloured by wishful thinking. Moreover, there may be a certain lack of psychological truth, for *Work Suspended* shows that real growth must involve a reconciliation with the world of fathers. And since Basil and Angela never achieve such a reconciliation, neither their maturation nor their creator's can be considered complete at this point.

Waugh's ambivalence about the past is especially evident in his "dedicatory letter" to Randolph Churchill. There he claims that *Put Out More Flags* deals with "a race of ghosts, the survivors of the world we both knew ten years ago, . . . where my imagination still fondly lingers. . . . These characters are no longer contemporary in their sympathy; they were forgotten even before the war; but they lived on delightfully in holes and corners and, like everyone else, they have been disturbed in their habits by the rough intrusion of current history." In *Put Out More Flags* Waugh sacrifices these creatures of fond memory by forcing them to adapt to "current history"—but it is evident that he does not like doing it. After *Put Out More Flags* and the huge disappointment of the war, Waugh never again looked ahead with optimism. The ambivalent tone of *Put Out More Flags* prefigures the darker outlook of *Brideshead Revisited*, in which Waugh regards the future with grim foreboding, the present with distaste, and repudiates the most joyous aspects of the past. Embedded in Waugh's most "committed" novel lie the germs of his future misanthropy.

## CHAPTER 12

*I had better make up my mind and settle down to the humble rut which fate
had ordained for me. I must write a book. . . . But I am not utterly enslaved.
I still have dreams of shaking off the chains of creative endeavour. Rimbaud
got away from it and became a gun runner. Vanbrugh gave up writing plays
to build the most lovely houses in England. . . . John Buchan is lording it in
Quebec. . . . Perhaps there is a chance of freedom.*

Evelyn Waugh, "General Conversation: Myself . . ."

# *Brideshead Revisited: The Sacred and Profane Memories of Captain Charles Ryder*

In *Brideshead Revisited* the theme of vocation moves to the fore with
particular clarity as Waugh depicts Charles Ryder's arduous journey toward the right kind of art. Ryder is the first Waugh protagonist who successfully matures, and his maturation depends upon his acceptance of his
unique purpose in God's design. What may appear merely chaotic from
man's perspective is orderly from God's, and so Waugh presents Ryder's
"profane" memories in a "sacred" frame which reveals the pattern inherent in disorder and the good latent in evil. It would be wrong to say that
Ryder struggles toward his vocation; in fact he struggles violently against
it, repeatedly refusing to conform to the plan God has for him. But like a
fish on a hook, his resistance is in vain, for as Cordelia says, "If you
haven't a vocation it's no good however much you want to be; and if you
have a vocation, you can't get away from it, however much you hate it." [1]
Charles Ryder sceptically watches the Flytes wrestle with their vocations,
but he does not realize that he is one of those who "can't get away from
it," and he tries to follow his own path. The central conflict in *Brideshead*, therefore, is between the will of man and the will of God: an unequal contest, it might appear, but Waugh always found the drama of
capitulation more gripping than the spectacle of revolt. Despite the headstrong and wayward spirit which leads Ryder astray into the jungles of
secular art, Providence reclaims him, and in the process of being "brought
up short, like a horse in full stride" (p. 272), Ryder learns that art must

serve God, not man. He escapes the tyranny of his earthly father by at last responding to the reins of a heavenly one. As an artist-novel, *Brideshead Revisited* invites comparison with that very different representative of the genre, *A Portrait of the Artist as a Young Man.* Waugh's portrait faces in the opposite direction from Joyce's: where Stephen Dedalus rejects religion on his way to artist-hood, Charles's successful maturation as an artist depends upon his religious awakening, an awakening which comes about through his repudiation of secular art and action.

In "Charles Ryder's Schooldays," the intended sequel to *Brideshead* which Waugh abandoned in 1945 after twenty-three pages, we find a useful description of Ryder as an adolescent.[2] In "Schooldays" the young Ryder lives at "Spierpoint College," a product of "the Oxford Movement and the Gothic Revival," a school which had been founded with "definite religious aims" but which now, in 1919, retains only an "ecclesiastical flavour." Its magnificent neo-Gothic chapel rises "like an ice-berg triumphantly over the surrounding landscape" (as, indeed, Lancing College chapel still does today), but it is incomplete. "At the west it end[s] abruptly in concrete and timber and corrugated iron, while behind, in a wasteland near the kitchens . . . [lies] a nettle-and-bramble-grown ruin" (the remains, one suspects, of some more authentic edifice). Ryder's surroundings are appropriate, for, like his school, he too has fallen away from the stricter religious practices of the past. The war has set its seal upon the decay of his faith: when it began, Ryder's father gave up family prayers, explaining that there was now "nothing left to pray for." A bomb has killed Charles's mother in Serbia.

Charles once experienced a religious phase, during which he wanted to become "a priest of the Anglican Church"; but that phase "had passed and lingered now only in Charles's love of Gothic architecture and breviaries." Young Ryder loves the outward show of religion but, like Spierpoint College itself, he is no longer genuinely religious. As the fragment opens, Charles sits beneath a Gothic frieze which equates the love of God with brotherly love, and in his diary he writes bitterly of Apthorpe, his house-captain. A master reminiscent of J. F. Roxburgh urges him to send an "ornate" illuminated manuscript to "Crease." After Communion, Charles contemplates with vague dissatisfaction "the secular, indeed slightly anti-clerical lyric which, already inscribed, he was about to illuminate"; he finds no incongruity between Hodgson's "'Twould ring the bells of heaven" and the "compressed thirteenth-century script" in which he has printed it. Not long after, a voice interrupts Charles's reverie, a "detached, critical" Mr. Hyde who intrudes on his pose as the "respectable" Dr. Jekyll. Here, then, is the distortion of religious art in the hands of a young man of split temperament who has lapsed from religion into religiosity: precisely Waugh's condition when he entered Lancing College in May 1917.

In his first edition "Warning," Waugh describes the theme of *Brideshead Revisited* as "an attempt to trace the workings of the divine purpose in a pagan world, in the lives of an English Catholic family, half-paganized themselves, in the world of 1923–1939."[3] The reader who approaches *Brideshead* with no preconceptions concerning what novels ought to be about should find no difficulty with Waugh's subject, which is a legitimate one. But the evidence shows that Waugh found it difficult to implement such an ample theme, and that he was never wholly satisfied with the result, revising his novel at the manuscript stage, in the 1960 edition, and at a number of intermediate stages.[4] The manuscript is riddled with false starts and emendations,[5] and bound at the rear there stands a section entitled "ms. interpolations in second draft." There are thirty-three of these often quite lengthy interpolations, and they include some of the most celebrated passages in the novel: descriptions of Anthony Blanche, part of the account of Sebastian's luncheon-party, the eulogy of youth and languor, the description of Lady Marchmain's room, Charles's dinner with Rex at Paillard's, his departure from Brideshead into the "light of common day," and Julia's farewell to Ryder at the end of the novel. Many of the interpolations replace pre-existing passages, and almost all of them serve to strengthen the novel's structure.

As in all of Waugh's novels, setting is extremely important in *Brideshead Revisited*, for it lends special significance to the characters who move about in it. Brideshead House is the main setting; the novel's main scenes occur there and the characters repeatedly "revisit" it. Brideshead House is so manifestly central that the temptation to regard it as the novel's organizing metaphor is hard to resist, and indeed it has not been resisted. Rodney Delasanta and Mario D'Avanzo have written the most detailed analysis of the house as a guide to the novel's meaning.[6] They argue that the Brideshead estate in the novel "is representative of the Roman Catholic Church in the modern world, and Charles Ryder's entrance into it is symbolized by his sexual entrance into the 'brideshead' of Julia."[7] They continue:

> The most impressive evidence resides in the name itself and in the ambiguous relationship of the name to the people and events in the novel. In Christian symbolism, anticipated in the Old Testament in the Canticle of Canticles and explicitly mentioned in St. Paul's Epistle to the Ephesians (5 : 22 ff.) as well as in the Apoc-

alypse (21 : 2), the Church is repeatedly referred to as the Bride of
Christ and Christ as her Bridegroom. In the Church Fathers too the
perfect love of Christ for his Church and his intimate dwelling
therein is figured by the connubial love of a man for his bride.
Brideshead, therefore, in this novel is the *bride* of the *Head*, the
Church of Christ who is the Head of the Mystical Body. And the
members of Brideshead are in some mysterious manner participants of this intimate life, participants that in a composite way
make up the total picture of the Church on earth.[8]

The argument is persuasive. In the authors' view, the characters' actions
consist of departures from and returns to the Roman Catholic Church as
symbolized by Brideshead House, a fount of purity. So far, so good; but a
little later Delasanta and D'Avanzo remark, "At every turn in the spiritual
odyssey of Charles Ryder . . . Waugh constructs a series of appropriate
architectural settings mirroring the spiritual state of Ryder, the main
character."[9] Here we must pause, for Brideshead House itself is one of
those settings, and Ryder is an agnostic, if not an atheist. How can
Brideshead mirror Ryder's spiritual state, if it is "representative of the
Roman Catholic Church"? We can best find our way out of this apparent
impasse by seeing that there is no contradiction: Brideshead *does* mirror
Ryder's spiritual state because it does *not* represent the Roman Catholic
Church, contrary to what Delasanta and D'Avanzo say. The error they
make is in assuming that Waugh approves of Brideshead; it is the familiar
error of failing to perceive Waugh's irony.

What, then, *does* Brideshead House represent? It will be best to begin
with the account of the house and family which Waugh submitted to the
MGM directors who wished to film *Brideshead*:

> Brideshead is one of the historic English houses, the ancestral home
> of the Flyte family, of whom the head is the Marquis of March-
> main. Two architectural features are used in the story to typify the
> conflicting characteristics of the English aristocratic tradition.
> These are the Chapel and the fountain. . . . The Chapel in the book
> is a new one, and Lord Marchmain is represented as a recent and
> half-hearted convert to Catholicism. For the purpose of the film the
> Chapel should be old and part of the original castle on the site of
> which the baroque palace has been built. The Flytes should be rep-
> resented as one of the English noble families which retained their
> religion throughout the Reformation period. The Chapel should
> therefore be small and medieval, and should contain the Flyte

tombs which in the novel are described as standing in the parish church. The fountain represents the worldly eighteenth century splendour of the family. It has been brought from Italy and I see it as a combination of three famous works of Bernini at Rome, photographs of which may be found in any architectural handbook. These are the Trevi and Piazza Navona fountains and the elephant bearing the obelisk in the Piazza Minerva which the Romans fondly call "the little pig." [10]

Written "for the purpose of the film," Waugh's account is useful, for it dramatically alters certain aspects of the story, thereby throwing the theme of the novel itself into high relief. Waugh says that Brideshead House is "the ancestral home of the Flyte family." In fact, it is not their ancestral home at all, but a "New House," built some 250 years ago out of the stones of the old castle, which stood on a hill near the village church, in what is now waste land. Sebastian Flyte prefers the new house because it is gentler and more sequestered than the old one. Beauty is what matters to him: "What does it matter when it was built," he says, "if it's pretty?" (p. 72). The new house has come into being gradually; it is the product of generations of Flytes. It is one of those "buildings that grew silently with the centuries" (p. 198), buildings which Charles Ryder loves to paint. But despite its venerable appearance to Charles—and to most readers—Brideshead is really quite new in terms of English history. And despite the leisurely pace of its construction, it is evident that it is still in some way unfinished. It is, one suspects, one of those houses of which Charles Ryder thinks when he says, "I have always loved building, holding it to be not only the highest achievement of man but one in which, at the moment of consummation, things were most clearly taken out of his hands and perfected, without his intention, by other means, and I regarded men as something much less than the buildings they made and inhabited, as mere lodgers and short-term sub-lessees of small importance in the long, fruitful life of their homes" (p. 198).[11] Although it is now manifestly in decline, Brideshead still awaits its completion.

We turn now to the family which, with the exception of the exiled Lord Marchmain, Brideshead shelters. In his MGM "Memorandum," Waugh says that the Flytes "should be represented as one of the English noble families which retained their religion throughout the Reformation period." But a moderately attentive reading of the novel reveals that only Lady Marchmain's side of the family is "old Catholic." Her husband's side, which was Catholic some centuries ago, has lapsed into an Anglicanism which Waugh regards as a form of neo-paganism.

The physical characteristics of the two sides of the family are important. Lord Marchmain's line is handsome, graceful; he himself looks young even at his advanced age. Lady Marchmain's line, on the other hand, is grim-faced and stern, traits which manifest themselves more in her three brothers than in Lady Marchmain herself. Charles Ryder looks at photographs of the Marchioness's brothers in the little book which Mr. Samgrass has edited for Lady Marchmain: "The frontispiece reproduced the photograph of a young man in Grenadier uniform, and I saw plainly revealed there the origin of that grim mask which, in Brideshead [Marchmain's elder son], overlaid the gracious features of his father's family; this was a man of the woods and caves, a hunter; a judge of the tribal council, the repository of the harsh traditions of a people at war with their environment. There were other illustrations in the book . . . and in each I traced the same archaic lines; and remembering Lady Marchmain, starry and delicate, I could find no likeness to her in these sombre men" (p. 123). Grace and grimness are present in the Flytes' children: Sebastian and Julia resemble each other in their enchanting beauty, while Brideshead and Cordelia are alike in their homeliness.

When Lord Marchmain marries, he tells his wife that she has brought his family back to the faith of their ancestors (p. 194). But as in other matters, Lord Marchmain is not reliable on this point, for only half of his family has returned to the faith. As Sebastian says, Cordelia and Brideshead, the plain children, are "both fervent Catholics," while he and Julia are "half-heathen." Nor does Lord Marchmain remain in the Church. After the war he stays in France with Cara, a dancer, thereby abandoning his duties and becoming a figure of absentee authority, like most Waugh fathers.

At the outset of the novel, then, the half-heathen family of an apostate father inhabit a derivative and only partly finished house. That house does not represent the Roman Catholic Church, the house of divine love; rather, it represents its divided legacy: the house of aberrant worship and profane love which still shelters, here and there, a few remnants of a better age. Built out of the stones of the "original castle" by erring fathers, the "baroque palace" is post-Reformation England itself. It is really two houses in one: it is the house of wrong-headed patriarchs, within which there still survives a waning maternal influence. With its "bondieuserie" and chintz, Lady Marchmain's "intimate, feminine" sitting-room differs markedly from the "august, masculine atmosphere" of the rest of Brideshead: "This room was all her own; she had taken it for herself and changed it so that, entering, one seemed to be in another house" (p. 112). Brideshead House is an emblem, then, not of orthodoxy, but of schism; it stands for the diminution of Mother Church by neo-pagan fathers. Through Anthony Blanche, Waugh points out the contrast between husband and wife: Lady Marchmain, Blanche says, uses "no artifice," while her husband is "fleshy" (p. 49). The dual nature of Brideshead House anticipates that of the medieval church at Broome in *Unconditional Surrender* (p. 73); one side is for Anglicans, the other for Roman Catholics, and a wall stands between them. But if time can divide the unity of the Church, grace can restore it. If the purely divine has been profaned, the profane can serve as an avenue back to the divine, for as Ryder says, "to know and love one other human being is the root of all wisdom" (p. 41). To go a step further, Brideshead represents not only the result of heresy but also the way out of it. It is simultaneously the epilogue and prologue to undivided Catholic worship in England, and in Waugh's view, what lies in between is merely a digression. Since, as Waugh says elsewhere, "the Catholic structure still lies lightly buried beneath every phase of English life,"[12] it is only a question of time before Brideshead House is "twitched" back to the faith.

Waugh conveys his sharp criticism of Brideshead House through subtly charged language. Set in a "new and secret landscape," Brideshead is an Arcadia, "a sequestered place" (p. 18) in which "the rest of the world [is] abandoned and forgotten" (p. 282). Sebastian wants it to be a *locus amoenus*: "If only it could be like this always—always summer, always alone, the fruit always ripe and Aloysius in a good temper" (p. 71). Here everything is play: "with a pantomime of difficulty" Sebastian moves "through the succession of hot-houses, from scent to scent and climate to climate" (p. 71). As the novel opens, Sebastian and Charles approach this "man-made landscape" of pagan bliss through "fool's parsley and meadowsweet"; they pass a clergyman "pedalling quietly down the wrong side of High Street"; they smoke Turkish (that is, culpably heathen) cigarettes in the shade, and they pass through "twin, classical lodges" to visit the shadowy house with its "tricky ceilings" and "vast twin fireplaces." While appearing to praise the house, Waugh condemns it, for its joys are illusions—just the first of many which Charles Ryder will experience in the course of the novel.

Two architectural features stress Brideshead's delusive beauty: its dome and its fountain. The "high and insolent" dome, to which Sebastian immediately leads Charles on his first visit, is inhabited by Sebastian's beloved nanny. Although Waugh describes the dome and Nanny Hawkins in the same ostensibly approving tones, his language is heavy with veiled criticism: "It was a charming room, oddly shaped to conform with the curve of the dome. . . . laid out on the top of the chest of drawers and carefully dusted, were . . . carved shell and lava, stamped leather, painted wood, china, bog oak, damascened silver, blue-john, alabaster, coral, the souvenirs of many holidays" (p. 34). Motley taste is an established Waugh cue for lack of reason and discipline; as if in confirmation of this, Nanny Hawkins's rosary lies "loosely" between her open hands. Later she stitches "complacently" while indulgently calling Charles and Sebastian "a pair of children" (p. 71). Her room is "charming," and in subsequent pages this word will be applied repeatedly to the Flytes themselves who, because of their precarious theological status, seem to operate as if by magic. In the fourth British edition (1946), Waugh pointed his criticism of enchanted Brideshead by making the dome a false one which resembles the cupolas of Chambord. (In 1926 Waugh and the Grahams travelled to France and Waugh noted in his diary that Chambord was "a monstrous building. With what the book of Touraine calls 'a dream city' on its roof.") [13]

Waugh describes the great fountain with a similarly veiled hostility. It stands right in the middle of the stage-like terrace, where many of the novel's most poignant scenes are set. Imported from a piazza in southern Italy, the fountain consists of "an oval basin with an island of formal rocks at its centre; on the rocks grew, in stone, formal tropical vegetation and wild English fern in its natural fronds; through them ran a dozen streams that counterfeited springs, and round them sported fantastic tropical animals, camels and camelopards and an ebullient lion all vomiting water; on the rocks, to the height of the pediment, stood an Egyptian obelisk of red sand-stone" (p. 72). "Natural," "counterfeit," and "fantastic," the miscellaneous taste of the pagan fountain connotes fraud, and Ryder compounds the fraud by painting a picture of it. Such a picture is not a suitable gift for Lady Marchmain, so Charles gives it to Nanny Hawkins who, in characteristic Waugh fashion, unthinkingly adds it to her collection.

Waugh's treatment of the art nouveau chapel is similar. It is a recent addition, built as a wedding present for Lady Marchmain when her husband married back into the faith, and its "arts-and-craft" and "plasticine"-like décor is as bogus as the design of the dome and the fountain. Yet despite its tasteless design, the sanctuary lamp holds the "small red flame" of the faith, which has endured despite the vicissitudes of time. The chapel and the sanctuary lamp encapsulate the novel's theme: the operation of grace through the inauthentic. We are now in a position to move closer to the meaning of Brideshead Revisited.

Brideshead is a book about love, and Waugh asserts that the worthiest expression of man's love is his love for God as expressed through membership in the Church, Christ's bride. The Ryder of the Epilogue at last knows about divine love, but he has bought that knowledge only at the expense of other, more shadowy loves. Sebastian is the first of these, then Celia, then Julia; Ryder even expresses his disenchantment with the army in terms of marital love. Waugh regards Ryder's preliminary loves as shadows; indeed, the theme of the novel may be expressed as the search for substance through shadows. The most explicit articulation of this idea comes when Ryder muses, "'Perhaps . . . all our loves are merely hints and symbols; a hill of many invisible crests; doors that open as in a dream to reveal only a further stretch of carpet and another door; perhaps you and I are types and this sadness which sometimes falls between us springs from disappointment in our search, each straining through and beyond the other, snatching a glimpse now and then of the shadow which turns the corner always a pace or two ahead of us'" (p. 265). Shadows, the novel's major leitmotif, are evils which harbour potential good: they are evil if they are valued as ends in themselves, but good if used as means toward God. Although Ryder does not wish to abandon his shadowy loves, circumstances compel him to do so; and so, outgrowing "bride" after "bride," he passes through the shadows to the light, to the red flame in the sanctuary lamp of "deplorable" design.

There is an additional bride whom Ryder must relinquish as an end in herself, and whom he must learn to treat as a pathway to God. She is secular art, the most Circean of all the novel's brides. Unflaggingly seductive, she is Charles's first profane love, and she is the last to go. Waugh attacks secular art by making Ryder outgrow it, and in so doing he takes up an unfamiliar and unfashionable position in the history of twentieth-century taste. Waugh's major image for secular art is Brideshead House itself, which rose out of the ruins of the "old house" of Christian art. Brideshead is a palace of art; according to Ryder, "It was an aesthetic education to live within those walls, to wander from room to room, from the Soanesque library to the Chinese drawing-room, adazzle with gilt pagodas and nodding mandarins, painted paper and Chippendale fretwork, from the Pompeian parlour to the great tapestry-hung hall" (p. 72).

An examination of the history of Brideshead, from Inigo Jones to art nouveau, reveals an allusive history of post-Reformation secular art. And Charles Ryder himself is the current admirer of this art; he finds his inspiration in contemplating the houses of man rather than the House of God. Waugh makes Ryder speak modestly about his success in painting the works of man, but Waugh implies that the merely human is a dubious and risky source of inspiration. Here, for example, is Ryder painting the florid fountain: "By some odd chance, for the thing was far beyond me, I brought it off and by judicious omissions and some stylish tricks, produced a very passable echo of Piranesi" (p. 73). And when he succeeds in painting Marchmain House, he feels lucky, "like a gambler." Indeed, Ryder never again experiences "the intensity and the singleness . . . in a word, the inspiration" which he has known in the drawing-room at Marchmain House (p. 199), and in a desperate hunt to recover it he goes to the South American jungle to seek "inspiration among gutted palaces and cloisters embowered in weed" (p. 199). The desolation he beholds only confirms the transience of human endeavour, but instead of rejecting the ruins in favour of some worthier source of inspiration, Ryder paints them. Like Tony Last he intensifies his plight by travelling into the jungle, and like John Plant he becomes a second-rate artist. His art serves the world of change and decay; he paints imitations of illusions.[14] The enigmatic Anthony Blanche knows that Ryder's work is false: "My dear, let us not expose your little imposture before these good, plain people. . . . We know, you and I, that this is all t-t-terrible t-t-tripe" (p. 236).

Ryder himself admits that his work is a "mirage" (p. 199), but his engaging modesty should not disarm the reader. Through Ryder, Waugh intimates that works without inspiration, the "authentic impulse to action" (p. 71), are not unique but in some way double; they belong to the world of shadows. Waugh's severity does not of course extend to a dismissal of all works of secular art, but he does maintain that few such works can attain the highest levels of genius. In an important passage which stands at the core of Waugh's commentary on art, Ryder reflects on his memories, memories which are of course *Brideshead Revisited* itself:

> These memories are the memorials and pledges of the vital hours of a lifetime. These hours of afflatus in the human spirit, the springs of art, are, in their mystery, akin to the epochs of history, when a race which for centuries had lived content, unknown, behind its own frontiers, digging, eating, sleeping, begetting, doing what was requisite for survival and nothing else, will, for a generation or two, stupefy the world, commit all manner of crimes, perhaps, follow the wildest chimeras, go down in the end in agony, but leave behind a record of new heights scaled and new rewards won for all mankind; the vision fades, the soul sickens, and the routine of survival starts again.
>
> The human soul enjoys these rare, classic periods, but, apart from them, we are seldom single or unique; we keep company in this world with a hoard of abstractions and reflexions and counterfeits of ourselves—the sensual man, the economic man, the man of

reason, the beast, the machine and the sleep-walker, and heaven knows what besides, all in our own image, indistinguishable from ourselves to the outward eye. We get borne along, out of sight in the press, unresisting, till we get the chance to drop behind un-noticed, or to dodge down a side street, pause, breathe freely and take our bearings, or to push ahead, outdistance our shadows, lead them a dance, so that when at length they catch up with us, they look at one another askance, knowing we have a secret we shall never share. (pp. 197–98)

This remarkable first-edition passage is an account of art and the hu-man spirit locked in the world of mutability. There, life's "vital hours" are those "rare, classic periods" when one is "single or unique"; those moments are "the springs of art," comparable on the level of history to epochs of high civilization. They occur infrequently, and after they pass, the human spirit tumbles all too quickly from uniqueness into "routine," where it is plagued by "shadows." If life in the uninspired routine world is shadowy, then the art based on that life extends the unreality to one more remove.

Since most of life is routine (here Waugh's chronic boredom colours his attitude), the artist's problem is to achieve a more lasting kind of "sin-gleness." That, no doubt, is what Waugh sought to find in religion, which he regarded as a more "authentic impulse to action" than any merely sec-ular stimulus. Waugh treasured the beautiful works of man; indeed, his house at Stinchcombe was crowded with them. But he resisted the temp-tation to see them as ends in themselves, and could always relinquish them in favour of a higher beauty.[15]

Waugh was interested in religious art as early as his fourteenth year, when he composed "The World to Come"; more important still, there is a preoccupation with religious art in his first book, *Rossetti: His Life and Works* (1928). Here Waugh adopts the view that Rossetti was a second-rate artist, but that he somehow managed to transcend his "spiritual in-adequacy" to create great works like *Beata Beatrix*: "here and there in his life he seems, without ever feeling it, to have transcended this inade-quacy in a fashion that admits of no glib explanation."[16] Rossetti's sim-ilarity to Ryder is plainly evident. "Here and there" in their lives, they both transcend their inadequacies to produce masterpieces. In each case secular inspiration manages to overcome the limitations of the world of mutability, but eventually that sadly limited inspiration dries up.

According to Waugh, Rossetti's work is for the most part derivative rather than authentic. In the *Damozel of the San Grail*, for example, "the Grail itself . . . has become a modern chalice, straight from the windows

of any ecclesiastical outfitter." [17] And Rossetti's poetry "is all a sonorous
re-echoing of dark perceptions . . . rich, odorous, picturesque, with not a
statement that any child may not understand, not an emotion that any
man may not share. Despondency, desire, sense of loss, realization of
transience and of mortality, hope, all the common emotions ornamen-
tally expressed." [18] Except for a few successes, then, Rossetti is bogus. He
paints religious subjects without religious feeling; beneath the ornamental exterior there is no new or vital emotion. Like Charles Ryder, Rossetti
represents the best that art can do without religion; they are both secular
artists in the service of inadequate ideals.

If we look for the source of Rossetti's and Ryder's spiritual inadequacy,
we find, in each case, an irresponsible father. Rossetti's father was a Catholic who had become a free-thinker, a reader of Swedenborg and the sacred lore of the Brahmins. His private religion "left his children very little
but a mild and muddled awe with which to confront a very difficult
world." [19] With such weak guidance, Rossetti was fated to live amid the
second-rate and the insubstantial, like Ryder, whose decrepit and atheistical sire virtually orphans him. But important as the elder Rossetti is as
a precursor of the irresponsible fathers of Waugh's fiction, the ultimate
source is Arthur Waugh himself. Arthur Waugh introduced his son into
the Anglo-Catholic rite, which Evelyn later came to regard as a mere parody of Roman Catholicism. In Waugh's rejection of his father's allegedly
spurious religion in favour of the more authentic faith of his forefathers,
one can clearly see the genesis of Charles Ryder's spiritual odyssey in
*Brideshead Revisited*. Waugh's passing interest in Anglo-Catholicism is
the source of the ambivalent shadows of *Brideshead*, whose value depends upon whether they are ends or means.

So long as it is regarded as an end in itself, Brideshead is an insubstantial house of art. The stimulus it provides may provoke "singleness," but
not for long. One of the most telling pieces of information about Brideshead is embedded in Ryder's apparently innocuous observation that "the
ground led, still unravished, to the neighbourly horizon" (p. 18). As Delasanta and D'Avanzo rightly observe, the line suggests that we ought
to look at Keats's "Ode on a Grecian Urn." When we do, we find that
Waugh has relied on it heavily—but as before, there are problems with
Delasanta's and D'Avanzo's account of the way Waugh uses it. Here is
their contention: "Like Keats's urn, Brideshead is an unravished bride
not only because it is a work of art eminently beautiful, but also because
it is Christ's Church which is eminently true . . . Waugh's *Brideshead*,
therefore, is his brilliantly subtle synthesis, or reconciliation, of the Romantic with the Christian credo." [20] But there are several difficulties here.
As we have seen, the Marchmains do *not* retain their faith, and Brides-

head is *not* the Roman Catholic Church but schismatic post-Reformation England. It therefore cannot represent a reconciliation, however "brilliantly subtle," between the Christian (which in Waugh's eyes means the Catholic) and the Romantic credos. But it can and does indicate that the twin manifestations of the English Reformation, its religion and its art, are equally insubstantial. Despite Ryder's ostensible approval of Brideshead House (a curious narrative problem in itself, as he knows better by the time he tells the story),[21] it should be borne in mind that Waugh himself does not regard it as the highest form of truth or beauty. Despite appearances, Brideshead is neither "eminently beautiful" nor "eminently true." Keats and religion are indeed conjoined in the image of the house, but not as Delasanta and D'Avanzo suppose: Waugh "reconciles" the "truth and beauty" which Brideshead represents by rejecting them both.

The similarities between Brideshead House and the urn are apparent. Both are "foster-children of silence and slow time," and both feature scenes of "happy, happy love." Sebastian is the "fair youth, beneath the trees," and Charles is the "Bold Lover." But the differences between house and urn are far more important. Keats's urn pictures a frozen Arcadia, which stands in stark contrast to changing, time-worn Brideshead; and the macabre inscription on the skull amid Sebastian's roses well suits Brideshead itself: "*Et in Arcadia Ego*"—"even in Arcadia there am I [Death]." Unlike the static scene on the urn, Brideshead is not a *locus amoenus* but an ordinary house locked in the world of change and decay; it stands upon unchanging hills but is not itself "still unravished." In contrast to the figure on the urn, Sebastian, the "fair youth," leaves his song and becomes old, bald, and an alcoholic. Nor does Ryder, the "Bold Lover," remain frozen in eternal anticipation; instead he passes through a succession of unhappy loves until he finally achieves his goal. His passion is not "all breathing human passion far above," nor, to judge from the amount of wine he consumes, does he entirely escape "a burning forehead and a parching tongue."

By implicitly contrasting Brideshead House and Keats's urn, Waugh rejects the notion that secular art can be truly permanent, and the same veiled hostility is evident elsewhere. Against Keats's assertion of the permanence of secular art, Waugh presents the image of the frozen but melting swan on the transatlantic liner. A little man, who resembles a cartoon character and who pretends to be a guest at Celia's party, counts the drops falling from the swan's beak: fraud contemplates fraud. Below decks there is a whole "Noah's Ark" of such frozen creatures, but eventually they too will melt.

There is an even more important discrepancy between Brideshead and the urn. Although it may be true for Keats that "Beauty is truth, truth beauty," it is not so in Waugh's novel. Sebastian and Julia, the beautiful children, are farthest from the truth, while the plain Cordelia and Bridey possess it. Thus, while truth is always morally beautiful, it may not be physically prepossessing, and physical beauty may conceal error and immaturity.

Waugh's attitude to beauty is distrustful, and there can be little doubt that it was dictated by his almost pathological sense of transience and decay. As a young man Waugh certainly loved beauty and was himself beautiful. Harold Acton recalled that he had "wide-apart eyes," "curved sensual lips," and "hyacinthine locks of hair."[22] But all that beauty had to die, "changed past recognition" by the infirmities of age which, even in 1944, Waugh rightly sensed near at hand. In *Brideshead* Waugh resolves the desolating problem of the death of beauty in a manner not everyone can endorse. He tenderly calls forth the notion of perpetual beauty and exorcises it as a snare and a delusion. A cruel Florimund, he wakes the Sleeping Beauty and sends her packing. Waugh emphatically rejects Keats's pagan heaven of art. In Waugh's view, it is not true that "a thing of beauty is a joy for ever"; a thing of beauty is a joy only if it is a way-place on the road to God. Thus Ryder "needs to know" more than Brideshead House and "happy love" if he wishes to achieve lasting "singleness." He must renounce all earthly brides as ends in themselves. It is not by chance that in the *Brideshead* manuscript Waugh speaks of Julia in terms of the Mona Lisa, and alludes slightingly to Walter Pater, who believed that the Mona Lisa embodied "the return of the Pagan world" and was "the symbol of the modern idea."[23] By exchanging all his preliminary brides for the Bride of Christ, Ryder escapes his "dead years" and creates a non-derivative work of art animated by an authentic "impulse to action." That work is *Brideshead* itself.

Brideshead is the house of schism and secular art; it is half-pagan, immature, incomplete, and, it should be observed, overwhelmingly masculine. But in the heart of the great house, Lady Marchmain has a room which is "all her own"; it is full of chintz, lambskin bindings, views of Florence, bowls of pot-pourri, petit-point, a plaster St. Joseph, and an ivory Madonna. It is a mother's room, from which the unperceptive Charles Ryder escapes after his "talks" into the "masculine atmosphere" of what he mistakenly thinks is "a better age" (p. 122). Lady Marchmain's room is the last bulwark of the faith in Brideshead House and from it she tries to stave off the decay of her family. She tries to restrain Julia from her godless marriage with Rex, and Sebastian from his escape into alcoholism. But she fails, for she is not severe enough with her wayward children. Even while trying to discipline Sebastian, she admits her leniency to Charles: "When you left he was so sweet to me, just as he used to be as a little boy, and I agreed to all he wanted" (p. 127). When Charles advocates freedom of choice for Sebastian, she says, "But he's been free, always up till now, and look at the result." Significantly, Lady Marchmain does not resemble her grim-faced brothers, but is "starry and delicate"; she is "charming," perhaps even infected by her husband's weakness. She likes "the Alice-in-Wonderland side of religion." Her favourite reading matter is *The Diary of a Nobody*, the story of the too-tolerant and ridiculously ineffectual Victorian paterfamilias, Mr. Pooter. When she tries to paint, the colours merge into khaki. These nudges are Waugh's way of saying that Lady Marchmain's feminine softness is no match for the massive decay of Brideshead House, which is the result of the apostasy of fathers; nothing can be done to reverse it until a father returns to the faith.[24]

The story of Lord Marchmain's side of the family is virtually the same tale Waugh tells in his early satires. Lord Marchmain and his son Sebastian are only romanticized versions of Colonel Blount and Adam Symes or John Plant and his father. They languish at the foot of a long cultural decline, and they have arrived there through the vitiating weakness of fathers. But *Brideshead* marks the appearance of a startlingly new set of characters: it is the presence in the novel of Lady Marchmain's family which makes *Brideshead* radically different from all Waugh's previous fiction, for the Marchioness's family personifies the affirmative values which until now Waugh has adumbrated only through innuendo.

For dramatic effect Waugh arranges things so that the imminent eclipse of Lord Marchmain's line follows close on the extinction of his wife's family. Lady Marchmain's three brothers, about whom Waugh strategically says very little, all die in the Great War. Both families perish: Lady Marchmain's has just done so and her husband's will soon follow. After all, neither Cordelia nor Bridey, who marries the matronly Mrs. Muspratt, is likely to have children, nor will Sebastian ever be a father, fleeing as he does from change and responsibility. And Julia is prevented by misfortune from bearing children, although that fact is not revealed until later in the novel. So it is that as the story reaches its nadir at the end of Book II, the old Catholic line is defunct and the new "pagan" line is on the verge of extinction.

In keeping with his old theme, heresy, and his new one, the redeeming action of Providence upon heretics, Waugh now focuses his attention upon those who err rather than upon the faithful. According to the MGM "Memorandum," "the second half of the story . . . shows how the Grace of God turns everything in the end to good, though not to conventional prosperity." In the "Memorandum" as in the novel Waugh uses the metaphor of the fisherman's line for the operation of grace. It comes from

G. K. Chesterton's story, "The Queer Feet," in which the "club of the Twelve True Fishermen" lose their celebrated set of fish-cutlery to the notorious criminal, Monsieur Flambeau. Flambeau performs his theft by masquerading, in rapid alternation, as a waiter and as a gentleman. He is about to make good his escape when Father Brown apprehends him, recovers the cutlery, and then surprisingly, releases the criminal. Later one of the "fishermen" questions him:

> "Did you catch this man?" asked the colonel, frowning. Father
> Brown looked him full in his frowning face. "Yes," he said, "I
> caught him, with an unseen hook and an invisible line which is
> long enough to let him wander to the ends of the world and still to
> bring him back with a twitch upon the thread." [25]

Once having caught Flambeau, Father Brown may reclaim him in due course, like God reclaiming Jonah. What happens to Flambeau also happens to the erring Flytes, to Charles Ryder, and will happen, Waugh hopes, to the great, divided "house" which shelters them all.

Sebastian is the first of the Flytes to be "twitched" back to God. Waugh's imagination is intensely engaged with him: he personifies youth, grace, love, and whimsey, and he is delineated with a captivating charm. But despite his beauty, Sebastian is sharply criticized, for he represents chronic immaturity and a blighting selfishness. Like Peter Pan, he flees his home, luring others, notably Charles Ryder, into a Never-never-land of carefree youth, "an enclosed and enchanted garden, which was somewhere, not overlooked by any window, in the heart of that grey city" (p. 29). Later, when Sebastian's flight from responsibility leads him into alcoholism, he rides a horse named Tinkerbell. He also represents a new, worldly paganism (he reads the *News of the World*), and the decay of the faith. Like Augustine, he wants to be "good, but not yet" (p. 77). His undiscriminating taste reflects his lack of discipline: "His room was filled with a strange jumble of objects—a harmonium in a gothic case, an elephant's foot waste-paper basket, a dome of wax fruit, two disproportionately large Sèvres vases, framed drawings by Daumier—made all the more incongruous by the austere college furniture and the large luncheon table. His chimney-piece was covered in cards of invitation from London hostesses" (p. 29).

Sebastian's only desire is for solitude: "His constant, despairing prayer," Ryder tells us, "was to be let alone" (p. 113). When the odious Samgrass takes him away on a tour of the East, he escapes, later telling Charles, "I shall go on running away, as far and as fast as I can" (p. 120). But the farther Sebastian flees from responsibility, the more he moves into the shadows. On the way to Brideshead, Sebastian and Charles dine in a shadowy parlour; the great house itself is full of shadows; on their way home they seem to be in pursuit of their own shadows. Cara speaks to Charles about Sebastian and love "in the shade"; at Oxford the following year they live "more and more in the shadows" (p. 94), and after his drunkenness at Easter,[26] "the shadows [close] round Sebastian" (p. 124). After his journey to the East, Sebastian speaks "like an echo" from "the shadows beyond the lamplight, beyond the warmth of the burning logs, beyond the family circle and photographs spread out on the cardtable" (p. 132). Inevitably, Sebastian rejects Charles, whom he wrongly suspects of conspiring with his mother; Charles thereupon exchanges the "enchanted garden" for the "light of common day" and the first phase of his education is over. But Sebastian stays behind, resolutely adolescent, and his intense desire for solitude leads him into self-love; a "Narcissus with one pustule," he refuses responsibility and conformity. Eventually his flight into solitude leads him to the shadowy Kurt, who resembles "the footman in 'Warning Shadows'" (p. 180). But here is where *Brideshead* differs from the early fiction: shadows, evil in themselves, can lead to good. *A Handful of Dust* concludes with Tony the slave of the shadowy Mr. Todd; but Sebastian escapes Tony's fate by loving his shadow. His newly acquired charity, learned in circumstances which seem sordid to Charles, nevertheless leads him at last to a renewed love for God. As Ryder himself has said, "to know and love one other human being is the root of all wisdom" (p. 41). To Ryder, Sebastian's love for Kurt looks like the end of the line, but it is in fact the beginning of the way back. Although Sebastian remains the slave of his addiction and, as the manuscript tells us, "charming" to the end, he finds holiness. One of the last things we hear about him is that he wants to become a missionary. Despite Sebastian's long and exhausting struggle against his vocation, it finds him at last; and the key is charity.

There can be little doubt that Lord Marchmain's "attractive, wayward and helpless younger son"[27] is the character readers of *Brideshead* remember most clearly; indeed, he is beyond a doubt the most successful character Waugh ever created. He is by no means purely fictional, however. He is a composite drawn from Richard Pares, Hugh Lygon, and Alastair Graham, for whom Waugh formed attachments while at Oxford. Other friends are incorporated in minor ways. For example, Sebastian's arrest for drunk driving stems from that of Matthew Ponsonby, whose sister, Elizabeth, was the leader of the Bright Young People. And it was Keith Douglas, a contemporary of Waugh's at Oxford, who carried around a toy bear. But Alastair Graham is the main original. Like Sebastian, Graham had a pathological aversion to his mother, a very different

sort of woman, it should be said, from Lady Marchmain, who in her resemblance to a "Reinhardt nun" possibly owes something to Diana
Cooper as she appeared in Max Reinhardt's production of *The Miracle*.
Fleeing from his mother on one occasion, Graham was found drunk at
the Lotti in Paris; at a relatively tender age he rented a house of his own
to escape his mother's dominating influence. The name Alastair even appears instead of Sebastian at several points in the manuscript. Waugh was
devoted to Graham, and their friendship endured until well into the
1930s; but Waugh eventually realized that the relationship was harmful
to him. Looking back in *A Little Learning* on Graham, or "Hamish Lennox," as he calls him, Waugh remarks, "I could not have fallen under an
influence better designed to encourage my natural frivolity, dilettantism
and dissipation or to expose as vulgar any promptings I may have felt to
worldly ambition." [28] There can be no doubt that in describing Ryder's
"outdistancing" of Sebastian, Waugh was trying to lay to rest his affection for Alastair Graham and for the debilitating aestheticism he represented. Indeed, Waugh's loss of Graham was tantamount to the loss of his
youth, the painful but necessary loss of part of his personality: "As I
drove away and turned back in the car to take what promised to be my
last view of the house, I felt that I was leaving part of myself behind, and
that wherever I went afterwards I should feel the lack of it, and search for
it hopelessly, as ghosts are said to do, frequenting the spots where they
buried material treasures without which they cannot pay their way to the
nether world" (p. 149). But material treasures must go by the board,
however alluring they may be; although Waugh never says so explicitly,
he regards Charles's love for Sebastian as a gorgeous mistake and a *felix
culpa*. Despite the fact that Ryder's love is misguided, "its naughtiness
high in the catalogue of grave sins" (p. 41), it adumbrates his love for
Julia and his eventual love for God. Like many another "shadow" in
*Brideshead Revisited*, Sebastian is pernicious when loved as an end in
himself but valuable as an avenue to the divine. Although Anthony
Blanche is undoubtedly motivated by malice, he is right when he warns
Ryder that Sebastian is dangerous. Because of his association with Sebastian, Ryder's early life and art are "strangled with charm" (p. 52).

Sebastian is unquestionably the most vivid character in *Brideshead Revisited*. Unfortunately, his brilliance constitutes a liability for the novel
after he leaves it. As a forerunner of Ryder's love for Julia, and of the
Church, he must be rejected, but he is so sympathetic a creation that
Charles's other loves seem pale by contrast. The risk, therefore, is that
the reader's attention will linger on Sebastian rather than focusing on
Julia, who is the subject of the next part of the book.

While it is true, as Christopher Sykes claims, [29] that there is no distinct model for Julia, there is a general similarity of situation. Writing in *A Little Learning* of the events of 1924, Waugh remarks, "In the course of the autumn I had fallen in love. I had in fact fallen in love with an entire family and, rather as Mr. E. M. Forster describes in *Howards End*, had focused the sentiment upon the only appropriate member, an eighteen-year-old daughter."[30] The family were the Plunket-Greenes who, in the sense that Waugh loved them all, correspond to the Flytes. Biographical evidence suggests that Waugh found his own home life unsatisfactory and wanted to be part of the Plunket-Greene family, just as Ryder rejects his malicious father in favour of the sympathetic Flytes. Like Lady Marchmain, Gwen Plunket-Greene was separated from her husband; Waugh was a good friend of her son Richard, whose sister Olivia became the focus of Waugh's love and then rejected it. It would be false to argue that Olivia Plunket-Greene was the sole original for Julia, for as we have noticed, Waugh was adept at merging similar real-life situations to produce fictitious composites. The Flytes also owe a great deal to the Lygon family—especially to its head, Lord Beauchamp, who like Lord Marchmain was exiled from England. Unlike Lord Marchmain, however, Lord Beauchamp was forced into exile by charges of pederasty levelled against him by an angry relative. Neither Richard Plunket-Greene nor his tall, dandyish brother David was particularly devout, but their mother was, and so was Olivia. Although the analogy is admittedly not exact, the Plunket-Greenes helped lead Waugh to the Church, just as the Flytes lead Charles Ryder. It was Olivia who found Father Martin D'Arcy, s.j. to instruct Waugh.

Julia and Charles live together for two years at Brideshead. Their defiant and private love makes them hate both God and the world who, Julia remarks, "are in a conspiracy" against them. Although Waugh's romantic tone is ostensibly sympathetic, his charged language shows that their secular solitude is wrong-headed. Near the fountain, where "the shadow of the obelisk spanned the terrace" (p. 243), Ryder paints Julia in her Chinese gown, still the wrong subject for his art. Here, after Lord Brideshead reminds them of the forgotten concept of sin, they meet in the moonlight, and Ryder compares Julia's stricken face with the one in Holman Hunt's "The Awakened Conscience." The dialogue hints at their imposture:

Once more we stood by the fountain.
"It's like the setting of a comedy," I said. "Scene: a baroque fountain in a nobleman's grounds. Act one, sunset; act two, dusk; act three, moonlight. The characters keep assembling at the fountain for no very clear reason."

"Comedy?"

"Drama. Tragedy. Farce. What you will. This is the reconciliation scene."

"Was there a quarrel?"

"Estrangement and misunderstanding in act two."

"Oh, don't talk in that damned bounderish way. Why must you see everything second-hand? Why must this be a play? Why must my conscience be a pre-Raphaelite picture?" (p. 255)

The following night they stand again by the fountain (p. 258), surrounded by deceptiveness: the moonlight lies "like hoar-frost"; the picturesque fountain plays; the park resembles the Greek camp where "false" Cressid lay. Charles and Julia make the pagan response of *carpe diem* to their prevision of disaster, but throughout the passage there is the sense that their illicit seclusion must yield to something more genuine. The master-image for the destruction of autonomous and therefore false joy is the trapper's hut; it appears to be a "neat and warm" sanctuary from the cold, but it is in fact a snow-covered prison which is about to be crushed by an avalanche.

Into this atmosphere of impending catastrophe comes Lord Marchmain, who returns to Brideshead House to die. Everything about his preparation for death is heavy with the aura of falseness. The room he chooses is the Chinese drawing room, "a splendid, uninhabitable museum of Chippendale carving and porcelain and lacquer and painted hangings," with a "grotesque, chinoiserie chimney-piece" (pp. 277,279). And his bed is "an exhibition piece, a vast velvet tent like the baldachino at St. Peters." Although Lord Marchmain's death is modelled on that of Waugh's friend Hubert Duggan, his theatricalism is Arthur Waugh's. His taste for effect leads him to stage a little boy's romanticized version of an adult death-scene:

"It looks very well, does it not?"

"Very well."

"You might paint it, eh—and call it the *Death Bed*?" (p. 279)

Lord Marchmain prepares to die amid the sham and the pseudo: "the gold plate . . . and the gilt mirrors and the lacquer and the drapery of the great bed and Julia's mandarin coat gave the scene an air of pantomime, of Aladdin's cave" (p. 279).

Waugh's vivid picture of "waspish" Lord Marchmain gasping for breath amid the delusive "gilt" mandarins is moving because it represents the truth behind the old man's whole way of life. In an early Waugh novel

Lord Marchmain would have died oblivious to the irony of his surroundings. But *Brideshead* is a parable of return as well as of departure, and so grace recovers him at the eleventh hour. Lord Marchmain's return to the faith is a pivotal moment, for it reverses the course both of *Brideshead Revisited* and all of Waugh's fiction. In his youth Lord Marchmain had thought that he was "free as air," and "committed a crime in the name of freedom" (p. 292). The crime was his neglect of his duties as a husband and father in favour of an easy life amid the fleshly consolations of Venice. Now, on his deathbed, Lord Marchmain receives what has been denied to every other father in Waugh's previous fiction: moral insight. As he struggles for breath, he realizes that neither the air, nor he himself, is free. He sees, or at least we assume he does, for we are not at this dramatic moment given access to his mind, that his freedom has only been God's delay. Marchmain's perception that he is God's creature marks the end of a series of linked errors. It marks the end of his long apostasy, the end of his grotesquely prolonged childhood, and the end of his tolerant irresponsibility. For the first time in Waugh's fiction we get a story of successful maturation: an advance which is achieved by means of a return, in the midst of the pseudo, to the authentic. Marchmain's return terminates the first half of Waugh's career, which has consisted of satire against the blindness of fathers. On the level of the parable his return is prophecy, for it counteracts the apostasy of Mr. Todd's father and restores the neopagan digression of Anglicanism to the Roman Catholic mainstream.

It is perhaps indicative of Waugh's desire for personal heroism, thwarted by official obstructionism, that the real hero of the return is not Lord Marchmain but his nearly adopted son, Charles Ryder—who, of course, is also Waugh's persona. As the priest urges Lord Marchmain to make the sign of the Cross, Ryder reverses his earlier attitude and prays that Marchmain may do so. Granted, Charles prays sceptically, but this is a novel in which the genuine operates through the spurious. We cannot know whether Ryder's prayer is instrumental in restoring Lord Marchmain, but Waugh wants us to entertain the thought as a probability. Ryder's affirmative act reverses the flow of degenerate paternal influence which cripples all the sons in Waugh's fiction: Ryder, a spiritually impoverished son, restores the father who, figuratively, has caused his moral bankruptcy.[31] The act is no small achievement on Waugh's part, for it formally concludes the hatred for fathers which has fuelled his fiction throughout nearly two decades. How was such a dramatic reversal now possible? While it is evident that the change was heralded by *Work Suspended*, it is probable that a personal event now made it psychologically right. In the summer of 1943, six months before Waugh began *Brideshead*, his father died. That Ryder should lead Marchmain to the faith is appropriate, for in *Brideshead* spiritual continuity is more important than temporal continuity, and it upsets all temporal causality. In the War Trilogy too (and in *Howards End*, one of Waugh's favourite novels), spiritual continuity outweighs dynastic considerations.

Because of Lord Marchmain's example, Julia is gripped by the conviction that she is made for a greater purpose, and she terminates her relationship with Charles. The avalanche sweeps their "little lighted place" into the valley, liberating them from their ornate prison. Grace subordinates their personal happiness to the divine purpose—a theme which many readers find disagreeable but which is clearly prefigured by Waugh's hostile treatment of secular privacy in earlier novels. Charles Ryder does not become a member of the Marchmain family, to share a family life he never had; nor does he inherit Brideshead House, as he seemed sure to do before Lord Marchmain's dramatic return to the faith. Had Charles married Julia and inherited Brideshead (as he would have done but for Lord Marchmain's last act), the great house would have become one of the spiritless manors so common in Waugh's early fiction. But grace intervenes and "revisits" it. Like its occupants, the house is "twitched" back to orthodoxy; to use Waugh's religio-sexual language, Brideshead's return to the undivided mainstream is its "moment of consummation."

Brideshead House is the product of many builders, but grace is its ultimate architect. It is grace which prevents Ryder from becoming Lord Marchmain's son and Julia's husband, and it is grace which expels Ryder into the cold world to become "homeless, childless, middle-aged, loveless" (p. 303). If we compare Charles's fate with Paul Pennyfeather's we can see that Waugh's treatment of his personae has exactly reversed itself. In his loss of Brideshead and his material expectations, Ryder resembles Paul and Tony Last. But in his spiritual enrichment Ryder is an affirmative parody of those early, homeless waifs; furthermore, the shaping genius of grace emerges as a divine parody of the contingency and chance which govern the early fiction.

Unlike Paul Pennyfeather and Adam Symes, who succumb to disasters which crush their ambitions, Ryder is overtaken by the creative catastrophes of grace, which give him the apotheosis of all his desires. He has wished for inspiration, and for a wife and a family and a home; grace destroys his hopes for these and gives him the Holy Spirit and the Bride of Christ and the Household of the Faith and the City of God. The wheel comes full circle: the faith has nearly expired in World War I with the deaths of Lady Marchmain's stern brothers. Now, in the darkness of a second war, their spirit is reborn in Charles Ryder, who becomes the spiritual son of Lady Marchmain rather than the actual heir of Lord Marchmain.

Waugh held a dual view of World War II. On the one hand it was a prison created by the excesses of the Twenties and Thirties—excesses which had turned England into an asylum full of encaged lunatics like the ones Ryder contemplates in the Prologue. On the other hand, influenced perhaps by Eliot in "Little Gidding," Waugh regarded the war as the purgatorial fire which would cleanse England and return it to the path it had left in the reign of Elizabeth I. On a national plane, Ryder's return to Catholicism looks forward to the end of the Anglican digression in England. And on a personal level it represents the return of the house of Waugh to the Catholicism of its forefathers; Evelyn Waugh, the right-minded father, supersedes Arthur Waugh, the last of the apostate fathers.

## CHAPTER 13

# Scott-King's Modern Europe

If *Brideshead Revisited* is Waugh's ambivalent elegy for "the odorous gardens of [the] recent past,"[1] *Scott-King's Modern Europe* is his unequivocal attack on the drab new Europe which he saw emerging from the "lightless concentration camp" of war. The novelette does not rank with Waugh's best work, but it clearly articulates the mood of cynicism and rage which settled on its author after 1945. Who could have guessed before the war that "all that seeming-solid, patiently built, gorgeously ornamented structure of Western life was to melt overnight like an ice-castle"? In the aftermath of battle the spacious palace of civilization shrank to the mean dimensions of a prison-house, and "there [was] no room for tourists in a world of 'displaced persons'."[2]

Waugh sends forth a dim, shabby tourist into the grim postwar world. Bald, corpulent, middle-aged and unknown, Scott-King has been twenty-one years a classical master at Granchester, and has witnessed the slow decay of interest in his field. But he does not "repine."[3] Indeed, he finds "a peculiar relish in contemplating the victories of barbarism," and rejoices in his "reduced station, for he . . . is fascinated by obscurity and failure" (p. 3). By associating Scott-King with Pater's Mona Lisa ("He was older . . . than the rocks on which he sat," p. 9), Waugh seems to establish him as a dispassionate and experienced observer who will take adversity in his stride.[4] But the comparison is ironic, for insular Scott-King has not been abroad since 1939. When, in a fit of nostalgia for the Mediterranean that he once knew, Scott-King accepts an invitation to Neutralia, nothing in his real or imagined experience prepares him for the chaos he finds.

Conquered successively by the Athenians, Carthaginians, Romans, Hapsburgs, and Napoleon, Neutralia is now "a typical modern state" (p. 4) under the control of "a dominant Marshal" (p. 5) whose major achievement has been to keep his secluded country out of World War II. When Neutralia convenes an international conference in order to regain contact with the world, it chooses as a pretext the tercentenary of its obscure seventeenth-century Latin poet, Bellorius, who devoted his life to describing a utopian island in the New World. Bellorius's reasonable community seems far removed from totalitarian Neutralia, yet not really, for Waugh implies that any attempt to set up a merely rational utopia will issue in a repressive dystopia. Since Scott-King has translated Bellorius into Spenserian stanzas—his "monument to dimness"—and has composed a monograph on the poet's work, the Neutralians invite him to their conference.

The junket of the gentle academic is modelled on Waugh's trip to Spain with Douglas Woodruff to attend the 1946 celebrations in honour of Francisco de Vittoria, the sixteenth-century Dominican jurist. The Spanish government withdrew its hospitality the moment the festivities ended, and Waugh and Woodruff were stranded, with very little cash in hand. They experienced some anxious moments before British officials in Madrid made room for them on a government aircraft.

Like Waugh and Woodruff, the fatigued and hungry Scott-King suffers the anguish of the air traveller, endures boring official oratory, and buckets across the dusty republic to assorted points of interest. The authorities trick him into laying a wreath at the base of a controversial war memorial, and his fellow delegates leave, some on principle, others abducted by ferocious partisans. One, a Swiss Calvinist, is murdered. In the end, only Scott-King remains to honour Bellorius. Standing before the draped statue of his poet, Scott-King speaks from his heart, in Latin: "He . . . said that a torn and embittered world was that day united in dedicating itself to the majestic concept of Bellorius, in rebuilding itself first in Neutralia, then among all the yearning peoples of the West, on the foundations Bellorius had so securely laid. He . . . said that they were lighting a candle that day which by the Grace of God should never be put out" (p. 66). After this echo of ill-fated Latimer, Scott-King tugs at the cord and undrapes the statue, which in its gross bad taste epitomizes the fraudulence of the entire conference and underscores the perversion of Bellorius's utopia. The inappropriate statue has not been made for Bellorius at all, but for the tomb of "a fraudulent merchant prince" with an "illusory" estate (p. 65). Finally Scott-King gives up the belief "that in Neutralia Western Culture might be born again" (p. 77), perceiving that the whole thing is a charade. After a quick jaunt back to Bellacita, the stagey Dr. Fe bids Scott-King farewell with tell-tale "Arcadian grace" and abandons him to pay super-tax in his trumpery hotel under the broiling Neutralian sun. But thanks to a chance encounter with Miss Bombaum, the redoubtable American journalist, he learns about "the underground"—"the new ultra-national citizenship" (p. 74) which disregards and perverts traditional political boundaries. Through it, Scott-King escapes with a motley crowd of imprisoned refugees dressed as Ursuline nuns. Like Noah's animals before the cleansing flood, they enter a dark hold, and when they emerge they are in "No. 64 Jewish Illicit Immigrants' Camp, Palestine" (p. 86). As before, the quest for a utopia leads to prison, and once again the perverted is the gateway to the genuine.

When Scott-King returns to Granchester he is silent about his adventures, but admits that he needs "a new subject," having "come to the end of old Bellorius at last" (p. 87). Utopias and their distorted successors no longer interest Scott-King, who now turns his back on the modern world and refuses, more than ever, to participate in it. When his headmaster offers him the chance to preserve his position at Granchester by teaching eonomic history, he declines:

> "I think it would be very wicked indeed to do anything to fit a boy for the modern world."
> "It's a short-sighted view, Scott-King."
> "There, headmaster, with all respect, I differ from you profoundly. I think it the most long-sighted view it is possible to take." (p. 88)

The novelette's conclusion marks no real advance over its beginning. Although Scott-King exorcises Bellorius, a delusive "shade" who demands "placation" (p. 6), he does not profit much from his disillusionment. He does not exchange his threatened secular refuge for something more stable, and the barricade he builds against the modern world is made only of dead languages. We shall notice a similar lack of an unambiguously affirmative conclusion in *The Loved One* and *Love Among the Ruins*.

With its tart and formal diction, *Scott-King's Modern Europe* is a stylistically superb little work; nevertheless it is marred by weaknesses which suggest that Waugh's powers of invention were flagging. There is too much undigested personal experience, and too much similarity to Waugh's other books.[5] Moreover, there is a problem with clarity of motivation: Waugh does not make it sufficiently plain that Scott-King really does expect to find a happy utopia in modern Neutralia, and that it is a profound disillusionment with his utopian dream which causes him to abandon Bellorius. Waugh himself admitted in a 1950 interview that he was not satisfied with his novelette, which had taken him but a month to write.[6] He had not "done it," he said. He admitted that he had placed "too much emphasis on fretful detail": "If I had rewritten it now I should get into it more of the real horror, less of the fascination of travel."

Waugh's little book is redeemed in part by its many funny moments, it is true,[7] but on the whole it is a minor work, the product of his growing impatience with the world. Previously Waugh had worked with his tongue in his cheek. Now he sticks it out, and the result of his explicitness borders too closely on invective to rank as satire of the first order.

## CHAPTER 14

# *The Loved One*

Despite mixed reviews from the critics, *Brideshead Revisited* soon became a best seller. In the United States it became the January 1946 "Book of the Month" and earned Waugh "£10,000 down and a probable further £10,000 from ordinary sales and cinema rights."[1] On 14 November 1946 Waugh noted in his diary: "This morning a long cable from Peters in America offering these terms: a month's trip to Hollywood for Laura and myself, all expenses paid, for me to discuss the film treatment of *Brideshead*. If we cannot agree, they forfeit their money. If we agree, they pay $140,000 less what they have already spent. These terms are acceptable and funny because I was under contract to this very firm to let them have the rights of any novel I wrote for $20,000 and they paid me £3,000 free of tax to be released from this contract." Waugh accepted the invitation, but he was uneasy, as he said to Christopher Sykes, about "what these people might want to do to my book."[2]

In Hollywood discussions of the film were "infrequent and futile."[3] Waugh found that the script-writer saw *Brideshead* "purely as a love story" and that "none of them see the theological implications";[4] accordingly, he prepared a "Memorandum" carefully outlining his intentions.[5] The director "lost heart as soon as I explained to him what *Brideshead* was about, until in the end when the censor made some difficulties he accepted them as an easy excuse for abandoning the whole project."[6] Waugh, who had been drugging himself with "cocaine, opium and brandy"[7] to dull the pain of an operation for piles (performed for reasons of "perfectionism"), began to enjoy himself much more "as soon as the danger of the film was disposed of."[8] He never had any serious intention of allowing the project to succeed; as he had written to Peters right at the start, "the object of the Hollywood project is to give Laura a jaunt."[9]

Waugh had come to the United States seeking new material for his fiction (he feared that after *Brideshead* he might be written out), and in that quest he was successful. An acquaintance, Lady Milbanke, "told Evelyn that she had been shown a graveyard, just outside Los Angeles, which for sheer exquisite sensitive beauty surpassed anything she had seen of that kind. In its power of faith and consolation it was unique. It was religion and art brought to their highest possible association." [10] Waugh went to the marvellous necropolis, lunched with "The Dreamer," [11] and when he returned to England he noted in his diary, "I found a deep mine of literary gold in the cemetery of Forest Lawn"; [12] to Peters he wrote that he was "at the heart of it" while Huxley (in *After Many a Summer*) had only flirted with the "superficialities" of the place. [13] By July 1947 he had finished the first draft, and was using a new, more rapid method of composition. [14] By December Stuart Boyle had begun the illustrations, and in February 1948 the story appeared in *Horizon*, with an urbane introduction by Cyril Connolly. [15]

With its cool, cruel humour and its imaginative "over-excitement with the scene," *The Loved One* recalls Waugh's early satires. It is a slim volume, but behind its spare, clean lines there is a satisfying thematic fullness; indeed, it is distinctly a work of Waugh's later years. Instead of mysteriously disappearing, its protagonist matures—or at least *partly* matures, for he is a notably secular hero—in a manner which might prompt us to think of John Plant in *Work Suspended*.

Explaining the origin of *The Loved One* to Cyril Connolly, Waugh wrote: "The ideas I had in mind were 1. Quite predominantly, over-excitement with the scene. 2. The Anglo-American impasse—'never the twain shall meet.' 3. There is no such thing as an 'American.' They are all exiles uprooted, transplanted and doomed to sterility. The ancestral gods they have abjured get them in the end. 4. The European raiders who come for the spoils and if they are lucky make for home with them. 5. *Memento mori*." [16]

Let us begin with point three, "there is no such thing as an 'American'." Far from approving of the great American melting-pot, Waugh blames it for everything that is aesthetically and spiritually wrong with American culture. Inspired by an American dining-car attendant who said, "We are all foreigners in this country," [17] Waugh came to regard the United States as a limbo of expatriates who have lost all of their sustaining individuality. They have been dehumanized and have lost their identities, like the film-star Juanita del Pablo, who loses her accent, her teeth, and her name. Plastic and interchangeable, Aimée Thanatogenos is another typical American: "She was the standard product. A man could leave such a girl in a delicatessen shop in New York, fly three thousand miles and find her again in the cigar store at San Francisco, just as he would find his favorite comic strip in the local paper." [18] Aimée's *in-*

*amorato* Mr. Joyboy is equally featureless: "He had scant eyebrows and invisible eyelashes; the eyes behind his pince-nez were pinkish-grey; his hair, though neat and scented, was sparse. . . . It was as though there were an amplifier concealed somewhere within him and his speech came from some distant and august studio" (p. 57). Mr. Joyboy's ghastly "Mom" has "a shapeless body" and, her son claims, it is a sign of high approval that she treats Aimée "natural" (p. 99).

Waugh was no lover of "nature" in the sense of the original, uncivilized condition of man unaffected by grace; thus Joyboy's criterion of excellence could hardly appeal to him. But nature in the sense of "the particular combination of qualities belonging to a person, animal, thing, or class by birth, origin or constitution"[19] was a concept that Waugh very warmly endorsed, for, following Augustine, he believed that each nature had its own unique combination of properties.[20] These properties, Waugh liked to maintain, were abused in America:[21] in *Officers and Gentlemen*, for example, pious Mr. Crouchback muses over the significance of a bottle labelled "Cocktail Onions" in an American care package: "Could it be that . . . this people whose chief concern seemed to be the frustration of the processes of nature—could they have contributed an alcoholic onion?"[22] The tendency to disregard the "right properties of things" becomes a manifestation, on the level of taste, of the perversion which occurs when a culture turns away from God.

Echoes of the East—the Grand Sanhedrin, the Garden of Allah Hotel, the Guru Brahmin—confirm that California has become a lotus-land of bizarre cults. Aimée's father has lost his money in the "Four Square Gospel" and her mother has turned to Free Thought. Large numbers of self-ordained ministers compete in the lucrative religion market as "non-sectarian" clergymen who, like Mr. Prendergast in *Decline and Fall*, are not required to believe in anything. The perversion of religion has infected death itself, which in California has become a consolation rather than a warning. In their lack of discernment, Californians belong to Augustine's City of Man; poor Mr. Joyboy, uncomprehending medium for Waugh's irony, says, "I try not to discriminate, but I am only human" (p. 60). Waugh's point is that a society which is only human is really less than human, and its spiritual bankruptcy is manifested in its aesthetic poverty. One might say of the shapeless Joyboys and ubiquitous Heinkels what Dennis Barlow says of his "nutburger": "It is not so much their nastiness but their total absence of taste that shocks one" (p. 120).

Barlow is a former RAF squadron leader and war poet who has come to Hollywood to write a film life of Shelley. Repelled by the "monotonous and makeshift" life of the studios (p. 17), he takes a job with a local pets' cemetery, for he is a romantic in pursuit of inspiration: "For the first time he knew what it was to 'explore an avenue'; his way was narrow but it was dignified and umbrageous and it led to limitless distances" (p. 18). After the suicide of his host, Sir Francis Hinsley, Dennis is delegated to make funeral arrangements at Whispering Glades Memorial Park. Impressed by the pseudo-religion of the place, and, a little later, by the expensive obsequies of Mrs. Joyboy's pet parrot, Dennis decides to become a "non-sectarian" minister. Aimée Thanatogenos, a cosmetician, fascinates him, and he becomes Mr. Joyboy's rival for her hand. His unconventional way of life soon scandalizes the English colony and, when Aimée commits suicide rather than fulfilling her vow to marry him (it would not be "ethical"), Joyboy and the Englishman Abercrombie send him home first class.

All those who step westward risk hurtling into the vortex of the melting-pot. Among the many who fail to emerge again is Sir Francis Hinsley, once a belle-lettrist in London but now an aging Hollywood scriptwriter. His now fatally "blurred" face shows that he has abandoned himself and his art to the vapid tastes of his adoptive land. He no longer cares about the literary events of Europe, nor is he even interested in the poetry of his own protégé, Dennis Barlow. Referring to a children's play called *Where the Rainbow Ends*,[23] Sir Francis admits, "I am deep in thrall to the Dragon King. Hollywood is my life" (p. 10). Sir Francis has become an insubstantial shade in a childish heaven, "a peach without a stone" (p. 73). He has forfeited his individuality, and his refuge has become his prison. The most colourful thing about his life is his death, which, after the crucial failure of his debased art, he encompasses by stringing himself to the rafters with his braces.

Although much more recently arrived in California than Sir Francis, Dennis rapidly falls under its spell. In the silent stretches of the night-shift at the Happier Hunting Ground, he slips ever further into narcosis by reciting romantic poetry to himself, "as a monk will repeat a single pregnant text, over and over again in prayer" (p. 12). Art becomes his religion; moreover, the "rhythms from the anthologies" which Dennis especially prefers are poems about acquiescence in death. "I wither slowly in thine arms, / Here at the quiet limit of the world," he intones; "Now more than ever seems it rich to die, / To cease upon the midnight with no pain." In his "tranquil joy," he verges on spiritual death. Under the influence of poets inspired by classical beliefs, he fails to see that the Christian's death is by no means "easeful." In the classical tradition (and in the debased neo-paganism of California) the soul goes directly to Elysium. But in the Christian tradition the soul undergoes a painful separation from the body and is rigorously judged. The dead are not all "happier," as Tithonus fondly imagines.

Waugh says that Dennis "came of a generation which enjoys a vicarious intimacy with death" (p. 31) and that he therefore found Sir Francis's suicide "the kind of thing to be expected in the world he knew." As Dennis drives to Whispering Glades to arrange Sir Francis's last rites, "his conscious mind [is] pleasantly exhilarated and full of curiosity." Waugh shares Dennis's curiosity about death but he criticizes him sharply, for he is insufficiently serious: in Waugh's view, death is the most significant event in life, and under no circumstances should its gravity be diminished.

Whispering Glades is in the business of minimizing the importance of death and relieving everyone of responsibility for it. The cosmeticians paint the dead until they look healthier than they were in life, and they replace death's "grim line of endurance" (p. 85) with a radiant cardboard smile. Then, in the Slumber Room, attendants prop the bodies on rafts of flowers in imitation of their habitual poses in life. At the "leave-taking," the living nod "into the blind mask of death" (p. 66) oblivious to the dread face behind it. Throughout the proceedings, Whispering Glades carefully removes any sense of physical discomfort by replacing all real words with a pabulum of euphemisms: does one wish to have a corpse buried? Then he must consider "inhumement, entombment, inurnment or immurement" or, perhaps "insarcophagusment. That is *very* individual" (p. 36).

In the quasi-religion of Whispering Glades, death differs from life only in the sense that it is better. Writing in *Life* magazine about the moribund denizens of Southern California, Waugh observes, "They are gently spinning the cocoon which will cover their final transition. Death is the only event which can now disturb them, and priests of countless preposterous cults have gathered round to shade off that change until it becomes imperceptible."[24] In the fruity terms of Wilbur Kenworthy, "the Dreamer," only a "narrow stream" separates the dead from the living who are "Happy in the certain knowledge that their Loved Ones [are] very near; in Beauty and Happiness such as the earth cannot give" (p. 33). Death is only a happier life; it is "the greatest success story of all time. The success that waits for all of us whatever the disappointments of our earthly lives" (p. 67). Or, one might add, whatever the misdemeanours of those lives: because crosses carry disquieting overtones of sin and punishment, Whispering Glades replaces them with evergreen shrubs. In every respect the grimness of the supernatural is offset by a hyped-up "natural" joy. As Waugh venomously noted in "Death in Hollywood,"

There is usually a marble skeleton lurking somewhere among the marble draperies and quartered escutcheons of the tombs of the high Renaissance; often you find, gruesomely portrayed, the corpse half decayed with marble worms writhing in the marble adipocere. These macabre achievements were done with a simple moral purpose—to remind a highly civilized people that beauty was skin deep and pomp was mortal. In those realistic times hell waited for the wicked and a long purgation for all but the saints, but heaven, if at last attained, was a place of perfect knowledge. In Forest Lawn, as the builder claims, these old values are reversed. The body does not decay; it lives on, more chic in death than ever before, in its indestructible Class A steel-and-concrete shelf; the soul goes straight from the Slumber Room to Paradise, where it enjoys an endless infancy.[25]

By eliminating any hint of pain, Whispering Glades turns the dead into sources of consolation for the living. Thus, at the private moment when the dead should be honoured, they are exploited and desecrated. The gravest moment of life becomes a source of sentimental joy. Waugh contends that death has an identity and a purpose, which is "to remind a highly civilized people that beauty [is] skin deep and pomp [is] mortal." But in California death has been distorted: it ceases to be a reminder of transience and becomes a reminder of life. Waugh bitterly attacks America's perversion of death and regards it as the central failure in taste from which all its other grievous lapses stem. In his view, if a civilization makes death look like life, it will turn life into a form of death. The unwitting Aimée says more than she knows when she declares that the imitation "Works of Art" at Whispering Glades are "an epitome of all that is finest in the American Way of Life" (p. 88).

Whispering Glades is the high shrine of the tasteless culture around it, and it is toward this holy place that Dennis directs his steps after Sir Francis's death: "As a missionary priest making his first pilgrimage to the Vatican, as a paramount chief of equatorial Africa mounting the Eiffel Tower, Dennis Barlow, poet and pets' mortician, drove through the Golden Gates" (p. 32). Like a church, Whispering Glades has its holy orders: Mr. Joyboy, who is "kinda holy" (p. 81) is "the incarnate spirit of Whispering Glades—the mediating Logos between Dr. Kenworthy and common humanity." Aimée, who works "like a nun, intently, serenely, methodically" (p. 59), is "the nautch girl and vestal virgin of the place." Dennis is the novice, and, as if in parody of *Brideshead*'s Platonic ascent to the absolute through love and art, he moves through ever higher levels of unreality towards the suggestively named Dr. Kenworthy.

But Whispering Glades is more than a shrine in the religion of consolation. It is also a gallery and school for its art. Throughout its exclusive acres stand replicas of old world art, and around each art work cluster the adoring dead. The prospective client may arrange to have his rubberized effigy interred near a reproduction of an English parish church, an old English manor, or Rodin's *The Kiss*. Or he may choose to spend eternity on a facsimile of the Lake Isle of Innisfree, improved by such innovations as the electrically simulated hum of bees. But it is within the concealed workshops that the true art of Whispering Glades is created. There, amid the gurgle of the taps and the low calls for surgical instruments, Mr. Joyboy, "a true artist" (p. 47), passes among his admirers "like an art-master among his students" (p. 85). There, Aimée Thanatogenos works on each "crucial phase of her art" (p. 59), art which, significantly, lacks permanence. Impressed that Dennis is a "live poet," she confides her misgivings about the transience of her "poetic" work: "Sometimes at the end of a day when I'm tired I feel as if it were all rather ephemeral. . . . My work is burned sometimes within a few hours. At the best it's put in the mausoleum and even there it deteriorates, you know. I've seen painting there not ten years old that's completely lost tonality. Do you think anything can be a great art which is so impermanent?" (p. 76). Waugh's view, already emphatically dramatized in *Brideshead Revisited*, is that no art which serves only man can be either lasting or great. Aimée's art, painted on the very face of death, is Waugh's gruesome symbol for all art which serves "change and decay" rather than God.

As well as being an artist, Aimée is a species of false muse. She inspires Mr. Joyboy to fix ecstatic smiles on the faces of the corpses he sends her. She also inspires Dennis to work on a mysterious opus. As Joyboy's rival, Dennis courts Aimée by letting her believe that some of the best-known poems in the English language are his own. From Waugh's point of view, Dennis's courtship through borrowed art is no worse than Joyboy's courtship through ornamented death: Aimée is an undiscriminating girl and in Waugh's eyes deserves no better. She is spiritually descended from the high Greek artists who "had deserted the altars of the Old Gods" (p. 129), and in Aimée their apostasy is complete. She is art without grace (she would have "majored" in art had her father not lost his money in a quack religion) and an alcoholic journalist now guides her spiritual welfare under the pseudonym of the "Guru Brahmin." In vying for the favours of this modern Eurydice in her Californian Hades, Dennis and Joyboy compete for the bride of moribund art—a situation which recalls *Brideshead Revisited*.

Ostensibly about death, then, *The Loved One* is really about the abuse of art, an abuse which Waugh finds at its worst in the film studio and the morticians' workroom. These two sources of corruption dove-tail when Aimée goes to work on Sir Francis, one misguided artist practising on another. Waugh describes the result of Aimée's handiwork in trenchant language, euphony of style correcting grossness of content: "The complete stillness was more startling than any violent action. The body looked altogether smaller than life-size now that it was, as it were, stripped of the thick pelt of mobility and intelligence. And the face which inclined its blind eyes toward him—the face was entirely horrible; as ageless as a tortoise and as inhuman; a painted and smirking obscene travesty by comparison with which the devil-mask Dennis had found in the noose was a festive adornment, a thing an uncle might don at a Christmas party (p. 65)." So moved is Dennis by Aimée's plasticized replica of Sir Francis that he composes a parody of a poem by W. J. Cory on the subject:

> *They told me, Francis Hinsley, they told me you were hung*
> *With red protruding eyeballs and black protruding tongue*
> *I wept as I remembered how often you and I*
> *Had laughed about Los Angeles and now 'tis here you'll lie;*
> *Here pickled in formaldehyde and painted like a whore,*
> *Shrimp-pink incorruptible, not lost nor gone before.*      (p. 73)

Thus, in a remarkable compounding of fraudulence, Aimée the ephemeral artist transfigures Sir Francis the apostate artist, who becomes in his own person a work of art for the consolation of others.

By poisoning herself, Aimée becomes a loved one in fact as well as in name, thereby giving ultimate expression to the suicidal culture which she serves. She gives consolation too, for on every anniversary of her unceremonious cremation, a postcard will go to Mr. Joyboy: "Your little Aimée is wagging her tail in heaven tonight, thinking of you" (p. 143). It is appropriate that Aimée is cremated in a pets' cemetery, for as Waugh wrote elsewhere, "man without God is less than man." [26]

Sir Francis and Aimée represent attitudes which Dennis must outgrow. Sir Francis represents misguided aestheticism, acquiescent in its eclipse, and as such, he recalls Ambrose Silk in the west of Ireland. Aware of Dennis's danger, Sir Francis does his best to warn him away, citing himself as an example and a "*memento mori*" for Dennis. But before he can be a truly effective example for Dennis he must become an actual *memento mori*. Fatherly Sir Francis must die so that Dennis may live, for Sir Francis represents the bad artist that Dennis could easily become. The gruesome reminder which Sir Francis provides acts as the first stage in Dennis's reclamation, but it also leads him directly into Whispering Glades and the lethal embrace of Aimée. Here Dennis runs the risk of succumbing to the object of his scrutiny, death. Aimée fascinates him because she is the last example of a once-high civilization; but this degenerate Eurydice must die too; she is a false muse who represents the moribund art which Dennis loves too much.

Throughout Waugh's narrative there are hints about the growth of Dennis's art. At first, "Whispering Glades held him in thrall. In that zone of insecurity in the mind where none but the artist dare trespass, the tribes were mustering. Dennis, the frontierman, could read the signs" (p. 68). The bogus has a way of leading to the authentic, and even though he has been delegated to compose a eulogy for a false artist, Dennis gradually falls under the sway of true art: "There was also another voice speaking faintly and persistently, calling him to a more strenuous task than Frank Hinsley's obsequies. . . . All the while his literary sense was alert, like a hunting hound. There was something in Whispering Glades that was necessary to him, that only he could find. . . . The Muse nagged him. He had abandoned the poem he was writing, long ago it seemed, in the days of Frank Hinsley. That was not what the Muse wanted. There was a very long, complicated and important message she was trying to convey to him. It was about Whispering Glades, but it was not, except quite indirectly, about Aimée. Sooner or later the Muse would have to be placated. She came first" (pp. 69,90). The placation which Dennis offers the true Muse is *The Loved One* itself—a book which appears secular but is in fact deeply Christian.

Having intuited art's "long, complicated and important message"— that is, that secular art will not endure—and having abandoned his plans to become the priest of a false faith, Dennis is able to make a narrow escape from "Shadowland," his debased and confining Elysium. He is still little more than a happy pagan, but he is rich with potential:

> On this last evening in Los Angeles Dennis knew he was a favourite of Fortune. Others, better men than he, had foundered here and perished. The strand was littered with their bones. He was leaving it not only unravished but enriched. He was adding his bit to the wreckage; something that had long irked him, his young heart, and was carrying back instead the artist's load, a great, shapeless chunk of experience; bearing it home to his ancient and comfortless shore; to work on it hard and long, for God knew how long. For that moment of vision a lifetime is often too short. (pp. 143–44)[27]

In his "moment of vision" Dennis sees that man-centred art is immature and ephemeral. No longer an adolescent Orpheus, he rejects the false father and the false bride of transient art, and he *begins* to discover something that "only he" can find: his vocation as a genuine artist. Although the less-than-candid narrator says that Dennis is a "favourite of Fortune," his escape is not fortuitous but providential. His good taste and his reason have already moved him beyond the perverted art of Aimée and Sir Francis, and beyond the influence of Sir Ambrose, this novel's figure of Fortune. But he is still young, and the task of conforming completely as an artist to the will of God will be "hard and long." *Helena* will demonstrate what a difficult task it is.

## CHAPTER 15

*Style is what makes a work memorable and unmistakable. We remember the false judgements of Voltaire and Gibbon and Lytton Strachey long after they have been corrected, because of their sharp, polished form and because of the sensual pleasure of dwelling on them.*

Evelyn Waugh, "Literary Style in England and America"

# Helena

Waugh conceived the idea of writing about St. Helena at Christmas 1935, when he visited Jerusalem on his way home from "embattled Abyssinia." *Helena* was to be one in "a series of books—semi-historic, semi-poetic fiction . . .—about the long, intricate, intimate relations between England and the Holy Places"[1] as embodied by such figures as Richard Lionheart, Stratford Canning, and General Gordon. But in the end *Helena* was the only one of the series to come to fruition. According to Christopher Sykes, Waugh initially envisioned his study of Helena as "a history of the age of Constantine centred on her,"[2] but soon abandoned that approach in favour of "semi-historic, semi-poetic fiction." In May 1945 Waugh noted that he had done enough research to start the next day on *Helena*. But the summer passed in inactivity. In London he led "the life of an old man" and commiserated with cronies over the "prodigious surprise" of the Conservative defeat. At Stinchcombe he and Laura repaired the damages Piers Court had suffered in its five years as a convent school. On 18 September Waugh was demobilized, and soon afterwards he read his Lancing diaries "with unmixed shame" and began "Charles Ryder's Schooldays."[3] He quickly abandoned the novel, and following the Christmas holidays he noted, "I began the New Year without previous resolutions by resuming work on *Helena*."

According to Waugh's initial conception, *Helena* was to fall into three "books." By 26 January 1946 he had finished the first book and was "reading hard" for the second and third, but then the wave of attention generated by *Brideshead* swept his new novel off course. His visits to Spain and California further distracted him. Early in 1948 he wrote to A. D. Peters, "I am finishing the life of St. Helena. That will be a very difficult work to publish—[it] falls between all stools."[4] It was not until the end of 1949 that he at last completed the book, and he was ecstatic about it. It replaced *Brideshead*, which he had come to dislike, as his favourite. "I am an enthusiast for it all," he serenely wrote to Peters.[5] He told Sykes, "It's far the best book I have ever written or ever will write."[6] He informed Harvey Breit that it was a "masterpiece" and he gloated over the "hidden humour" in it.[7] To John Freeman he said that it was "the best written" of his books and had "the most interesting theme."[8]

The general reader will hesitate to concur with Waugh's euphoric pronouncements, for *Helena* was, and remains, one of Waugh's least popular books. Sykes notes, "The indifferent reception given to what Evelyn believed to be by far his best book was the greatest disappointment of his whole literary life."[9] One understands Waugh's disappointment: he had worked long and hard on intractable material and transformed it into art. But it should not have surprised him that the novel was not to the public's taste, for it was too doctrinaire and lacked both the subtlety of his satires and the romance of *Brideshead Revisited*.

Although *Helena* marks a departure from Waugh's earlier styles, it is ideologically connected with its predecessors through the themes of taste and vocation. In *Brideshead* Waugh dramatizes the idea that God endows each of his creatures with a unique identity and purpose. He shows that recognizing the unique identities of things is good, and distorting them is evil. Evil is perverted good: orthodox Christian doctrine. The plot of *Brideshead* shows that man's attempts to pervert "the right properties of things" is counteracted by Providence, which can educe good from evil. Waugh disliked the modern world—not because there was no good in it, but because the good was everywhere distorted by bad form and bad style. In *Helena* as in *Brideshead* and other novels, Waugh liberates the good by attacking the distorted forms it often takes.

As we have seen, moral and stylistic goodness are closely linked in all of Waugh's early satires about the modern world. In *Helena* Waugh shifts the focus of his scrutiny from the twentieth to the fourth century, and he finds the same problem: the abuse of the right properties of things—in this case, Christian doctrine itself. *Helena* takes place at the time when Christianity was pushing aside a proliferation of sects and cults to become Rome's state religion. Its very success was exposing it to danger, and no sooner had it become established than theorists began to muddy the clear waters of the well-head with ingenious speculations. To reinforce his theme of doctrinal distortion, Waugh emphasizes that Rome is a place of aesthetic perversion. Behind the ancient temples and historic buildings of the Republic rise "huge, new, shabby apartment houses, island-blocks ten storeys high made of rubble and timber;"[10] and Constantius reports that at the divine Aurelian's triumph, "everything was got up to look like something else, partridges made of sugar, peaches of mincemeat; you couldn't tell what you were eating" (p. 76). Crank reli-

gions abound. Rome is proof that, contrary to Constantius's belief, there
is barbarism inside the wall as well as outside of it. Yet despite its "gross
and haphazard" appearance (p. 144), and despite the bad taste of the
new Emperor Constantine, whose embroidered collar tells "indifferently
the stories of the gospel and of Mount Olympus" (p. 165), Rome becomes the Holy City of Christianity. As in *Brideshead Revisited*, Providence perpetuates the truth amid surroundings of distorted faith and
taste.

As one of the twentieth century's leading heresimachs, Waugh believed
that it was evil to violate the nature of things, especially in matters of
faith; and he constantly inveighed against men's tendency to establish
private realms where they might carry out such distortions. These realms
were not the paradises they seemed to be: because their aberrations pre-
cluded the full realization of potential, they were in fact prisons of the
spirit. Early in his novel Waugh endows Helena with the same insight. As
she challenges her young husband's praise of "the Wall," which fences
out barbarians and disorder, she intuitively perceives a central truth. In
asking Constantius whether the City might not one day break out of its
own protective wall, she sees that the entire Roman Empire is an immature "lush place," and, almost alone among the characters in the novel,
she avoids striving for such a retarding kind of security. Helena prefers
privacy of a more obscure kind—at Nish, at Trèves, in Dalmatia—but it
is precisely this privacy that she must give up in order to conform to the
will of God and find the Cross. "Odi profanum vulgus et arceo," Waugh
muses on Helena's behalf as his heroine enters the fishy world of the corrupt Fausta, and forfeits her treasured solitude among the teeming throngs
of Rome.

In the fourth century as in the twentieth, the defence of the good is a
question of style and vocation. Lactantius, a Christian and "the greatest
living prose stylist," articulates the situation; comparing martyrs and
writers, he says:

> "It needs a special quality to be a martyr—just as it needs a special
> quality to be a writer. Mine is the humbler rôle, but one must not
> think it quite valueless. One might combine two proverbs and say:
> 'Art is long and will prevail.' You see it is equally possible to give
> the right form to the wrong thing, and the wrong form to the right
> thing. Suppose that in years to come, when the Church's troubles
> seem to be over, there should come an apostate of my own trade, a
> false historian, with the mind of Cicero or Tacitus and the soul of
> an animal," and he nodded towards the gibbon who fretted his
> golden chain and chattered for fruit. "A man like that might make

it his business to write down the martyrs and excuse the persecutors. He might be refuted again and again, but what he wrote would remain in people's minds when the refutations were quite forgotten. That is what style does—it has the Egyptian secret of the embalmers. It is not to be despised." (pp. 122–23)

Edward Gibbon was not to be alone among those who would mistake their vocations and give the wrong form to the right thing. In Helena's time there were Arius and Donatus and the Eusebiuses, and in the modern world there would be people like Aimée Semple McPherson or, as Waugh dubbed her, Mrs. Melrose Ape.

As the martyr's vocation is to die for his faith, so the writer's is to write for it. The writer's is "a humbler role" but "not quite valueless": he refutes error "again and again" in the hopes of disengaging the good from the distorted forms it has assumed. Sixteen centuries ago, St. Helena helped disperse the mists of speculation by knocking the heads of the faithful against "a solid chunk of wood." She showed that the good was rooted in the simple form of the Cross, not in the convoluted theories of aberrant intellectuals. Waugh sees an analogy between Helena and himself. His service, humbler than the saint's, but "not to be despised," is to give enduring form to Helena's blunt message that "God became man and died on the Cross; not a myth or an allegory; true God, truly incarnate, tortured to death at a particular moment in time, at a particular geographical place, as a matter of plain historical fact." [11]

Waugh calls his book a novel, but it is of course a saint's life cast in novelistic form: a hagiographical romance, as it were. Historical fiction has its own set of pitfalls, but to these were added the special difficulties of Waugh's particular subject. His great problem was to sustain the reader's interest in Helena herself, for during her long and otherwise uneventful life she seems to have performed only one saintly act—the "invention" of the Cross. The fact that Helena's obscure early life was all preparation for her one great act imposed large demands on Waugh. He had to invent for her "a quiet private life" (p. 111) of everyday adversity, through which she would make a gradual approach to the truth.

But Waugh could not allow Helena's routine life to bore his audience. He found two solutions to his problem. First, he invented freely, expanding history through fiction. He invented Helena's sophistical tutor Marcias ("a modern intellectual," Waugh called him)[12] and, with an interesting touch of fantasy, made Old King Coel her father (Coel is another of Waugh's wayward fathers, and the celebration of his genealogy is really a eulogy of the City of Man). Moreover, Helena's various aspirations and disappointments are all fictitious. Secondly, Waugh diverted the reader's attention from Helena to the ambitions of her husband, Constantius and her son, Constantine. He allowed Helena to travel—in keeping with the little that is known of her life—and to discuss the ebb and flow of power within the Roman Empire with fictitious friends, or with historical figures in imaginary circumstances. Throughout the novel, Helena sees only what it is plausible for her to see, and it is only gradually that her own private story assumes pre-eminence over the vast machinations of Empire which she beholds.

But it is not merely through the accumulation of imagined events that Waugh holds the reader's attention. By means of the powerful cluster of motifs that surround the Troy theme, Waugh is able to invest his narrative with shape and resonance. For example, at the outset of the novel, the eunuch Marcias reads the Troy story to Helena and we learn that both she and her tutor are in search of a city. Marcias wants to go to Alexandria, the "ancient asparagus bed of theological controversy" of *Officers and Gentlemen*, and Helena wants to "go and find the real Troy" (p. 5) in order to verify that it actually existed. Since Coel traces his descent back through Brutus and Aeneas to Troy, Helena's quest will consist of a return to her forefathers, a return from exile: "After all, papa, we Trojans are always in exile, aren't we—poor banished children of Teucer?" (p. 34). She identifies herself with Helen of Troy and Constantius with Paris. But Providence has other plans for Helena. Rather than going to Troy to verify the existence of an earthly city, she goes to Jerusalem in order to prove the basis of the City of God. As in the War Trilogy, family ties prove to be less important than spiritual ties.

Unlike Waugh's early protagonists, Helena gives up her youth without struggle or regret. As she ages, she enters into a prolonged gentle apathy, and she gives up her dream of visiting Troy. Marcias, meanwhile, has allowed his pursuit of the false City of Man to lead him into the hocus-pocus of Gnosticism. "All things are double one against another" in his world, but not in hers (p. 126). Just as Charles Ryder gives up the delusive charm of Brideshead House, so Helena gives up her dream of Troy in favour of things which are progressively more real: Rome, Jerusalem, and the City of God. She stands in instructive contrast to Marcias who, even as a great Gnostic preacher, fails to reach Alexandria, let alone the fabulous dream cities of Asia. "Slaves," says Pope Sylvester, "like to imagine such cities" (p. 207). The statement is Waugh's trenchant dismissal of earthly utopias then and now.

Another allusion to the Troy story helps shape Waugh's narrative. It is the image of the horse. In her youth Helena sees herself as both horse and rider: "There was the will of the rider that spoke down the length of the rein, from the gloved hand to the warm and tender tongue under the bit.

. . . And there was the will of the animal to shrink and start, to toss aside the restraint of bridle and saddle and the firm legs across her. . . . Then at the height of the play, in sweat and blood-flecked foam, came the sweet moment of surrender, the fusion, and the two were off together, single" (pp. 22–23). But as a young woman Helena becomes the horse, standing in the stable with the bit in her mouth: "Helena trotted on and Constantius bestrode her in triumph" (p. 25). Waugh uses the horse metaphor for erotic effect (he modelled Helena on Penelope Betjeman and interrogated her about adolescent sexual fantasies),[13] but his main point is that headstrong Helena must be ridden, first by Constantius and eventually by God if she is ever to make the leap of faith. In *Brideshead* Charles Ryder compares himself to a horse balking at an obstacle, and shortly before her own conversion, Helena echoes Ryder's words when she says, "It all seems to make sense up to a point, and again beyond that point. And yet one can't pass the point. . . . Well, I am an old woman, too old to pass the point now" (p. 136). But Helena eventually passes the point, exchanging her earthly father and husband for heavenly ones, and adding faith to her innate common sense. Thus tamed, she finds the True Cross. Delayed in reaching her goal by error and by learned speculation, Helena prays for the Magi in the stable-cave in Bethlehem: "You are my especial patrons," said Helena, "and patrons of all late-comers, of all who have a tedious journey to make to the truth, of all who are confused with knowledge and speculation, of all who through politeness make themselves partners in guilt, of all who stand in danger by reason of their talents" (p. 240). The most moving passage in the novel, Helena's prayer also marks the culmination of the motif of the horse. The woman of horse-sense praying in the manger vanquishes the sophists whose disregard of fact threatens the early Church with heresy. Furthermore, the scene in Christ's stable reduplicates and corrects the one in Coel's stable. No longer ridden by Constantius, or "power without Grace," Helena is guided by God to a goal more important than Troy.

The confluence of Helena and the Cross marks the book's climax and provides a useful example of the way Waugh's fiction has evolved. *Helena* is a delicately structured work, built like *Brideshead* and the later novels as an affirmative parody of the chance-ridden early books. At the heart of those early novels there is always a collision of wrong with wrong or of fraud with fraud—Tony meets Mr. Todd; Atwater meets John Plant Senior; Basil meets Ambrose. *Helena* reverses this pattern, for the idea which guides Waugh throughout is the slow but purposeful convergence of two pure natures: Helena and the "solid chunk of wood." Out of their intersection comes no zany dance of shadows, but a forthright statement about the unique nature of Christian religion.

By casting off error and apathy on her long journey to the truth, Helena actualizes the identity which has long been latent within her. The performance of her vocation is an act of self-realization—an act which profoundly attracted Waugh. Waugh believed in the uniqueness of each human individual, and he also maintained that it took heroic effort to elude the shadowy, false selves which so often obscured man's true sense of purpose. In "The Holy Places," Waugh writes:

> There are evident dangers in identifying ourselves with Saint Francis or Saint John of the Cross. We can invoke the help of the saints and study the workings of God in them, but if we delude ourselves that we are walking in their shoes, seeing through their eyes and thinking with their minds, we lose sight of the one certain course of our salvation. There is only one saint that Bridget Hogan can actually become, Saint Bridget Hogan, and that saint she *must* become, here or in the fires of purgatory, if she is to enter heaven. She cannot slip through in fancy-dress, made up as Joan of Arc.[14]

Waugh concludes with an important statement about the uniqueness of all vocations: "What we can learn from Helena is something about the workings of God; that He wants a different thing from each of us, laborious or easy, conspicuous or quite private, but something which only we can do and for which we were each created."[15] Bluff and commonsensical, like Shaw's St. Joan, Helena is an exemplary figure in Waugh's work. Despite the perversion and barbarism all around her, she "had completely conformed to the will of God. . . . to gather wood . . . was the particular, humble purpose for which she had been created. And now it was done" (pp. 259–60). Helena's realization of her true nature through the performance of her vocation deeply appealed to Waugh; it was the quintessential act of good faith, good taste, and self-discovery.

While by his own admission Waugh could not hope to be another Helena, he was entirely captivated by her example. He regarded her correction of error as irrefutable, but perceived that her act needed proper literary shape because the "wrong form" constantly distorts the "right thing." For example, the Wandering Jew[16] sells trashy relics, and Helena's own son, the green-wigged, shadowy-minded Constantine, grossly distorts the faith he claims to profess, producing a fake Labarum, "forging" one of the holy nails into a bit for his horse, and building a city in his name to rival Rome. Like Helena but in a "humbler" way, Waugh would help correct such distortions. Like her he had blundered into a false, public vocation: she had become an empress and he had become a soldier.

But by writing about Helena's belated fulfilment of her vocation, Waugh would help to realize his own—and this in an age even more barbaric than hers. Waugh's diary entry for 6 May 1945 shows how strongly he felt about his long-delayed acceptance of his proper vocation:

> I have done enough reading to start tomorrow on *Helena*. . . . It is pleasant to end the war in plain clothes, writing. I remember at the start of it all writing to Frank Pakenham that its value for us would be to show us finally that we were not men of action. I took longer than him to learn it. I regard the greatest danger I went through [as] that of becoming one of Churchill's young men, or getting a medal and standing for Parliament; if things had gone, as then seemed right, in the first two years, that is what I should be now. I thank God to find myself still a writer and at work on something as "uncontemporary" as I am.

*Helena* may be unpopular, but its lucid exposition of the difficult and belated fulfilment of a vocation makes it one of Waugh's most important works.

*Every act of free will, good or bad, attenuates its consequences to the end of time.*

*Diaries of Evelyn Waugh*

# Love Among the Ruins

Like *Helena*, *Love Among the Ruins* is a product of the sporadic work habits which characterized Waugh's later years.[1] He began the short novel in 1950; three years and at least two drafts later[2] he finished his book, complete with "some collages from Moses's engravings after Canova."[3] Critical response was uniformly cool[4] and, having been invited by the *Spectator* to "review the reviews," Waugh wrote, rather plaintively, "It was begun as a longer work three years ago . . . As it stands it is designed purely to amuse. . . . Either it comes off or it fails."[5] Waugh admitted to Graham Greene that his novelette was "a bit of nonsense begun three years ago and hastily finished and injudiciously published."[6]

Waugh's "phantasy about life in the near future"[7] is an attack on the secularized and featureless welfare state. It is the sad story of a decadent heir of past greatness, Miles Plastic, "the Modern Man."[8] Waugh's plastic soldier is an underprivileged orphan who has been expensively moulded by "Constructive Play" and psycho-analysis and then given a job tending a dishwasher in an air force base. Bored, he burns the place down, but instead of being punished, he is commended by his psychiatrist and sent by an indulgent magistrate to Mountjoy Castle, once a country house and now a plush new jail.

In the eyes of the court, Miles is merely maladjusted, for it is an article of faith in the "New Law" that no man is responsible for "the consequences of his own acts" (p. 8). In the New Britain there are no evils, only anti-social acts for which the doer cannot be blamed. Waugh attacks all this, of course, because he believes people ought to accept responsibility for their actions. In his essay on *The End of the Affair* Waugh agrees with Graham Greene's conviction, which "lies at the root of all morality, that the consequences of every human act for good or ill are an endless progression."[9] And in *Robbery Under Law* he inveighs against man's tendency to shift the blame for his faults elsewhere: "individually and collectively [man] is always in search of an oppressor who will take responsibility for his ills. . . . Anything will do so long as he can focus on it his sense of grievance and convince himself that his own inadequacy is due to some exterior cause." [10] By blaming subjective evils on an "exterior cause," people try to place the fault in the material world, where it can be eliminated. By perfecting the material world, they theorize, they can perfect human nature. But to Waugh such an aim is wrong-headed: man is "aboriginally corrupt," not a noble savage with infinite potential.

Mountjoy is this novel's lush place. Its antique glories sum up a noble past now pressed into the service of a tawdry present. At last the house of England has become an actual prison, and here Miles is rehabilitated according to the tolerant precepts of the New Penology. There are no criminals in the New Britain, "only the victims of inadequate social services" (p. 10), and these "victims" are compensated for what they have lost rather than punished for what they have done. Murderers and sex offenders live in the utmost luxury, and even as a mere arsonist Miles is coddled by "every agreeable remedial device" (p. 8). Like Paul Pennyfeather, he finds jail more pleasant than the world he has left, and vestigial traces of good taste induce in him "an incomprehensible tidal pull towards the circumjacent splendours" of Mountjoy (p. 2). Despite his conditioning he loves the past, much as Orwell's Winston Smith loves his vellum diary and Huxley's John Savage loves Shakespeare. His attraction to Mountjoy and the unique things of the past results from vestigial traces of reason and good taste that the State has been unable to eradicate. Stunted though he is, Miles is still more sensitive than the brain-washed brutes who surround him. [11]

Miles's sensitivity to uniqueness attracts him to a ballerina whom he meets while working in the Euthanasia Department, where he has been sent as "the first success, the vindication of the Method" (p. 10). If the Euthanasia service epitomizes the death-loving New Britain, then Clara, with her antique fans and embroideries, embodies the vitality of the unique things of the past. Her voice is "all unlike the flat conventional accent of the age" (p. 23). But it is her "long, silken, corn-gold beard" which most enchants Miles; its incongruity appeals to primal forces which his conditioning has not yet eradicated.

Like Dennis Barlow and Aimée Thanatogenos, Miles and Clara fall in love in a moribund and featureless society. For a time their affair flourishes; then Clara discovers that despite her "Klugmann's Operation" she is pregnant. She is inconsolable, for motherhood means the end of her dancing career. She vanishes, and by the time Miles discovers her, she has had an abortion and her beard has been replaced by "a tight, slippery mask, salmon pink" (p. 40), an emblem of her sudden conformity and sterility. Appropriately, her operations have taken place at "Santa-Claus-Tide," now a quaint celebration preserved only "as a matter of historical interest" (p. 37).

Clara's beauty and the tasteful pleasures of prison have become associated in Miles's mind; and now that one has been destroyed the other must follow. By incinerating Mountjoy—significantly, perhaps, under a changing moon—Miles exorcises his memories of Clara. "Once before he had burned his childhood. Now his brief adult life lay in ashes; the enchantments that surrounded Clara were one with the splendours of Mountjoy; her great golden beard, one with the tongues of flame that had leaped and expired among the stars; her fans and pictures and scraps of old embroidery, one with the gilded cornices and silk hangings, cold and sodden" (p. 43).

Now that he has demolished the nostalgia-laden beauty of the secular past, where can Miles turn? Since he knows nothing about the Church, he embraces, or seems to embrace, the bleak ideals of the New Britain. As the only graduate of Mountjoy, he is pressed into service by the authorities, who want him to lecture to a populace which is fast losing confidence in the New Penology. His first glimpse of the model for the new Mountjoy—a standard packingcase—seems to expunge all trace of his nostalgia for the past. "In perfect peace of heart" Miles agrees to marry the gruesome Miss Flower, for as the Minister of Rest and Culture says, "Folks like a bloke to be spliced" (p. 51). But Miles is unregenerate to the last. During the marriage ceremony his conformist mood changes, and he fidgets with his trusty cigarette-lighter, which produces "a tiny flame—gemlike, hymeneal, auspicious" (p. 51).

What does the conclusion mean? Robert Murray Davis finds it affirmative: "Given the society, destruction is itself a creative and laudable act. For one thing, it is an act of will, and . . . free choice of a lesser good (since we cannot choose evil *per se*) is better than no choice at all." [12] Davis's interpretation needs some qualification. It is true that Miles makes a free choice, and it is true that his unregeneracy is a good thing, for it shows that the anomalies of human nature can resist manipulative governments. But before we invest the ending with too much "creative" rebellion, we must determine just what it is that Miles chooses. In the first draft, Miles is last seen on board a train in the American Midwest appraising wooden houses with the discerning eye of a pyromaniac. But the second draft and published text are quite different, and far darker. In them, Miles presses the catch of his lighter—while it is still in his pocket. Surely, therefore, it is suicide, not creative rebellion against a repressive society that Waugh envisions in the second version. The second ending is more in keeping with Waugh's usual way of thinking: when a society perverts distinctiveness and love, and fosters no awareness of a divine alternative, it becomes a prison. And the only way out of that prison is through suicide. Miles himself, not the repressive society around him, will burn with a "gemlike" flame. It is a death of Miles's own choosing, but hard to accept as unambiguously "laudable."

Like Adam Fenwick-Symes in *Vile Bodies*, Miles is the last representative of the old order; in him something human lingers on. That something human is original sin: paradoxically, the incorrigible defect that has kept him imperfect in God's eyes is the saving grace that preserves him from becoming a perfect machine in the eyes of the State. But now Miles is gone, and with him have passed away all redeeming vestiges of imperfect, unconditioned humanity. Even *Nineteen Eighty-Four* is a less sombre book than *Love Among the Ruins*, for it suggests that the unregenerate "proles" will never succumb to Big Brother's brainwashing. In contrast, those who remain in Waugh's Satellite City are plastic humanoids conforming completely to the will of an imprisoning State.

In *Brideshead* Waugh tolerated the ornate secular past because he was able to regard it as Charles Ryder's imperfect means toward a divine end. But *Love Among the Ruins* shows Waugh in a darker mood: he destroys those secular glories, burns up his protagonist, and turns in contempt from the City of Man. Like *Scott-King*, *Love Among the Ruins* is an anomaly among the late novels, for its spiritually undernourished hero finds no authentic alternative to his lush prison and escapes, it would seem, only into death.

*Love Among the Ruins* is not a great book, but Waugh was right in refusing to think it "quite as bad as most reviewers do." His targets may appear innocuous when compared with the horrors envisioned by Huxley, Orwell, and other dystopians,[13] and his sarcasm may seem excessive. But in criticizing bad taste and the conformist welfare life, Waugh attacks a very great evil: the dehumanization which results when men and women are deprived of their sense of a unique purpose in life. Waugh always believed in the "vast heterogeneity of mankind."[14] He constantly reiterated his view that "there is no such thing as a man in the street, there is no ordinary run of mankind; there are only individuals who are totally different."[15] Furthermore, he believed that the spark of individuation came from God and that each man is "God's creature with a defined purpose."[16] According to Waugh, when people lose their belief in God, they forfeit their purposive behaviour, and falseness shrouds their vital selves. In attacking the conformism which drives the unregenerate Miles into self-destruction, Waugh implies that spiritual suicide is the ultimate end of a secularized culture. It is strong medicine, harshly administered.

## CHAPTER 17

*I know that one goes into a war for reasons of honour & soon finds oneself
called on to do very dishonourable things.*

*Letters of Evelyn Waugh*

# The War Trilogy: Introduction

Even before the outbreak of hostilities, Waugh had noted in his diary,
"There is a symbolic difference between fighting as a soldier and serving as a civilian, even if the civilian is more valuable."[1] When the war began, he could have devoted himself to "semi-literary, semi-bureaucratic
tasks"[2] at the Ministry of Information, but he strove instead to join a
fighting unit, believing that the war would provide him with a belated
opportunity to find his vocation as a man of action. After unsuccessful
attempts to join the Yeomanry, the Navy, and the Welsh Guards, Waugh
eventually found his way into the Royal Marines with the assistance of
Brendan Bracken and Winston Churchill. As a Marine he participated in
an abortive raid on Dakar in 1940. In 1941 he secured a transfer to Robert Laycock's Commando, and took part in a botched landing at Bardia
and in the rout of the Allied armies from Crete. After the disaster on
Crete he rejoined the Marines, but by May 1942 he was back in a Commando unit. Later he was transferred to the Royal Horse Guards. As a
member of William Stirling's Special Air Service Regiment in 1943 he
took a course in parachuting, and in 1944 he flew with Randolph
Churchill to Yugoslavia as part of Fitzroy Maclean's Military Mission to
Tito's Partisans.

It surprised no one when after four years Waugh became completely
disheartened with his new vocation. His gloom had grown steadily since
1940, for his impossibly high standards had led him to expect a degree of
perfection which no modern army could achieve. He was disappointed
by lack of promotion, angered by his remoteness from the front lines,
and frustrated by "the measureless obstructive strength" of the "vast uniformed and bemedalled bureaucracy."[3] Where he had expected to find
devotion to a just cause, he found cowardice, avarice, and treachery. To
his chagrin, he saw action only four times, and on the sole occasion when
he actually met the enemy (a lone German motor-cyclist on Crete), no

shot was fired. But Waugh's disenchantment must not colour any assessment of his career as a soldier. In fact, Waugh was unhappy with a record that almost anyone else would have been proud to own. He was already thirty-six when he joined the Marines—virtually an old man where active combat was concerned—yet he underwent arduous Commando and parachute training, and acquitted himself well in hazardous operations which might have exhausted much younger men.

After Crete Waugh's abrasive and idiosyncratic manner led him into disfavour with his superiors. He lost his "adventurous spirit" and Col. Robert Laycock told him that he had become "so unpopular as to be unemployable";[4] others feared that his own men might shoot him if he went into action again, and a special guard was posted on his sleeping quarters. The turning point came in the summer of 1943 when, contrary to what Laycock had promised, he left Waugh behind when the Commando went to North Africa on Operation "Husky." After an acrimonious correspondence with "Shimi" Lovat and an interview with Gen. Charles Haydon, Waugh was forced to resign from the Special Service Brigade "for the Brigade's good."[5] Lovat (an extraordinary character in his own right) said, "Nobody wished to have him,"[6] and he later wrote that Waugh was adept at "veiled sarcasm . . . of a very high order," and had "infuriated his immediate superiors."[7] Matters came to a head when after his father's death Waugh allegedly spent two weeks drinking at White's Club. When Lovat learned how Waugh was spending his leave, he commanded him to return to Commando depot and work himself back into shape. Justified though Lovat's directive may have been, it is unlikely that it was devoid of malice, for it threatened Waugh's prospects of joining Laycock on Operation "Husky" in North Africa. He had planned to sail in early August, but Lovat's order would have delayed him until October. When Lovat remained adamant in his decision, Waugh reported to General Haydon for an interview. "When I saw the GOCO he was already in a highly excited condition," he wrote afterwards to Laycock, complaining of "personal malice." But according to Lovat, it was Waugh who was "already . . . excited": "There was a painful scene," he wrote. "Waugh could not contain himself and stormed unannounced into General Haydon's office. Nobody, Waugh said, could interfere with the arrangements made for his departure overseas. It was a rash speech. He was sacked on the spot for insubordination." A "fine pompous" appeal to Lord Mountbatten on the grounds of unfair treatment "failed abysmally." (In his diary Waugh says that he "saw Lord Louis Mountbatten on terms so cordial as to be almost affectionate. Result, none.")[8]

Waugh returned in low spirits to the Royal Horse Guard barracks at Windsor. "My military future is vague," he wrote disconsolately. Soon he had lost all desire to succeed as a man at arms, and his chronic *tedium vitae* overwhelmed him:

> I have got so bored with everything military that I can no longer remember the simplest details. I dislike the Army. I want to get to work again. I do not want any more experiences in life. I have quite enough bottled and carefully laid in the cellar, some still ripening, most ready for drinking, a little beginning to lose its body. I wrote to Frank [Pakenham] very early in the war to say that its chief use would be to cure artists of the illusion that they were men of action. It has worked its cure with me. I have succeeded, too, in dissociating myself very largely with the rest of the world. I am not impatient of its manifest follies and don't want to influence opinions or events, or expose humbug or anything of that kind. I don't want to be of service to anyone or anything. I just want to do my work as an artist.[9]

It was the end of his love affair with the army and a turning-point in his life. Looking back on it in letters to Nancy Mitford, he remarked, "You still have the delicious gift of seeing people as funny which I lost somewhere in the highlands of Scotland circa 1943. . . . My life ceased with the war."[10]

Letting go of the active life was a slow and painful process for Waugh. Even after the brutal lesson of July 1943 he hankered for public service, hoping in 1945 to return to Yugoslavia as a consul. Not surprisingly, he was rejected, and he noted with relief, "Honour is satisfied. I am glad to have done all I could to go back and glad not to be going."[11] At heart Waugh had always been a civilian and an artist, and his difficulties with the army stemmed from the incompatibility of his real and assumed vocations: at every step army discipline and conformity offended Waugh's taste for the unique. After 1945 the public life never again tempted Waugh; like Gilbert Pinfold's, his life became "strictly private."[12]

Pinfold envied painters because they were "allowed to return to the same theme time and time again, clarifying and enriching until they have done all they can with it."[13] The War Trilogy constitutes Waugh's final return to a number of his favourite themes: Fortune, Providence, vocation, withdrawal, the family, and it dramatizes his final attempt to be "a man of the world."

The voices of three distinct aspects of Waugh contribute to the War Trilogy's curious harmonics. There is the voice of Waugh's persona Guy Crouchback, the voice of the narrator, who sometimes pretends to share Guy's naiveté, and, unassimilated into the latter, occasional undertones from the real-life Waugh. In the early sections of *Men at Arms* Guy Crouchback unaffectedly loves the military life, but an undercurrent of irony shows that the narrator no longer wholly shares Crouchback's affection. The narrator prefers the private life, yet without advocating complete withdrawal. But behind it all there is the felt presence of the Waugh who has turned his back on the world. There are thus three attitudes, not always sufficiently separate, perhaps, to the important new theme of *caritas*. Persona and narrator eventually agree that a limited form of private charity is the best way to work for good in the world, but there is the sense throughout that Waugh himself was never fully able to achieve the ideal he enshrined in his narrative voice.

Some readers find it hard to reconcile the comic cruelty of Waugh's early satires with the theme of charity in the trilogy. Others remark, in his repeated acts of rudeness and intolerance, a lack of *caritas* so profound that it contradicts the essence of his professed faith. Waugh had, there can be no doubt, more faith than he had hope or charity. Compassion did not come easily to him, and it is certain that his chronic lack of charity was his cardinal fault. He admitted that he found it "impossible . . . to love mankind in general,"[14] but he tried very hard to behave charitably towards individuals. He believed that real charity should be personal: "organized charity, in the form of a welfare state," was "a pure fraud."[15] True charity, he said, was "the job of private associations among people, primarily of religious bodies," and the A. D. Peters files show that he contributed extensively to such bodies.[16] He gave the serial rights of *Scott-King* to Father D'Arcy and the Jesuits, along with the profits from the de luxe edition of *The Loved One*. A handsome chunk of Waugh's profits from the MGM *Brideshead* fiasco went to the Church; the proceeds from his *Life* essay on Forest Lawn went to the Convents' Aid Society, and he signed over his French bank balance to a convent in Grasse; after 1948 he gave the proceeds from all translations of his books to Catholic charities in the countries concerned. There are many other examples of Waugh's charity, but the strange thing about them is the way they coexist with demands for "more dollars," "fine big retaining fees," and "whacking advances." Present also are blunt instructions about lawsuits for late payment and failure to "cough-up," and demands that Peters should "investigate and castigate" with "the utmost rigour of the law" unhappy persons suspected of "plagiarism" and "get the hand-cuffs on" them. Giving to charity—especially in the post-*Brideshead* years—made good business sense. As Waugh wrote to Peters on one remarkable occasion in 1949, "I can't afford to earn like this. . . . This is getting desperate. We must get rid of the whole of the cinema rights of *Scoop* on the Jesuits if the deal goes through." Waugh often gave to charity, but it is not easy to maintain that he was often charitable in the fullest sense of the word.

When after the war Waugh turned away for the last time from the life of action, he tried to maintain a link with the world by acting upon it through religious bodies and the family. Indeed, the War Trilogy is a celebration of the family which, being at once private and communal, provides Guy Crouchback with a mature form of solitude denied to Waugh's earlier protagonists. But one may doubt whether even the restricted charity Guy achieves was ever more than an ideal for Waugh himself.

In general outline, the trilogy depicts the course of Guy's slow realization that his father's maxim is right: "Quantitative judgments don't apply." [17] As Waugh said, "I shall deal with Crouchback's realization that no good comes from public causes, only private causes of the soul." [18] Waugh wrote to Cyril Connolly, "The theme . . . is the humanizing of Guy." [19] Despite the fact that Waugh had a general plan for the trilogy before he began (the theme of "private causes" and the images of the swords of Sir Roger and Stalingrad were "there from the beginning"),[20] the history of its composition is long and irregular. The trilogy "appeared at intervals throughout a decade" [21] and Waugh plainly found his task a difficult one. It was a far more enterprising work than any he had undertaken before and, as *Scott-King* and *Love Among the Ruins* show, his creative powers were beginning to fail. The first volume, *Men at Arms* (entitled "Honour" in manuscript), appeared in 1952 with the announcement that the author "hopes to complete a trilogy of novels, each complete in itself, recounting the phases of a long love affair, full of vicissitudes, between a civilian and the army." [22] But by 1955 Waugh appeared to have abandoned the idea of a trilogy. *Officers and Gentlemen* (or "Happy Warriors," as Waugh at first called it), would be the final volume: "*Officers and Gentlemen* completes *Men at Arms*. I thought at first the story would run into three volumes. I find now that two will do the trick," Waugh wrote.[23] "It is short and funny & completes the story I began in *Men at Arms* which threatened to drag out to the grave." [24] *Unconditional Surrender* (entitled "Conventional Weapons" in its early stages) did not appear until six years later. Waugh wrote: "I knew that a third volume was needed. I did not then feel confident that I was able to produce it. Here it is." (Waugh had not felt able to produce the third volume because of the difficulties so vividly described in *Pinfold*.) When an interviewer inquired whether he had carried out a plan which he had "made at the start" of the trilogy, Waugh replied, "It changed a lot in the writing. Originally I had intended the second volume, *Officers and Gentlemen*, to be two volumes. Then I decided to lump them together and finish it off. There's a very bad transitional passage on board the troop ship. The third volume really arose from the fact that Ludovic needed explaining. As it turned out each volume had a common form because there was an irrelevant ludicrous figure in each to make the running."[25] Initially the Crouchback saga was to have been "four or five"[26] novels long, and "all the subsidiary characters, like 'Trimmer' & 'Chatty Corner' & 'de Souza' [were] each [to] have a book to himself."[27] A volume dealing with Dunkirk was to have followed *Men at Arms*. Waugh interviewed a veteran of that battle in order to get his impressions, but although the veteran was cooperative, the Dunkirk volume was never written. "It was useless," Waugh said. "I should have realized that one cannot live other people's experiences."[28] Finally, in 1965 there appeared a "recension" under the title of *Sword of Honour*. In his preface Waugh admitted that he had been "less than candid" in assuring his public that each novel was "to be regarded as a separate, independent work. . . . The product is intended . . . to be read as a single story. I sought to give a description of the Second World War as it was seen and experienced by a single, uncharacteristic Englishman, and to show its effect on him."

In the new Uniform Edition Waugh adds very little (he tells us, for example, that Mugg and his niece blow themselves up) but removes "repetitions," "discrepancies," and "tedious" passages, mainly from *Men at Arms* (a novel which he privately described as "unreadable and endless," "slogging, inelegant," and "interminable").[29] He removes extraneous characters, like Prentice, Roots, Slimbridge, and Smiley, reduces confusingly detailed summary (especially from the weak "Interlude" section of *Officers and Gentlemen*) and smoothes the flow of the narrative by reorganizing the chapter divisions and in some cases giving them new titles. Waugh reduces Trimmer's early importance by attributing a number of his speeches to Frank de Souza, and he changes Kilbannock's occupation from racing columnist to gossip columnist. In the revised version Ritchie-Hook is given less attention, and the scene in which Guy returns Chatty's possessions is abbreviated, as are the parachute-school episode and the airplane crash in Croatia. Gilpin becomes slightly less odious.

Some of the changes make certain characters and situations less ambiguous. Throughout, Waugh omits details about saintly Mr. Crouchback's fortune and possessions which might be unfavourably construed. Uncle Peregrine is no longer parsimonious, and no longer responds with displeasure when Virginia announces her intention to become a Catholic. Guy himself is presented as slightly less naive through the omission of some of his more romantic reflections on the justice of the war and the certainty of victory. There is less insistence on his poverty, and one important passage which could be construed as critical of Guy's escape from Crete is omitted. Even the old tenor is made more sympathetic by the removal of any suggestion that he is an alcoholic.

In one kind of change which Waugh does not mention, he eliminates several passages which could be interpreted as insulting to religion. Cuts of this sort include the apathetic Catholic chaplain's unenthusiastic sermon; the "not over scrupulous" Catholic, Hemp; and even the alleged abuses of the confessional at Staplehurst. Throughout, Waugh confers capital letters on Church rites and activities while reducing secular titles to lower case.

Many readers will regret the more important deletions as serious aesthetic losses. As a result of the cuts there is no trace of the symbolic painting at Kut-al-Imara House; Ambrose Goodall's fascination with Guy's ancestry; Air Marshal Beech's song about Elinor Glyn; the officers' bingo game; the over-technicoloured film of Bonnie Prince Charlie; Captain Truslove, Congreve, and the Pathans; the Loamshire officers' episode; the soldier with the hot-potato voice on Crete; General Miltiades and his obsolete courtesy; the English composer who announces that Guy has "the death-wish"; the description of Ludovic's book which links it with *Brideshead Revisited*.

The most important change comes at the end, where Waugh wisely decides not to let Guy and Domenica have any "children of their own." By making little Trimmer their sole heir, Waugh places unambiguous emphasis on the pre-eminence of spiritual ties over mere family ties, and on the importance of new blood-lines in carrying on old institutions. There can be no doubt that this is a change for the better, and it is hard to imagine how Waugh missed it in the first place. Indeed, he did catch it very early, making the revision (which he then revised again in 1965) in the 1961 Chapman and Hall second edition of *Unconditional Surrender*.[30] With the notable exception of the new conclusion, Waugh's changes are rarely improvements; indeed, the trilogy loses far more than it gains through the omissions noted above. After weighing the alternatives, I have decided to accept the original text of the trilogy as aesthetically superior and biographically more revealing, but also to accept the second edition ending as logically right and theologically more satisfying.

## CHAPTER 18

# *Men at Arms*

As *Men at Arms* opens, Guy Crouchback is ready to leave Italy for the defence of his "endangered kingdom." [1] He is motivated by thoughts of patriotic adventure but, above all, by an intense loneliness: his great craving is for vocation, brotherhood, and a place to belong. He is an outcast and a dreamer. He has lived alone in easeful Santa Dulcina ever since his divorce, eight years previously, from his unfaithful wife, Virginia. Before that, he lived with her in "Eldoret," an African utopia which resembled a parody of Restoration England. As an expatriate, Guy is severed from his native land, from his family, and from his English Catholic faith. In the absence of "loyalties that should have sustained him" (p. 5), he has become solitary and apathetic. His soul now languishes in a waste land, and he has lost his sense of purpose: "It was as though eight years back he had suffered a tiny stroke of paralysis; all his spiritual faculties were just perceptibly impaired" (p. 7). Conscious of his inner emptiness and in need of some form of commitment, Guy responds enthusiastically to the outbreak of war, but he does not realize at this early stage that the brotherhood he seeks in war is really to be found in rededication to his family and his faith.

Guy belongs to an illustrious old family. Throughout all the penal years, the Crouchback chapel at Broome always had a priest, and devout forebears died on the scaffold. But although the Crouchbacks have suffered for their faith, there has always been a successor in the male line, and as late as the 1890s the lands of Broome "stretched undiminished and unencumbered from the Quantocks to the Blackdown Hills" (p. 1). The Crouchbacks' material circumstances are now sadly altered, but Guy's father Gervase, a widower, is still moved by an intense family pride:

> Only God and Guy knew the massive and singular quality of Mr.
> Crouchback's family pride. He kept it to himself. That passion,
> which is often so thorny a growth, bore nothing save roses for Mr.
> Crouchback. He was quite without class consciousness because he
> saw the whole intricate social structure of his country divided
> neatly into two unequal and unmistakable parts. On one side stood
> the Crouchbacks and certain inconspicuous, anciently allied fam-
> ilies; on the other side stood the rest of mankind . . . all of a piece
> together. Mr. Crouchback acknowledged no monarch since James
> II. (p. 34)

Powerful as his family pride may be, however, it "was as a schoolboy
hobby compared with his religious faith" (p. 36). Because he values his
faith over his family pride, Mr. Crouchback is untroubled by the imminent extinction of his ancient name.

Eclipse is near. Angela, the eldest Crouchback child, has married the
Protestant Arthur Box-Bender, and has a son, Tony. Gervase, the eldest
son, who would have inherited the family name and what remained of its
fortune, has been killed in World War I, "picked off by a sniper . . . fresh
and clean and unwearied" (p. 12). Ivo, the next brother, was a recluse
who tried to starve himself to death in his rented lodgings and who "died
. . . stark mad" (p. 12). As the last surviving male Crouchback of mar-
riageable age, Guy is the custodian of the family name and fortune. But
he appears to be "*fin de ligne*," for he is divorced and, as a Catholic, cannot remarry to produce an heir. This grave state of affairs does not disturb Mr. Crouchback: "it did not occur to Mr. Crouchback . . . that Guy
should marry by civil law and beget an heir and settle things up later with
the ecclesiastical authorities as other people seemed somehow to do.
Family pride could not be served in dishonour" (p. 36).

Guy shares his father's views about the pre-eminence of faith over family, but unlike his father he is not in fact very deeply moved by spiritual
matters. Despite Guy's many visits to church, he merely goes through the
motions of worship, for he possesses only "a few dry grains of faith,"
practises "a dry and negative chastity" (p. 11), and takes no joy in his
religion. To avoid disturbing the "wasteland" in which his soul "languishes" he confesses in Italian, iterating mechanically and without nu-
ance "his few infractions of law" (p. 7). Guy suffers from *accidie*, the
spiritual sloth which Aquinas defines as "sadness in the face of spiritual
good";[2] it stunts his charitable fellow-feeling, eliminating all "sympathy
between him and his fellow men" (p. 11). He avoids the brotherhood his
faith can offer, wishing he had lived at Broome when it was "a solitary

outpost of the Faith," and imagining himself serving "the last Mass for the last Pope in a catacomb at the end of the world" (pp. 10–11). He worships alone, attending "very early on weekdays when few others were about" (p. 11). Childish habit rather than genuine feeling motivates Guy's confession on the fateful morning of his departure from Santa Dulcina: "On an impulse, not because his conscience troubled him but because it was a habit learned in childhood to go to confession before a journey, Guy made a sign to the sister and interrupted the succession of peccant urchins" (p. 7). Guy is himself a "peccant urchin," an infant in the faith; the trilogy records his growth from younger brother to father, and his escape, limited though it is, from *accidie* into charity.

What accounts for the decline of the house of Crouchback in the two generations since Gervase and Hermione? And what accounts for Guy's lack of mature religious feeling? Characteristically, Waugh offers no explicit answer, but we may confidently trace the source of the decline to semi-pagan Santa Dulcina delle Rocce, and to the romantic Castello Crouchback itself. In the parish church the effigy of Santa Dulcina lies "languorously" in a glass case, and, although the Arciprete denies it, the inhabitants believe that there is "a pre-Christian thunderbolt . . . in the back of the altar." Three generations of Crouchbacks have spent their honeymoons and holidays in the seductively veiled paganism of Italy and Guy has lived there for eight years; thus there can be little doubt that the sweet life of Santa Dulcina has influenced his and his family's decline. In the War Trilogy as in *Brideshead Revisited*, idyllic earthly happiness is incompatible with spiritual success, and at the end of *Unconditional Surrender* Guy's spiritual rejuvenation takes place in the austere setting of the "Lesser House" at Broome. Waugh never makes his puritanism explicit (indeed, there are many who still think him a hedonist); nevertheless, his diagnosis of the Crouchbacks, as of the Flytes, is that they need to suffer more, for out of suffering comes renewal.

Rather than looking for brotherhood in his family or in his faith, Guy seeks it in an adolescent vision of chivalry, represented by Sir Roger de Waybroke, the knight whose tomb stands in the parish church near Santa Dulcina and the thunderbolt. Eight hundred years before, Sir Roger had set out from England on the Second Crusade but, shipwrecked on the Italian coast, he entered the service of a "local" Count and fell in battle, "a man with a great journey still all before him and a great vow unfulfilled" (p. 6). Waugh says that Guy has felt "an especial kinship" with Sir Roger all his life (p. 7), and with characteristic reticence, Waugh leaves it to the reader to conclude that an expatriate knight canonized "despite all clerical remonstrance" and with his vocation unfulfilled is a poor object of emulation. Sir Roger is in fact a false idol, and the crusade to which Guy dedicates himself on Sir Roger's sword is a wrong-headed quest for a false vocation. The gentle irony extends to Guy's euphoric view of the implications of the Molotov-Ribbentrop pact: "But now, splendidly, everything had become clear. The enemy at last was plain in view, huge and hateful, all disguise cast off. It was the Modern Age in arms. Whatever the outcome there was a place for him in that battle" (p. 5). As the trilogy unfolds, Guy discovers his error. He learns that disguise only conceals disguise, and that the temporary and shifting alliances of nations cannot make sense of "the old ambiguous world."[3] He learns that his own "endangered kingdom" can be as corrupt as any Fascist or Communist state. And despite his repeated attempts, Guy finds no "place . . . in that battle" for he "crouches back" into a cage of romantic but graceless aspirations.

Where do Waugh's real sympathies lie? Against the value-free modern world and the incomplete values of Sir Roger, Waugh sets up the private values of Guy's father. Mr. Crouchback eschews crusades against infidels, medieval and modern. He is content to perform charitable acts in the small world of family and friends. In Waugh's words, "The abiding values which co-existed with and survived all the political clap-trap are personified in the hero's father."[4]

We have seen that Waugh's early protagonists suffer because of the moral bankruptcy of their heritage and try, without success, to escape from the debilitating influence of their fathers. The War Trilogy reverses this pattern. When it begins, Guy has drifted away from his father, and the narrative depicts his gradual return to his father's house and values. As in *Brideshead*, the pattern of the trilogy consists of repeated rejections of the false in a quasi-Platonic ascent to absolute reality. And, as in *Brideshead* again, the agency presiding over the return is grace. The trilogy begins at the eleventh hour, with Guy sunk in grandiose dreams and at the mercy of Fortune in a lotus-land far from the saving centre of things. As his misfortunes multiply, the reciprocal action of grace—which resembles Herbert's pulley more than Ryder's thread—steadily draws good out of evil. Although war and Guy's illusions about war are in themselves pernicious, they are the means through which grace will save the house and name of Crouchback.

Guy's reclamation depends upon his rejection of Sir Roger and his acceptance of Mr. Crouchback. Both aspects of Guy's education begin simultaneously. Soon after his unsuccessful attempts to join the war in London, Guy visits his father at the Marine Hotel in Matchet. Here Mr. Crouchback provides Guy with an entrée into the Halberdiers, but he also gives Guy his brother Gervase's medal of Our Lady of Lourdes, a gift which emblemizes the transmission of the family heritage and responsibility from elder to younger son. It is a crucial moment, for if Guy had not returned to England, the medal would have gone to Tony and the "ancient name" of Crouchback would have descended through the female line to be absorbed into the Box-Bender family. Indeed, Arthur Box-Bender has long "considered the addition of Crouchback to his own name, in place of either Box or Bender, both of which seemed easily dispensable" (p. 13).

Quite apart from considerations of name, Tony Box-Bender is a poor heir to the Crouchback heritage because he manifests a taste for excessive solitude and inaction. He prefers to have no company on the eve of his departure for France; he sees nothing wrong in the Abercrombies' flight to Jamaica at the outbreak of war, and he can't see the advantages of being with "one's own people" in wartime (p. 27). His ardent wish is to get a neat wound and spend the rest of the war "being cosseted by beautiful nurses" (p. 29). He thinks that Santa Dulcina would be "just the place to spend the war" (p. 24). Tony's taste for withdrawal resembles Ivo's—indeed, Tony asks Guy about Ivo—and it eventually leads him to become a monk. If the ideal of the trilogy is private and charitable action rooted in family life, then Tony is a bad heir.

The glamorous prospect of army life leads Guy into romantic illusion. He returns to England expecting high drama, but instead of "a rain of poison or fire" (p. 22) there are only broken bones and routine muggings in the blackout. In the congenial atmosphere of the Halberdier barracks Guy finds comradeship and a sense of purpose, but his loyalty generates unrealistic expectations in him. He talks constantly about the absolute justice of the British cause, adopting the dangerous view that "there was in Romance great virtue in unequal odds" (p. 220). He is curt with a priest who says that it is a time of doubt and danger rather than glory and dedication; he snubs an old tenor who forgets the Corps' nickname; he becomes scornful of failure, especially his own; he repeatedly contrasts himself with Sir Roger and with his childhood hero, Captain Truslove, measuring himself against the stuff of fantasy; he believes that the Halberdiers can do no wrong, and feels a "serene confidence" in their capabilities. This confidence is in fact a dream which is doomed to be destroyed.

Guy is very far from real war. On guest night he sits in the comfortable mess-hall "bemused by wine and company" listening to the musicians play: "It all seemed a long way from . . . no-man's land" (p. 87). Even after Dunkirk, when the war begins in earnest, the Halberdiers "did not know where the biffs came from. . . . For those who followed events and thought about the future, the world's foundations seemed to shake. For the Halberdiers it was one damned thing after another" (pp. 250,256). As we have seen in the early satires, the consecutive world of "one damned thing after another" is the insubstantial realm of Fortuna. Mere chance governs Britain's incompetent military effort, and Guy Crouchback, shuttled back and forth, is its pawn.

When the Halberdiers move to bleak Kut-al-Imara House, Guy believes that at last "this was war" (p. 109). But despite Guy's brave thoughts, he and his fellows continue to play at being soldiers. Waugh pokes fun at their little fraud by alluding to them as schoolboys. Kut-al-Imara House is a former preparatory school, and the officers duplicate their young predecessors' routine, sleeping in the dormitories, using the school bell instead of a bugler, dividing themselves into "day-boys" and "boarders," and eating food which reminds Guy of his schoolday fare. In short, "the preparatory school way of life was completely recreated" (p. 139). Guy's "Barrack batch" joins a group from the Training Depot, and the result is a set of mutually degrading caricatures: "It was as though in their advance the Barrack batch had turned a corner and suddenly been brought up sharp by a looking-glass in which they found themselves reflected. . . . To Guy it seemed that there were just twice too many young officers at Kut-al-Imara House. They were diminished and caricatured by duplication" (p. 111).

When ferocious Brigadier Ritchie-Hook arrives, he is quick to scent the fraud. Like a furious headmaster "in a wax," he terminates the program and sends the offenders packing. Waugh sums up the episode: "Regimental pride had taken them unawares and quite afflated them" (p. 145). From this time on, Guy slowly outdistances his prideful illusions and moves steadily closer to real combat. At the end of the novel he at last sees action when he leads the Dakar raid. His heroism merits a Military Cross, but instead of being rewarded, Guy "blots his copy-book" and flies away with Ritchie-Hook to England. He is not yet wholly disillusioned, but is well on the way.

A better way of charting Guy's development in *Men at Arms* is to examine the rise and fall of Apthorpe, who personifies the grandiose notions that bedevil Guy.[5] "Burly, tanned, moustached," master of military jargon and possessor of a vast accumulation of tin trunks and leather cases, "Apthorpe alone looked like a soldier" (p. 46). But Apthorpe is not as solid as he looks, for everything about him proves to be spurious. He recommends a hotel that no one can find, and his preparatory school has vanished. By his own account a seasoned African hunter, he turns out to have been a clerk in a tobacco firm. "There was about Apthorpe a sort of fundamental implausibility. . . . Apthorpe tended to become faceless and tapering the closer he approached. Guy treasured every nugget of Apthorpe but under assay he found them liable to fade like faery gold" (p. 131). Pretentious and evasive, Apthorpe is appearance without substance, a proud cardboard imitation of a great soldier. Waugh calls Apthorpe a "doppelgänger" (p. 128), but Guy never perceives him as such. As Waugh says in his diary, "Doppelgängers don't recognize each other."[6]

Christopher Sykes finds Apthorpe the greatest flaw in the novel after Guy himself. According to Sykes, he is "a bore who bores."[7] Sykes says Waugh told Nancy Mitford that Apthorpe had taken "the bit between his teeth,"[8] and he theorizes that Waugh killed off Apthorpe at the end of the novel because "he found that otherwise one whom he had invented as a minor character would grow out of all proportion and dominate the whole work." But Sykes, whose estimate of *Men at Arms* is far too low, misunderstands Apthorpe, who had to die for more artistic reasons.

Upon Apthorpe's advent the narrative swerves from realism into surrealism. At the end of the Prologue Guy drifts off to sleep wishing he could say "here's how" like a soldier. As the next section opens, he says "here's how" to Apthorpe. An important bifurcation has occurred; in the space between the sections Waugh has split Guy into two by personifying his illusions in Apthorpe. In *Brideshead Revisited* Waugh writes, "We keep company in this world with a hoard of abstractions and reflexions and counterfeits of ourselves."[9] Apthorpe is one of these abstractions; he represents the phoniness of the Phoney War and the falseness of Guy's expectations about war. It is not merely that Apthorpe is a fraudulent soldier; the whole vocation he embodies is false for Guy, who must escape from Apthorpe's web before he may discover his true occupation in life.

Guy first meets Apthorpe sitting "opposite" him in the train at Charing Cross Station. The two men arrive together at Halberdier barracks and because of their advanced age (thirty-six—Waugh's age in 1939), each earns the nickname of "Uncle." Their friendship is not unusual in the Halberdiers, where the officers march in "pairs" and "double" to their quarters. Even Trimmer has "a poor reflexion of himself," named Sarum-Smith (p. 49). Apthorpe is impressive. He masters complicated drill instructions, memorizes the Corps history, shouts authoritatively at impertinent subordinates, and persists in taking P.T. even though given permission to miss it. Guy's achievements are far less imposing; on one occasion he gets a "rocket" for bad marksmanship, for disobeying range discipline, and for failing to clean his rifle.

Apthorpe competes with Guy for prestige. In contrast to Guy, who is shy and has a "recurring need for repose and solitude" (p. 64), Apthorpe is often "lonely" and "can't do without company" (p. 66). The manner in which they enter the ENSA concert clarifies their inverse relationship— "Guy seeking to withdraw, Apthorpe rather timidly advancing" (p. 59). Apthorpe flourishes on recognition: when Ritchie-Hook mistakes Guy for Apthorpe, Apthorpe complains that Guy has impersonated him and is "never again quite off his guard in Guy's company" (p. 84). Guy and Apthorpe do everything together; indeed, Guy does begin to imitate Apthorpe. At the guest night the officers play rugger with a waste-paper basket: "Apthorpe leapt. Guy leapt. Others leapt on them" (p. 89). Guy emerges with a sprained knee and a limp, and throughout the Christmas holidays is "lonely and dispirited" without Apthorpe. Alas, when Apthorpe returns, he too is injured in the knee: "like a pair of twins," Guy says (p. 116). When Guy and Apthorpe appear for dinner, "each leaning on his stick," the officers laugh and applaud. "I consider it's in pretty poor taste," says Apthorpe, himself the incarnation of bad taste.

As Apthorpe's fortunes wax, Guy's wane, recalling the reciprocal action of "The Balance." Guy becomes still more fascinated by Apthorpe, learning with pleasure of Apthorpe's High Church aunt, and visiting the moonlit site of his High Church preparatory school. He tries to become a *miles gloriosus*, like Apthorpe. He buys a monocle (in a "false-leather" purse) to improve his marksmanship and this, together with his now-flourishing moustache, makes him look "every inch a junker" (p. 129). Guy's transformation enhances his image among his brother-officers— but on false premises, for he is now in full masquerade, beguiled by the "faery gold" of Apthorpe's "dreamlike universe" (p. 131).

Ambrose Goodall of St. Augustine's Church allays Guy's misgivings about Apthorpe. He corroborates Apthorpe's story about having been goalkeeper at Staplehurst and provides other "nuggets" about Guy's friend. But Goodall plays an even more important role in Guy's life. He tells a story about a "blameless and auspicious pseudo-adultery" (p. 148) which prompts Guy's attempted seduction of Virginia. However, upon inspection the apparently reliable Goodall proves to bear the tell-tale Waughian marks of error. Although he is a student of English Catholicism in penal times and is a former teacher of Church history, he is a convert; before becoming a Roman Catholic he was an Anglo-Catholic. Because he is still under the sway of his Anglo-Catholic background, Goodall errs by taking an excessively romantic view of the English Catholic aristocracy. And in *Officers and Gentlemen* he entertains highly romantic notions about a modern-day Pilgrimage of Grace.[10] Waugh's

Chesterbelloc is unrealistic in the performance of his new faith. He prays, "popping in and down and up and out and in again assiduously, releasing *toties quoties* soul after soul from Purgatory."[11] Goodall is by no means a liar nor is he in himself evil. For example, the story he recounts about the husband who "committed no sin in resuming sexual relations with his former wife" is theologically sound. But Mr. Goodall is an enthusiast who lacks a well-developed sense of evil. As he speaks he is "flown with wine and looser than usual in his conversation"—and under his heady influence Guy moves ever more deeply into illusion.

By the time he goes to London, as if in emulation of the husband in Mr. Goodall's story, Guy has all unwittingly become a full-fledged fraud. He is motivated by Goodall's idealism and disguised as a combination of Apthorpe and Ritchie-Hook (he wears both a moustache and a monocle). But Virginia, a realist, finds Guy's new appearance comically bogus. Guy gazes into the mirror and realizes that she is right: "After all, he reflected, his whole uniform was a disguise, his whole new calling a masquerade" (p. 152). He shaves his moustache but perseveres in his charade as a soldierly lover. Although "two husbands in a day" might seem excessive (even here the doubling is operative), Virginia proves amenable to Guy's advances. But three inopportune calls from Apthorpe soon disrupt her amorous mood. Apthorpe wants Guy's company for himself. During his first call he says, "I couldn't join you anywhere?" During his second he suggests, "We might all join forces." During his third he announces that he has just put a civilian under close arrest and says, "I hope you aren't going to take his part" (p. 164). The civilian whom Apthorpe has arrested is Guy himself.[12] Virginia leaves, furious that Guy has chosen her because she "was the only woman in the whole world [his] priests would let [him] go to bed with." Although Apthorpe's calls are outrageous, his prevention of a renewed relationship between Guy and Virginia is, as we shall see, providential.

In Book Two, "Apthorpe Furibundus," Guy seems certain to sink irretrievably into dream: "the spell of Apthorpe would bind him, and gently bear him away to the far garden of fantasy" (p. 166). Apthorpe now grows tremendously powerful, earning a company and his captaincy, while Guy becomes merely a platoon commander. But Apthorpe's success marks the beginning of his decline, for just as it appears that Guy will succumb forever to Apthorpe's spell, Brigadier Ritchie-Hook intervenes to save Guy through the explosively funny thunder-box episode.

Apthorpe's thunder-box is a massive Edwardian field latrine, the absurd possession of a bogus personality, and it brings him into conflict with that boyish tyrant, Ben Ritchie-Hook. A "tense personal drama" (p.

176) ensues, as fraud and *enfant terrible* join battle over the ownership of the cumbersome convenience. By means of devious strategems, Apthorpe preserves his property for his own especial use, pressing Guy into service as "joint custodian of the thunder-box" (p. 188). Apthorpe needs Guy's help, for "he was pitted against a ruthless and resourceful enemy and must hold fast to Guy or go down" (p. 192). Apthorpe succeeds until the last day before Easter. Then, impeccable in appearance and triumphant in demeanour, he sallies forth to use the thunder-box, wearing his tin helmet; like Charles I, he "nothing common did or mean" on that fateful day. A sharp report rings out as a bomb dislodges the closeted Apthorpe and destroys the thunder-box. "Biffed," says Apthorpe (p. 196).

The bomb that catches Apthorpe in the "rears" marks the beginning of the end for him and for Guy's illusions. At Penkirk pride bloats Apthorpe's ego; he tries to take control of a detachment of signallers quite outside his jurisdiction, and when promoted to captain he insists on being saluted. Apthorpe's absurdities contrast with the increasing gravity of the military situation. As Apthorpe and Dunn squabble over the case of the boot, the British army is on the run in France. Boulogne, Calais, and then Paris fall, but Apthorpe the false knight fades into a remote world of fantasy, challenging Dunn to a "Trial by Combat" in Morse and offering to lecture the men on "the Jurisdiction of Lyon King of Arms compared with that of Garter King of Arms" (p. 260). Such is the vanity that goes before a fall.

Like Apthorpe, Guy too is far gone in fantasy. He dreams of Sir Roger's paynims and Captain Truslove's Pathans; once, his imagination overstimulated by a tale about fifth-columnists, he spends "a night alone with Halberdier Glass, armed to the teeth, on the sands of a little cove" (p. 264). His unfounded suspicions nearly prove fatal to two innocent Loamshire officers (p. 265). Long overdue for destruction, Guy's romantic notions persist until after his night-time raid on Dakar. "This was true Truslove-style," he thinks (p. 282) when invited to lead the landing party. But the raid proves to be the ultimate illusion. Although Guy acquits himself bravely, Fortune again perverts his high intentions: Ritchie-Hook has secretly accompanied him, has been wounded, and the unauthorized attack comes to official notice.

Apthorpe has retreated from the narrative. But now, in Guy's moment of disgrace, he re-enters the story on a stretcher borne by native boys from up-country. Even in his extremity he looks bogus, resembling "a Victorian wood-cut from a book of exploration" (p. 299). Waugh scrupulously avoids any suggestion that there is a connection between Guy's disillusionment and Apthorpe's moribund state. But there is a connection: Guy's illusions are fading, and so, therefore, is Apthorpe. Waugh reserves the *coup de grâce* for Guy himself. The bed-ridden Apthorpe consumes the whisky Guy brings him, and he dies. Guy receives a sharp reprimand for his role in Apthorpe's death; shaken but unashamed, he is possessed by a sense of disaster, for the military powers above have twisted his good intentions into disgrace.

Guy should now be free of illusion, but the memory of Apthorpe lingers on. He discharges Apthorpe's nine-shilling debt for Dunn's boot (the running joke is a Firbankian touch), and he agrees to hand over Apthorpe's gear to Chatty Corner. (With his usual wicked eye for detail, Waugh makes Apthorpe select an ape-man as his heir rather than his High Church aunt.) Apthorpe's death coincides with the departure to England of Guy and Ritchie-Hook. As "the two men who had destroyed Apthorpe" fly away (p. 313), Apthorpe, pretentious in life, is treated with ostentation in death. When Guy's double is laid to rest, the bugles sound "in perfect unison" and the rifles fire "as one." But Guy's future is in doubt: an "alien" once again, he has failed to achieve the brotherhood he sought. Moreover, he has blotted his copy-book twice and has fallen under the influence of a new incubus in the person of Ritchie-Hook. As the novel ends the reader is left to wonder whether Guy will ever shake off his illusions and find the comradeship he seeks. *Officers and Gentlemen* provides a partial answer to this question.

## CHAPTER 19

# Officers and Gentlemen

As Waugh grew older, he grounded his fiction ever more solidly in personal experience; there can be little doubt, for example, that he wrote the Crouchback saga with his diaries at his elbow. Why did Waugh rely so heavily on real life? Was it because of failing imagination? Egocentricity? A desire for authority which could come only from "experience totally transformed"?[1] Some readers, noticing the loose organization of Guy Crouchback's adventures, may find that *Officers and Gentlemen* lacks coherence and unity;[2] they may decide that there are liabilities in Waugh's method, or conclude that real life is too dull and disorganized for "transformation" into satisfying fiction. But to complain about the fragmented narrative sequence of *Officers and Gentlemen* is to overlook the likelihood that it is the product of an implicit organizing principle—that is, it can be argued that the world of battle is incoherent, in Waugh's view, because it is governed by incompetent military authorities who are the embodiments of chance. Yet the trilogy is more than a mere expression of disorder; when Providence finally prevails against Fortune, design asserts itself in Guy's life and in the plot-line, and the trilogy ends on a note of personal order. Like many another modern writer, Waugh uses form to reflect his metaphysics.

In *Officers and Gentlemen* (which Waugh began "excellently" on 25 March 1953),[3] Guy continues his quest for a heroic vocation, but he finds only the perversion of his high expectations. Above all, he remains alone, for values like his are shared by few. In "Happy Warriors" he sees mock-epic "heroes" engaged in war games and lounging at their ease, while in "In the Picture" he sees them in actual combat. Four doggy characters bear the brunt of Waugh's attack: in Ivor Claire and Trimmer, Waugh depicts the decline of aristocratic bravery and the rise of the spurious proletarian hero. And in Major Hound and Ludovic he portrays the pragmatism and cowardice which is now the norm. Guy's adventures unfold against the elaborately counterpointed stories of these and other characters.

As *Officers and Gentlemen* opens, Guy has left the "false emotions" and unwarlike lushness of Dakar behind, and the prospect of real combat exhilarates him. He responds with enthusiasm to the bombs and search-lights of the Blitz, for he is "fresh to these delights" (p. 1). But even the Blitz is somehow unreal: an atmosphere of high farce surrounds its lethal splinters and pitchy clouds. The "ochre and madder" sky reminds Guy not of war but of Turner; the "incongruous façades" of the clubs are "caricatured by the blaze" as progressive novelists dressed as fire wardens squirt "a little jet of water" into the briskly burning Turtle's Club. Behind the blacked-out windows of Bellamy's, the night-porter grossly over-acts "the part of a stage butler" in a mood of "high drama." At the centre of this caricature of war, cowardly Air Marshal Beech crouches under the billiard table and Ian Kilbannock, trying to avoid him, behaves like a character "in a stage farce."

The Commandos on Mugg provide an even better parody of heroism. Unsung in ballad or story because of its unrhymable name, Mugg is a northern facsimile of Crete, the site of "a dress rehearsal for an opera-tion" (p. 105). Allusions to Hector, Philoctetes, Miltiades, Jason, Her-cules, and Achilles indicate that Waugh thought of X Commando in terms of the Heroic Age; specifically, he seems to have had the Trojan War in mind. But the Commandos are only parodies of those antique he-roes, and Hector Campbell of Mugg, with his smoky castle, "infernal brutes"of dogs, and obsession with high explosives, provides a comic foretaste of the Cretan "nether world" which they are planning to attack.

Soon after Guy's arrival, "as in an old-fashioned, well-constructed comedy, . . . characters began to enter" (p. 58). "An enormous Grenadier Captain in the tradition of comedy" brings news of Captain Anstruther-Kerr's "fall." In fact, almost all the officers have fallen on the icy rocks of Mugg, and their tumbles presage their collective fall on Crete. Foremost among the fallen is Ivor Claire, whom Guy soon comes to admire. But Guy is mistaken, of course, for with his turban, his pekinese, and his sofa of Turkey carpet, languid Claire is not a crusader but an infidel (p. 57).[4] A horseman and an aristocrat, Claire appears to be this century's Sidney; but before the novel is over effete Ivor will prove a coward and a traitor, thereby completing Guy's disillusionment with modern heroism. Trim-mer makes "the final entry," dressed in the uniform of a highland reg-iment and operating under the alias of "Ali" McTavish. He proves to be Claire's similar opposite. Soon to be a proletarian hero, Trimmer rises as Claire falls. Trimmer eventually disappears into the egalitarian West while Claire escapes to the heathen East.

If Claire is an infidel, Trimmer is an outright impostor. Doubly disguised in name and in rank, "Major McTavish" takes an unauthorized leave amid the fog and darkness of Glasgow. Like a mongrel among dustbins, "ears cocked, nose a-quiver," he finds female companionship in the person of Virginia Troy, Guy's former wife, now sadly declined from former affluence. The well-matched couple meet amid the trumpery décor of the station hotel restaurant, where a phony French waiter serves them. Their liaison results in the birth of little Trimmer, a birth which has far-reaching consequences for Guy.

Guy moves among the "happy warriors" of Book One unaware that not all officers are gentlemen. At first he is under a cloud for his part in the Dakar raid, and, stationed at Southsand, despairingly sees himself "make a hermitage of Apthorpe's tent and end his days encamped on the hills . . . a gentler version of poor mad Ivo" (p. 47). By alluding here to Ivo, and elsewhere to reclusive Tony Box-Bender, Waugh keeps the spectre of excessive withdrawal before the reader. Will Guy become another Ivo? Or will he be more like Gervase, who is "in Paradise perhaps, in the company of other good soldiers" (p. 47)? Even as Guy loses heart, Fortune intervenes; Churchill himself absolves him from any wrong-doing at Dakar, and Jumbo Trotter arrives to rescue Guy and "to draw him back into the life of action" (p. 247) with X Commando on Mugg. By coincidence Mugg also shelters Chatty Corner himself, whose castle resembles "a set by Gordon Craig for a play of Maeterlinck's" (p. 67). After receiving an "acquittal" for Apthorpe's gear, his impediment to action, Guy is free to "follow his fortunes in the king's service" (p. 18). But no sooner does Guy placate Apthorpe's spirit than he falls prey to another illusion: Ivor Claire and the Commandos.

Waugh's attitude towards the newly formed Commando units is highly ambivalent. In his *Life* article, "Commando Raid on Bardia," Waugh adopts an approving tone, but there are traces of criticism. He writes:

> The officers were mostly from the Household Brigade. They got the
> reputation of being exclusively recruited from the very rich and
> very gay but there was a fair proportion of industrious professional
> soldiers to preserve the balance. I remember well my impression on
> first joining. The Commando was at that time living in Scotland
> and the officers' mess was at a seaside hotel. I had come home from
> the austerity and formality of the Royal Marines. In a Marine mess
> it is thought disgraceful to sit down before 6 in the evening; those
> who have nothing to do must pretend that they have. I found a
> young troop leader wearing a military tunic and corduroy trousers.
> He was reclining in a comfortable chair, a large cigar in his mouth.

Then I noticed above the pocket of his coat the ribbon of the Military Cross, and later when I saw him with his troop I realized that his men would follow him anywhere.[5]

Waugh published the "Bardia" article without the proper authorization; the War Office then issued it as a bulletin, prompting Waugh to think about sueing for plagiarism. In his diary (highly illegal, in wartime), he noted that No. 8 Commando was composed of a "smart set" of congenial company, whom he liked because they were resourceful, individualistic, and dandified: "The whole thing was a delightful holiday from the Royal Marines. . . . No. 8 Commando was boisterous, xenophobic, extravagant, imaginative, witty, with a proportion of noblemen which the Navy found disconcerting."[6] But Waugh did not admire them unreservedly. The extreme variety of these "odds and sods" bothered him (they were drawn from at least ten different regiments), and their lack of discipline was their greatest fault:

> The standard of efficiency and devotion to duty, particularly among the officers, is very much lower than in the Marines. There is no administration or discipline. The men are given 6s a day and told to find their own accommodation. If they behave badly they are simply sent back to their regiments. Officers have no scruples about seeing to their own comfort or getting all the leave they can. . . .
> When formed they had been exceptionally zealous; discipline was already deteriorating when I joined. After R M Brigade the indolence and ignorance of the officers seemed remarkable, but I have since realized they were slightly above normal Army standards. Great freedom was allowed in costume; no one even pretended to work outside working hours. . . . Two night operations in which I acted as umpire showed great incapacity in the simplest tactical ideas. One troop leader was unable to read a compass.[7]

Waugh's "Memorandum on Layforce" is a bitter indictment of the Commandos. In Egypt, says Waugh, "the morale of B Battalion [No. 8 Commando] began to deteriorate very rapidly." He noted, "During this period I met a Grenadier subaltern in . . . the Union Bar; he had been given sick leave by the Church of England chaplain in order to go into hospital but felt better in Alexandria and so was engaged in courting a Greek lady. At Marsa the Commando gave up all pretence of military work and spent the day bathing and fishing. A Scots Guard sergeant came on parade with a fishing rod." He also wrote, "The feelings of the

battalion were well summed up by an inscription found on the troop-
decks of *Glengyle*: 'Never in the history of human endeavour have so few
been buggered about by so many'." [8]

In *Unconditional Surrender* Waugh writes, "Most of those who volun-
teered for Commandos in the spring of 1942 had other motives besides
the desire to serve their country. A few merely sought release from regimental routine; more wished to cut a gallant figure before women; others had led lives of particular softness and were moved to re-establish
their honour in the eyes of the heroes of their youth—legendary, historical, fictitious—that still haunted their manhood." [9] Guy belongs to the
last group. At first he is not close to the Commandos, but when they become part of Hookforce under Ritchie-Hook, Guy formally joins the
"happy warriors" as brigade intelligence officer.

Lord Ian Kilbannock, the two-faced journalist and creator of modern
heroes, congratulates Guy on his good fortune; he says that Guy's aristocratic unit provides an admirable way of soldiering among friends, but
adds that Guy's élite Commando fails to embody the new, democratic
ideal of heroism: "They just won't do, you know. Delightful fellows, heroes too, I daresay, but the Wrong Period. Last-war stuff, Guy. Went out
with Rupert Brooke. . . . We want heroes of the people, to or for the people, by, with and from the people" (p. 130). Kilbannock's important if
inebriated remarks make the theme of heroism explicit and set the stage
for the rise of Trimmer and the fall of Claire in the second half of the
book. Implicit in Waugh's far graver treatment of heroism in "In the Picture" is the view that the new heroism is a hoax, and that the fall of Crete
is the result of the old heroes' neglect of their duties.

Commando training on Mugg ends abruptly when the authorities,
having arrived on board Mrs. Stitch's yacht *Cleopatra*, "shanghai" their
men into action. "Interlude," set in Cape Town (not on board a troop-
ship, as Waugh mistakenly told Julian Jebb) synopsizes the Commandos'
preparations for Operation "Badger." It also presents a preliminary
sketch of the decay of authority which Waugh later portrays so vividly in
"In the Picture." The two Commandos in Hookforce are examples of de-
ficiency and excess. B Commando is led by the "fleshless, glaring figure"
of the draconic Colonel Prentice. Members of X Commando, on the
other hand, saunter through the bright streets of Cape Town too much at
ease. With a joke about "*esprit de corps*," two of them nonchalantly drop
their bottle of "Kommando" brandy into the sea. Ivor Claire smokes
"with conscious luxury"; his man Ludovic wears bedroom slippers all
day. His drawling admission that he has scarcely ever been sober on
board ship does not prevent Guy from regarding him as "quintessential

England"; neither does his ominous desire for disaster and solitude on "some nearby island" (p. 141). Like Tony Box-Bender, Claire wants to spend the war in an isolated "lush place." Disrespect for authority soon causes X Commando's decline. At Scapa Flow Guy's aristocratic friends dub Ritchie-Hook "the Widow Twankey" and his influence wanes. Now that he has disappeared altogether—he and his brigade major are lost in the Congo—his command descends to the more tolerant Tommy Blackhouse. Claire approves: it is another present from Ali Baba's lamp. "Interlude" ends with Guy lost, as usual, in ill-founded love. X Commando, and Guy's illusions about them, are now ripe for destruction.

Still called "Hookforce" despite the loss of their commander, the Commandos sail into a "picture" overshadowed by threats from friends and foes alike. Benghazi and Greece have fallen, the Commandos have lost their ships and their purpose—Operation "Badger" has been cancelled—and at home the War Office clamours to have them disbanded. Pending a decision on their future, the Commandos languish in their tents at Sidi Bishr near Alexandria.

Help comes from an unexpected quarter. As the Easter bells ring out in London, Egypt and Matchet, linking the three settings of chapter 1, General Whale decides to create a hero who will redeem the Commandos' reputation. From now on the narrative has a double and carefully counterpointed thrust: the fabrication of a proletarian hero in the person of Trimmer, and the disgrace of upper-class heroism as embodied in Ivor Claire. Trimmer's story shows vice rewarded, and Claire's shows virtue betrayed. Together they represent the supersession of traditional values by a base new pragmatism, a process soon to be embodied on the international level by that ultimate injustice, the alliance of Britain with Russia.

Waugh carefully orchestrates the rising action. In the first two sections of chapter 1, he counterpoints the events of Easter week with the activities of infidels, figurative and real: General Whale and the army brass are as faithless as the paynims Sir Roger once sailed against, and these infidels now stand at the very heart of the British war effort. The second and longest section is an intricate prelude to the massive betrayals of Crete. This prelude begins and ends with Major Hound, who as Blackhouse's brigade major is a portrait of another kind of incompetent officer: the dogmatic administrator who loses his nerve under pressure. Although Waugh had heard of "Colonel Hound" and his cowardice as early as the Bardia raid, it seems that he did not meet him personally until he delivered Laycock's orders to him on Crete and found him "under the table . . . sitting hunched up like a disconsolate ape." [10] Waugh brings him into the novel early in order to prepare the reader for his pusillanimity. At first he provides just enough detail to make Hound disagreeable (curiously, Hound dislikes the Commandos for the same reasons Waugh did), and he adumbrates the hostility between Hound and Ludovic which he will develop later.

By stationing the Commandos near Alexandria, "ancient asparagus bed of theological absurdity" (p. 161), Waugh places modern military disorder in a context of ancient heresy. Guy goes to Alexandria to make his Easter duties, avoiding the priest at the camp because "he had begun to dissociate himself from the army in matters of real concern" (p. 161). But Guy finds treachery even in the confessional where the priest questions him on confidential military matters. After confession Guy visits Claire, who is now comfortably sequestered in a private nursing home, having sustained a trivial injury to his knee. While Guy is there, an important figure arrives. She is Mrs. Stitch, the Cleopatra of modern Alexandria. In a scene which deftly prefigures her protection of Claire and her disposal of the red identity disc, Mrs. Stitch "inclined the huge straw disc of her hat over Claire and kissed his forehead" (p. 166). Wife of the commander-in-chief[11] and "a mine of indiscretion," Julia Stitch is the aristocratic guardian of aristocratic heroes, an example of the English nobility looking after its own: "X Commando felt her presence as that of a beneficent, alert deity, their own protectress. Things could not go absolutely wrong with them while Mrs. Stitch was about" (p. 208). Waugh's remark is purely ironic, for Julia is caprice itself, a contemporary Fortuna whose actions are constricting rather than liberating. Earlier, for example, she has been described imprisoning a minotaur-like "underground cow" in a cell beneath the Castello Crouchback. Under the influence of this whimsical deity, the Commandos' fortunes fall very low indeed.

Mrs. Stitch spirits Guy away for shopping and luncheon in a fine comic romp in the early Waugh manner. Oblique language establishes Mrs. Stitch's values. Before leaving Claire she offers him Turkish delight; then she goes off to buy "a pair of crimson slippers which were both fine and funny, with high curling toes" (p. 169). The oriental slippers link Julia with Ivor, who affects monogrammed velvet slippers, and with Ludovic, who wears bedroom slippers. As she darts through the traffic in a little open car which recalls the world of *Scoop*, Mrs. Stitch discourses volubly on the history of Alexandria. She halts in the middle of a busy intersection to point out the Soma and Alexander's tomb, and to comment on the Gates of the Sun and Moon, and Hypatia. A zany modern Cleopatra, Mrs. Stitch presides over the decayed grandeur of Alexandria.

The bad taste which stems from bad faith marks Mrs. Stitch's incongruous villa: "She enjoyed change and surprise, crisp lettuce-freshness and hoary antiquity" (p. 317). Only the Berber servants are African;

everything else "smacked of the Alpes Maritimes" (p. 170). The luncheon party is "heterogeneous": two Egyptian millionairesses speaking French and English, a Maharaja, an English cabinet minister, a Pasha, and Algernon Stitch himself, hardly changed since he exited from the pages of *Scoop* holding a newspaper in his mouth. The Pasha is asked to explain Cavafy, and Algernon Stitch recites W. J. Cory's "Heraclitus," the "best poem ever written in Alexandria" (p. 172). The whole boisterous episode is Waugh's allusive elegy on the supersession of ancient Greek civilization by its debased modern counterpart. A Greek lady proudly tells Guy that her husband has given up cards and that she herself has given up cigarettes: all for Greece. Heraclitus is dead indeed.

The eventful first chapter of "In the Picture" ends with a brief glimpse of Mr. Crouchback smoking "his first pipe of Easter" at Matchet and thinking about "that morning's new fire" (p. 175). Waugh characteristically avoids any explicit comment on Mr. Crouchback, but his brief reappearance provides a reminder of "the abiding values" in which he believes. Mr. Crouchback is the trilogy's only reliable figure of authority.

Chapters II and III concern Trimmer's reunion with Virginia and his meteoric rise to fame as the hero of Operation "Popgun." En route in a submarine to his staged heroics, Trimmer melodramatically writes that he has found "the real thing" in Virginia, who is now disgusted by the events of Glasgow. The raid is pure farce, a travesty of the Dakar raid and of the Hookforce landing on Crete. Trimmer and his twelve disciples land by mistake on the coast of occupied France, and in the "delusive moonlight" the stagey Kilbannock swigs whiskey, quotes from Noël Coward and from Latimer, and lends support to the shirker he later extols as a hero. Trimmer's medal recalls the one Guy should have received at Dakar and stands in contrast with two others: the red identity disc of the dead soldier on Crete, and Guy's medal of Our Lady of Lourdes. Instead of disbanding the Commandos, the War Office decides to raise three more; meanwhile Trimmer the modern hero goes on a lecture tour.

Waugh now proceeds with graver business: the Allied withdrawal from Crete, "island of disillusion" (p. 241). Waugh's account of the evacuation is the showpiece of *Officers and Gentlemen* and it remains the best prose he ever wrote. Its excellence is not in the least diminished by the fact that it is a near-transcription of the "Memorandum on Layforce"; here real-life experience forms the basis of an exciting narrative nearly one hundred pages long. Waugh judiciously suppresses his rage at the Allies' ineptitude. Coolly, and with a carefully restricted point of view, he details the cowardice and treachery which Guy Crouchback observes on every side during his five days on Crete.[12]

The withdrawal from Crete dramatizes a crisis in leadership which

Waugh traces to the very highest levels of authority. Episode after episode demonstrates the staggering incompetence of those who have been trained to command. "We did not once, in the five days' action," Waugh writes, "receive an order from any higher formation without going to ask for it."[13] Waugh does not try to give a full-scale account of the operations, but restricts himself to the role of Hookforce and to the actions of four men: Hound, Ludovic, Claire, and Guy himself. Hookforce's role, like that of Layforce, is to provide a rearguard defence through which the broken armies can fall back to their waiting ships at Sphakia. They are to remain on the island to the end, even if that means surrendering to the Germans. Already weakened because of the presumed death of Ritchie-Hook, the force loses his replacement, Blackhouse, who falls and breaks his leg. Command therefore devolves upon Major Hound, who fails utterly to rise to the occasion. In disorder itself, Hookforce enters an even greater "shambles," which is more the result of Allied incompetence than of German superiority.

Major Hound quickly assumes prominence as Waugh's focal point, and his personal fall epitomizes the fall of Crete. He graduated from Sandhurst at the time when no one believed that England would ever again fight a European war, but nothing in his rigid training has prepared him for Crete, where courage and flexibility are more important than staff-solutions. A caricature of an officer, Hound merely goes through the motions of performing his duty; his salvation lies in "bumf," and his only faith is in "the magic of official forms" (p. 268). At first he stays afloat, "like Noah, sure in his own righteousness" (p. 231), but he soon goes under. The cataclysm on Crete proves that faith in official papers is not enough.

As acting commander of Hookforce, Hound must keep his brigade headquarters in touch with his own men and with Creforce, and Guy and Ludovic assist him in this duty. In a rising panic, Hound races back and forth between his men and the constantly shifting Creforce headquarters, but soon he loses his nerve, the defection of all but eight members of headquarters precipitating his flight. After an all-night retreat, "Fido" hides in a culvert "like an air marshal under a table" (p. 257), leaving Guy in charge of the remnants of headquarters. From this point on, Hound's fortunes diverge from Guy's and Waugh counterpoints their actions; eventually Guy escapes from his Cretan prison but Hound does not.

Hound's perversion of his duty degrades him by degrees to a level below that of the animals. In a sense his fall represents the crucifixion of the honourable vocation. It begins when he chooses "the heady precipice of sensual appetite" over "the steep path of duty" (p. 235); he loses his soul by bartering cigarettes for bully beef and biscuits. Accompanied by General Miltiades, the sleepy representative of almost-obsolete chivalry, Hound and Guy reach X Commando lines and divide "the cheese, the wafers, the sardines" (p. 249). Hound will not listen to the courtly Miltiades. Deserted by his men, Hound believes that he has "fallen among thieves" (p. 254); like Ishmael he believes that "every hand was against him" (p. 267). After his all-night retreat he believes he "heard a cock crowing once" (p. 256). At Creforce headquarters he receives bundles of currency from his "headmen," who squat "like chimps in a zoo" and behave like cannibals. So it is that the caves of modern Crete harbour something even more destructive than a Minotaur: generals given over to defeat. Clutching his money, Hound goes into the "wilderness" where in a crucially important scene he falls through the branches of a tree into an "Arcadian vale." Having descended to the level of the merely pagan, Judas-like Hound is robbed by a Cretan patriarch[14] who wears "trousers in the style of Abdul the Damned" and who looks at him "as though he were a fractious great-grandson" (pp. 266, 267). Hound's valley is the lush place of escape from duty, and the robbery is a subtle symbolic recapitulation of the long decay which has produced him. That is to say, when the heathen patriarch strips Hound of his money and possessions, he re-enacts Adam's theft of his children's innate rectitude. That remote and catastrophic theft took place when Adam tried to turn Eden into a lush place independent of God's will; in falling back through the branches of his genealogical tree, Fido returns to the source of his moral bankruptcy and suffers the fateful robbery all over again. Adam's attempt to turn Eden into a secluded lush place led him into the prison of the appetites, and as if in demonic repetition, the same thing soon happens to Hound.

After the Cretan's departure, "Fido wept" (p. 267). Stripped of his possessions, he splashes in a parody of baptism through the waters of a consecrated but abandoned spring, and meets Ludovic, who is in search of an unattached officer. In "prayerless abandon" he follows the smell of cooking; it calls to him as clear as the horn of Roland and leads him to a cave where a dishevelled crowd of defectors communes around a heterogeneous stew. Many of the "congregation" were once Hound's men. Now he joins them: his obedience has made him their slave. As Ludovic dictates terms to the imprisoned Hound, a colony of bats comes to life "for no human reason" and then settles again, "head-down" (p. 272). The image of the bats confirms the inversion of hierarchy which has overtaken Hound and all the spiritually blinded authorities on Crete. The story of the fall of Major Hound shows that the bestial now reigns supreme; it is also one of the finest examples of the allusive language and symbolic recapitulation which characterize all of Waugh's work.

After Hound's defection Guy marches on alone, "eased at last of the lead weight of human company" (p. 273). After gazing at his "mocking reflection" in a well, he discovers a young warrior who lies motionless, "like Sir Roger in his shadowy shrine" (p. 275). Although the unknown soldier reminds Guy of Sir Roger, he is in fact far closer to Gervase, for he is "undamaged," and like Gervase he has a medal: a red identity disc. Guy pockets the disc and later, adrift in the Mediterranean, he confuses it with Gervase's medal while praying, "preposterously," to "Saint Roger of Waybroke" (p. 305). There is accuracy in Guy's confusion, for the dead soldier is more relevant to the times than Sir Roger is; his crusade is unfinished and he will remain forever unknown because of the infidels within the British power structure itself. Unlike Trimmer, who gives nothing yet rockets to fame, the soldier gives his life and achieves anonymity. He symbolizes the crucifixion of honour by Judases like Hound; in a sense, he is Guy himself. In his presence Guy and the two Greek girls stand by the body, "stiff and mute as figures in a sculptured Deposition" (p. 275). Circumstances prevent him from burying the soldier, "one of the corporal works of charity." And he takes the red disc because of military "precept," not because of compassion. Only after he exchanges his romantic view of heroism for the austerer view of his father does Guy achieve a fuller awareness of charity.

After a poignant encounter with the Halberdiers (this is pure invention, for Waugh did not meet the Marines) who will not let him join their war, Guy continues towards his headquarters and then towards Sphakia. He brings the "last grim orders" to the Hookforce commanders: they are to surrender. To Guy the orders are shameful, but he is ready to comply with them. Ivor Claire, in contrast, is not prepared to spend years of his life in a prison camp like a "young prince of Athens sent as sacrifice to the Cretan labyrinth" (p. 311), so he strides forward out of the night and converses with Guy about honour: "It's a thing that changes, doesn't it?" he says (p. 295). Guy never sees him again. "Well, the path of honour lies up the hill," Claire says ambiguously, and departs into the moonlight. Guy learns later that he has boarded a ship without his men and has sailed back to Alexandria in comfort.

Is there any basis in real experience for Claire's cowardly escape? Let us examine Waugh's account of his own departure from Crete:

> Bob and I had resigned ourselves to being captured but now got
> slightly more hopeful of escape. Weston [the Royal Marine General

commanding the rearguard action] said that we [Layforce] were to cover the withdrawal and that a message would be sent to us by the embarkation officer on Sphakia beach when we could retire.

At about 10 o'clock that evening [May 31] there was no sign of the enemy and the approaches to the beaches were thronged with non-fighting troops. Bob and I and Freddy, with servants, therefore set off to find the beach officer, Colonel Healy, and ask authority to withdraw. We pushed our way through the crowds who were too spiritless even to resist what they took to be an unauthorized intrusion and arrived on the beach to find that there was no one in charge, Colonel Healy having left earlier by aeroplane. Bob then took the responsibility of ordering Layforce to fight their way through the rabble and embark. My servant Tanner took this order back. The beach was a little harbour approached by narrow lanes through the village of Sphakia. . . . As there was nothing further he could do, Bob ordered brigade HQ to embark, which we did in a small motor boat. We reached the destroyer *Nizam* at about midnight and sailed as soon as we came aboard. (*Diaries*, p. 509)

What would have happened to Laycock, who embarked ahead of his troops and without official permission to withdraw, if Tanner had not reached Layforce or if Layforce had not been able to penetrate the "rabble" choking those "narrow lanes"? For the answer we need only glance at Ivor Claire's alibi as presented by Mrs. Stitch:

"What happened," said Julia as though at repetition in the schoolroom, "was an order from the beach for Hookforce to embark immediately. Ivor was sent down to verify it. He met the naval officer in charge who told him that guides had been sent back and that Hookforce was already on its way. His ship was just leaving. There was another staying for Hookforce. He ordered him into the boat straight away. Until Ivor reached Alexandria he thought the rest of Hookforce was in the other cruiser. When he found it wasn't, he was in rather a jam. That's what happened. So you see no one can blame Ivor, can they?" (p. 314)

One imagines that Laycock too would have been in "rather a jam" if he had embarked to find that his men had not followed him. As things turned out, that did not happen, but the risk Laycock ran seems to have coloured Waugh's account of Claire's actions.

Is Ivor Claire based on Sir Robert Laycock? At first glance it seems unlikely, in view of the fact that Waugh dedicated *Officers and Gentlemen* to Laycock, "that every man in arms should wish to be." Moreover, most of Waugh's intimates believed that he used Laycock as the model for Tommy Blackhouse. But in his diary Waugh transcribes a telegram from Ann Fleming (wife of the creator of James Bond): "Presume Claire based on Laycock dedication ironical." Although Mrs. Fleming a little later claimed that she was being facetious, Waugh did not actually deny the charge: "I replied that if she breathes a suspicion of this cruel fact it will be the end of our friendship." Waugh's odd disclaimer goes far towards confirming Ann Fleming's allegation. On the other hand, Lady Diana Cooper has said that Claire was modelled on "Shimi" Lovat.[15] Waugh certainly had a motive for using Lovat, who had helped to force his resignation from the Special Service Brigade in 1943. Waugh's hostility to Lovat notwithstanding, his horrified response to Ann Fleming's telegram about Laycock carries much force; moreover, if the allegation was unfounded, it seems inconceivable that Waugh, usually so careful in such matters, would have recorded it in diaries which he knew might be published. At the very least it is likely that Claire is a composite of Laycock and Lovat.

If it is true that Waugh perceived some parallel between Laycock's withdrawal and Claire's escape, what did he make of the fact that he himself accompanied Laycock? Did his close association with Laycock's withdrawal influence his treatment of Guy Crouchback's escape? Apparently so, for Waugh's attitude toward Guy's departure is highly ambivalent. When we examine Waugh's account of the escape, we find that Guy is at first prepared to surrender, even though he finds the thought disgraceful. He watches a sapper captain preparing a fishing boat for his escape, and he observes another man seeking company for a getaway into the hills. A sergeant asks, "Is there anything in that, sir?" And Guy responds, "Our orders are to surrender" (p. 297). Guy rejects the idea of escape—but then he meets Ludovic, who has been contemplating suicide: "Would moralists hold it was suicide if one were just to swim out to sea, sir, in the fanciful hope of reaching Egypt?" (p. 299). Waugh does not say so, but Ludovic's "theological speculations" fascinate Guy, for they contain an acceptable proportion of hope and death-wish.[16] Guy impulsively decides to go with the sapper captain in the fishing boat. He scrambles on board, closely followed by Ludovic, and they sail "out of the picture" just in time to avoid a lethal shower of German bombs.

There is nothing illicit about Guy's escape from the labyrinth. He is not responsible for his intelligence section in the same sense that Claire is responsible for his troop; he consults his men and invites them to go with him; furthermore, escape by small boat has been endorsed by Creforce headquarters. But Waugh's attitude to Guy's escape is curiously defensive. He explains that Guy is very feeble when he makes his decision, and that in his fatigue "he was aware only . . . of the satisfaction of finding someone else to take control of things" (p. 301). If we see that Waugh is in fact critical of Guy's escape, then (and only then) can we make sense of the remark which prefaces the whole episode: "[Guy] had no clear apprehension that this was a fatal morning, that he was that day to resign an immeasurable piece of his manhood" (p. 296).[17] The point is that Guy escapes when he might have remained with his men. His act is not illegal; but at a crucial moment he passes up the opportunity to share adversity with his fellow men at arms. Although Waugh's attitude is ostensibly approving (he even has Blackhouse consider recommending Guy for a Military Cross), there is an undercurrent of disapproval which connects Guy's flight with Claire's, just as (though in a more immediate way) Waugh's was associated with Laycock's. In 1955 Waugh denied that Guy had "funked"; but in 1962 he described his own escape as "my bunk from Crete."[18] Evidence from previous novels shows that Waugh approved of some sorts of prisons and disapproved of others. In this case, it appears that he was not able to decide: he had been ordered to surrender, but surrender was disgraceful. Like everything else about the war, Waugh regarded his escape from the Cretan labyrinth as "ambiguous" (p. 322).

Ludovic is an important figure in Guy's escape. Six feet two inches tall, of mysterious origins, with two tones of voice and oyster-tinted eyes, Ludovic is the chronicler and later the embodiment of the defeatism of the age. He claims, "we live . . . in the Age of Purges and Evacuation. . . . Cultivate the abhorred vacuum" (p. 207). Ludovic is preoccupied with a more than Apthorpian inner emptiness. He epitomizes what Waugh has earlier described as "the vacuum, the spasm, the precipitation" of army life (p. 53). He approves of the universal death-wish (p. 211), observes that "all gentlemen are now very old" (p. 249), and refuses to drink when General Miltiades proposes a victory toast. Ludovic is a shadow, an "*éminence grise*" (p. 144) who attaches himself first to Claire, then to Hound, and finally to Guy. Claire eludes the leech-like Ludovic by promoting him upstairs, but Hound is less fortunate. When Hound balks at going ashore on Crete, Ludovic escorts him, and he eventually proves to be the death of Hound: "I was with him until—as long as he needed me, sir" (p. 299). After bleeding Hound dry, the parasitical Ludovic fixes on Guy: "I'll follow you round, sir" he says (p. 300), and when Guy is about to climb into the fishing boat he notices that Ludovic is "close behind him" (p. 301). Ludovic gradually gets stronger and more independent as the Commandos disintegrate. At one point he moves a truck "without waiting for an order" (p. 242). And at sea he remains lucid and as "strong as a horse" (p. 315) while the others are racked with delirium. At the end of the ordeal he carries Guy ashore and recovers after only two days in hospital. He receives a commission and a Military Medal for his efforts. Initially Claire's servant but soon a captain and then a major, Ludovic is the rank growth which flourishes in the decay of heroism and traditional values (in the open boat, he sits "godless at the helm" while the others pray for help). In setting out to sea with Ludovic, Guy gives expression to the death-wish which has motivated him from the beginning, and which he does not acknowledge until the end of *Unconditional Surrender*. Guy even prevents the sapper from shooting Ludovic, thereby making his own contribution to Ludovic's uncanny advance. We may conclude that Guy's escape from Crete is not altogether heroic, for he is motivated and saved by the embodiment of his own death-wish.

When Guy regains consciousness in hospital, he stays silent, for he does not wish to re-enter the ignoble "picture" he has left. Here again is the motif of withdrawal; now Guy very nearly becomes another Ivo.[19] Not until Julia Stitch speaks to him with her deceptively "clear voice" does Guy respond to the outside world. From Julia he learns of Claire's desertion and of Blackhouse's refusal to prosecute him. But despite his realization that "the man who had been his friend has proved to be an illusion" (p. 320), he still believes in justice. Disillusion finally arrives with the German invasion of Russia, soon to be followed by an unholy alliance between Britain and the Soviets. Waugh describes it as "a day of apocalypse for all the world for numberless generations" (p. 320). Guy's idealism has died hard: "Now that hallucination was dissolved, like the whales and turtles on the voyage from Crete, and he was back after less than two years' pilgrimage in a Holy Land of illusion in the old ambiguous world, where priests were spies and gallant friends proved traitors and his country was led blundering into dishonour" (p. 322). Compared with the Anglo-Russian alliance, Claire's treachery is a trifle, so Guy incinerates the evidence against him. The ignoble alliance marks his farewell to arms.

The crescendo of treachery rises with the impending return of the old-fashioned hero, Ritchie-Hook, who has "biffed" his way across Africa and has turned up in western Abyssinia, another "ancient asparagus bed" of theological controversy. Now Mrs. Stitch hears of his intended return, and of his habit of hounding and breaking those who "let him down" (p. 323). Because she thinks he will tell Ritchie-Hook of Claire's desertion, she has Guy shipped home by the slowest possible route. On the day of his departure Guy encloses the unknown soldier's identity-disc in an envelope and gives it to Mrs. Stitch to forward to GHQ. She, thinking the envelope contains documents which will incriminate Claire, fondly kisses Guy farewell and then discards the envelope, her eyes an "immense sea, full of flying galleys" (p. 327).[20] Her protection of Claire capriciously relegates the young soldier, and the honourable values he represents, to eternal oblivion. The episode crystallizes the message of the trilogy's first two novels, which is that innocence has no place in modern warfare: in his naiveté, Guy is unwittingly involved in destroying the values he has fought to defend. At last (to borrow a line from *Scott-King*), the war has "cast its heroic and chivalrous disguise and [has become] a sweaty tug-of-war between teams of indistinguishable louts."[21]

## CHAPTER 20

# *Unconditional Surrender*

After his return from Crete, Guy rejects a post with the Commandos and "soldiers on" for "two blank years" with the Halberdiers, sinking steadily into apathy. The war has defeated his expectations and has perverted his good intentions at every turn. The narrative resumes in August 1943 with his new brigadier's refusal to let Guy go abroad with the Halberdiers. This crucial disappointment finally ends Guy's love affair with the army, and sets the stage for his all-important realization that "personal honour alone remains."[1]

Waugh's activities during 1942–43 differ substantially from the fictional form he gives them in *Unconditional Surrender*. For Waugh, 1942 and 1943 were not entirely blank years. After returning from Crete he rejoined the Marines and went on a company commander's course near Edinburgh. Laycock requested his services and Waugh rejoined the Commando at Ardrossan, Scotland. Soon after, he was cross-appointed to the Royal Horse Guards. Once again he was "soldiering among friends,"[2] but he was losing Laycock's esteem. Later in 1942 Waugh took a course in photographic interpretation. He noted, "I get steadily worse as a soldier . . . but more patient and humble."[3] By March 1943 he began to suffer from "dreams of unendurable boredom" and soon after decided to go to London as Laycock's liaison officer at Combined Operations H.Q. If Scotland bored him, London exasperated him: "Restaurants crowded; one is jostled by polyglot strangers, starved, poisoned and cheated by the management; theatres at an early hour of the afternoon when it is unnatural and inconvenient to go; even so they are all crowded."[4] Then on 24 June two important events coincided: his father died and the Commandos left without him for North Africa and Operation "Husky." Waugh was enraged. Embittered at the army, he went in December for a course in parachuting at "a secret house near Ringway," and in January 1944 he sought and received leave to write *Brideshead Revisited*.

In "transforming" fact into fiction, Waugh alters several details. He makes Guy's appointment to HOO H.Q. follow his rejection by the Commandos and precede his father's death. Guy is not forced to resign, as Waugh was, and his failure to go abroad is explained as a lingering effect of Apthorpe's "jungle magic." The display of piety which surrounds the death and burial of Guy's father has no parallel in the diaries or letters, for Waugh's attitude towards Arthur Waugh differed markedly from that of Guy towards Mr. Crouchback. Instead of being merely "unfortunate," Mr. Crouchback's death is the occasion for a full-scale elegy on the passing of a way of life. Waugh tinkers further with fact by turning the "charming" commandant of the parachute school, "a songwriter in private life,"[5] into the lugubrious Ludovic. Moreover, he transfers to Ludovic aspects of his own experience, such as the keeping of a journal and the writing of a novel. And—a less felicitous touch, perhaps—he turns Randolph Churchill's decision to take him to Yugoslavia into the choice of an "Electronic Personnel Selector." Like Mrs. Stitch and the anonymous Major, like anti-espionage agent Grace-Groundling-Marchpole and "Loot" Padfield, the gadget is one more manifestation of the principle of chance which governs the contingent universe of war.

After the Operation "Husky" episode of 1943, Waugh's enthusiasm for the war turned sour. So it is that Guy Crouchback tells his father, "It doesn't seem to matter now who wins" (p. 8). But his father responds, "That sort of question isn't for soldiers." When Guy approves of the defeat of Italy because it means the end of the undignified and compromising Lateran Treaty, Mr. Crouchback writes that Guy is too devoted to appearances and has too little charity. He points out that while the Lateran Treaty may have caused the Church to lose face, it nevertheless helped it to go about its chief concern—the saving of individual souls: "When you spoke of the Lateran Treaty did you consider how many souls may have been reconciled and have died at peace as the result of it? How many children may have been brought up in the faith who might have lived in ignorance? Quantitative judgments don't apply. If only one soul was saved that is full compensation for any amount of loss of 'face'" (p. 10). Mr. Crouchback's pivotal remarks set the stage for the rest of *Unconditional Surrender*, which depicts Guy's retreat from the intractable world of "quantitative values" into the more manageable domain of personal and family relationships, and into the hierarchical world of qualitative values. Although Mr. Crouchback soon dies, his influence lingers on, and by painful stages Guy comes to emulate him.

The "state sword," costly gift of the people of Britain to their new comrades, the "steel-hearted people of Stalingrad," dominates the novel's opening pages.[6] An image of the ignoble expediency which now dictates

Britain's war policy, it stands on a table "counterfeiting an altar" right next to "the shrine of St. Edward the Confessor and the sacring place of the kings of England" (pp. 18, 19). This sword and Sir Roger's were in Waugh's plan from the outset and they provide a frame for the story. The state sword is both like and unlike Sir Roger's. Like his, the "sword of Stalingrad" is worshipped, though with "no formal act of veneration" (p. 35). And like his again, it will never strike the foe, for Stalin will not use it. But here the resemblance ends, for the new sword is merely cere-monial: "the escutcheon on the scabbard will be upside down when it is worn on a baldric" (p. 23). The reversed sword of Stalingrad perverts ev-erything that Sir Roger's sword represents, and epitomizes everything that is ignoble in the inverted world of quantitative values. The king, we are told, was inspired to create the decorative weapon after seeing Trim-mer's Commando dagger in a film of Operation "Popgun"; most of these Commando daggers were given away to prostitutes, and none was ever used in action except to stab a policeman (p. 48).

Guy refuses to pay homage to the sword, but Ludovic goes to see it because he plans to celebrate it in a literary competition. It reminds him of the sword which, as a youthful member of the Horse Guards, he held over the heads of a society bride and her wealthy groom on the day he met Sir Ralph Brompton.[7] Waugh points the parallel between the two swords by having Ludovic jump the queue to get in, just as Guy, four years before, had interrupted the stream of young penitents in the church at Santa Dulcina. In the twelfth century Sir Roger was thwarted in his desire to smite the enemy with his sword. In the twentieth century the people of England go a step further by giving away their sword, and with it, their honour. Swords belong to the past. Sir Ralph finds swords merely "picturesque"; and as Lady Perdita says, "That was a long time ago. Think of it; *swords*" (p. 41).

Through Sir Ralph, Ludovic, Everard Spruce, and the ubiquitous "Loot" Padfield, Waugh explores the nascent egalitarian world. Sir Ralph, apparently modelled on Harold Nicolson, is a former bourgeois dandy whose taste now runs to Communism. In days gone by he began a liaison with young Ludovic and taught him psychology and Marxist eco-nomics. Now that he is a diplomatic adviser to HOO H.Q., Sir Ralph is "a figure of obsolescent light comedy rather than of total war" (p. 27). He edits a journal devoted to Communist propaganda, and through him Waugh satirizes corruption in diplomatic circles. His Turkish cigarettes link him with other modern infidels like Ivor Claire and Ludovic. Ludo-vic is already familiar from *Officers and Gentlemen*, and in *Uncondi-tional Surrender* he receives the "explaining" Waugh felt he needed. A romantic in real life and now a classicist (he uses Roget and Fowler and polishes his *pensées* with care), Ludovic is guilt-ridden by his sinister activities on Crete. In Everard Spruce (almost certainly based on Cyril Connolly),[8] Waugh pokes fun at upper-class bohemians and the New Left; Spruce is another Roger Simmonds. Although he believes the human race is "destined to dissolve in chaos," Spruce does not find it hypocritical to edit a journal dedicated to the survival of values. His publication is pessimistic in tone and filled with pages of "squiggles": *Horizon*, obviously, in thin disguise. The reader first encounters Spruce in a typical pose, entertaining leftist literati with precious talk and noxious distillations; Ludovic, with his *pensées*, is his newest discovery. Padfield, for his part, represents American democracy, another form of egalitarianism.[9] He knows everything and everyone. A lawyer, he obtains the evidence used when Hector Troy divorces Virginia, and he is indirectly responsible for Virginia's renewed interest in Guy, for he tells her that Guy is to inherit £200,000. Spruce, Brompton, Ludovic, Padfield: all are symptomatic of the sterile and undifferentiated secular order, the bad taste and bad faith which are eclipsing the house of Crouchback.

When Mr. Crouchback dies, it seems that the old order has finally vanished. Waugh describes the funeral in elegiac tones, setting the scene with care. He describes the small, predominantly Catholic village of Broome, the parish church with its wall dividing the Anglican and Roman Catholic areas, and the chapel which Gervase and Hermione built back in the days when "the conversion of England seemed something more than a remote, pious aspiration" (p. 77). Opposite the Catholic Church stands the "Lesser House," which has fulfilled a variety of functions, its "older structure" now masked by a stucco façade and porch. Hundreds of condolences have been received and many mourners attend, some bearing names famous in the region since recusant times. The catafalque dressed, the dirge sung, the hatchment—inappropriately, Ivo's—displayed, the Requiem begins. It is a lament for the passing of Mr. Crouchback and of the values he embodied.[10] As the ceremony proceeds, Waugh contrasts Guy, who is "*fin de ligne*," with Box-Bender, into whose family the Crouchback line and legacy is to be diverted. Self-conscious and uncomfortably aware of the differences between "your" cardinals and "our" bishops, Box-Bender mouths clichés and scrupulously observes the outward forms. Guy on the other hand "followed the familiar rite with his thoughts full of his father." It is a poignant moment: Guy, in the bosom of his family and his faith, is to be superseded by an upstart.

But even as the fortunes of the house of Crouchback sink towards their nadir, Providence (which with a flair for the dramatic always delays, in

Waugh, until the last moment) asserts itself against chance to provide the beginning of the way back. Until now Guy's prayers have been mere acts of respect, apathetic offers to be of use in the unlikely event that God should need him. But as Guy prays, he now sees that God requires each man "to ask" before he may discover his true vocation, his "chance to do some small service which only he could perform, for which he had been created" (p. 81). Guy's prayer is Waugh's own, taken almost verbatim from his diaries (p. 722): "Show me what to do and help me to do it" (p. 81).

Guy does not have long to wait, for Virginia soon learns that she has conceived a child by Trimmer. It is that event, the least likely of all possible opportunities, that provides Guy with his first chance to serve others. When he agrees to marry Virginia so that Trimmer's child may have a father, Kerstie Kilbannock reproaches him: "You're being *chivalrous*—about *Virginia*. Can't you understand that men aren't chivalrous any more." But Guy replies:

> "Knights errant . . . used to go out looking for noble deeds. I don't think I've ever in my life done a single, positively unselfish action. I certainly haven't gone out of my way to find opportunities. Here was something most unwelcome, put into my hands; something which I believe the Americans describe as 'beyond the call of duty'; not the normal behaviour of an officer and a gentleman; something they'll laugh about in Bellamy's.
> "Of course Virginia is tough. She would have survived somehow. I shan't be changing her by what I'm doing. I know all that. But you see there's another—" he was going to say "soul"; then realized that this word would mean little to Kerstie for all her granite propriety—"there's another life to consider. What sort of life do you think her child would have, born unwanted in 1944?" (p. 193)

When Kerstie objects that it is not Guy's business, that "one child more or less" among the homeless millions of Europe will make no difference, Guy reponds: "It was made my business by being offered. . . . I can't do anything about all those others. This is just one case where I can help. And only I, really. I was Virginia's last resort" (p. 193).

In the face of the quantitative world's defeatism, Guy recalls his father's letter and asserts the value of the individual soul.[11] He accepts sacrifice and loses face in the eyes of the world in order to carry out the charitable act which he alone can perform. His act marks the end of his apathy. Now Guy is about to discover a vocation more suitable than that of modern crusader—a vocation to which he comes even closer when the interfering Sir Ralph Brompton sends him to Croatia.

In 1944 Waugh went to Croatia as a member of Fitzroy Maclean's 37th Military Mission to Tito's Partisans. His immediate superior there was Randolph Churchill. They crashed on their first attempt to land, and they were lucky to escape alive. After recuperating for two months in Italy, they tried again, successfully, and in September moved into mission headquarters in Topusko. Throughout his Yugoslavian assignment Waugh was very low-spirited. As a Catholic, he detested Communism, yet he was acting as liaison between the allies and Tito (who, he liked to maintain, was a lesbian). Randolph Churchill did not make things easier for him. According to Waugh's diary, Churchill was often "uproariously" and "paralytically" drunk, full of bluster, and garrulously quoted the sayings of his father and passages from Macaulay, Hilaire Belloc, and John Betjeman. In order to silence Churchill, Waugh and the Earl of Birkenhead each bet him £10 that he could not read the Bible from cover to cover. This only prompted Churchill to quote choice passages and to exclaim, "God, isn't God a shit." [12] Waugh found his companion a "flabby bully" and a "bore" with no self-control and no independence of character. [13] He observed, "His coughing and farting make him a poor companion in wet weather." [14] Yet Waugh noted, with uncharacteristic self-awareness, "the conclusion is always the same—that no one else would have chosen me, nor would anyone else have accepted him. We . . . must make what we can of it." [15] For his part, Churchill later wrote: "Waugh possesses both physical and moral courage in a very high degree. . . . His courage, coupled with his intellect, might have won him a distinguished military career. But he was usually more interested in driving his immediate superiors mad than in bringing about the defeat of the enemy." [16]

Guy does not go directly to Croatia but pauses at Bari for briefing. Here he meets the obnoxious Gilpin and the unknown Major who has often appeared at other crucial points in his career. The Major, who turns out to be the brother of Grace-Groundling-Marchpole, "secret bigwig" in London, heaps scorn on "romantic" Italy and destroys Guy's fond memories. The "Loot" is there too, of course, and so is a celebrated English composer who announces, "Crouchback has the death wish" (p. 219). The composer is right, and Guy confesses soon after to a priest that he wishes to die. His four years away from Italy have brought him nothing but frustration; like Sir Roger he has "never struck the infidel," and "in his heart he felt stirring the despair in which his brother, Ivo, had starved himself to death" (p. 217). Before Guy can triumph over his despair he must perceive that his desire to emulate Sir Roger is in fact a death-wish: in the modern world as in Sir Roger's day, knight-errantry issues in failure—not because it is bad, but because it is ineffective in a world so twisted by Fortune. Guy must abandon all notions of public honour and move farther along the road toward private compassion. The opportunity to do so presents itself in Yugoslavia with the arrival of a band of Jewish displaced persons.

Waugh mentions the Jews only fleetingly in his Yugoslavian diary, which, where it concerns compassionate matters, is primarily concerned with the welfare of Croatian Roman Catholics.[17] In fictionalizing his Croatian adventures, Waugh omits any reference to Catholics and writes instead about the Jews. He delineates them in terms far more moving than those he used in the diary: they are dressed in rags but retain their dignity and bourgeois civility; they have been bundled from camp to camp by one oppressor after another and now they think they see their salvation in the British. Guy commits himself to their welfare: "he felt compassion; something less than he had felt for Virginia and her child but a similar sense that here again, in a world of hate and waste, he was being offered the chance of doing a single small act to redeem the times" (p. 248). He sends two Jewish representatives to Bari and arranges to have the others follow: "It seemed to Guy . . . that he was playing an ancient, historic role as he went . . . to inform the Jews of their approaching exodus. He was Moses leading a people out of captivity" (p. 293). Guy is a refugee too. In the past he has sought refuges which have proved to be spiritual prisons; now, in selflessly freeing others, he frees himself from the paralysis which has severed him from his fellow men. On three occasions fog prevents the departure of the Jews, and they must wait for spring. Guy leaves in mid-winter, but before doing so he visits Mme Kanyi and promises to continue to help the Jews.

Woven into the strands of the Kanyi story is another: the death of Ritchie-Hook. Guy's old hero has appeared seldom after the "thunderbox" episode, but now the *enfant terrible* of World War I steps back into the narrative, sadly changed. "Grey-faced, stiff," with a lustreless eye, Ritchie-Hook now looks like a ghost (p. 271). He is to "play second fiddle as an observer" in a staged assault on a blockhouse, formerly a Christian fort. In a last demonstration of foolhardy heroics the revitalized old soldier (in disguise once again) advances to his death, deserted by the cowardly partisans but accompanied by a photographer. The passing of Ritchie-Hook marks the demise of the Truslove style of heroism, a heroism which, Waugh intimates, is glorious but immature, and in the end lethal. Ritchie-Hook personifies the death-wish at the heart of romanticism. As his servant says, "More than once he's said to me right out:

'Dawkins, I wish those bastards would shoot better. I don't want to go home.' One thing for him; different for me that's got a wife and kids and was twenty years younger" (p. 289). Ritchie-Hook's immaturity is prefigured by Waugh's description of his original: "Our brigadier St. Clair Morford looks like something escaped from Sing-Sing & talks like a schoolboy in the lower fourth."[18] When Guy visits Mme Kanyi soon after the brigadier's death, she provides an important gloss on Ritchie-Hook's example:

> "Is there any place that is free from evil? It is too simple to say that only the Nazis wanted war. These communists wanted it too. It was the only way in which they could come to power. Many of my people wanted it, to be revenged on the Germans, to hasten the creation of the national state. It seems to me there was a will to war, a death wish, everywhere. Even good men thought their private honour would be satisfied by war. They could assert their manhood by killing and being killed. They would accept hardships in recompense for having been selfish and lazy. Danger justified privilege. I knew Italians—not very many perhaps—who felt this. Were there none in England?"
> "God forgive me," said Guy. "I was one of them." (p. 300)

After his tour of duty in Dubrovnik, Guy returns at last to Italy and seeks the Kanyis, much to the surprise of military officials who fail to see how two refugees more or less can make any difference. Soon he learns the grisly truth: although all the other Jews have reached Italy, the Kanyis have been executed, the husband charged with sabotaging the electric light plant and his wife accused of being the mistress of a British agent— in other words, of Guy himself. Once again Guy's good intentions have been thwarted and perverted, and he returns to England in gloom. But while Guy's act is partially frustrated, it is by no means fruitless. In "Compassion," the 1949 short story on which the Kanyi episode is based, Major Gordon is also appalled at the distortion of his good intentions. He talks about it with his chaplain:

> "A fat lot of good it did the Kanyis."
> "No. But don't you think it just possible that *they* did you good? No suffering need ever be wasted. It is just as much part of Charity to receive cheerfully as to give."
> ". . . I'd like you to tell me a bit more about that," said Major Gordon.[19]

Waugh omits the passage from *Unconditional Surrender*, but we may be confident that, like Major Gordon, Guy has profited from his compassionate action.

Guy does not return to the Castello after the war. Instead, he sells it to Ludovic, who goes to live there with Padfield. All along, as we have already noticed, an obscure reciprocal relationship has existed between Ludovic and Guy.[20] In *Officers and Gentlemen* Ludovic flourishes as Guy grows weaker, and at the end, strong as a horse, he carries the unconscious Guy ashore. Guy's frailty stems from his romanticism; consequently it is no surprise to find that Ludovic's new power is associated with classical restraint. In *Unconditional Surrender* Waugh depicts him "curtailing, expanding, polishing" his journals, "often consulting Fowler, not disdaining Roget; writing and re-writing in his small clerkly hand" (p. 41). But as Guy gradually becomes more realistic, Ludovic undergoes a curious change: he assumes a more romantic frame of mind—assumes, in fact, both Guy's romanticism and his lush Italian retreat. While Guy painfully achieves true freedom through self-abnegation, Ludovic's self-indulgence leads him into the lush prison that Guy has escaped.

Ludovic's "last two years had been as uneventful as Guy's," says Waugh (p. 40), pointing obliquely to the parallel between the two characters. Ludovic believes, wrongly, that Guy knows the truth about Hound and the murdered sapper captain. After fleeing in horror from Guy at Spruce's soirée, he is appalled to learn that Guy is to be a student at his parachute-training school in remotest Essex. Ludovic avoids an encounter by remaining upstairs during Guy's stay, a tactic which stimulates de Souza to fantastic speculations about international politics and unnatural vice. When Guy parachutes to earth, he experiences an ecstatic sense of liberation; but this false freedom is short-lived and leads to his virtual imprisonment in hospital with an injured knee.[21] In his absence Ludovic or "Major Dracula" descends "like the angel of death" to "eat graceless" with the eleven remaining men. Ludovic's funereal manner provokes concern for his sanity. So does his purchase of a dog which he names "Fido" and addresses in baby-talk. In the hope of killing Guy, he recommends that he be sent into action even though his training is incomplete.

Now, it seems, chance intervenes to frustrate chance—or is it Providence intervening in the guise of chance? In any event, Colonel Grace-Groundling-Marchpole thwarts Ludovic's machinations, rejecting for security reasons the plan to send Guy to Italy. Fact here undergoes a curious Waughian transformation. In real life Waugh failed to reach Italy because of his own unpopularity; in contrast, his persona's fate is dictated by external forces like the sinister Ludovic and the dotty Marchpole. Despite Waugh's repeated pronouncements about accepting responsibility for one's own sins, he was human enough to disown it when he transmuted fact into fiction.

Ludovic fades from the narrative as Waugh turns his attention to Guy's convalescence, his reconciliation with Virginia, and his increasingly more charitable behaviour. By the time Ludovic reappears he too is dramatically altered. Instead of filing and polishing his aphorisms with the help of Fowler and Roget, he now writes effusively and without discrimination: "His manner of composition was quite changed. . . . He never paused; he never revised. He barely applied his mind to his task. He was possessed, the mere amanuensis of some power. . . . His book grew as little Trimmer grew in Virginia's womb without her conscious collaboration" (pp. 206–7). But books—good ones—seldom grow like babes in the womb. They are consciously and arduously crafted. Ludovic's lack of taste and precision is an indication of his moral decay; as early as 1934 Waugh ridiculed "the bluff about inspiration" and expressed his preference for the regular habits of Trollope over "the romantic legend of inspired genius" as embodied by the "wicked artists" Rossetti and Swinburne.[22] In letters to Nancy Mitford in 1951 he stressed that revision must be done *"con amore"* and that he was abandoning the experiment of writing without revising.[23] Ludovic adopts the method which Waugh gives up.

Ludovic's rapid method of composition, his Scottish typist,[24] and his completion date (June 1944) all suggest that his novel, *The Death Wish*, is an allusion to *Brideshead Revisited*. *Brideshead* is Waugh's single, uncharacteristic excursion into romanticism; similarly, *The Death Wish* is a lush book, unlike anything Ludovic has written before, "a very gorgeous, almost gaudy, tale of romance and high drama set . . . in the diplomatic society of the previous decade" (p. 242). Just as *Brideshead* culminates in the ceremonial passing of Lord Marchmain, so Ludovic's "whole book had been the preparation for Lady Marmaduke's death." Moreover, since "the heroine was the author," *The Death Wish* is Ludovic's ritualistic account of his own death—a framework familiar in Waugh's own novels.

Waugh does not spell out the relationship between Guy and Ludovic; nevertheless we may conclude that Ludovic is an externalization of the evil in Guy. Since evil is perverted good, Ludovic has no independent existence and must decline when Guy ceases to be evil—that is, when he abandons his romantic illusions and his death-wish. In *A Handful of Dust* Tony Last succumbs to Mr. Todd because he fails to take responsibility for the failure of his marriage and the death of his son. In *Unconditional Surrender* Guy outdistances Ludovic because he confesses to Mme Kanyi that he was one of the men whose misguided desire for manly combat caused the war. Guy is freed when he acknowledges his share in the

universal death wish; death-loving Ludovic vanishes to lush Santa Dulcina while Guy, loving life, remarries and dwells at Broome.

The Epilogue shows the gross, tasteless world of quantitative values
triumphant: "monstrous constructions" of steel and concrete litter the
South Bank, heralding the dismal rise of postwar British architecture;
"ill-conditioned young people" in soft shirts and hired evening dress attend Box-Bender's daughter's débutante ball and drink "the cheapest
fizzy wine in the market." Box-Bender has lost his seat in Parliament,
while Gilpin, a socialist, has been elected. Air Marshal Beech, a coward,
has penned a book of memoirs and Ivor Claire, another coward, has received a DSO. Guy no longer hopes to stem the rising tide of mediocrity.
Instead, he withdraws from it—from the Castello, from Eldoret, from
London—to the Lesser House at Broome, the home of his ancestors. In
so doing he at last finds the "place" he had vainly sought in war. Guy's
is neither the withdrawal of Ludovic, into romantic isolation, nor that
of Ivo, into madness and death, nor that of Tony Box-Bender who,
by becoming a monk, completes the collapse of his father's dynastic
pretensions.

By choosing the Lesser House over the Castello, Guy elects mundane
reality over romance, charity over heroism, maturity over adolescence,
and the brotherhood of family and faith over that of the Round Table.
He values the ideal of the paterfamilias over that of the knight errant, for
in an age when crusades are futile, the gentle Mr. Crouchback presents a
saner example than Sir Roger. The family circle provides a *true* refuge
from the bewildering multifariousness of the drab modern world. Guy's
retirement into his West Country fastness recalls a remark Waugh made
in 1949: "I believe that we are returning to a stage when on the supernatural plane only heroic prayer can save us and, when on the natural plane,
the cloister offers a saner and more civilized life than 'the world'." [25] But
the "cloister" of Broome is not a final end in itself. Guy's withdrawal does
not constitute a permanent rejection of the world, like the retreats of Paul
Pennyfeather and, say, Candide. Waugh almost certainly sees it as a period of recuperation which forms the basis for future action: from its
stronghold in the west, the house of Crouchback, so nearly extinguished
by its digression into error, will rise again.

The new beginning of the house of Crouchback, or (if the reader wishes
to accept the parallel Waugh probably had in mind) the Household of the
the Faith in England, is embodied in little Trimmer. At first glance the
adopted infant heir might seem to represent the end of the line of
Crouchback and its supersession by coarser modern values. It might
seem, too, that when Guy remarries Virginia to provide a father for her
child, he flies in the face of his own father's "massive and singular" family

pride. But Waugh forestalls this objection in *Men at Arms*, where Mr. Crouchback's family pride is "a schoolboy hobby compared with his religious faith" (p. 36). Dynastic considerations go by the board where matters of faith are concerned, and when Guy remarries Virginia, only his religion motivates him. Had Mr. Crouchback known about little Trimmer, he would have endorsed Guy's decision to remarry:[26] like the self-effacing behaviour of the Church in the matter of the Lateran Treaty, Guy's act is a "loss of face" which results in the salvation of a soul. His charity is costly in material terms: in order to rescue little Trimmer, Guy makes him heir to the Crouchback name and fortune. He bestows the impeccable genealogy of the Crouchbacks on the illegitimate offspring of obscure outsiders, and he marries a woman he no longer loves.

But here inscrutable Providence intervenes to make the consequences of Guy's selfless action bear fruit. "There's a special providence" in the fall of the bomb that kills Virginia (p. 261); now freed at last from his damaging marriage, Guy eventually weds Domenica Plessington and establishes a stable new household at Broome. In his affirmative new context, which is now God-centred rather than man-centred, little Trimmer takes on a positive significance: rather than representing the end of the Crouchback dynasty, he becomes its means of perpetuation. Seen in one light, little Trimmer's gestation parallels the monstrous growth of Ludovic's tasteless book; seen in a better light, it parallels the birth of Guy's charity—indeed, the birth of Guy himself as a complete human being.[27]

Like the Household of the Faith, the Crouchback household becomes an adoptive institution: there is a need for converts in both. Just as little Trimmer's new blood perpetuates the name of Crouchback, so new vigour constantly floods into the Church from unexpected quarters. As Waugh remarked in "The American Epoch in the Catholic Church,"

> Again and again Christianity seems dying at its center. Always Providence has another people quietly maturing to relieve the decadent of their burden. . . . No loss is impossible, no loss irretrievable, no loss—not Rome itself—mortal. It may well be that Catholics of today, in their own lifetime, may have to make enormous adjustments in their conception of the temporal nature of the Church. Many indeed are already doing so, and in the process turning their regard with hope and curiosity to the New World, where, it seems, Providence is schooling and strengthening a people for the heroic destiny long borne by Europe.[28]

It may amuse American Catholics to find themselves described as unlikely sources of renewal, the Trimmer's children of Church history, but the point stands. Providence finds good in unlikely sources, and no mortal can foretell what obscure race might harbour new light. All manner of misfortune befalls Guy Crouchback—divorce, delusion, frustrated love, the perversion of his good intentions—but through it all, Providence quietly works to turn his death-wish into new life. Waugh's trilogy does not appear to be exceptionally well structured and the reader might say of it what Spruce says of Ludovic's *pensées*: "The plan is not immediately apparent" (p. 57). But there is a plan. Even when Guy finds himself most victimized by its secular parodies (like Grace-Groundling-Marchpole and his web of espionage), he is most under the protection of divine Providence, which constitutes a justice larger than the one he has mistakenly tried to serve. Robertson Davies says that the War Trilogy is "a book of hopelessness" written by a man who had "outlived his soul."[29] But the trilogy's conclusion is by no means hopeless: temporarily misled by Guy's immature love of utopian seclusion, the house of Crouchback will rise again, on firmer foundations than before.

Despite Guy's afflictions Providence produces an heir at the eleventh hour—and from the one acceptable womb. Little Trimmer is the child of Virginia's bad faith and Trimmer's bad taste, but he will be the sole means of restoring the house of Crouchback and, figuratively, the Household of the Faith in England. In the first edition Waugh weakened his point somewhat by allowing Guy and Domenica to have two boys of their own. He rectified his error in the second edition by making little Trimmer their only child, thereby strengthening the implication that only through new blood can the Crouchbacks perpetuate their name and values.[30]

With his revitalizing powers, little Trimmer, offspring of aristocrat and plebeian, performs a synthesizing role reminiscent of other important fictional children. Leonard Bast's child in *Howards End* is a case in point; yet despite Waugh's admiration for Forster's novel, there is a fundamental difference, since the child of Leonard and Helen represents a future quite unlike anything which has gone before. A better analogy—indeed, perhaps even a source—is little Chrissie Tietjens in Ford Madox Ford's *Parade's End*, for Chrissie represents a future which is really a return to the past. Certain similarities suggest that Waugh knew *Parade's End* and, unconsciously perhaps, echoed it in his own World War II trilogy.[31]

The continuance of Guy's family and faith by means of an outsider is anticipated by Mr. Goodall's story in *Men at Arms*.[32] As we have already noticed, Mr. Goodall tells Guy about "an historic Catholic family" whose "last heir" married a wife who proved to be unfaithful. "They had two daughters and then the wretched girl eloped with a neighbour," whom she married. As a result, her first husband was left with no male heir, but ten years later he met his former wife again, and there was a "rapprochement." Then "she went back to her so-called husband and in due time bore a son." Although the child was "in fact" the divorced husband's it was "by law the so-called husband's, who recognized it as his." Mr. Goodall concludes, "And so under another and quite uninteresting name a great family has been preserved."

To Mr. Goodall, a genealogist, the perpetuation of a noble family is more interesting than the continuance of its faith. Mr. Goodall's view is antithetical to Mr. Crouchback's, and for that reason the reader must be wary of it. If good can sometimes masquerade as evil, evil can sometimes appear in the guise of good, and it does so in Mr. Goodall's story, which foreshadows, *in reverse*, what eventually happens to Guy. Its immediate effect is to inspire Guy to go to London and attempt a travesty of what Providence has prepared for him. If Apthorpe had not telephoned when he did, Guy might well have provided Hector Troy with an heir, and had he done so, he would have debased his own blood in the service of Troy's materialism and would have fallen into the position of Trimmer in a grotesque parody of the role prepared for him. Happily for Guy, Providence, in the unlikely person of Apthorpe, prevents such a gross perversion of its aims.[33]

Readers of the trilogy and *Brideshead Revisited* will remark similar family configurations in both works. In *Brideshead* Lady Marchmain is the daughter of an old Catholic family, and her husband is a former Anglican, whose new faith soon lapses. Her three craggy-faced brothers have been killed in World War I, and the novel shows how Charles Ryder, an outsider, perpetuates their values by becoming the Marchmain's spiritual son. None of Lady Marchmain's children begets an heir, so the family name dies out; only their faith survives in Charles Ryder. The trilogy improves upon this only partly satisfactory state of affairs. In the later work Waugh explores a similar situation, but from a different point of view. Instead of posting the reader in the consciousness of an outsider, Waugh places him right within the dying family of the faith, which once again comprises three brothers and a sister who has married out of the faith. This time Waugh is less interested in the female line (Lady Marchmain/Angela Box-Bender), so he leaves one of the three brothers (Guy) alive but verging on spiritual death, and focuses on him. In both works spiritual kinship outweighs blood ties (as it does in *Howards End, Ulysses, Lady Chatterley's Lover, The Great Gatsby,* and Faulkner's "The Bear," to give a few obvious examples), but the conclusion of the trilogy is much more affirmative than that of *Brideshead*. This time the newcomer to the faith, little Trimmer, plays a fuller and more satisfying symbolic role than Charles Ryder does. Rather than achieving spiritual succession, through conversion, to a decaying family whose name vanishes, he is born into a distinguished family and inherits both its faith and its name. And in contrast to "homeless, childless, middle-aged, loveless" Ryder, little Trimmer presumably will beget heirs to continue the Crouchbacks' name. A child will lead them out of a father's prison of error. In *Brideshead* Waugh leaves the reader with the painful image of Ryder, whose salvation is purchased at the cost of great unhappiness. But in the trilogy Waugh leaves Guy fulfilled and little Trimmer potent with promise; furthermore, he shifts the reader's interest toward the future resurgence of the Crouchback family and away from the small joys and griefs of its individual members. Apart from *Put Out More Flags* and *Helena*, it is the closest Waugh permitted himself to come to a happy ending.

The unsullied succession of the truth from generation to generation is one of Waugh's central themes, and in the War Trilogy he gives it final expression. It is evident, too, that Waugh thought his own personal religious history resembled the adoptive process by which the Church survives. In *Brideshead Revisited* his persona is an outsider newly admitted to the faith. By the time of the War Trilogy his persona has grown into an established Church member who ensures his own salvation by admitting others. Moved by the chance arrival of little Trimmer (which, depending upon one's attitude, is also the providential arrival of little Gervase), Guy rejects the immature world of Fortune where he is dogged by shadows; now he liberates others from their imprisoning false refuges by letting them "come inside" the true refuge of the Church. Guy makes an "unconditional surrender" by accepting important changes to the surface, but not to the substance, of his faith. As representatives of the Catholic Church in England, the Crouchbacks fight a battle "that can never be lost and may never be won until the Last Trump." [34] Whenever danger threatens, Providence ensures survival through a return to the well-head, the Mystical Body sustaining itself through rejuvenation of the Visible Body.

At the end of *Unconditional Surrender* Waugh's persona seems resigned, composed, almost happy in "defeat." But how accurately does Guy Crouchback reflect Waugh himself in his rural seat in deepest Somerset? Is the portrait realistic or is it, perhaps, only an ideal state which Waugh never achieved? And—a related question—is it significant that the withdrawal Guy achieves is that of the retired army captain and country gentleman rather than that of the artist? For answers to these and other questions we must turn to *The Ordeal of Gilbert Pinfold*.

## CHAPTER 21

# *The Ordeal of Gilbert Pinfold*

"The book is too personal for me to be able to judge it," Waugh confided to his diary.[1] But he made no secret of the fact that *The Ordeal of Gilbert Pinfold* was firmly rooted in his own experience. He talked freely to friends and even to interviewers about his brief spell of madness in 1954, proudly calling it "my late lunacy."[2] He admitted to Nancy Mitford that he had suffered "a sharp but brief attack of insanity"[3] and jauntily informed Lady Dorothy Lygon that he had "lost [his] reason in February but got some of it back in March."[4] After seeing *King Lear* he wrote, revealingly, to Ann Fleming, "Lear's sufferings seemed no sharper than mine."[5] To Robert Henriques he wrote, "Mr. Pinfold's experiences were almost exactly my own. In turning them into a novel I had to summarize them. I heard 'voices' such as I describe almost continuously night and day for three weeks. They were tediously repetitive and sometimes obscene and blasphemous. I have given the gist of them. . . . My voices ceased as soon as I was intellectually convinced they were imaginary."[6] Although Margaret Morriss has provocatively argued that Mr. Pinfold may be in part a satire on Waugh's public reputation,[7] I think there can be little doubt that Waugh was striving in complete sincerity to give an accurate and complete self-portrait. As he wrote in a prefatory note for the American first edition, "Mr. Waugh does not deny that Mr. Pinfold is a portrait of himself. Subsidiary characters are fictitious."

Waugh's hallucinations had been incubating for many years. In the Thirties he liked a house in Ireland because there were "no conspiracies" there.[8] As early as 1944 he was writing to Laura about the clarity of his "nut";[9] in 1949 he wrote to Nancy Mitford, "I am jolly near being mad and need very careful treatment if I am to survive another decade without the strait straight? jacket."[10] In the long and often hilarious correspondence with A. D. Peters over the cigars the latter was obtaining for him, he betrays a disproportionate sense of persecution: "Is it fanciful to think that Matson [his American agent, who was sending the cigars] may be acting with malice as well as with sloth?"[11] In September 1953 he wrote to John Betjeman, "I remember everything wrong these days so I thought now I have lost my reason. . . . My memory is not at all hazy—just sharp, detailed and dead wrong. This affliction leads me into countless humiliations."[12] Even after he ceased to have hallucinations, he continued to complain to Peters about intercepted letters and the possibility that British customs agents were stealing his "CIGARS."[13] He told Peters that he would complete *Ronald Knox* by 1958 "if I keep my reason" and apologized to Margaret Stephens for wrongly addressing her "by a Pinfoldian aberration."[14] In 1958 he bitterly wrote to Peters, "I like to keep track of the extent to which my powers are failing," having earlier announced that he would avoid "hack-work" and write a novel "while I have inventive strength left."[15] In 1960 he refused to promise two books a year to Little, Brown because that would make him feel "claustrophobic and Pinfoldian."[16]

Driven, as always, to turn experience into art, Waugh announced to Peters in 1955, "I have fully formed in my mind an account of my late lunacy this time last year."[17] He believed it would be popular, "as 42% of the country's population, I read, fall into the hands of alienists at one time or another."[18] The first draft was more revealing than the final one, and was destroyed at Waugh's own request because he feared that it might damage his chances of winning the bitter court battle he was then waging against Nancy Spain: "Please destroy any copies you hold of the first draft. . . . In view of my forthcoming reappearance in the courts I have to be careful what I publish. It is therefore important that no version of *Pinfold* appear anywhere with the injudicious statements I have here corrected."[19]

Gilbert Pinfold is a novelist with a large family who leads a "strictly private"[20] life in the West Country. An "idiosyncratic" Tory, he has never voted in a parliamentary election; he is a pessimist of antique tastes, intolerant and easily annoyed. In matters of religion he burrows "ever deeper into the rock" of the catacombs while the leaders of his church seek the forum. Only a "tiny kindling of charity" reaches him from his religion, muting his disgust with the world into mere boredom. His most valued possession is his privacy, and in order to protect it, he assumes "a character of burlesque" which eventually dominates "his whole outward personality." Although Pinfold is neither a scholar nor a regular soldier, the mask he chooses is "a combination of eccentric don and testy colonel"; Pinfold assumes it whenever he ceases to be alone, for the presence of other people makes him feel defensive. His memory is beginning to fail him. Time passes very slowly, and at night he has boring dreams of doing

*The Times* crossword puzzle or of reading a tedious book to his family. Words revolve in his head, driving him from his bed to make minute corrections to his manuscript. He is troubled by rheumatism and is an insomniac; he finds his nightly chloral and bromide more palatable in *crème de menthe*. He is a man of refined tastes who has retired from the world. He has not, however, lost his sting.

*The Ordeal of Gilbert Pinfold* is the story of a civilized and pious man's brief exposure to savagery. In his youth Waugh had travelled to remote places and "gadded among savages." Now, at "the notoriously dangerous age" of fifty (as he said to Stephen Black, the original of Mr. Angel, the sinister BBC interviewer),[21] he explores the barbarism within his own mind. Most of the action takes place on board the *Caliban*, where Pinfold expects privacy and silence but finds noisy music and menacing voices. Waugh skilfully orchestrates the crescendo of annoyances which afflict Pinfold. With the insight born of personal experience,[22] he shows how Pinfold's paranoia makes him invent intricate theories whereby he may attribute his imagined persecution to external causes. When he hears jazz music nearby, he attributes it to his neighbour; overhearing an evangelical church meeting, he decides that the sound is coming to him through a concealed amplifier on the ship's deck. When the "voices" start, he blames them on a faulty communications system running through his cabin: because of the movement of frayed wires, the mechanism conveys conversations from all parts of the ship. Soon, as the voices begin to assail his personal reputation, Pinfold conceives the idea that the BBC is hooked up to the hypothetical communications system, and that Captain Steerforth, who smiles like Hamlet's uncle, is responsible for the harassment. Abusive voices named Goneril and Angel accuse him of being a decadent writer, a usurer, a homosexual, an insincere and social-climbing Catholic, a fascist, a communist, an income-tax evader. Another voice, belonging to a species of good angel named Margaret, falls in love with him.[23] As the attacks increase in virulence, Pinfold concludes that Mr. Angel, the BBC interviewer from Lychpole, is on board continuing his interrogation. He thinks that the interviewer is using a sophisticated form of "the Box," a device used in the country to cure assorted maladies and now, Pinfold believes, perfected by the Germans, the Russians, and "the existentialists in Paris" (p. 158). At first Pinfold refuses to believe that he can be wrong. Is there no Spanish cruiser waiting to take him on board? Then the "international incident" is a hoax by "the hooligans." Has Margaret not come to his bed? Then she has been offended because he fell asleep. Pinfold's overheated mind works hard on the wrong premises, as if he were inside "an ingenious, old-fashioned detective novel" (p. 147). He divides his fellow passengers into friends and foes; he assembles "the intricate pieces of a plot," following "false clues" to "absurd conclusions" (p. 157). He hears voices coming from "quite near him" and he marvels that the Angels can read his mind. But he is not prepared to admit that he himself is the source of the voices until Mrs. Pinfold proves to him that Angel has been in England all the time. Father Westmacott denies that "the existentialists or psychologists" have a secret invention, and Dr. Drake traces the whole problem to Pinfold's medication. Only then does Pinfold realize that the anarchy he has attributed to the outside world has emanated from within.[24] But he silently rejects poisoning as the cause. Enigmatically he observes, "He knew, and the others did not know—not even his wife, least of all his medical adviser— that he had endured a great ordeal, and unaided, had emerged the victor. There was a triumph to be celebrated, even if a mocking slave stood always beside him in his chariot reminding him of mortality" (pp. 183–84).

Pinfold's bizarre adventure is an expedition into the bestial regions of his own mind. His very name and residence provide clues about the direction of his journey, for a pinfold is an enclosure for animals, and a lych (O.E. lich) is a body or corpse.[25] As his body deteriorates under the influence of drugs and drink, and as his spelling becomes more "wildly barbaric" (p. 23), Pinfold decides that he must escape the steely English winter. As chance would have it (since he chooses at random), he sails in a ship named after Shakespeare's "savage and deformed slave," Caliban, skippered by a man bearing the name of Dickens's villainous Steerforth. The Caliban[26] appears to be "a very decent sort of ship" (p. 36), but it is not: there are no private baths or private dining facilities, there is no chaplain, and the ventilator makes an annoying "insect-hum." It is a place, first of all, of barbaric taste. Among the first things that Pinfold "hears" are the strains of a jazz band and the "beastly" rhythms of the "Pocuputa Indian dance," used by the Gestapo to drive their prisoners mad. Mr. Pinfold's own good taste suffers. When he comes on board, he orders a brandy, disregarding the steward's question about trademark and demanding only a "large one"; later when ordering champagne he asks simply for half a bottle: "Don't worry about the name" (pp. 31, 42).

The Caliban is also a place of barbaric faith. Mr. Pinfold overhears an evangelical religious meeting conducted by a "pseudo-priest." A little later he overhears a nurse saying the rosary and murmuring the Angelic Salutation for an injured lascar. But Mr. Pinfold's own good faith is infected; he has been uncharitable to his mother; he has missed Mass the Sunday before embarking and it is not until he reaches Colombo that he attends again. He has tumbled "prayerless" into bed on his first evening aboard, and soon he gives up "any attempt at saying his prayers" because "the familiar, hallowed words provoked a storm of blasphemous parody from Goneril" (p. 154).

A prison of bad taste and bad faith, the *Caliban* forms the setting for a dreadful confrontation in Pinfold's mind. Just as "hag-born" Caliban, "got by the Devil himself," tries to overthrow Prospero, who has imprisoned him on Setebos, so Pinfold's animal impulses try to usurp his higher faculties. Goneril tries to overturn the right order of things in order to reduce Lear-like Pinfold to the condition of a Caliban. So relentless is the assault that Pinfold verges on entering "a beastly state"; he is on a "beastly ship" and is the victim of a "beastly joke." At the centre of all this beastliness stands the ironically named Angel. Under his direction Steerforth takes revenge on a mutinous sailor by shipping him off to a "Hell-spot" of a hospital; Goneril tortures a prisoner with "horrific, ecstatic, orgiastic cries" (p. 63); and gentle Margaret's bluff old father urges her into Pinfold's bed: "I'd like dearly to be the one myself to teach you, but you've made your own choice and who's to grudge it you?" (p. 132). Margaret's father, whom Waugh later said he based on Lady Chatterley's father,[27] is typical of the grossness that pervades the *Caliban*.

Pinfold leaves the *Caliban* at Port Said and experiences an ecstatic sense of liberation, feeling himself "the sole inhabitant of a private, delicious universe" (p. 165). But as we have seen, Mr. Pinfold's taste for a private universe is the root of his problem, and within hours the voices return to pursue him across Arabia and India to Ceylon. Pinfold decides to go home only when his frantic wife cables that she is flying to join him. He goes to Mass, then he boards a plane and, still pursued by Angel and the voices, flies back across the Moslem world: "It was when they reached Christendom that Angel changed his tune" (p. 174). Angel now promises never to bother Pinfold again on the condition that his "experiments" are kept secret. It is a tempting offer—but Pinfold rejects it, and the voices dwindle and vanish. Angel has tried to imprison Pinfold but, aided by Christian discipline (he has been to church for the first time in weeks), Pinfold turns the tables on him. Upon his return, Pinfold's wife, physician, and priest explain Angel away as an hallucination. But Pinfold silently disagrees, for he knows that Angel is the centre of his animal nature. He is the Prince of Darkness himself, a force that can be withstood but not ignored.

Pinfold does not dismiss the bad Angels as fragments of a drug-disordered imagination. He has learned that the evils of the outside world have their counterparts within, and that no amount of privacy can fence them out. When Pinfold sits down to commit his "fresh, rich experience" to paper, he acknowledges inward evil and takes responsibility for it. He has had a narrow escape, far narrower than that of Basil Seal from Azania or

Dennis Barlow from the moral jungle of California. He defeats evil by accepting its existence within him and then refusing to have commerce with it. It is what Tony Last could not do when he fell prey to Mr. Todd.

Despite Pinfold's scorn for psychiatrists, Waugh did have contact with Dr. Eric Strauss, whom Father Philip Caraman summoned to the Hyde Park Hotel on the evening Waugh returned to England. According to Sykes, Waugh "said he was being tormented by devils" and wanted Caraman to exorcise them. But Caraman insisted on calling Strauss, who was able to stop the voices by changing Waugh's sleeping draught. When Waugh returned to Strauss for a friendly visit, Strauss "suggested to Evelyn that he should write an account of his hallucinations. . . . Eric's suggestion was the origin of *Pinfold*." [28] Despite the fact that a psychiatrist had cured him and a specialist had ruled that the "recent hallucinations of hearing were due to bromide poisoning," Waugh preferred to believe that he had been the victim of diabolic possession. [29]

In a penetrating article entitled "What Was Wrong with Pinfold," J. B. Priestley accuses Waugh's protagonist of "what we may call Pinfolding— the artist elaborately pretending not to be an artist." [30] Priestley claims that Pinfold's madness has sprung from the tension between his pose as a gentleman and his real calling as an artist:

> What is on trial here is the Pinfold *persona*. This *persona* is inadequate. . . . [Pinfold] is not a Catholic landed gentleman pretending to be an author. He is an author pretending to be a Catholic landed gentleman. But why, you may ask, should he not be both? Because they are not compatible. And this is not merely my opinion. It is really Pinfold's opinion too.
>
> Let Pinfold take warning. He will break down again, and next time may never find a way back to his study. The central self he is trying to deny, that self which grew up among books and authors and not among partridges and hunters, that self which even now seeks expression in ideas and words, will crack if it is walled up again within a false style of life. . . . Pinfold must step out of his role as the Cotswold gentleman quietly regretting the Reform Bill of 1832, and . . . discover an accepted role as an English man of letters.

Priestley's observations are astute, for Waugh often spoke disparagingly of his vocation as a writer, noting on one occasion that he had been "reduced to the family trade of writing" and on another that there was "a chance" of escaping it. [31] But regardless of whose diagnosis we accept— Priestley's, Strauss's, Dr. Drake's, or Waugh's own—the result of his decision to write about his affliction remains a remarkable novel, brilliant at the outset, uneven in its account of "the voices," but in the final analysis the most revealing book he ever wrote. It is a powerful and frightening work which in 1977 formed the basis of a highly acclaimed stage adaptation starring Michael Hordern.

Although Waugh closely resembles Pinfold, he undoubtedly wished that he could have been more like Guy Crouchback, whose life at Broome seems to promise modest happiness. One may conjecture that some lesson drawn from Pinfold's too uncharitable pursuit of privacy—and even, perhaps, from his boredom with his vocation—eventually helped give *Unconditional Surrender* the affirmative qualities implicit in little Gervase and his charitable foster father.

## CHAPTER 22

# Epilogue

Only a very rash critic would presume to "sum up" the work and character of the complex figure who is the subject of this study. As a man Waugh had failings which he himself often exaggerated; as an artist he remains a very great prose stylist, a defender of Palladian grace and Apollonian values in a century which he believed to be in the last throes of Dionysian disorder. He advocated discipline, yet the anarchy that he deplored was firmly rooted within his own deeply divided nature, so that he fought savagely against savagery and warred immoderately in the name of moderation. In his satires he attacks appetency and irrationality, but his own diaries form a devastating catalogue of his own unreasonable indulgences. As a boy at Lancing he scorned his fellow students but wanted to be like them; as a young man he attacked stuffed shirts but eventually posed as the stuffiest of them all. In an attempt to combine security with freedom, he publicly advocated order but remained a "bolshie" who feuded with every authority from ticket-taker to tax-man. While he was bitterly critical of the flaws of others, he often seemed innocent of any adequate perspective upon his own failings. Father Martin D'Arcy remarks, "It would seem . . . that he did not realise fully how splenetic or atrabilious his conduct could appear to some who met him."[1] And Anthony Powell points out that Waugh's brief desire to stand for Parliament after World War II is an "example of his complete lack of self-awareness regarding himself and his own behaviour."[2]

Yet as *Pinfold* clearly shows, Waugh possessed surprising insight into his own shortcomings, and he made genuine attempts to remedy them. He knew, for example, that he was lacking in charity. He found "the obligation of charity to love mankind in general . . . impossible to meet,"[3] but tried hard to overcome his fault on a personal basis. When Moray McLaren lost his health and his income, Waugh helped him back to a productive life with "persistent generosity."[4] When Hubert Duggan lay on his death-bed, Waugh was a constant source of strength.[5] He also took pleasure in encouraging fellow-writers like Henry Green, Angus Wilson, Nigel Dennis, Muriel Spark, Alfred Duggan, Thomas Merton, Alexander Comfort, and Nancy Mitford. According to Dom Hubert van Zeller, Waugh was not the ogre that many people imagined: "There were differences certainly, down-right rows, with many of his friends but . . . in almost every case his charm won in the end and the friendships were renewed."[6] Waugh's wartime batman Ralph Tanner maintains that Waugh was not a tyrant, did not exploit him, was not irascible nor rude, never got roaring drunk, and never fell asleep in evening dress in a cold bath: "This reputation he's supposed to have for rudeness is totally alien to the Waugh I knew."[7] Tongue-in-cheek though Tanner's remarks may have been, John Montgomery of A. D. Peters's literary agency was in earnest when he criticized Sykes's biography of Waugh: "He missed the boat. He didn't get under the skin of the man. Also he didn't quite show what a very warm-hearted and human person Evelyn was. And so there are almost no jokes at all in the book, and yet the man was one of the wittiest and funniest people in the literary world."[8]

The "warm-hearted" and "human" side of Waugh emerges in his own correspondence, sensitively edited in 1980 by Mark Amory. The *Letters* surprised and enchanted many readers who had believed that there was no more to Waugh than his crusty public image, and who felt that their worst suspicions had been confirmed in Michael Davie's 1976 edition of the far more sombre *Diaries*. In his preface, Amory suggests that the "difference in tone" between the letters and the diaries stems from the fact that Waugh's letters were written "in the morning, when he was sober," while the more vitriolic diaries were composed in the evening, when he was not.[9] A more probable explanation is that the tonal difference is a question of audience: Waugh wrote his diaries to himself, an audience for which he often felt an intense loathing. His letters, on the other hand, were written to people he for the most part liked.

Waugh's letters to his beloved "Whiskers," Laura, are unfailingly loving and often tenderly moving; in the early stages of the war he writes that she has profoundly changed him "because [he can] no longer look at death with indifference."[10] Often they are comic in the extreme, as in the minor classic about Lord Glasgow's tree stump.[11] His effervescent and facetious correspondence with the Lygon sisters is full of manic verve, friendly impudence, genial exaggeration, and is sprinkled with worldly allusions to "koks," "rogering," and Moroccan brothels. His many letters to Ann Fleming are affectionate, and his sparkling correspondence with Nancy Mitford is revealing and funny. Here Waugh puts his dignity far enough aside to admit that it was "blissikins" to be with "the Master," Sir Max Beerbohm.[12] His letters to his children are wisely and lovingly written: "I love you and will not let you be really unhappy if I can prevent it . . . darling little girl," he writes when Margaret reports trouble at school.[13] Whimsically, he hopes that his "sweet Pig" has "given up swearing and smoking and drinking for Lent."[14] In a teasing mood of macabre humour, he writes to Margaret and Harriet that Laura has brought all fourteen cows to Teresa's débutante ball, and that some near relatives have been imprisoned, one having stolen "five watches, six diamond rings and some silver spoons."[15] As for Teresa herself, she is missing: "I suppose she was crushed to death and the corpse too flat to be recognized."[16] These letters are serious too; to Margaret he writes, "The whole of our life is a test and preparation for heaven—most of it irksome."[17]

Waugh's letters—poised, impudent, witty, and never dull—are an introduction into a small, tight-knit world inhabited by people who rejoice in the names of Preters, Jump, Dig, Sponger, Blondy, Poll, Boom, Frisky, Bloggs, Prod, Boots, Tanker, Honks, Pug, Lavatory-Chain, Pig-Walloper, and Boofy. The affectionate zest which produced these absurd nicknames irradiates Waugh's letters, and should help dispel the image of the eccentric monster which Waugh himself publicly fostered.

However, despite the favourable evidence of the *Letters*, and despite the discreet treatment he receives from Sykes, Waugh will not be remembered as the most amiable of men. Although he was capable of kindness and gaiety, his greatest failing was a profound lack of joy in life. His low blood pressure, he claimed, meant that he would live "absolutely for ever in deeper and deeper melancholy."[18] Waugh was a pessimist, convinced that all change was for the worst and that it took all of a civilization's energies simply to maintain the status quo. Seeing himself as a battleground for the eternal war between Fortune and Providence, he was stricken by a deep sense of powerlessness and loss; and that in turn was aggravated by a profound conviction of personal sinfulness. One detects in Waugh's frequent utterances about original sin, and his own sins, a relish which verges upon the masochistic; like Ludovic thumbing through his thesaurus, Waugh must have pondered frequently the synonyms of "doom."

Waugh habitually undervalued the present. He was much more intent upon the past, which contained certainty, and the future, which contained disaster. He scrutinized the here and now from a remote perspective—"*sub specie aeternitatis*," as he called it—and found it boring, annoying, and absurd. His world-weariness was so precocious that at Lancing he was moved to write a cynical little poem punningly entitled "Tedium."

What accounts for Waugh's blighting *tedium vitae*? His intense pursuit
of his vocation provides one answer: for him, self-realization lay in the
future and the present was merely an "irksome" obstacle on the route to
something better. But there was another cause: Waugh lived more fully in
fiction than he did in life, and he treated experience too often as a source
for future art. It is apparent that his diaries are in part a writer's note-
book—in fact, many of his entries are well on the way to fiction even at
the diary stage. Eventually Waugh tired of salting away amusing memories, and by the age of forty he wearied of experience itself. Three years
later, in 1946, he played with the idea of removing to Ireland, where he
could enjoy "the luxury of . . . completely retiring from further experience and settling in an upstairs library to garner the forty-three-year harvest." [19] After the war Waugh lost interest in the future and devoted himself to transforming the past into art. The present became an only mildly
interesting spectacle, full of human absurdities. In 1947, on his forty-
fourth birthday, Waugh wrote in his diary, "Mentally I have reached a
stage of non-attachment which if combined with a high state of prayer—
as it is not—would be edifying." [20] Time passed with excruciating slow-
ness, and ailments crowded upon him: rheumatism, failing memory,
piles, obesity, insomnia, bad teeth, hallucinations. "The scientists might
blow up the world," Bowra warned. "I wouldn't mind if they did,"
Waugh replied.[21] He told Lady Diana Cooper that he wanted to be an old
man hitting people with a stick.[22] The faun-like "Gremlin," the once-
energetic "Mr. Wu" was drawing further away from the world with each
passing year. In 1955 he resolved "to regard humankind with benev-
olence and detachment." [23] In 1963 he observed, "It was fun thirty-five
years ago to travel far and in great discomfort to meet people whose entire conception of life and manner of expression were alien. Now one has
only to leave one's gates." [24] But he seldom left; he lowered the portcullis
against the modern jungle at his doorstep and took refuge from the world
behind a moat of deep and bitter exasperation. The State had changed
beyond recognition and now his Church seemed about to follow. At
Easter 1956 Waugh found himself "in violent disagreement" with the
new Catholicism and "resentful of the new liturgy." [25] Later he argued
that the Church should "transmit undiminished and uncontaminated the
creed inherited from its predecessors," [26] but his voice went unheeded.
Good taste had long since decayed; now good faith was crumbling: it was
too much to bear. "The Vatican Council has knocked the guts out of me,"
he lamented.[27] Crusty and cranky, a celebrated curmudgeon and a self-
confessed "mugwump," Waugh had become a legend in his own time.
Now bad health and bad habits took their toll and "the vicious spiral of
boredom and lassitude" [28] of bygone years intensified. In April 1965, just

a year before he died, Waugh told Sykes, "My life is roughly speaking over. I sleep badly except occasionally in the morning. I get up late. I try to read my letters. I try to read the paper. I have some gin. I try to read the paper again. I have some more gin. I try to think about my autobiography. Then I have some more gin and it's lunch time. That's my life. It's ghastly." [29] To Ann Fleming he wrote, "I just do not much like being alive." [30] It was by now apparent that Waugh's practice of fencing the world out was really fencing him in; his sanctuary at Combe Florey was really a jail, and indeed all of life had become a prison.

Waugh's release from his "ghastly" life was not far off. By Lent 1966 he was in poor physical and mental condition, and his brother-in-law Alick Dru wrote asking Dom Hubert van Zeller to pass Holy Week at Combe Florey. According to Dom Hubert, Waugh "knew I liked the Latin and particularly wanted the Easter Sunday Mass said in the house according to the Latin Tridentine rite." [31] Alick Dru urged the priest to come, giving "as a reason for this the lamentable state poor Evelyn was in. He had lost weight, was eating hardly anything, and though he was keeping his alcohol-free Lent as usual, was taking massive doses of drugs to make him sleep. Dru's letter also said that he felt he was being cold-shouldered by his friends and had developed what amounted almost to a mania about the Church's hostile attitude towards his anti-progressive views openly expressed." Waugh hoped, Dru said, that Dom Hubert would "stand by him to the end." Dru also "hinted at a persecution complex." As it turned out, Dom Hubert was unable to accept Waugh's urgent invitation, and he never saw him alive again. Waugh died on Easter Sunday 1966, having had occasion, as Sykes discreetly observes, to "raise his arms" in "the back parts of the house." [32] As Dom Hubert wrote, "The only consolation was that Evelyn had had his Easter Mass in Latin in the house and that Fr. Caraman had received permission to say it. So at least our friend died knowing that he had not been completely deserted." He had wanted to die: "Don't worry," Laura told Diana Cooper, "he is totally happy to be dead." [33]

From here we may glance back and see Waugh's long retreat from the world as his fiction mirrors it, a quest for sanctuary and "unique achievement" manifested in a see-saw contest between art and action. In *Decline and Fall* and *Vile Bodies* naifs who are men neither of taste nor of action are relegated to oblivion, for they are mere caricatures and have no sustaining uniqueness. In *Black Mischief* the man of action triumphs in the person of Basil Seal, and in *Scoop* the artist wins, but since he glorifies the "lush places" of mere nature, he is dangerously immature. In the unfinished *Work Suspended* Plant the mature artist would almost certainly have ousted Plant the immature writer of second-rate thrillers. *Put Out*

*More Flags* reflects the about-turn dictated by the war: here the man of action expels the still-immature artist as Basil Seal tricks Ambrose Silk into exile in Ireland. But the euphoric patriotism and worldliness of this novel vanish in the blighting cross-winds of war. Waugh believed that World War II would purge the decadence of the interwar years, and that justice, honour, and piety would reassert themselves. In this fond hope he was mistaken; in *Brideshead*, therefore, the disenchanted warrior reviews his early life and rejects both action and secular art in favour of an art which shows "man in relation to God." In *The Loved One* Dennis Barlow follows a similar course: a former RAF squadron leader and war poet now exiled in Hollywood like Orpheus in Hades, he develops a taste for death-loving romantic art. This he must outgrow before he is able to transform his experience into mature Christian art: *The Loved One* itself. By the late Forties Waugh stood in no doubt that the pen was mightier than the sword, provided that it explicitly served God and not the world. Waugh's new vocation as literary defender of the faith animates every page of *Helena*. And in the War Trilogy Guy Crouchback's failure as a soldier and his withdrawal to Broome reflect the "unconditional surrender" of the public man of action to the private man of good taste and good faith. After Guy's long series of false refuges in Eldoret, Santa Dulcina delle Rocce, and the British army, the austere and modest life of Broome is to be his true refuge.

Unfortunately for Waugh, Guy Crouchback was not a wholly accurate self-portrait, and in the end Waugh's life imitated his early satires rather than his "serious" fiction. For various reasons, Waugh in his refuge at Combe Florey failed to achieve even the limited contentment which he conferred upon Guy Crouchback at Broome. Illness and constant exasperation played their roles, but there were two major problems—his Church, which was changing, and his vocation, which he seems never to have fully accepted. Even after spending a lifetime in search of his "defined purpose," the "something which only [he could] do," Waugh was not at ease as a writer. Had he discovered what God wanted him to do, only to find that even that was not enough? J. B. Priestley says that Waugh never accepted the hard-won mantle of the artist, "Pinfolding" instead as a country gentleman and thereby deflecting his energies from their proper goal.[34] Perhaps it was so, for the gloom of Waugh's last years indicates that one of the finest novelists of our time found little fulfilment in his vocation.

"Oh for the Marshalsea," Waugh lamented to Nancy Mitford in 1950, predicting that he would "have to go to prison" for debt. While he often made similar quips to A. D. Peters, he was not merely joking, for the metaphor of life as a prison dominates Waugh's view of the world. He frequently speaks of "escaping"—from Holland, from Cyprus, from life itself. ("Longevity is one of the greatest curses introduced by the scientists"; "The awful prospect is that I may have more than 20 years ahead.")[35] "*L'enfer—c'est les autres,*" he wrote to Nancy Mitford, echoing Sartre in *No Exit*; and to Graham Greene he wrote about "the need to hide."[36] At Combe Florey he was conscious of a nearby asylum for the retarded, and upon reading Wilde's letters he remarked, "The saddest thing is his euphoria in the first few days after leaving prison, all turning to dust immediately."[37] Waugh knew that feeling well and recorded it often in his novels, which are also informed by the metaphor of the prison. In *Decline and Fall* Paul Pennyfeather moves from one "house" to another, but despite their different names and appearances those houses are all prisons. After the war Waugh's sense of the world as a prison deepened and darkened, and he found postwar Europe a "lightless concentration camp." In 1937 he had retired to the West Country, and for a short time after the war he contemplated a further withdrawal to Ireland. In an uncharacteristically introspective diary entry, he wondered why he wanted to do it:

> Why do I contemplate so grave a step as abjuring the realm and changing the whole prospects of my children? What is there to worry me here in Stinchcombe? I have a beautiful house furnished exactly to my taste; servants enough, wine in the cellar. The villagers are friendly and respectful; neighbours leave me alone. I send my children to the schools I please. Apart from taxation and rationing, government interference is negligible. None of the threatened developments of building and road-making have yet taken place. Why am I not at ease? Why is it I smell all the time wherever I turn the reek of the Displaced Persons' Camp?[38]

In asking himself why he wanted to retreat to Ireland, Waugh put his finger on the pattern which had characterized his life: his tendency to withdraw into "dark and musty seclusions"[39] and to shun the world. Waugh seems to have noticed this pattern without being able to break out of it. Although he repeatedly dramatizes it in his novels he never seems to have perceived its dangers to the full, ignoring, it would appear, the lesson implicit in the fates of characters like Paul Pennyfeather and Tony Last. He appears to have thought that he was withdrawing only from the deceptive "City of Man," but in fact he was backing away from everything—and soon his back was against the wall. Repeatedly he gave up ground, retreating from refuge to refuge, but as in *Decline and Fall* each refuge unexpectedly proved to be another prison. All options were traps. He had seen it happening to Paul Pennyfeather, but he did not seem to realize that it was still happening to himself. Perhaps intuiting that seclusion in Ireland would really mean immurement there, Waugh did not go. But he did not break out of his pattern.

By settling at Combe Florey Waugh seems to have thought that he had finally found a refuge that was not also a prison—but in that delusion the master-ironist of the twentieth century fell victim to an irony that even he could not have anticipated. Just like Scone College, King's Thursday, Hetton Abbey, and Boot Magna, Combe Florey itself proved to be another cage; it was but one in an infinite regress of traps. And now it became evident that the ultimate *oubliette* was not Waugh's house but his mind. In responding with superiority and intolerance to a world which he saw as a dungeon, Waugh built up massive defences; and once settled behind those ramparts he couldn't get out again. In 1929 he had argued, "freedom produces sterility,"[40] and he had imposed strict discipline upon his wayward impulses, believing that true freedom could be achieved only by conformity to God's will. But in the end his discipline was confining rather than liberating, and it created an inner version of the vast jail he sought to avoid. Waugh's use of the names Pinfold (a place of confinement or restraint) and Caliban (the prisoner of Prospero) shows that he was at least partly aware of the extent to which the "shades of the prison-house" had closed around him.

But beyond Stinchcombe and Combe Florey there was another refuge: the Church itself. At Easter 1965 Waugh complained bitterly about changes to the Church which, in his eyes, would "reduce the priest's unique sacramental position" and would turn the Mass into a mere "social meal." He told Lady Mosley, "Church going is a pure duty parade."[41] He wrote in his diary, "Pray God I will never apostatize, but I can only now go to church as an act of duty and obedience."[42] He did not say, "as an act of compulsion," but one wonders what he might have said had he lived longer. Waugh seems to have felt that his ultimate refuge was turning into a place of constraint. The dawning suspicion must have filled him with dread, for in the Church he thought he had found an unchanging haven. For years he had written about the double nature of sanctuary, and he implied through all he wrote that secular refuge issued in spiritual bondage. But Waugh did not adequately perceive that *any* place of total concealment, secular *or* religious, would ultimately turn into a prison.

At the end of *Decline and Fall* Paul Pennyfeather, recently liberated from disorder, smugly condemns the "ascetic Ebionites" and the heretical Bishop of Bithynia and falls asleep in a refuge which is really a prison. At the end of his life Waugh, like a tragic parody of Paul, condemned "heretical" innovations in his Church and "burrowed ever deeper into the rock,"[44] thereby turning his room in the Household of the Faith into solitary confinement. Now there was only one refuge left, and there can be little doubt that Waugh's dread of changes in the unchangeable was instrumental in driving him there.

# Textual Note

Changes of varying degrees of importance appear at almost every stage in the line of transmission of almost every Waugh novel,[1] and the serious scholar will want to know about such variants before deciding upon a text. Waugh composed all his work in a tight, crabbed longhand which led his typist to complain that it was hard to read even after recourse to the magnifying glass, the encyclopedia, and the public reference library. Waugh himself admits that his handwriting is "full of illegibilities."[2] His agent A. D. Peters sent the typescripts to Chapman and Hall (or, if they were travel books, to Duckworth),[3] and after Waugh had checked and sometimes altered the proofs, American first editions (at first Doubleday, then Cape, Farrar and Rinehart, and Little, Brown) were usually based on the British first editions. Variations often crept in at this point. Sometimes the difference is no more than a change in title: for example, in the United States *Remote People* is entitled *They Were Still Dancing; Robbery under Law: The Mexican Object-Lesson* is *Mexico: An Object-Lesson;* and *Unconditional Surrender* is *The End of the Battle.* At other times there were substantial changes: to take an extreme case, the American text of *Pinfold* varies so much from the British text that it nearly constitutes a separate version.[4]

Always alert to the financial advantages of advance publication, Waugh sometimes pre-released his novels in serial form (*A Handful of Dust* and *Brideshead Revisited* appeared this way), and sometimes (as with *Vile Bodies* and *Scoop*) he made segments into short stories. Conversely, short stories which had appeared on their own sometimes became incorporated into novels, as in the case of "The Man Who Liked Dickens" and "Compassion," which were adapted respectively to *A Handful of Dust* and *Unconditional Surrender.* In some cases, notably *Decline and Fall, Work Suspended, Brideshead Revisited,* and *Unconditional Surrender,* Waugh had immediate second thoughts and revised his work soon after its initial publication. A Uniform Edition in 1948 and 1949 gave him a chance to make further modifications to novels published before that time.

By the early Fifties Waugh's works had appeared in Penguin paperbacks, which often have an interesting textual history of their own. Then in the early Sixties a new Uniform Edition began to appear, with prefaces by Waugh and revisions of different degrees of significance. Waugh died in 1966 before completing his task of revision, so that while *Pinfold*, *Love Among the Ruins*, "Mr. Loveday's Little Outing," and *Scott-King's Modern Europe* appeared unprefaced in one volume of that series in 1973, these versions cannot be considered to have final authority. *Work Suspended* and *Helena* do not appear at all in the new Uniform Edition, which therefore is not uniform.

Close scrutiny of the revisions which appear in the line of transmission of Waugh's novels reveals that his attitude to his work changed and developed as he matured. A novel which reflected his state of mind in 1944, for example, no longer did so in 1959, and he made changes accordingly; but only infrequently were these revisions very significant. It is important to pause over this point, for while it is always fascinating to trace a writer's evolving attitude to his work, it is possible to exaggerate the significance of his revisions. It is equally possible to regard them, unquestioningly, as changes for the better which after all must be accepted because they were the author's final thoughts on the matter. In fact, the revisions which Waugh incorporates in the new Uniform Edition go beyond the cosmetic only in the cases of *Brideshead Revisited* and the War Trilogy, and very often even these are not improvements.

When Waugh revised *Brideshead* and the trilogy, he added very little, preferring for the most part to prune passages and to reorganize (and in some cases retitle) chapters, books, and sub-sections. In *Brideshead*—a book which he began to dislike as time went on—he removed passages which had come to seem lush and fatuous. There are important deletions involving Anthony Blanche, who is made less bizarre and therefore more trustworthy as a commentator on the Flytes; other significant omissions (at the beginning of "A Twitch Upon the Thread") involve the paragraphs about the "vital hours of a lifetime" and shadowy doubles. Waugh reduces his account of the "Pollock diggings" and his description of Mulcaster, decides against comparing Charles's round of parties to "romping cupids in a Renaissance frieze," and no longer lets Blanche describe Julia as a "fiend" and a "killer." He prunes the eulogy on "the languor of Youth," is less explicit about Charles's secular education, and removes the self-indulgent description of the burgundy at Paillard's. He omits the passage describing human beings as "sub-lessees" of buildings and the description of Charles taking possession of Julia's "narrow loins." He deletes some of Julia's frenzied remarks about "living in sin" and cuts some of the more improbable remarks which Lord Marchmain makes on his deathbed. Except for the first-mentioned deletions concerning Blanche and "counterfeits" the revisions are of minor importance. Waugh himself told A. D. Peters, "They don't amount to much." [5]

In revising the War Trilogy Waugh tried hard to make it read as a single, unified novel. He argued (with a candour he had not displayed earlier), "It was unreasonable to expect the reader to keep in mind the various characters; still more to follow a continuous, continued plot." [6] While Waugh succeeded in imposing greater unity on the trilogy, it can be strongly argued that the passages he cut constitute too great an aesthetic sacrifice to justify the story's new form. (The deletions are discussed in greater detail in chap. 17.) Waugh minimized the importance of these changes when in a letter to Lady Diana Mosley he wrote, "It is not much different but slightly pulled together." [7]

In opting amid a jungle of later variant readings to follow British first editions rather than the new Uniform Edition, I have decided to value Waugh's first thoughts over his last—as, indeed, he himself did in the new Uniform Edition when he restored the manuscript readings of *Decline and Fall*. My first reason for doing so is consistency: since *Pinfold*, *Love Among the Ruins*, "Mr. Loveday's Little Outing," and *Scott-King's Modern Europe* are unprefaced and lack final authority, and since *Work Suspended* and *Helena* do not appear at all, there is a large gap in the new Uniform Edition. Second, in the cases of *Brideshead Revisited* and the trilogy, the two most radically revised fictions, I believe that Waugh's deletions represent a serious aesthetic loss, dictated by what may even be ultimately commercial considerations. One may observe in passing that Waugh did not initiate the idea of a revised *Brideshead*; John Mac-Dougall of Chapman and Hall prompted him to revise it, and the same may well be true of the trilogy. [8]

There is some reason to distrust Waugh's judgment in the late Fifties and early Sixties, when he was working on the new Uniform Edition. All of his revisions took place after his *Pinfold* hallucinations when his faculties were enfeebled and his creative powers were on the wane. Evidence from the A. D. Peters files shows that at the very time Waugh was revising the new Uniform Edition he was losing his grip on his personal affairs: on one occasion he promised an article on P. G. Wodehouse to two rival editors, and on another forgot that he had agreed to a paperback edition of *Ronald Knox* [9] (for a fuller discussion of this period see the chapter on *Pinfold*). A look at Waugh's revisions in the trilogy (made in red ink in Penguin paperbacks) shows that on several occasions he mistakenly deleted the wrong material and inserted other material in the wrong place.

All but one of the items on the errata slip are his own fault. If at this time Waugh could make mechanical errors it is not unreasonable to suppose that he could also make aesthetic errors; indeed, the disjointed manuscript of *A Little Learning* shows that he had lost his youthful fluency of composition, and he candidly admitted to John Montgomery that in *Basil Seal Rides Again* he had lost much of his creative faculty.[10]

Finally, the present book is a critical and biographical study of Waugh. It seeks to show, among other things, how Waugh transmuted his own experience into literature, and it uses his novels as biographical data. While a 1948 revision of a 1942 novel can show how Waugh's attitudes evolved, it is not the best version to choose if one seeks to examine the state of mind the author was in when he wrote it. In choosing to rely on British first editions, I do not wish to scant the interest (even the biographical interest) of his later revisions, nor the painstaking labours of those who have studied those revisions. I do argue, however, that the principles of consistency, aesthetic superiority, and, above all, historical accuracy, give us licence to value Waugh's first thoughts over his final revisions, especially since Waugh made those revisions when in rapidly deteriorating health. If it is argued that first editions are not as accessible as the new Uniform Edition, it may be answered that where they exist, the Penguin editions—which are the most accessible of all—are closer to British first editions than to the new Uniform Edition in every case except *Brideshead*.

# Notes

## Chapter 1

1. Evelyn Waugh, *A Little Learning* (London: Chapman and Hall, 1964), p. 44. Subsequent references appear parenthetically in the text. Waugh's love of the sequestered life has been noticed by others. See, for example, Nigel Dennis, "Evelyn Waugh: the Pillar of Anchorage House," *Partisan Review* 10 (July–August 1943): 350–61; A. E. Dyson, "Evelyn Waugh and the Mysteriously Disappearing Hero," *Critical Quarterly* 2 (Spring 1960): 72–79; James F. Carens, *The Satiric Art of Evelyn Waugh* (Seattle and London: University of Washington Press, 1966), pp. 35–45; Jerome Meckier, "Cycle, Symbol and Parody in Evelyn Waugh's *Decline and Fall*," *Contemporary Literature* 20 (1979): 51–75; and especially Richard Wasson, "*A Handful of Dust*: Critique of Victorianism," *Modern Fiction Studies* 7 (1961–62): 327–37. Wasson's important article marked a major advance in Waugh criticism, and while the present study did not start from his premises, it has arrived, in some instances, at related conclusions.

2. Evelyn Waugh, "Out of Depth," in *Mr. Loveday's Little Outing and Other Sad Stories* (London: Chapman and Hall, 1936), p. 122.

3. Wyndham Lewis, *The Doom of Youth* (London: Chatto and Windus, 1932).

4. Ibid., p. 99.

5. See Susan Ganis Auty, "Language and Charm in *Brideshead Revisited*," *Dutch Quarterly Review* 6 (Autumn 1976): 291–303.

6. Evelyn Waugh, "The War and the Younger Generation," *Spectator*, 13 April 1929, p. 570.

7. Evelyn Waugh, "A Call to the Orders," *Country Life*, 26 February 1938, Supplement, p. xiv.

8. Evelyn Waugh, preface to Francis Crease, *Thirty-Four Decorative Designs* (London: privately printed, 1927), p. vii.

9. Evelyn Waugh, "Palinurus in Never-Never Land," *Tablet*, 27 July 1946, p. 46.

10. Evelyn Waugh, "Fan-Fare," *Life*, 8 April 1946, p. 56.

11. Evelyn Waugh, "St. Helena Empress," *The Holy Places* (London: Queen Anne Press, 1952), p. 13.

12. Mark Amory, ed., *The Letters of Evelyn Waugh* (London: Weidenfeld and Nicolson, 1980), p. 339. Hereafter cited as *Letters*.

13. Jeffrey M. Heath, "*Decline and Fall* in Manuscript," *English Studies* 55 (December 1974): 529.

14. Evelyn Waugh, "Come Inside," in *The Road to Damascus*, ed. John A. O'Brien (New York: Doubleday, 1949), p. 21.

15. Saint Augustine, *The City of God*, ed. Vernon J. Bourke (New York: Doubleday Image, 1958), p. 250. Waugh's outlook was also influenced by the work of St. Thomas Aquinas. In his diary for 11 December 1932 Waugh notes that he read the Thomist philosopher Jacques Maritain's *Introduction to Philosophy* while en route to British Guiana. His early but hostile interest in Bergson may well have been stimulated by Maritain's *La Philosophie Bergsonienne* (first published in 1913). Waugh often refers to St. Thomas, notably in "Bioscope," *Spectator*, 29 January 1962, pp. 863–64, where he writes, "As may be said of the scholastic proofs of the existence of God, the argument from Design fails; the argument from contingency stands." Waugh's work seems to reflect many concerns of "the Angelic Doctor": finality (the view that all activities are directed toward some end or purpose and that a good action occurs when a man's action proceeds to its end according to reason and eternal law); the specific and unchanging nature of things; the importance of right reason in action and in art. Father Martin D'Arcy said that Waugh's art embodies St. Thomas's three requirements for beauty (*integritas, consonantia,* and *claritas*). (Interview with Father Martin D'Arcy, S.J., 25 June 1969.) In *Vile Bodies* (pp. 97–98), the facetious debate about "the exact status of angels" may refer to St. Thomas, just as the warning against "multiplying social distinctions indefinitely" may allude to William of Ockham.

16. Ibid., p. 256.

17. Ibid., p. 255.

18. Evelyn Waugh, *A Handful of Dust* (London: Chapman and Hall, 1964), p. 131.

19. Waugh's letters to Dudley Carew are at the Humanities Research Center Library, University of Texas at Austin.

20. See "The Rich Boy" and "The Diamond as Big as the Ritz." A comparison of Waugh and Fitzgerald on the subject of vocation (Dick Diver's, for example), would make a useful study.

21. *Letters*, p. 466.

22. Evelyn Waugh, "The Claim of Youth or Too Young at Forty: Youth Calls to Peter Pans of Middle-Age Who Block the Way," *Evening Standard*, 22 January 1929, p. 7.

23. Michael Davie, ed., *The Diaries of Evelyn Waugh* (London: Weidenfeld and Nicolson, 1976), p. 630. Hereafter cited as *Diaries*.

24. "Fan-Fare," p. 56.

25. *Diaries*, p. 6.

26. John Freeman, interviewer, "Face to Face," BBC TV, 26 June 1960.

27. Cecil Beaton, *The Wandering Years: Diaries: 1922–1939* (London: Weidenfeld and Nicolson, 1961), p. 173. Beaton wrote to me, "Evelyn W. and I really hated one another so much that I don't know if it is fair of me to have a last word . . . he certainly was exceptionally cruel." In Waugh's novels Beaton appears as David Lennox, society photographer, who takes artistic shots of the backs of people's heads.

28. Interview with Henry Yorke (Henry Green), 23 February 1969. This and other interviews cited herein (apart from BBC and CBC programs) were conducted by the author.

29. Arthur Waugh, *One Man's Road* (London: Chapman and Hall, 1931), p. 334.

30. *Diaries*, p. 623.

31. Evelyn Waugh, *The Ordeal of Gilbert Pinfold* (London: Chapman and Hall, 1957), p. 28.

32. Arthur Waugh, *Reticence in Literature* (London: J. G. Wilson, 1915), p. xv.

33. In the University of London Library (U.L.L. Box 810/I/2118–2160).

34. See, for example, the sentimental dedicatory letter to Evelyn in Arthur Waugh's *Tradition and Change* (1919). See also Peter Hinchcliffe, "Fathers and Children in the Novels of Evelyn Waugh," *University of Toronto Quarterly* 35 (1966): 293–310.

35. *Diaries*, pp. 36, 116, 127.

36. Ibid., pp. 73, 143.

37. Ibid., p. 16 (Davie's phrase).

38. Ibid., p. 47.

39. C. L. Chamberlin, "De Mortuis Nil Nisi Bonum," *Lancing College Magazine* LV (Summer 1942): 126–27.

40. *Diaries*, pp. 33, 64, 123.

41. Ibid., pp. 131, 27.

42. Ibid., p. 44.

43. Ibid., p. 56.

44. Ibid., p. 132.

45. Ibid., p. 19.

46. See Jeffrey M. Heath, "A Note on the Waugh *Diaries*," *Evelyn Waugh Newsletter* 7 (Winter 1973): 7–8.

47. *Letters*, p. 12.

48. Ibid., p. 4.

49. Ibid., p. 435.

50. Harold Acton, *Memoirs of an Aesthete* (London: Methuen, 1948), p. 26.

51. One of these bears the inscription, "*Atqui sciebat quae sibi barbarus tortor pararet*" ("And yet he knew what the barbarian torturer was preparing for him"). The line from Horace (*Odes*, III.v.49–50) describes the return of Regulus to Carthage, false gods, and certain death.

52. *Letters*, p. 10.

53. Acton, *Memoirs*, p. 98.

54. Ibid., p. 121.

55. Peter Quennell, *The Marble Foot* (London: Collins, 1976), p. 117.

56. At the Humanities Research Center, University of Texas at Austin.

57. *Letters*, p. 12.

58. Ibid., p. 6.

59. *The Scarlet Woman—An Ecclesiastical Melodrama* was first shown at the Oxford University Dramatic Society, 22 November 1925. For a good description of the film, see Charles E. Linck, Jr., "Waugh–Greenidge Film—*The Scarlet Woman*," *Evelyn Waugh Newsletter* 3 (Autumn 1969): 1–7.

60. Julian Jebb, "The Art of Fiction xxx: Evelyn Waugh," *Paris Review* 8 (Summer–Fall 1963): 76. See Alain Blayac, "Evelyn Waugh's Drawings," *Texas Library Chronicle* NS 7 (Spring 1974): 40–57.

61. *Diaries*, p. 183.

62. Ibid., p. 190.

63. Ibid., p. 199.

64. Ibid., p. 203.

65. Ibid., p. 208.

66. Ibid., p. 211.

67. Ibid., p. 214. The moon may symbolize Fortune; see pp. 76, 134, 137, 148, 180.

68. Evelyn Waugh, "The Balance: A Yarn of the Good Old Days of Broad Trousers and High-Necked Jumpers," in *Georgian Stories, 1926*, ed. Alec Waugh (London: Chapman and Hall, 1926), pp. 253–91. (In *My Brother Evelyn and Other Profiles*, Alec Waugh states that he edited the collection.)

69. The accident probably stems from the "*affaire* Ponsonby" of the 1925 Easter vacation when Waugh and Matthew Ponsonby were arrested for drunk driving and "had to sit for about four hours in an awful cell just like an urinal" (*Diaries*, p. 206).

70. Ibid., pp. 225–26.

71. Ibid., p. 240.

72. Ibid., pp. 211, 249–50.

73. Ibid., p. 265.

74. Ibid.

75. Ibid., p. 273.

76. Ibid., p. 281.

77. Evelyn Waugh, "The Tutor's Tale: A House of Gentlefolks," in *The New Decameron: The Fifth Day*, ed. Hugh Chesterman (Oxford: Basil Blackwell, 1927), pp. 101–16.

78. Byng, who teaches George to smoke in the saddle-room, prefigures Ben Hacket, who in *A Handful of Dust* teaches John Andrew to swear. There, as in "The Tutor's Tale," only the wrong sort of teaching takes place. Waugh's preoccupation with the dangers of seclusion is apparent in a 1929 letter to A. D. Peters in which he proposes a serialized novel (never to be published): "I would also write an humorous serial called 'Grand Young Man' dealing with the arrival in London of a young, handsome & incredibly wealthy marquess hitherto brought up in seclusion and the attempts made by various social, religious, political bodies & ambitious mothers to get hold of him" (*Letters*, p. 30). The sketch re-

calls "The Tutor's Tale" and anticipates *Vile Bodies*. Christopher Sykes (*Evelyn Waugh*, p. 92) reads "Gilded" for "Grand."

79. Waugh later drew upon his description of Stayle for his account of Colonel Blount's Doubting 'All in *Vile Bodies*.

80. *Diaries*, p. 282.

81. Ibid., p. 284.

82. Ibid., p. 290.

83. *Rossetti: His Life and Works* (London: Duckworth, 1928) was not warmly received, and it made Waugh himself "shiver" (*Letters*, p. 27). An anonymous reviewer in the *Times Literary Supplement* criticized it harshly and, mistaking its author's gender, referred to Waugh as a "dainty Miss of the Sixties." It turns out that the reviewer was T. Sturge Moore. On the fly-leaf of his copy of *Rossetti* in the University of London Library there appears a pencilled inscription in the hand of his daughter, Riette (identification by Joan Gibbs, University of London Library): "Subject of a quarrel with Bruce Richmond *TLS*; Papa thought the author was a young woman." Moore's letters confirm him as the unfortunate reviewer. In a letter of 9 March 1928 to Miss Sybil Pye, Moore wrote, "I am working at a centenary article on Rossetti which I want to make worthy of the subject, which means that it will be very difficult." On 11 May he wrote, "You will have guessed the authorship of the Rossetti article in the Lit. Sup." Two days later Sybil Pye replied, "I . . . realized the authorship of the Lit. Sup. article—too full of large ideas & memorable sentences for anyone else to produce. I am glad they gave it at such length & hope it will get at least some of the attention it deserves. (By the way, did you ascertain that the book you review was by a woman? I have certainly seen the author referred to as Mr. Waugh, & 'Evelyn' is often a man's name in England—but I don't know that it matters much.)" It did matter. In the following week's *TLS*, Waugh, acrimonious from the start of his career, condemned the author for his opinions and for his negligence. The Moore-Pye correspondence is in the University of London Library: U.L.L. Box 21/123 (i); 21/129; 22/154B (i–ii); 22/156 (i–ii).

84. Lady Pansy Lamb to J. M. Heath, 19 August 1979.

85. Interview with Lady Pansy Lamb, 29 August 1979.

86. Lady Pansy Lamb to J. M. Heath, 23 September 1979.

87. Dudley Carew, *A Fragment of Friendship: A Memory of Evelyn Waugh When Young* (London: Everest Books, 1974), p. 77.

88. Lady Pansy Lamb to J. M. Heath, 19 August 1979.

89. *Diaries*, p. 293.

90. Ibid., p. 294.

91. Christopher Sykes, *Evelyn Waugh: A Biography* (London: Collins, 1975), p. 94. Hereafter cited as Sykes.

92. *Diaries*, p. 294.

93. Ibid., p. 295.

94. Sykes, p. 95.

95. *Letters*, p. 38.

96. Lady Pansy Lamb to J. M. Heath, 19 August 1979. Heygate lost his job at the BBC when Sir John Reith heard of his actions, and he and Evelyn Gardner

were forced to live in penury "in a Sussex cottage." If she-Evelyn had faults, greed was not one of them. Indeed, Pansy Lamb has remarked, "Whenever her husbands looked like making money she left them." Evelyn Gardner eventually married John Heygate, and in their household "she did all the work." She "was tremendously devoted," but the marriage failed. When in 1936 John Heygate wished to be received into the Church of England, he was required to ask Waugh's forgiveness for the injury he had done him. Heygate received his absolution by postcard: "O.K.E.W.," it read (Sykes, p. 163). After she separated from her second husband, Evelyn Gardner wrote to her old friend Pansy Lamb that she was thankful her name was no longer Heygate, and that she was now married to a man named Nightingale. Ronald Nightingale was a real estate agent in Tunbridge Wells; he refused to speak a word to Pansy Lamb when she visited them in 1950. A year or two later Nightingale left his wife, who was now very much changed from the "light" and uncommitted débutante of the Twenties. "She became a heroic wife and mother," Pansy Lamb remembers; "she spent her whole life working. Her favorite expression was 'I think it's time something nice happened'."

Evelyn Gardner has said little about the matter. She wrote, "Christopher Sykes when writing his memoir of Evelyn—in my opinion it cannot be called a biography—did not trouble to come to see me altho' Anthony Powell had written to say that I would be willing to talk to him. He interviewed John Heygate instead & altho' I am sure John did his best I do not think he would have been entirely reliable. . . . I have written a full account of my marriage & more importantly the background i.e. my opinion of Evelyn's and my upbringing and the effect it had on the marriage, which has been placed with my will so that my children, if they wish, can give it to any biographer of their choice" (Evelyn Gardner to J. M. Heath, 13 August 1980).

97. *Letters*, p. 39.

98. Evelyn Waugh, *Labels: A Mediterranean Journal* (London: Duckworth, 1930), p. 206.

99. Evelyn Waugh, *The Life of the Right Reverend Ronald Knox* (London: Chapman and Hall, 1959), p. 314.

## Chapter 2

1. Evelyn Waugh, *A Little Learning* (London: Chapman and Hall, 1964), p. 68.

2. See Alain Blayac, "Evelyn Waugh's Drawings," *Texas Library Chronicle* n.s. 7 (Spring 1974): 40–57.

3. *Diaries*, pp. 8, 11.

4. Evelyn Waugh, "Come Inside," in *The Road to Damascus*, ed. John A. O'Brien (New York: Doubleday, 1949), p. 12.

5. *The World to Come: A Poem in Three Cantos* (London: privately printed, 1916).

6. "Come Inside," p. 14.

7. Interview with Tom Driberg, 25 February 1969.

8. "Face to Face," BBC TV, 26 June 1960.

9. *Letters*, pp. 268, 318, 243.

10. Evelyn Waugh, "Unacademic Exercise," *The Cherwell*, 19 September 1923, pp. 152–53.

11. *Letters*, pp. 4, 11.

12. At the Humanities Research Center Library, University of Texas at Austin.

13. *Diaries*, pp. 163, 178, 180, 202, 218, 224, 249, 292.

14. "Face to Face."

15. "Come Inside," p. 15.

16. Evelyn Waugh, "Converted to Rome: Why it has Happened to Me," *Daily Express*, 20 October 1930, p. 10.

17. "Come Inside," p. 15.

18. Stephen Black, interviewer, "Personal Call, No. 14," BBC radio, 29 September 1953.

19. *Letters*, p. 245.

20. Evelyn Waugh, "Matter-of-Fact Mothers of the New Age," *Evening Standard*, 8 April 1929, p. 7.

21. Evelyn Waugh, "The War and the Younger Generation," *Spectator*, 13 April 1929, pp. 571, 570.

22. Evelyn Waugh, *Rossetti* (London: Duckworth, 1928), p. 227.

23. Evelyn Waugh, "More Barren Leaves," *Night and Day* 1 (23 December 1937): 24.

24. Evelyn Waugh, *Edmund Campion: Jesuit and Martyr* (London: Longmans, 1935), pp. 3–4.

25. Evelyn Waugh, Foreword to William Weston, *The Autobiography of an Elizabethan*, trans. Philip Caraman (London: Longmans Green, 1955), p. vii.

26. *Edmund Campion*, p. 11.

27. "Come Inside," p. 16.

## Chapter 3

1. Evelyn Waugh, "A Call to the Orders," *Country Life*, 26 February 1938, Supplement, p. xii.

2. *Letters*, p. 553.

3. Evelyn Waugh, "Fan-Fare," *Life*, (8 April 1946), pp. 53–54, 60.

4. Evelyn Waugh, *Rossetti* (London: Duckworth, 1928), pp. 227, 226.

5. *Letters*, p. 215.

6. Ibid., pp. 176, 190, 243, 240, 251.

7. "Fan-Fare," p. 60.

8. *Diaries*, p. 791.

9. Julian Jebb, "The Art of Fiction XXX: Evelyn Waugh," *Paris Review* 8 (Summer–Fall 1963), p. 84.

10. Evelyn Waugh, *Remote People* (London: Duckworth, 1931), p. 183.

11. Evelyn Waugh, *A Tourist in Africa* (London: Chapman and Hall, 1960), p. 32.

12. Stephen Black, Jack Davies, and Charles Wilmot, interviewers, "Frankly Speaking," BBC radio, 16 November 1953.

13. Evelyn Waugh, *Ninety-Two Days: The Account of a Tropical Journey through British Guiana and Part of Brazil* (London: Duckworth, 1934), p. 234.

14. *Diaries*, p. 641.

15. Ibid., p. 643.

16. Ibid., p. 663.

17. Evelyn Waugh, "Mr. Waugh Replies," *Spectator*, 3 July 1953, p. 24.

18. "Frankly Speaking."

19. "Personal Call," BBC radio, 16 November 1953.

20. Evelyn Waugh, *The Ordeal of Gilbert Pinfold* (London: Chapman and Hall, 1957), pp. 1, 2.

21. "Frankly Speaking."

22. *Diaries*, p. 317.

23. *Rossetti*, p. 52.

24. *Remote People*, p. 110.

25. Evelyn Waugh, "A Fifth Study in Loyalty," *Time and Tide*, 12 December 1953, p. 1652.

26. *Diaries*, p. 548.

27. Ibid., p. 627.

28. Ibid., p. 640.

29. Ibid., p. 662.

30. "Face to Face," BBC TV, 26 June 1960.

31. Evelyn Waugh, *A Little Learning* (London: Chapman and Hall, 1964), p. 109.

32. Waugh's dislike of conformity recalls Beau Brummell's legendary individualism, as described by Max Beerbohm: "Even in Oriel, [Brummell] could see little charm, and was glad to leave it, at the end of his first year, for a commission in the Tenth Hussars. Crack though the regiment was—indeed, all the commissions were granted by the Regent himself—young Mr. Brummell could not bear to see all his brother-officers in clothes exactly like his own; was quite as deeply annoyed as would be some god, suddenly entering a restaurant of many mirrors." See Max Beerbohm, "Dandies and Dandies," *The Bodley Head Max Beerbohm*, edited and with an introduction by David Cecil (London: The Bodley Head, 1970), pp. 188–89. Like Brummell, Waugh disliked the uniformity of military life. In a diary entry for 18 January 1940 he characteristically observes, "The other detachment of officers from Deal, Portsmouth and Plymouth are so like ourselves in composition that it is like a 'hall of mirrors'." See also Barry Wicker, "Waugh and the Narrator as Dandy," *The Story-Shaped World* (London: Athlone, 1975), pp. 151–68.

33. Beerbohm, "Dandies and Dandies," p. 190.

34. Ellen Moers, *The Dandy* (London: Secker and Warburg, 1960), p. 13.

35. See David Pryce-Jones, ed., *Evelyn Waugh and His World* (London: Weidenfeld and Nicolson, 1973).

36. Sheridan Morley, "A Swift Look at Alec Guinness," *The Times*, 4 October 1976, p. 7.

37. Sykes, pp. 294-95.

38. *Ordeal of Gilbert Pinfold*, p. 9.

39. Richard Ellmann, *W. B. Yeats: The Man and the Masks* (New York: Dutton, 1948), p. 72.

40. Sharp assumed the name and personality of "Fiona MacLeod," wrote books under her name, "complained to friends who wrote to her that they never wrote to him, and eventually almost collapsed under the strain of double life." Ibid., p. 73.

41. Ibid., p. 72.

42. Ibid.

43. *Ordeal of Gilbert Pinfold*, p. 9.

44. Alec Waugh, *My Brother Evelyn and Other Profiles* (London: Cassell, 1967), p. 169.

45. *W. B. Yeats*, p. 74.

46. Evelyn Waugh, "Two Unquiet Lives," *Tablet*, 5 May 1951, p. 356.

47. Evelyn Waugh, *Scott-King's Modern Europe* (London: Chapman and Hall, 1949), p. 2.

48. Evelyn Waugh, *Robbery under Law: The Mexican Object-Lesson* (London: Chapman and Hall, 1939), p. 279. Waugh possibly absorbed this idea from Aldous Huxley, whose early work he admired. In *Antic Hay* (Harmondsworth, Middlesex: Penguin, 1962), p. 133, Huxley writes, "We need no barbarians from outside; they're on the premises, all the time."

49. *Ordeal of Gilbert Pinfold*, p. 9.

50. Sykes, p. 50.

51. Maurice Beebe, *Ivory Towers and Sacred Founts: The Artist as Hero in Fiction from Goethe to Joyce* (New York: New York University Press, 1964), p. 18.

52. Oscar Wilde, quoted in Ellmann, *W. B. Yeats*, p. 71.

53. Evelyn Waugh, *Ronald Knox* (London: Chapman and Hall, 1959), p. 314.

54. Christopher Saltmarshe, "Some Latter-Day 'Decadents,'" *Bookman* (London) 80 (1930): 196-97.

55. Evelyn Waugh, *Put Out More Flags* (London: Chapman and Hall, 1967), p. 45.

56. Evelyn Waugh, *Men at Arms* (London: Chapman and Hall, 1952), p. 111.

57. *Diaries*, p. 503.

58. Evelyn Waugh, *Brideshead Revisited* (London: Chapman and Hall, 1945), p. 198.

## Chapter 4

1. Harold Acton, *Memoirs of an Aesthete* (London: Methuen, 1948), p. 126.

2. Lady Pansy Lamb to J. M. Heath, 23 September 1979.

3. Sir Henry Channon, *Chips: The Diaries of Sir Henry Channon*, ed. Robert Rhodes James (London: Weidenfeld and Nicolson, 1967), p. 19.

4. Harvey Breit, *The Writer Observed* (London: Alvin Redman, 1957), p. 43.

5. Leo Rosten, "How I Met Evelyn Waugh," *Saturday Review/World*, 21 September 1974, p. 3.

6. Lady Pansy Lamb to J. M. Heath, 23 September 1979.

7. Evelyn Waugh, "Aspirations of a Mugwump," *Spectator*, 2 October 1959, 435.

8. Rose Macaulay, "Evelyn Waugh," *Horizon* 14 (December 1946): 360–76.

9. *Authors Take Sides on the Civil War* (pamphlet), ed. Louis Aragon (London: *Left Review*, 1937).

10. Evelyn Waugh, *A Little Learning* (London: Chapman and Hall, 1964), p. 122.

11. Ibid., p. 129.

12. Evelyn Waugh, *The Ordeal of Gilbert Pinfold* (London: Chapman and Hall, 1957), p. 8.

13. Nancy Mitford to J. M. Heath, 18 June 1969, *Evelyn Waugh Newsletter* 7 (Spring 1973): 9.

14. Kevin Burns, ed., "A Report on Evelyn Waugh," CBC "Nightcap," 9 November 1978.

15. Howard E. Hugo, "Vile Bodies," *Harvard Magazine* 80 (January–February 1978): 94.

16. Interview with Sir Cecil Maurice Bowra, 24 January 1969.

17. C. M. Bowra, *Memories: 1898–1939* (London: Weidenfeld and Nicholson, 1966), p. 173.

18. Interview with Henry Yorke (Henry Green), 23 February 1969.

19. Interview with Lady Diana Cooper, 11 March 1969.

20. Interview with Henry Yorke (Henry Green), 23 February 1969.

21. Waugh to Peters, [November] 1934, A. D. Peters file, Humanities Research Center Library, University of Texas at Austin.

22. Waugh to Peters, January 1932, December 1931, A. D. Peters file.

23. Waugh to Peters, [Autumn] 1933, A. D. Peters file.

24. Waugh to Peters, [Winter] 1935, A. D. Peters file.

25. Farrar to Hill, 3 May 1934, A. D. Peters file.

26. Hill to Peters, 10 August 1934, A. D. Peters file.

27. Waugh to Peters, [Spring] 1936, A. D. Peters file.

28. Hill to Peters, 7 January 1937, A. D. Peters file.

29. Waugh to Peters, 16 April 1937, A. D. Peters file.

30. Waugh to Peters, 30 September 1944, A. D. Peters file.

31. Waugh to Peters, received 3 July 1942, A. D. Peters file.

32. Waugh to Peters, letters of March 1946, A. D. Peters file.

33. Hill to Peters, 18 March 1947, A. D. Peters file.

34. Waugh to Peters, [July] and [August] 1948, A. D. Peters file.

35. Waugh to Peters, 4 July 1950, A. D. Peters file.

36. Waugh to Peters, 30 April, [May] 1957, A. D. Peters file.

37. Christopher Sykes, "Evelyn Waugh—a brief life," *The Listener*, 24 August 1967, p. 229.

38. Harold Acton, *More Memoirs of an Aesthete* (London: Methuen, 1970), p. 314.

39. Sykes, p. 228.

40. *Diaries*, p. 559.

41. Dom Hubert van Zeller, "The Agreeable Mr. Waugh," *The Critic* 35 (Fall 1976): 38.

42. Sykes, p. 334.

43. Ibid., pp. 284–85.

44. *Diaries*, p. 599.

45. Evelyn Waugh, "Apotheosis of an Unhappy Hypocrite," *Spectator*, 2 October 1953, p. 363.

46. "Frankly Speaking," BBC radio, 16 November 1953.

47. Interview with Lady Pansy Lamb, 29 August 1979. The *Letters* (840 of some 4,500) have since been edited by Mark Amory, and Lady Pansy Lamb's description is particularly true of Waugh's correspondence with Lady Dorothy Lygon and Lady Mary Lygon.

48. *The Observer* excerpts appeared at intervals between 25 March and 13 May 1973; the unabridged edition appeared in 1977. Nearly eight hundred pages long and spanning most of his life, Waugh's diaries represent a substantial portion of his literary output and deserve attention in their own right. They are extremely offensive. When Michael Davie edited the diaries for book-length publication, he and his publishers, Weidenfeld and Nicolson, found it advisable to excise "twenty-three libellous references" for fear of the British libel laws. "Another twenty phrases" were expunged because they might prove "intolerably offensive or distressing to living persons or surviving relations." Davie's fear of libel is a good indication of the amount of venom Waugh poured into his private journals, but it also distorts their true nature. Because the omissions are hidden, the reader loses both the offending passages and all trace of their location. Gone without a trace is the information that at Lancing a friend of Waugh's took dope; gone too is Waugh's explanation of how Cyril Connolly's mistress was "lamed for life." Discreetly suppressed is the entry in which a former gossip columnist confessed, on the brink of war, that he was happier than he had been since the Twenties. Also absent is the 1945–56 entry in which Waugh identifies an eminent man of justice, whose "only real pleasure in life is to be birched by a common prostitute. Perhaps his arse was at that moment smarting from the joys of the preceding evening." In other places (presumably where the context is less revealing), "instead of cutting out libellous or offensive passages altogether," Davie replaces names with dashes. In addition to Davie's omissions, the Waugh estate itself exercised its veto seven times, "making cuts in entries that might otherwise have caused unnecessary distress."

Waugh himself almost certainly made many deletions from these remarkable documents, but these were to protect himself, not others. In an entry for 10 October 1919 he admits to having torn out "all the first part of this diary" because it was "really too dangerous without being funny." In a letter to Dudley Carew Waugh says that he has destroyed part of his Oxford diary, and a similar fate no doubt befell the entries dealing with the collapse of his first marriage and his "Pinfold" hallucinations. But we must not jump to the conclusion that the large gaps in the diaries always resulted from their author's decision to suppress incriminating entries. We must also entertain the possibility that on many occasions Waugh simply neglected to record his impressions at all. It is useful to note his assertion, in an unpublished portion of his autobiography, that "in times of change and high excitement" he did not keep a diary at all. (See Jeffrey M. Heath, "A Note on the Waugh Diaries," *Evelyn Waugh Newsletter* 7 [Winter 1973]: 7–8.) Here, for example, is Waugh's diary comment on his 1926 return from Paris with a friend named Bill Silk: "The journey was disgusting, and I think that I am so unlikely to forget it that I will not write about it at all." And here is his youthful assessment of the value of his diary: "What a futile thing this diary really is. I hardly record anything worth the trouble. Everything important I think had better be stored in my memory and it consists chiefly of 'Shops in morning, cinema in afternoon.' I ought to try and make it more —— but it becomes so dangerous." (*Diaries*, p. 100. Davie says the deleted word is heavily crossed out; nevertheless, it looks like "profound." Waugh's small, crabbed handwriting is orderly but often illegible; in view of the difficulty of the script Davie does well in his transcription, but creates enough cruces to keep the scholars busy.) Evidently many "disgusting" or "important" matters were stored in Waugh's memory and thus never destroyed at all. What do we make of a man who is reticent to the point of keeping secrets from his own diary? And what of the diaries themselves?

The early diaries are the most revealing. In them Waugh develops from a precocious and censorious little boy who hated "trippers" and liked "spikey" churches into an ambitious and calculating youth who "kept his life in 'watertight' compartments." (Waugh reread his Lancing diaries in later life "with unmixed shame" yet used them as the basis for the unfinished "Charles Ryder's Schooldays.") After the earnest and self-advertising revelations of the Lancing diaries, the "mock-whimsical" and exaggeratedly objective style of the post-Oxford diaries comes as a shock. Here the reader forfeits what little he had of the diarist's mind and soul and gets instead, with a few exceptions, a hectic record of hangovers and flying lavatory seats, adversity and perversity. The reader remains in a world of surfaces throughout the laconic Thirties diaries until, quite suddenly, after the engrossing war entries, he runs into long, bleak pages of closely reasoned gloom. These are the pages which will shake and depress him as he watches the prancing faun become an ailing stag: alertness distorts into irritability, individuality into solitude, and youth and grace into peevish infirmity.

Except for a few tremblings of the veil, the reader of the diaries seldom regains access to Waugh's innermost thoughts after the Lancing period. Instead, he witnesses a long parade of outward life as seen through the eyes of a chronic caricaturist who has elevated scorn into a way of life. What, one wonders, did Waugh think when in 1925 he read *The Brothers Karamazov* and Plato? What did he feel when he fell in love with Evelyn Gardner? And what did he think about the poor creatures he so deftly slices into bundles of disconnected attributes? Here is an acquaintance, Lady N——: "She had a thick beard, a bald dog, a drunken husband and a paederastic son." And another, named Wallace: "very tall and misshapen with jet-black shingled hair and wrinkles." And three other wretches: "a woman with a face like a pie," "a low-born man with no legs and two daughters," and "a deaf man with second sight who rode a tricycle."

49. Evelyn Waugh, "One Way to Immortality," *Daily Mail*, 28 June 1930, p. 8.

50. Evelyn Waugh, "The Youngest Generation," *Lancing College Magazine* XIV (December 1921): 5.

51. Alec Waugh, *My Brother Evelyn and Other Profiles* (London: Cassell, 1967), pp. 166, 168, 177.

52. Wyndham Lewis, *The Doom of Youth* (London: Chatto and Windus, 1932), p. 107.

53. Father Martin D'Arcy, "The Religion of Evelyn Waugh," in *Evelyn Waugh and His World*, ed. David Pryce-Jones (London: Weidenfeld and Nicolson, 1973), p. 76.

54. Sykes, p. 50.

55. Evelyn Waugh, "Fan-Fare," *Life*, 8 April 1946, p. 60.

56. Evelyn Waugh, *Work Suspended* (London: Chapman and Hall, 1942), p. 83. Deleted from subsequent editions, probably because Waugh thought these and other passages too clearly showed his ironical attitude toward Plant.

57. "Fan-Fare," p. 56.

58. Frederick J. Stopp, *Evelyn Waugh: Portrait of an Artist* (London: Chapman and Hall, 1958), p. 192. See Steven Marcus, "Evelyn Waugh and the Art of Entertainment," *Partisan Review* 23 (Summer 1956): 230; D. S. Savage, "The Innocence of Evelyn Waugh," in *Focus Four: The Novelist as Thinker*, ed., Balachandra Rajan (London: Dobson, 1947), p. 35; Sean O'Faolain, *The Vanishing Hero: Studies in Novelists of the Twenties* (London: Eyre and Spottiswoode, 1956), p. 55; and George Mikes, "Evelyn Waugh," *Eight Humorists* (London: Allan Wingate, 1954), p. 136. Stopp is one of Waugh's friendliest critics. He lived with the Waughs while researching his book, and according to Laura the aroma of his hair-tonic lingered on for days after he left (interview with Laura Waugh, 25 July 1969).

59. Stopp, *Portrait of the Artist*, pp. 190–91.

60. See Mikes, p. 133; Donat O'Donnell [pseud. for Conor Cruise O'Brien], *Maria Cross: Imaginative Patterns in a Group of Modern Catholic Writers* (New York: Oxford University Press, 1952), p. 134; Graham Martin, *Pelican Guide to English Literature*, ed. Boris Ford, vol. 7, *The Modern Age* (Harmondsworth, Middlesex: Penguin, 1961), p. 398.

61. Malcolm Bradbury, *Evelyn Waugh*, Writers and Critics Series, No. 39 (Edinburgh and London: Oliver and Boyd, 1964), pp. 4, 5, 15.

62. James F. Carens, *The Satiric Art of Evelyn Waugh* (Seattle and London: University of Washington Press, 1966), p. 70.

63. Martin Green, *Transatlantic Patterns* (New York: Basic Books, 1977), pp. 78, 84.

64. Arthur Waugh, ed., *The Lives of the Poets*, by Samuel Johnson, The

World's Classics, (London: Oxford University Press, 1906), I: xv–xvi.

65. Wayne Booth, *The Rhetoric of Fiction* (Chicago and London: Phoenix Books, 1961), p. 20.

66. *Letters*, p. 574.

67. Peter Green, "Du Côté de Chez Waugh," *Review of English Literature* 2 (1961): 100.

68. George Greene, "Scapegoat with Style: The Status of Evelyn Waugh," *Queen's Quarterly* 71 (1964–65): 489, 491.

69. Evelyn Waugh, "Hands Off Smith," *Spectator*, 19 June 1959, p. 894.

70. Evelyn Waugh, "Travellers' History," ibid., 6 August 1932, p. 186.

71. Evelyn Waugh, "Desert Islander," ibid., 27 May 1938, p. 978.

72. *The Writer Observed*, p. 149.

73. Evelyn Waugh, *Ronald Knox* (London: Chapman and Hall), p. 75.

74. Lady Dorothy Lygon, "Madresfield and Brideshead," in *Evelyn Waugh and His World*, ed. David Pryce-Jones (London: Weidenfeld and Nicolson, 1973) p. 53.

75. Evelyn Waugh, "An Open Letter to the Hon. Mrs. Peter Rodd [Nancy Mitford] on a Very Serious Subject," *Encounter* 5 (December 1955): 15, 12.

76. Evelyn Waugh, "Drama and the People," *Spectator*, 6 November 1942, p. 438.

77. A. E. Dyson, "Evelyn Waugh: and the Mysteriously Disappearing Hero," *The Crazy Fabric: Essays in Irony* (London: Macmillan, 1965), pp. 195, 187.

78. Richard M. Ohmann, "Prolegomena to the Analysis of Prose Style," in *The Theory of the Novel*, ed. Philip Stevick (New York: The Free Press, 1967), pp. 191, 203.

79. Evelyn Waugh, "Literary Style in England and America," *Books on Trial* 14 (October 1955): 65.

80. Evelyn Waugh, "Ronald Firbank," *Life and Letters* 2 (March 1929): 192.

81. Like Eliot, Waugh endorsed traditional ways of being new—what one might call "renewedness": "One must distinguish between uses of 'new.' There is the Easter sense in which all things are made new in the risen Christ. A tiny gleam of this is reflected in all true art. Every work of art is thus something new. Just as within the moral framework there is space for infinite variations of behaviour, so within the aesthetic framework. Most so-called innovators have in fact thought themselves revivalists, appealing to an earlier and purer virtue against what they consider the corruption of their immediate predecessors" (*Letters*, p. 215).

82. Evelyn Waugh, "A Call to the Orders," *Country Life*, 26 February 1938, Supplement, p. xiv.

83. Evelyn Waugh, "The War and the Younger Generation," *Spectator*, 13 April 1929, p. 571.

84. Julian Jebb, "The Art of Fiction xxx: Evelyn Waugh," *Paris Review* 8 (Summer-Fall 1963): p. 76.

## Chapter 5

1. Edmund Wilson remarks on Waugh's ambivalence in *Classics and Commercials* (New York: Vintage, 1962), p. 146.

2. Evelyn Waugh, *Decline and Fall* (London: Chapman and Hall, 1928), p. 170. Subsequent page references appear in parentheses following each quotation. According to Anthony Powell, the original title (not preserved in the Texas manuscript) was "Picaresque: or the Making of an Englishman." See *Messengers of Day* (New York: Holt, Rinehart and Winston, 1978), p. 21.

3. *Diaries*, p. 199. Looking back in 1937 on his brief career as a schoolmaster, Waugh wrote, "However abominable one's record, though one may be fresh from prison or the lunatic asylum, one can always look after the silver or teach the young. I had not the right presence for a footman, so I chose the latter. I taught them about everything" (*Nash's Pall Mall Magazine* [March 1937]: 10).

4. *Letters*, p. 23.

5. *Diaries*, p. 249.

6. Ibid., p. 268. Waugh may have been inspired by Chesterton's "Wine and Water," a poem about Noah and the wine cellar aboard the Ark. (I am indebted to Professor David Dooley for this suggestion.) In 1929 Waugh told A. D. Peters that he wanted to write "a humorous confession of [his] own life called 'a career founded by drink' or something like that describing how [he] was saved from being a successful schoolmaster by a lapse into drunkenness and driven into authorship" (*Letters*, p. 47).

7. *Diaries*, p. 280.

8. Evelyn Waugh, *Robbery Under Law* (London: Chapman and Hall, 1939), p. 279.

9. *Diaries*, pp. 249, 211, 250.

10. In "Captain Grimes's Revenge," *London Magazine* n.s. 17 (April–May 1977): 65–73, T. M. Higham says that Grimes's original soon gave up schoolmastering to become first a lawyer and then the author of a thriller set in a school which closely resembles Arnold House. In the novel, entitled *A Preparatory School Murder*, "Grimes" seems to take revenge on Waugh by using him as the original for one of the suspects in the murder. Other information about Grimes may be found in *A Little Learning*, pp. 227 ff., and the *Letters*, p. 624.

11. See also Edward C. McAleer, "*Decline and Fall* as Imitation," *Evelyn Waugh Newsletter* 7 (Winter 1973): 1–4. McAleer notices the parodies of Pater, Shylock, Hamlet, and others.

12. Evelyn Waugh, "The American Epoch in the Catholic Church," *Life*, 19 September 1949, p. 135.

13. Nigel Dennis, "Evelyn Waugh: The Pillar of Anchorage House," *Partisan Review* 10 (July–August 1943): 350.

14. See the discussion of *Work Suspended*.

15. Fagan is almost certainly modelled on Waugh's Lancing College housemaster, J. F. Roxburgh, and not on "Mr. Banks of Arnold House" (or as Waugh calls him in *A Little Learning* in a possible allusion to Swift, "Mr. Vanhomrigh").

His *crêpe de chine* handkerchief indicates that he is an infidel (allusions to the Orient are always signs of heresy in Waugh). His original in literature is Dickens's Fagin, who in *Oliver Twist* teaches waifs and orphans to become pickpockets.

16. For the manuscript version of the school sports, see Jeffrey M. Heath, "Waugh's *Decline and Fall* in Manuscript," *English Studies* 55 (December 1974): 527–28.

17. Evelyn Waugh, "Changes in the Church: Questions for the 'Progressives'," *Catholic Herald*, 7 August 1964, p. 4. Scone was an abbey in Perthshire which was burned by a mob during the Reformation. (My thanks to Harriet White for this observation.)

18. In later editions, Martin Gaythorne-Brodie is Miles Malpractice (Eddie Gathorne-Hardy), and Kevin Saunderson is Lord Parakeet (Gavin Henderson). David Lennox was Cecil Beaton in real life. See "*Decline and Fall* in Manuscript," p. 526. Waugh did not restore the original names in the new Uniform Edition.

19. The passage appears to echo W. E. Henley's "To W.A.":

> Or ever the Knightly years were gone
> With the old world to the grave,
> I was a King in Babylon
> And you were a Christian Slave.

It might also be observed here that Margot's lover's name, "Chokey," is British slang for "prison."

20. *Diaries*, p. 285.

21. Evelyn Waugh, "The War and the Younger Generation," *Spectator*, 14 April 1929, p. 570.

22. One is reminded of the *Consolation of Philosophy*, where Boethius describes the imprisonment which results when we take Fortune as our mistress, and the liberty conferred by servitude to "divine reason." See my p. 282n67.

23. Waugh's interest in Silenus can be traced to many sources: to *The Golden Bough*, which he took with him to Arnold House; to James Branch Cabell's *Jurgen*, a mock-romance which had "quite captivated" Waugh at the age of nineteen (*A Little Learning*, p. 189), and to *The Brothers Karamazov* and Plato, both of which he read in 1925 (*Diaries*, pp. 221, 227). Silenus was a tutor, and so Waugh may have been thinking also of C.R.M.F. Cruttwell, dean and senior history tutor of Hertford College, Oxford. They intensely disliked one another. See *A Little Learning*, pp. 173–74, 177. Waugh's Silenus may also derive in part from Walter Gropius of the Bauhaus, and from Lawrence's Loerke in *Women in Love*. Both Silenus and Loerke are interested in the mechanical and the Dionysiac. Although he never says so, Waugh probably read Plato's *Symposium*, where Alcibiades compares the ironic Socrates to a hollow statue of Silenus filled with tiny idols of the gods. The idea of divinity hidden behind a drunken exterior may go far towards explaining Waugh's satiric method. (I am indebted to Professor Lee Patterson for this observation.)

24. See "*Decline and Fall* in Manuscript." Certain parts of Fagan's speech were "toned down" in editions subsequent to the first and restored in the new Uniform Edition.

25. In 1930 Waugh said that Hardy's view of a world governed by chance was immature. Hardy's influence is nevertheless evident in Waugh's early satires, where Fortune rules in the absence of Providence. There are other similarities: just as Tess ends up as a sacrificial victim of her forefathers' degeneracy, so Paul Pennyfeather suffers for the sins of his apostate ancestors and "mysteriously disappears."

26. As "Minister of Transport," Maltravers is probably based on Sir William Joynson-Hicks, who stood for anything but ecstasy. Maltravers later becomes Lord Metroland; "Metroland" was what Waugh and his cronies called the suburban areas opened up by the ever-expanding London Underground. See Charles E. Linck, "The Development of Evelyn Waugh's Career: 1903–1939" (Ph.D. diss., University of Kansas, 1962), p. 147.

27. Evelyn Waugh, "The Heart's Own Reasons," *Commonweal*, August 17, 1951, p. 458.

28. There is evidence that in writing *Decline and Fall* Waugh was working out the question of his own identity. Paul is part of Waugh, and since Paul is worried about his identity, we may conclude that Waugh is concerned about his own. In a passage which is present only in the manuscript, the imprisoned Paul meditates upon identity as follows:

> Paul's Meditations (This chapter may be omitted on the first reading)
> 1. Who am I?
> I am Paul Pennyfeather. For all I know there may be a hundred other people with the same name. I did not choose my name. The name Pennyfeather was preordained for me centuries ago; the name Paul was chosen by my mother, because she had an uncle Paul who had been kind to her as a child. Why was he called Paul? Perhaps for the same reason. What do I mean when I say that I am Paul Pennyfeather? A chain of consequences so obscurely connected and of such remote origins that it is impossible to trace what I mean. Here I am called D. 4. 12. That means that for twenty-two hours out of twenty-four I can be found in the twelfth cell of the fourth landing of block D. D. 4. 12 is the creature of order and purpose. Paul Pennyfeather is the creature of chaos.
> This is not quite true. D. 4. 12 has only extension in space. Paul Pennyfeather has continuity in time. How does continuity in time suggest itself to the imagination? In the form of a series of positions in space, Paul Pennyfeather at Scone, at Llannabba, at King's Thursday, etc. That is to say that Paul Pennyfeather is a series of which D. 4. 12 is an expression. This too is not quite true. Sometimes I am a part and sometimes a whole. It is very perplexing. Explain the position of D. 4. 12 in the series of Paul Pennyfeather.
> 2. Why Am I Here?

Paul has tried to achieve a sense of continuous identity through his ideals, but these are wrong and eventually lead him to prison. Soon he abandons the search for continuity, and his life becomes typical of those around him: mere discontinuous consecutiveness, like the newspapers which press on "with a series of events which never come to an end" (p. 184). Waugh gives visual form to Paul's sense of discontinuity in the drawing he designed for his novel's dust-cover. It shows Paul as a student, a bridegroom, a convict, and a minister: all of these are vocations which Waugh had tried or contemplated, and they reflect his sense of himself as a fragmented personality seeking a stable centre. In the end Waugh rejected the idea that the self derived continuity from anything within it; in his view, identity was the result of affiliation with enduring institutions.

29. Waugh shared a taste for innuendo with Ronald Firbank, of whose novels he wrote admiringly in 1929: "There is the barest minimum of direct description; his compositions are built up, intricately and with a balanced alternation of the wildest extravagance and the most austere economy, with conversational *nuances*. . . . The talk goes on, delicate, chic, exquisitely humorous, and seemingly without point or plan. Then, quite gradually, the reader is aware that a casual reference on one page links up with some particular inflexion of phrase on another until there emerges a plot; usually a plot so outrageous that he distrusts his own inferences" ("Ronald Firbank," *Life and Letters* 2 [March 1929]: 194, 195). Firbank's structural use of innuendo and allusion is evident in the running jokes about the fleas at the Ritz in *The Flower Beneath the Foot*, and the rats and the well in *Caprice*. Waugh borrowed the technique repeatedly: Tangent's gradual disintegration in *Decline and Fall* and the "drunk Major" in *Vile Bodies* are good examples. But in fact Firbank uses innuendo less often to shape plot than to create an unspoken dimension of naughtiness, something Waugh does in *Vile Bodies* but virtually nowhere else. In later years Waugh often expressed his admiration for allusive conversation, esoteric humour, concealed quotation, and private vocabulary, but he never confessed the main use to which he put these: the silent implantation of a moral level of meaning. In this he completely departs from Firbank, and from Nabokov, whose technique is similar. By scarcely ever mentioning his values explicitly and by keeping those values always in the back of his readers' minds, Waugh floods his fiction with a sense of their harmful absence. .

30. *Letters*, p. 29. See also D. Paul Farr, "The Novelist's Coup: Style as Satiric Norm in *Scoop*," *Connecticut Review* 8 (April 1975): 87–93.

## Chapter 6

1. Alec Waugh, *My Brother Evelyn and Other Profiles* (London: Cassell, 1967), p. 190.

2. *Letters*, p. 37.

3. *My Brother Evelyn*, p. 194.

4. Julian Jebb, "The Art of Fiction xxx: Evelyn Waugh," *Paris Review* 8 (Summer–Fall 1963): 77.

5. From the Waugh-Peters correspondence (early 1930), at the Humanities Research Center Library, University of Texas at Austin.

6. *Letters*, p. 39.

7. *My Brother Evelyn*, p. 191–92.

8. Evelyn Waugh, *Vile Bodies* (London: Chapman and Hall, 1930), p. 3. Subsequent page references appear in parentheses following each quotation.

9. Evelyn Waugh, *Labels* (London: Duckworth, 1930), p. 38.

10. *Diaries*, p. 241.

11. Evelyn Waugh, "The War and the Younger Generation," *Spectator*, 13 April 1929, p. 571.

12. See *Diaries*, p. 288, and *Rossetti* (London: Duckworth, 1928), p. 52.

13. *Letters*, p. 40.

14. See the discussion of *Decline and Fall* for Waugh's use of fireplaces, and "Ronald Firbank," *Life and Letters* 2 (March 1929), for his dislike of the rococo.

15. Evelyn Waugh, *The Ordeal of Gilbert Pinfold* (London: Chapman and Hall, 1957), p. 8.

16. In the Author's Note Waugh gives a time-scheme for his novel and pointedly remarks, "Christmas is observed by the Western Church on December 25th." The note is deleted from later editions.

## Chapter 7

1. *Diaries*, p. 329.

2. Evelyn Waugh, *Remote People* (London: Duckworth, 1931), p. 63.

3. Evelyn Waugh, *Robbery Under Law* (London: Chapman and Hall, 1939), p. 272; *Letters*, pp. 51, 55.

4. *Remote People*, p. 14.

5. See Waugh's correspondence with the Lygon sisters.

6. Ibid., p. 29.

7. Ibid., p. 240.

8. Evelyn Waugh, *Black Mischief* (London: Chapman and Hall, 1932), p. 12. Subsequent page references appear in parentheses following each quotation.

9. The "Wanda" probably owe their name to Wanda Baillie-Hamilton, née Holden. According to Michael Davie (*Diaries*, p. 794), she "inspired . . . Sonia Digby-Vane-Trumpington who (like Tallulah Bankhead) entertained young men in her bathroom while she bathed. According to Randolph Churchill, she threw a bun at the Mayor in her husband's constituency," after which he abandoned politics (see *Black Mischief* p. 103).

10. *Letters*, p. 52.

11. Dean Arthur Penrhyn Stanley, *The Eastern Church* (London, 1861), pp. 10–11. In a 1931 postcard to A. D. Peters, Waugh suggests "Further South" as a probable title for his novel. He also thought of calling it "Accession."

12. *Robbery Under Law*, p. 279.

13. Whenever Waugh mentions photographs, the reader may be sure that their subjects are in some way suspect. In *Decline and Fall*, for example, Paul Pennyfeather stupidly meditates on Margot's uniqueness while regarding her photograph in the newspaper. In *Scoop* (p. 9), the line of traffic in Piccadilly is "still as a photograph" and Mrs. Stitch avoids it.

14. Sir Samson's remark characterizes what Waugh earlier called "the romantic outlook." This was the "breezy, common-sense attitude to life, typified by Millais as 'one damned thing after another'." Its opposite was the "solemn per-

ception of process, typified by Holman-Hunt" (*Rossetti*, p. 52). One is "pictur-esque," the other is "mystical." Most people, Waugh says, act according to both of these contradictory attitudes at the same time. On 30 August 1927 Waugh and Alastair Graham attended "a revue called *One Damn Thing After Another*." Basil's mistress is named Lyne and he enters the novel down a flight of stairs cov-ered in linoleum; he is consecutiveness itself. One is reminded of "all that succes-sion and repetition of massed humanity" in *Vile Bodies* (p. 133).

15. Evelyn Waugh, *Put Out More Flags* (London: Chapman and Hall, 1942), pp. 59, 20.

16. Waugh's account of the Coronation Mass recalls his description of Ras Tafari's investiture at Debra Lebanos monastery in *Remote People* (p. 88).

17. Evelyn Waugh, "An Open Letter to His Eminence the Cardinal Archbishop of Westminster" (London and Tonbridge: The Whitefriars Press, May 1933), 19 pp. Never sold publicly, but now published in Waugh's *Letters*. Lady Diana Cooper's copy bears the inscription: "for Duff and Diana (one of five surviving copies) from Evelyn."

18. "An Open Letter," pp. 16—17.

19. *Letters*, p. 342.

20. Ibid., p. 2.

## Chapter 8

1. Evelyn Waugh, "Fan-Fare," *Life* (8 April 1946), p. 58.

2. Evelyn Waugh, *A Handful of Dust* (London: Chapman and Hall, 1934), p. 92. Subsequent page references appear in parentheses following each quotation.

3. *Letters*, p. 88.

4. Malcolm Bradbury, *Evelyn Waugh* (London: Oliver and Boyd, 1964), p. 66.

5. The staircase is an important motif, connoting the upward climb toward vocation, as in *Brideshead*, or its reverse, as in the linoleum-covered stairs in *Black Mischief* and Mr. Baldwin's step-ladder in *Scoop*.

6. See the discussion of *Scoop*. Sykes says that Evelyn Gardner was another pale "under-water" girl.

7. Jerome Meckier comments on Waugh's adaptation of the *Bildungsroman* in "Cycle, Symbol and Parody in Evelyn Waugh's *Decline and Fall*," *Contemporary Literature* 20 (1979): 51—75.

8. "The Claim of Youth or Too Young at Forty: Youth Calls to Peter Pans of Middle-Age Who Block the Way," *Evening Standard*, 22 January 1929, p. 7; "Matter-of-Fact Mothers of the New Age," ibid., 8 April 1929, p. 7; "The War and the Younger Generation," *Spectator*, 13 April 1929, pp. 570—71.

9. Evelyn Waugh, "Tolerance," in "The Seven Deadly Sins of Today by Seven Famous Authors," *John Bull*, 31 May 1932, pp. 22, 24.

10. Christmas was often a melancholy time for Waugh. On Christmas Day 1924 he wrote, "Christmas Day always makes me feel a little sad; for one reason because strangely enough my few romances have always culminated in Christmas

week—Luned, Richard, Alastair" (*Diaries*, p. 194).

11. "A white pekinese belonging to Phyllis de Janzé" (*Letters*, p. 85n). Waugh often uses oriental names and objects as tags to imply his disapproval: "For me Christianity begins with the Counter-Reformation and the Orientalism makes me itch" (*Letters*, p. 102).

12. See *The Ordeal of Gilbert Pinfold*, p. 121.

13. Chivalry always fascinated Waugh. He was an ardent reader of Spenser, and in 1924 he drew a "baroque Passing of Arthur." In the same year he considered renaming "The Temple at Thatch," "The Fabulous Paladins," after a passage from *A Cypress Grove* (*Diaries*, pp. 163, 182). The mock-chivalry of Cabell's *Jurgen* also fascinated him for a time.

14. Notice how Brenda is poised for the most part but often loses her balance, and how Dr. Messinger perishes when he loses his.

15. Raincoats are danger-signs. See the discussion of *Scoop*.

16. Doubleness is Waugh's recurrent metaphor for the falseness that occurs in the secular world.

17. Compare "The Balance," where in the end "circumstance decides." Waugh's emphasis on "nothing" and "nobody" as forces of oblivion recall the "Nil" of *Antic Hay* and the nothingness of the Marabar caves in *A Passage to India*. Both novels were favourites of Waugh's. The independent Mrs. Rattery may owe something to Lina Szczepanowska, the emancipated Polish aviatrix of Shaw's *Misalliance*. My thanks to Father Brian Hennessey for this suggestion.

18. Tony's attempts to phone Brenda bear a curiously inverted resemblance to Apthorpe's attempts to reach Guy Crouchback.

19. One wonders whether Waugh knew the Samarra legend, in which a man flees to Samarra to avoid Death only to find that it is the place where Death expects him. Somerset Maugham's *Sheppey*, which opened in London in the autumn of 1934, relies heavily on the legend. I am indebted to Professor Frederick Sweet for this suggestion.

20. Evelyn Waugh, *Ninety-Two Days* (London: Duckworth, 1934), p. 120.

21. Peter Fleming, *Brazilian Adventure* (Harmondsworth, Middlesex: Penguin 1957), pp. 15, 215.

22. "The Man Who Liked Dickens" first appeared in *Cosmopolitan* (September 1933). In "Fan-Fare" Waugh claims that the novel grew out of the short story, but it is interesting to note that while he was in Fez writing *A Handful of Dust*, Waugh twice wrote to A. D. Peters that he did not know how the novel would end. *Harper's Bazaar* published Waugh's novel serially but required a less melancholy conclusion. Waugh accordingly wrote a happy ending in which Tony travels only as far as the Caribbean and then returns to England, where he and Brenda tacitly agree to forget Brenda's adultery. Tony goes to London to settle the business of the flat, but Mrs. Beaver persuades him to keep it on, presumably for his own amours. The alternative ending is out of keeping with the spirit and logic of the original ending, although its brittle and conventional tone bears some similarity to that of the early portions of the book.

23. *Ninety-Two Days*, p. 90.

24. *Diaries*, p. 532.
25. Saint Augustine, *The City of God*, ed. Vernon J. Bourke (New York: Doubleday Image, 1958), pp. 206 ff. See also A. A. De Vitis, *Roman Holiday: The Catholic Novels of Evelyn Waugh* (New York: Bookman Associates, 1956), p. 32.
26. *Letters*, p. 81. Are there two sides of Teresa ("Baby") Jungman in *A Handful of Dust*? Thérèse de Vitré reflects her Roman Catholic self, but a less decorous side may be reflected in the person of "Baby," whom Tony meets at Brighton.
27. *Diaries*, p. 356.
28. *Letters*, p. 88.
29. Waugh's interest in overturned canoes recurs in *Scoop*, where Kätchen's prospector-husband recalls the iron-wood canoe which sank in the Matto Grosso.
30. See *Edmund Campion*, pp. 3–4.
31. See Evelyn Waugh, "Apotheosis of an Unhappy Hypocrite," *Spectator*, 2 October 1953: 363–64.
32. Evelyn Waugh, *Robbery Under Law* (London: Chapman and Hall, 1939), p. 109.
33. See Jerome Meckier, "Why the Man Who Liked Dickens Reads Dickens instead of Conrad: Waugh's *A Handful of Dust*," *Novel* 13 (Winter 1980): 171–87.
34. See *The Waste Land*, 1. 330: "With a little patience."
35. The first edition reads, "à côté de"—a mistake Waugh later corrected.
36. Northrop Frye, *Anatomy of Criticism* (Princeton: Princeton University Press, 1957), p. 233.
37. See Alvin Kernan, *The Plot of Satire* (New Haven: Yale University Press, 1965), pp. 143–67.

## Chapter 9

1. Waugh went to Spitzbergen in July 1934 with Sandy (later Sir Alexander) Glen.
2. Evelyn Waugh, *Waugh in Abyssinia* (London: Longmans, Green, 1936), p. 75.
3. Ibid., p. 181.
4. Phillip Knightley, *The First Casualty: The War Correspondent as Hero, Propagandist, and Myth-maker* (New York: Harcourt Brace Jovanovich, 1975), p. 175. See Knightley for other "originals."
5. *Letters*, p. 100.
6. Waugh to Peters, 2 October 1936, A. D. Peters file, Humanities Research Center Library, University of Texas at Austin.
7. *Diaries*, p. 420.
8. Ibid., p. 424.
9. Evelyn Waugh, "Memorandum for Messrs. Endfield and Fisz," typescript, Humanities Research Center Library, University of Texas at Austin.

10. Evelyn Waugh, *Scoop: A Novel about Journalists* (London: Chapman and Hall, 1938), p. 18. Subsequent page references appear in parentheses following each quotation.

11. Influenced possibly by lingering memories of Harold Acton's *Aquarium* (London: Duckworth, 1923), Waugh repeatedly uses marine imagery to describe the fallen, self-indulgent world. In *Brideshead Revisited*, for example, Charles Ryder comes "to the surface, into the light of common day and the fresh sea-air, after long captivity in the sunless coral palaces and waving forests of the ocean bed" (pp. 149–50). Various marine creatures float through the novel: the "queer fish" who interest Anthony Blanche (p. 227); the "fishes of silver and gold paper" above the linoleum floor of the "Blue Grotto Club" (p. 237); the "floundering fishes" from the shallows of Chioggia (p. 90); Rex Mottram with his bejewelled tortoise and his "own fish to fry" (p. 260); the "swan, moulded in ice and filled with caviar" on Charles's and Julia's transatlantic crossing (p. 211); and the disruptive image of war: "something coming out of the waters, a monster with sightless face and thrashing tail thrown up out of the depths" (p. 290). Sebastian writes whimsically to Charles, "And now I must try to catch a fish," (p. 40), while Charles himself, as a successful artist, "rises like a fresh young trout to the hypodermic injection of a new culture" (p. 200). In *Black Mischief* a woman eats sardines from the tin as Basil makes his first appearance; Margot Metroland keeps an octopus at King's Thursday; in *Put Out More Flags* Cedric Lyne collects grottoes, while fishermen—but seldom priests—visit Ambrose Silk's Irish refuge. In the War Trilogy Guy Crouchback sees marine creatures when he hallucinates on his return from Crete, and the fraudulent Apthorpe wears "porpoises." Arthur Atwater of *Work Suspended* owes his surname to his fishiness; there is also an Atwater in *Scoop*, which is riddled with references to fish, including the trout of Boot Magna which William recalls while en route to Ishmaelia. The motifs of fish, flight from vocation, and imprisonment may echo the Jonah story.

12. This is not as amazing as it sounds; an important London daily recently fired a reporter who for a long time covered the Washington scene by inventing interviews which he composed in England.

13. "The house was 16 Arlington St., Kent more than Hawksmoor looking on to Green Park with courtyard-garden, now [an] overseas club and ruined" (Lady Diana Cooper to J. M. Heath, 27 June 1977).

14. The valet in the tasteless and expensive hotel where William awakens on his second day in London makes "a High Anglican compromise between nod and genuflection" (p. 47); the typewriter keys in Copper's inner sanction make "no more sound than the drumming of a bishop's finger-tips on an upholstered prie-dieu" (p. 52).

15. *The First Casualty*, p. 174.

16. *Waugh in Abyssinia*, p. 161.

17. Christopher Hollis traces "Up to a point" to the villagers of Whatley, who habitually replied in those words to the eccentric Major Elderton (*Diaries*, p. 628).

18. See D. Paul Farr, "The Novelist's Coup: Style as Satiric Norm in *Scoop*," *Connecticut Review* 8 (April 1975): 42–54. Professor Farr's remarks about style in *Scoop* illuminate other early Waugh novels too.

302     NOTES TO PAGES 129–40

19. See Sykes, p. 116; Hector, in "On Guard," is another tribute to Granger.

20. The Boot family's eating habits may stem from those of E. S. P. Haynes, whom Michael Davie describes as an "eccentric lawyer" and "solicitor in Evelyn Waugh's divorce" who "at his end of his dining table, maintained a store of bottles, sauces, jars, garlic, tins, charcoal biscuits, etc." (*Observer*, "The Private Diaries of Evelyn Waugh," 25 March 1973, p. 26).

21. "The Novelist's Coup," p. 45.

22. *Waugh in Abyssinia*, p. 40.

23. In *Waugh in Abyssinia* (p. 147), Waugh remarks that he kept a "petulant and humourless baboon" at Frau Heft's pension; in *Scoop* (p. 214), Mr. Salter likens William's photograph to that of a baboon.

24. Boot Magna is figuratively under water too. When William daydreams of the trout in his "distant Canaan, . . . deserted Eden," the river and the Boot Magna dining-room merge in his mind (p. 91). See note 11.

25. Sykes, p. 139.

26. Ibid., p. 124.

27. *Diaries*, p. 354 (Davie's words).

28. Ibid., p. 355.

29. Ibid., p. 409.

30. See Jeffrey M. Heath, "*Scoop* in Manuscript," *Evelyn Waugh Newsletter* 11 (Autumn 1977): 9–11.

31. In Waugh the fallen world is always associated with linear things: Sir Samson's "one thing after another"; Mr. Baldwin's "undeviating" dinner; the name of Basil's mistress (Angela Lyne); and the linoleum on the floor of the Blue Grotto Club in *Brideshead Revisited*.

32. If the balanced man is the man with two boots, then Grimes's one-legged state takes on added significance.

33. *Diaries*, p. 422.

34. Compare the view from the terrace in *Brideshead*, where the "moonlight lay like hoar-frost" (p. 258). Boot Magna and Brideshead House are similar in several respects, and Nanny Bloggs and Nanny Hawkins both stem from Lucy Hodges.


## Chapter 10

1. Evelyn Waugh, *Work Suspended* (London: Chapman and Hall, 1942), p. 43. Subsequent page references appear in parentheses following each quotation.

2. Waugh to Roughead, December 1939, Humanities Research Center Library, University of Texas at Austin.

3. *Diaries*, p. 448.

4. In the 1948 edition Plant is thirty-four. For more on the differences between the first and second editions, see Robert Murray Davis, "Textual Problems in the Novels of Evelyn Waugh," *Papers of the Bibliographical Society of America* 62 (1968): 259–63; reprinted 63 (1969): 41–46.

5. His first child, Teresa, was born in March 1938.

6. Note, for example, the opinion of Robert Murray Davis, in "Textual Problems in the Novels of Evelyn Waugh" (p. 43): "John Plant['s] statements on fiction, like those on painting and politics, are quite similar to views expressed elsewhere by Evelyn Waugh. Two passages cut from later editions present opinions that Waugh expressed nowhere else during this period and that have significant implications in the study of his technique." Professor Davis does not see that Waugh is attacking Plant's views rather than endorsing them; see also his "Evelyn Waugh on the Art of Fiction," *Papers in Language and Literature* 2 (1966): 244–45.

7. Evelyn Waugh, "Fan-Fare," *Life*, 8 April 1946, p. 56.

8. Ibid., p. 56.

9. It is wholly typical of Waugh that he expresses Plant's truce with his father in aesthetic terms. It is also worth noting that Waugh's enthusiastic interest in Victoriana dates from about this time.

10. Nigel Dennis, "Evelyn Waugh: The Pillar of Anchorage House," *Partisan Review* 10 (July–August 1943): 354.

11. Evelyn Waugh, "A Call to the Orders," *Country Life*, 26 February 1938, Supplement, p. xii.

12. Evelyn Waugh, "The Youngest Generation," *Lancing College Magazine* XIV (December 1921): 85.

13. *Letters*, p. 638. Quoted in Sykes, p. 225. According to Lady Pansy Lamb, the new members of Lady Diana Mosley's circle included Brian Howard and his friends, whom Waugh disliked.

14. In all this we must remember that in the first edition the action is set in 1932, not 1939.

15. "Lucina," *Encyclopaedia Britannica*, 15th ed.

16. If Lucy is really Laura, then it is possible to argue that John Plant is an embodiment of the immature and anarchic side of Waugh which, because it was so intractable, was not "married" to Laura. At the same time, this anarchic self loved Laura and wished to win her recognition—perhaps even to win her away from the "other man" who had married her. This "other man" was Roger Simmonds, the newly domestic side of Waugh. Lucy's eventual rejection of Plant because of her domestic preoccupations may signal Laura's rejection of the anarchic side of Waugh.

17. The mackintosh connects her, unexpectedly, with the raincoated Atwater and the fishy, submarine world we have noticed in *Scoop*.

18. Sykes, p. 225.

19. Martin Stannard, in an article published when this chapter was in manuscript form, argues that Waugh failed to complete his novel not because of the war but because it lacked a supernatural dimension. I agree that Waugh's excuse about the pressures of war lacks candour. See Stannard, "*Work Suspended*, Waugh's Climacteric," *Essays in Criticism* 28 (October 1978): 302–20.

20. Sykes, p. 225.

21. *Work Suspended* highlights other Waugh techniques. When we get past the surface differences we perceive that the "Composed Hermitage" is a repetition,

with variation, of the house of Plant senior, of the hotel in Fez, and the secret "nest" where young Plant imprudently confessed that his father was an artist. Similarly, Plant is an intensification of his father and Atwater caricatures them both. Unexpected repetition with outrageous variation is one of Waugh's basic techniques, and in a corollary method, he brings the variations into conjunction: Atwater kills Plant senior and threatens Plant junior. Another device, essential to irony, becomes evident here; we might term it "the hidden parallel": thus Atwater is unexpectedly similar to Plant and both are morally analogous to Humboldt's Gibbon.

## Chapter 11

1. Evelyn Waugh, *Scott-King's Modern Europe* (London: Chapman and Hall, 1947), p. 5.

2. *Diaries*, p. 628.

3. Ibid., p. 637.

4. Ibid., pp. 661–62.

5. Evelyn Waugh, *Work Suspended* (London: Chapman and Hall, 1942), p. 49.

6. Evelyn Waugh, Dedicatory Letter, *Put Out More Flags* (London: Chapman and Hall, 1942). Subsequent page references appear in parentheses following each quotation. To his father Waugh described *Put Out More Flags* as "a minor work dashed off to occupy a tedious voyage" (*Letters*, p. 158). He wrote it while returning from Egypt by way of Cape Town in 1941. As usual, Waugh exaggerates in a self-deprecating manner. Some readers would disagree with his view that *Put Out More Flags* is a minor work while *Work Suspended* is major.

7. As a Communist artist standing in a "shadowy" relationship to Basil, Ambrose recalls the socialist novelist Roger Simmonds in *Work Suspended*, who stands in a similar relationship to John Plant.

8. Evelyn Waugh, "A Fifth Study in Loyalty," *Time and Tide*, 12 December 1953, p. 1652.

9. In the new Uniform Edition (p. 186), Waugh wrote "hermetic" for "cenobitic"; he appears to have forgotten to make the same change on p. 220, where "cenobitic" survives.

10. In an article published while this chapter was in manuscript form, John J. Riley also remarks on the split between art and action in *Put Out More Flags*. He suggests that the first epigraph refers to Basil, the second to Ambrose. See John J. Riley, "The Two Waughs at War," *Evelyn Waugh Newsletter* 12 (Autumn 1978): 3–7. Nigel Dennis makes a similar observation in "Evelyn Waugh: the Pillar of Anchorage House," *Partisan Review* 10 (July–August 1943): 360.

11. The other is Brian Howard. See Sykes, pp. 254–55.

12. Lin Yutang, *The Importance of Living* (London: Heinemann, 1938), p. 14.

13. Malcolm Muggeridge, *Chronicles of Wasted Time*, vol. 2, *The Infernal Grove* (London: Collins, 1973), pp. 77–78.

14. Nigel Nicolson, ed., *Harold Nicolson's Diaries and Letters, vol. 1, 1939–45* (London: Collins), p. 32.

15. Duff Cooper, *Old Men Forget* (London: Rupert Hart-Davis, 1953), p. 285.

16. *Diaries*, p. 461.

17. The Nollekens busts probably derive from the "enormous pair of portraits of George III and wife" which Waugh bought in 1939 and found "disconcerting." He hung the portrait of George III in his library and thought of putting "'scribble, scribble' on a ribbon across the top" (*Diaries*, pp. 435, 438).

## Chapter 12

1. Evelyn Waugh, *Brideshead Revisited: The Sacred and Profane Memories of Captain Charles Ryder* (London: Chapman and Hall, 1945), p. 196. Subsequent page references appear in parentheses following each quotation. In a May 1944 letter to A. D. Peters Waugh says, "I hoped the last conversation with Cordelia gave the theological clue" (*Letters*, p. 185).

2. The manuscript is in the Humanities Research Center at the University of Texas at Austin.

3. *Brideshead Revisited*, dustjacket of British first edition.

4. For an account of some of these changes, see the following: Alan Clodd, "Some Textual Variants in *Brideshead*," *Evelyn Waugh Newsletter* 3 (Spring 1969): 5–6; Gene D. Phillips, "The Page Proofs of *Brideshead Revisited*," *Evelyn Waugh Newsletter* 5 (Autumn 1971): 7–8, and especially Robert Murray Davis, "Notes Toward a Variorum *Brideshead*," *Evelyn Waugh Newsletter* 2 (Winter 1968): 4–6; idem., "The Serial Version of *Brideshead Revisited*," *Twentieth-Century Literature* 15 (April 1968): 35–43; idem., "Clarifying and Enriching: Waugh's Changing Concept of Anthony Blanche," *Papers of the Bibliographical Society of America* 72 (1978): 305–20. In the last-named article (p. 306), Davis lists twelve versions of the novel, but does not record a thirteenth version: the August 1946 Chapman and Hall fourth edition, which carries the important addition (p. 33) about the false dome which resembles the cupola of Chambord.

5. Originally the novel was subtitled "A Household of the Faith." Ryder is "Peter Fenwick," Cordelia is "Bridget," Beryl is "Cynthia," and Lady Marchmain's Christian names are "Marie Louise." The Prologue bears the epigraph "*Non hinc habemus manentum civitatem*"; Ryder's battle of wits with his father includes a second party, involving the "Angus Farthings" and a "Miss Pomfrey," whom the elder Plant hires from Harrods. In the important passage on shadows and routine, we learn that only the "saints of God" fail to cast shadows.

6. I have since seen an even better study. It is Susan Ganis Auty's excellent "Language and Charm in *Brideshead Revisited*," *Dutch Quarterly Review* 6 (Autumn 1976): 291–303. I had not yet had the pleasure of reading Auty's article when I wrote this chapter.

7. Rodney Delasanta and Mario L. D'Avanzo, "Truth and Beauty in *Brideshead Revisited*," *Modern Fiction Studies* 11 (1965/66): 142.

8. Ibid., pp. 142–43.

9. Ibid., p. 146.

10. See Jeffrey M. Heath, "*Brideshead*: The Critics and the Memorandum," *English Studies* 56 (June 1975): 227.

11. This is one of many passages Waugh cut from the 1960 new Uniform Edition because they were too self-indulgent—and, one suspects, too explicit.

12. Evelyn Waugh, "Come Inside," in *The Road to Damascus*, ed. John A. O'Brien (New York: Doubleday, 1949), p. 15.

13. *Diaries*, p. 264.

14. "He was a bad painter." See *Letters*, p. 196.

15. With characteristic exaggeration, Waugh said, "It is by having preposterous possessions that one can keep them at arm's length." *Letters*, p. 198.

16. Evelyn Waugh, *Rossetti* (London: Duckworth, 1928), p. 227.

17. Ibid., p. 196.

18. Ibid., p. 156.

19. Ibid., p. 14.

20. "Truth and Beauty in Brideshead Revisited," pp. 145–46.

21. George Orwell planned to analyse *Brideshead* and to "note faults due to being written in first person." See *The Collected Essays, Journalism and Letters of George Orwell*, 4 vols. (London: Secker and Warburg, 1968), 4: 576.

22. Harold Acton, *Memoirs of an Aesthete* (London: Methuen, 1948), p. 126.

23. Walter Pater, "Leonardo da Vinci," *The Renaissance* (New York: Boni and Liveright, 1919), pp. 103–4. Waugh attacks Pater's neo-paganism elsewhere too: in *Decline and Fall* he paraphrases Pater's description of the Mona Lisa in Paul's reverie on Grimes; and he compares crusty Scott-King to Lady Lisa in *Scott-King's Modern Europe*.

24. Waugh wrote to Nancy Mitford: "Lady Marchmain, no, I am not on her side; but God is, who suffers fools gladly; and the book is about God" (*Letters*, p. 196).

25. G. K. Chesterton, "The Queer Feet," *The Father Brown Omnibus* (New York: Dodd, Mead, 1935), p. 61.

26. "Drink is . . . bad because . . . it keeps the soul from God" (*Letters*, p. 459). Like Augustine, Sebastian is redeemed in North Africa.

27. "*Brideshead*: The Critics and the Memorandum," p. 227.

28. Evelyn Waugh, *A Little Learning* (London: Chapman and Hall, 1964), p. 193.

29. Sykes, p. 257.

30. *A Little Learning*, p. 216.

31. See the discussion of Mr. Todd in *A Handful of Dust*. Waugh criticizes lax fathers who have slid away from sustaining orthodoxy.

## Chapter 13

1. Evelyn Waugh, *Unconditional Surrender* (London: Chapman and Hall, 1961), p. 243.

2. Evelyn Waugh, *When the Going was Good* (London: Duckworth, 1946), pp. x, xi.

3. Evelyn Waugh, *Scott-King's Modern Europe* (London: Chapman and Hall, 1947), p. 2. Subsequent page references appear in parentheses following each quotation.

4. Walter Pater, *The Renaissance* (New York: Boni and Liveright, 1919), p. 103. Pater's Lisa is not as innocent as the "white Greek Goddesses" and "beautiful women of antiquity," for she has seen many changes; she sums up in herself the long ritual of supersession which is history, and the weight of change is heavy upon her weary eyelids: "All the thoughts and experiences of the world have etched and moulded there, . . . the animalism of Greece, the lust of Rome, the reverie of the middle age with its spiritual ambition and imaginative loves, the return of the Pagan world, the sins of the Borgias." Like Lady Lisa but in a later epoch, Scott-King gazes at the panorama of change, but he is unable to imitate her nonchalance.

5. The body of the book derives from Waugh's 1946 visit to Spain. Mrs. Antonic's demand that Scott-King take her family to England recalls the Yugoslavian family Mustapic with its "Palmerstonian ideas of the value of British citizenship" (*Diaries*, p. 603). And for Scott-King's escape to Palestine, Waugh is indebted to the Jews of the Yugoslavian diaries. In addition, there is repetition from other books, notably *Scoop*: the giantess Miss Sveningen, "like something in a film," knocking down the police "like nine-pins" (pp. 49-50), recalls the drunken Swede Erik Olafsen. And the meeting in which Miss Bombaum and others "vote a resolution" against Dr. Fe resembles the assembly of irate journalists who complain about Benito. The mistreated naif is also very familiar.

6. Harvey Breit, *The Writer Observed* (London: Alvin Redman, 1957), pp. 43-44.

7. One remembers the seedy noblemen retiring to their wives and subdivided palaces after being disappointed by Miss Sveningen's modest apparel; the splendidly inane conversation of Engineer Garcia about Salford and champagne; the description of Miss Bombaum, who "sat smoking a cigar with a man of repellent aspect" (p. 37); Scott-King essaying a grunt of sympathy while afflicted by hiccups; the deplorable table habits of the left-wing poet; Miss Sveningen modestly attired in bath towels and eating beefsteak the morning after a debauch.

## Chapter 14

1. *Diaries*, p. 628.

2. Sykes, p. 300.

3. Waugh to Peters, 19 February 1947, A. D. Peters file, Humanities Research Center Library, University of Texas at Austin.

4. *Diaries*, p. 673.

5. See Jeffrey M. Heath, "*Brideshead*: The Critics and the Memorandum," *English Studies* 56 (June 1975): 222-30.

6. *Diaries*, p. 675.

7. Ibid., p. 668.

8. Ibid., p. 675.

9. Waugh to Peters, 18 October 1946, A. D. Peters file.

10. Sykes, p. 306.

11. In 1961 "the Dreamer" (Dr. Hubert Eaton) wrote to Waugh, "asking [him] to sign a document disclaiming any intention of mocking him." *Letters*, p. 593.

12. *Diaries*, p. 675.

13. *Letters*, p. 247.

14. On 2 June 1947 Waugh wrote in his diary, "I have decided to try a new method of work. When I began writing I worked straight on into the void, curious to see what would happen to my characters, with no preconceived plan for them, and few technical corrections. Now I waste hours going back and over my work. I intend trying in *The Loved One* to push straight ahead with a rough draft, have it typed and then work over it once, with the conclusion firmly in my mind when I come to give definite form to the beginning" (p. 680).

15. Cyril Connolly, Introduction to *The Loved One*, *Horizon* 17 (February 1948).

16. Ibid., p. 76.

17. *Diaries*, p. 672.

18. Evelyn Waugh, *The Loved One* (London: Chapman and Hall, 1948), p. 45. Subsequent page references appear in parentheses following each quotation.

19. *The Random House Dictionary of the English Language* (New York: Random House, 1966).

20. See chap. 1, pp. 7–8.

21. Waugh modified this view considerably in "The American Epoch in the Catholic Church," *Life*, 19 September 1949.

22. Evelyn Waugh, *Officers and Gentlemen* (London: Chapman and Hall, 1955), p. 24.

23. The land the Dragon guards is an infantile Elysian Fields; as one character in the play says, "There blooms the flower of Happiness which grows in no other clime, and here all lost loved ones are found." See Clifford Mills and John Ramsay, *Where the Rainbow Ends* (London: Samuel French, 1951), p. 1 (first published in 1912).

24. Evelyn Waugh, "Death in Hollywood," *Life*, 29 September 1947, p. 83.

25. Ibid., p. 84. The passage of time has not improved matters. One wonders what Waugh would have said could he have seen a 1977 news item, entitled "Death Enters Computer Age": "U. S. scientists are working on a computerized tombstone with a video panel that lights up with the name and image of the deceased, plays a voice tape, dispenses incense and waters the grass."

26. Evelyn Waugh, "The Voice of Tito," *Commonweal*, 8 May 1953, p. 125.

27. The first edition's penultimate paragraph about Fortune and the escape from immaturity does not appear in the holograph "first ms. draft" which is preserved at the Humanities Research Center, Austin. An early version of it does appear in the *Horizon* version, and in the H.R.C.'s copy of that version the present paragraph appears as a holograph insertion. The addition adumbrates Dennis's development from a neo-pagan young bounder into a dedicated and (since his

book will be *The Loved One* itself) Christian artist.

The Texas manuscript differs in important respects from the *Horizon* version and the first edition. It contains a far fuller portrait of the youthful Sir Ambrose Abercrombie. On those evenings when Sir Ambrose came to Sir Francis for entertainment, he swam in Sir Francis's pool, courted the executives' wives, and canvassed people for advice about his own future; in a period of light taxation he prudently invested great sums of money. He married a "plain, garrulous wealthy lady of the country" and made the difficult transition from hero to sage, lover to father. Sir Ambrose suppresses the remoter and less flattering past when he was first a "toff" and then a young purser in Cunarder uniform who received cigarette cases from the wives of the mighty. A coward, he was frightened by the sinking of the *Titanic* and when World War I began he made "the great decision" to leave his ship in New York. Now began a new life of "women; the west, the movies; a new name, a new life . . . the talkies, the false, the fruity, the entirely captivating English accent." Waugh's description of Sir Ambrose recalls that of Trimmer, and his development has similarities with that of Basil in *Basil Seal Rides Again*. Moreover, this "handsome young mercantile marine . . . [who] boldly set out on the high road of fortune" is very much like Dennis Barlow himself. In refusing to become like Sir Ambrose, Dennis resists the allure of Fortune.

Also deleted from the *Horizon* version and the first edition is the information that Sir Francis invited Dennis to live with him when they met at the Megalopolitan Cafeteria. The manuscript also contains a fuller treatment of Sir Francis's lethargy and the inappropriateness of Californian life for an artist. Later in the manuscript we learn that when Aimée calls Mr. Slump for advice, the "Guru" tells her to "order . . . a nice big bottle of poison and drink it to [his] health." Aimée's death-scene is much reworked. There are two accounts of it in the Texas manuscript. In the first, she lies down in Joyboy's workshop and takes "a swig" of poison. A neglectful old watchman covers her in a sheet. The second version resembles the published version, except that it goes on, in colourful language, to describe the "sudden convulsion" and "spasm" which afflict her after she injects the poison. See also Robert Murray Davis, "*The Loved One*: Text and Context," *Texas Quarterly* (Winter 1972), 100–107.

## Chapter 15

1. Evelyn Waugh, *The Holy Places* (London: The Queen Anne Press, 1952), p. 2.

2. Sykes, p. 318.

3. See the discussion of *Brideshead Revisited*.

4. Waugh to Peters, n.d. [early 1948], A. D. Peters file, Humanities Research Center Library, University of Texas at Austin.

5. Waugh to Peters, [May] 1950, A. D. Peters file.

6. Sykes, p. 318.

7. Harvey Breit, *The Writer Observed* (London: Alvin Redman, 1957), pp. 148–49.

8. "Face to Face," BBC TV, 26 June 1960.

9. Sykes, p. 337.

10. Evelyn Waugh, *Helena* (London: Chapman and Hall, 1950), p. 143. Subsequent page references appear in parentheses following each quotation. The manuscript title is "The Three Quests of the Dowager Empress: a Legend Retold."

11. *The Holy Places*, p. 12.

12. Waugh to Peters, "Notes on Translating *Helena*," 18 March [1950], A. D. Peters file.

13. *Letters*, pp. 207, 221. Cf. Augustine: "Will is to grace as the horse is to the rider."

14. *The Holy Places*, p. 6.

15. Ibid., p. 13.

16. Waugh based the Wandering Jew on Brian Howard: once again the false leads to the genuine. See *Letters*, p. 221.

## Chapter 16

1. Waugh told Julian Jebb that he "used to be able to hold the whole of a book in [his] head" (*Paris Review*, 1963). But by the time he reached his fifties writing had become more difficult for him. "It's disagreeable work," he told Stephen Black, with "no release in a muscular way." He wrote everything "about twice" in longhand, tearing up the bad effort and starting again. It took him "longer and longer" to write a book as he got older. At one time he "used to be able to write a full-length book in about two months" but by 1953 it took him "something like a year" ("Frankly Speaking," 1953). He told Jebb, "I've got slower as I grow older. . . . One's memory gets so much worse. . . . Now if I take a walk whilst I am writing, I have to hurry back and make a correction, before I forget it." Gilbert Pinfold had similar problems: "There were periods of literary composition when he would find the sentences he had written during the day running in his head, the words shifting and changing colour kaleidoscopically, so that he would again and again climb out of bed, pad down to the library, make a minute correction, return to his room, lie in the dark dazzled by the pattern of vocables until once more obliged to descend to the manuscript" (*Ordeal of Gilbert Pinfold*, p. 11). But Pinfold did not work all the time: ". . . those days and nights of obsession, of what might without vainglory be called 'creative' work, were a small part of his year." Like Pinfold, Waugh worked irregularly. He told Harvey Breit, "My whole life's a vacation, interrupted by work" (*The Writer Observed*, p. 45).

2. See Robert Murray Davis, "Shaping a World: The Textual History of *Love Among the Ruins*," *Analytical and Enumerative Bibliography* 1 (Spring 1977): 137–54.

3. *Diaries*, p. 714.

4. As Waugh himself admitted, *Love Among the Ruins* has "certain obvious defects." In the first place, his subtlety has vanished, to be replaced by sarcasm, invective, and a jarring explicitness. A shrill note of bitterness shows how frayed Waugh's patience has grown. His intolerance of the modern world costs him his

eloquent neutrality and his delicate irony; he is now too close to his object of attack. There are other problems. Considered from the standpoint of plot, *Love Among the Ruins* is too elliptical—certain chains of cause and effect are weak, and there is too much ambiguity. What, for example, is the real significance of Clara's beard? It seems to represent the vitality of unregenerate human nature but the reader remembers that it is in fact the result of an attempt to sterilize Clara. In addition, it can be argued that the British welfare state of 1950 did not resemble Waugh's caricature of it, and that it was unlikely to do so in the "near future." And Waugh's condemnation of man's tendency to seek "an oppressor who will take responsibility for his ills" may indicate that Waugh is too insensitive to faults which lie outside the individual's control. Waugh's inflexibility on the question of personal responsibility was one of his least attractive traits, for it made him seem cruel, intolerant, and uncharitable. Finally—although this is less serious—*Love Among the Ruins* is somewhat repetitive. The attack on the legal system and on prisons echoes *Decline and Fall*; the juxtaposing of bad news with "tidings of comfort and joy" comes from *Vile Bodies*; the notion of love in a context of death comes from *The Loved One*. Once again the naive protagonist who represents the tail-end of past splendours goes forth into the cold world to reap the reward of his frailties.

5. Evelyn Waugh, "Mr. Waugh Replies," *Spectator*, 3 July 1953, p. 23.

6. *Letters*, p. 404.

7. "Mr. Waugh Replies," p. 23. In the manuscript the novel is entitled, "A Pilgrim's Progress—a tale of the Near Future." The manuscript title invokes Bunyan, but it also suggests *The Rake's Regress*, the Hogarthian subtitle of *Basil Seal Rides Again*. Hogarth's sequence of engravings, entitled *The Rake's Progress*, describes how a father's miserliness leads his son through a series of misadventures which lead him first to prison and eventually to the madhouse—a route often followed by the neglected children in Waugh's fiction.

8. Evelyn Waugh, *Love Among the Ruins* (London: Chapman and Hall, 1953), p. 5. Subsequent page references appear in parentheses following each quotation.

9. Evelyn Waugh, "The Heart's Own Reasons," *Commonweal*, 17 August 1951, p. 458.

10. Evelyn Waugh, *Robbery Under Law* (London: Chapman and Hall, 1939), p. 109.

11. The view that good taste is not entirely learned but is partially inborn is one which Waugh puts forward as early as "The Tutor's Tale" (1927), in which George Verney demonstrates "a natural fastidiousness" despite being oppressed by his miserly parents. In *Vile Bodies* Adam and Nina even have an argument on the subject. Waugh's position seems to be approximately this: after the Fall man retained only a small amount of his innate taste, reason, and other faculties. Because his will was now infected (to use Sidney's term), he could accomplish very little; in order to advance beyond the level of mere animal survival, he had to use faith to support his damaged nature. Miles is in the position of fallen man: he has only vestigial traces of taste and reason—but these preserve him from becoming a dehumanized robot. A related argument is found in Anthony Burgess's *A Clock-*

*work Orange.*

12. "Shaping a World," p. 152.

13. The dystopia is one of the twentieth century's most flourishing modes. *Love Among the Ruins* invites comparison not only with *Nineteen Eighty-Four* and *Brave New World*, but also with Zamyatin's *We*, Forster's "The Machine Stops," Mackenzie's *The Lunatic Republic*, Green's *Concluding*, and B. F. Skinner's *Walden II*.

14. Evelyn Waugh, "Machiavelli and Utopia—Revised Version," *Spectator*, 10 February 1939, p. 234.

15. "Frankly Speaking," BBC radio, 16 November 1953.

16. Evelyn Waugh, "Fan-Fare," *Life*, 8 April 1946, p. 56.

## Chapter 17

1. *Diaries*, p. 438.

2. Evelyn Waugh, *Men at Arms* (London: Chapman and Hall, 1952), dustjacket.

3. Ibid., p. 166.

4. *Letters*, p. 157; Sykes, p. 228.

5. *Diaries*, p. 543.

6. Ibid., p. 545n.

7. Lord Lovat, *March Past: A Memoir* (London: Weidenfeld and Nicolson, 1978), p. 233.

8. *Diaries*, p. 545.

9. Ibid., pp. 547–48.

10. *Letters*, pp. 343, 432.

11. *Diaries*, p. 627.

12. Evelyn Waugh, *The Ordeal of Gilbert Pinfold* (London: Chapman and Hall, 1957), p. 3.

13. Ibid., p. 2.

14. *Diaries*, p. 550.

15. "Frankly Speaking," BBC radio, 16 November 1953.

16. At the Humanities Research Center Library, Austin, Texas.

17. Evelyn Waugh, *Unconditional Surrender* (London: Chapman and Hall, 1961), p. 10.

18. Frederick J. Stopp, *Evelyn Waugh: Portrait of an Artist* (London: Chapman and Hall, 1958), p. 46.

19. *Letters*, p. 383.

20. Julian Jebb, "The Art of Fiction xxx: Evelyn Waugh," *Paris Review* 8 (Summer–Fall, 1963): 83.

21. Evelyn Waugh, Preface, *Sword of Honour* (London: Chapman and Hall, 1965), p. 9.

22. *Men at Arms*, dustjacket.

23. Bernard Bergonzi, "Evelyn Waugh's The *Sword of Honour*," *The Listener*, 20 February 1964, p. 306.

24. *Letters*, p. 433.

25. "The Art of Fiction xxx: Evelyn Waugh," p. 83.

26. *Letters*, p. 363.

27. Ibid., p. 383.

28. David Malbert, "Civil Waugh," *Evening Standard* (London), 19 September 1976, p. 19.

29. *Letters*, pp. 354, 363, 353.

30. See Winnifred M. Bogaards, "The Conclusion of Waugh's Trilogy: Three Variants," *Evelyn Waugh Newsletter* 4 (Autumn 1970): 6–7. See *Letters*, p. 599: "No nippers for Guy and Domenica" (1961).


## Chapter 18

1. Evelyn Waugh, *Men at Arms* (London: Chapman and Hall, 1952), p. 7. Subsequent page references appear in parentheses following each quotation.

2. In 1961 Waugh wrote, "Sloth is the condition in which a man is fully aware of the proper means of his salvation and refuses to take them because the whole apparatus of salvation fills him with tedium and disgust. . . . Man is made for joy in the love of God, a love which he expresses in service. If he deliberately turns away from that joy, he is denying the purpose of his existence" ("Evelyn Waugh on Sloth," *Sunday Times*, mag. sec., 7 January 1962, p. 21).

3. Evelyn Waugh, *Officers and Gentlemen* (London: Chapman and Hall, 1955), p. 322.

4. *Men at Arms*, dustjacket.

5. See also Frederick J. Stopp, *Evelyn Waugh: Portrait of an Artist* (London: Chapman and Hall, 1958), pp. 161, 197. Jerome Meckier makes a similar observation in "Evelyn Waugh," *Contemporary Literature* 18 (Winter 1977): 108. He rightly points out that Apthorpe's cumbersome baggage is a parody of Guy's "cumbrous romantic idealism." I had not yet had the pleasure of reading Professor Meckier's work at the time of writing this chapter.

6. *Diaries*, p. 783. Doubles had fascinated Waugh since "The Balance" and "The Tutor's Tale." It is interesting to note that in a letter to Nancy Mitford just after he had completed *Men at Arms* Waugh suggests a plot for her: it is the story of two mutually destructive doubles (*Letters*, p. 379).

7. Sykes, p. 418.

8. Ibid., p. 354.

9. Evelyn Waugh, *Brideshead Revisited* (London: Chapman and Hall, 1945), p. 198.

10. *Officers and Gentlemen*, p. 46.

11. Ibid., p. 47.

12. Stopp argues that the "civilian" is Virginia, not Guy.

## Chapter 19

1. Evelyn Waugh, *Officers and Gentlemen* (London: Chapman and Hall, 1955), dedication. Subsequent page references appear in parentheses following each quotation. Gene D. Phillips, in *Evelyn Waugh's Officers, Gentlemen and Rogues* (Chicago: Nelson-Hall, 1975), also discusses Waugh's use of actual experience.

2. In statements he made when *Officers and Gentlemen* was published, Waugh asserted a continuity between the two parts of *Officers and Gentlemen* and between *Men at Arms* and *Officers and Gentlemen*. Stopp quotes Waugh as having said, "*Men at Arms* ended with the death of Apthorpe. *Officers and Gentlemen* begins with the placation of his spirit, a ritual preparation for the descent into the nether world of Crete. . . . *Men at Arms* began with its hero inspired with an illusion. *Officers and Gentlemen* ends with its deflation" ("Waugh: End of an Illusion," p. 59). Nevertheless, the two sections of *Officers and Gentlemen* seem poorly connected (Waugh said to Julian Jebb, "There's a very bad transitional passage"). Furthermore, in the *Sword of Honour* preface Waugh admitted it was wrong to have claimed that *Men at Arms* and *Officers and Gentlemen* constituted a whole (on the dustjacket of *Unconditional Surrender* he said, "I knew a third volume was needed"). Evidently Waugh had some difficulty in completing the trilogy, but the main sources of the narrative "disorganization" are the informing themes of chance and military incompetence. Significantly, perhaps, Waugh was happier with *Officers and Gentlemen* than with *Men at Arms*. He glumly wrote to Graham Greene that *Men at Arms* "has some excellent farce" but that "the rest [is] very dull" (*Letters*, p. 370). When Kingsley Amis attacked *Officers and Gentlemen* in the *Spectator*, Waugh noted in his diary, "there is life in the old dog—more than in the young. I am quite complacent about the book's quality" (*Diaries*, p. 729).

3. Waugh to Peters, 25 March 1953, A. D. Peters file, Humanities Research Center Library, University of Texas at Austin.

4. See also B. W. Wilson, "*Sword of Honour*: The Last Crusade," *English* 23 (Autumn 1974): 92.

5. Evelyn Waugh, "Commando Raid on Bardia," *Life*, 17 November 1941, p. 64.

6. *Diaries*, pp. 491, 492.

7. Ibid., pp. 488, 491.

8. Ibid., pp. 494, 497, 495.

9. Evelyn Waugh, *Unconditional Surrender* (London: Chapman and Hall, 1961), p. 39.

10. *Diaries*, p. 502.

11. In real life, Duff Cooper; Mrs. Stitch is Lady Diana. See the discussion of *Scoop*, pp. 34, 37.

12. Waugh imposes shape on his experience in several ways. Much of it becomes exclusively Guy's, but other incidents, usually those witnessed jointly by Waugh and Major Hound, are narrated as if they happened to Hound alone. Examples of the latter are: Hound's visit to Creforce H.Q. in the coastal caves, the

gift of the Greek currency, and his visit to the runaway Spanish socialists with
their cauldron of aromatic stew. Hound becomes a focus for Waugh's attack on
cowardice, and Guy, in his quiet devotion to duty, is his foil. By means of allusion
and charged imagery, Waugh subtly elaborates other events and invests them with
significance they lack in diary form—for example, Guy's discovery of the dead
soldier and his meeting with General Miltiades. Where actual experience fails
him, as in Hound's strange encounters with the Cretan patriarch and with Ludovic, Waugh invents freely. But on the whole, the three long chapters which Waugh
devotes to the disaster on Crete are firmly rooted in fact, which, it should be said,
is by no means as fully "transformed" as Waugh lets on. Many passages are transplanted almost verbatim and in sequence from the "Memorandum on Layforce":
the terrified naval commander in shorts and greatcoat, the Italian prisoners carrying bedsheets, Guy's escape from the "lead weight" of human company, the
"breathless officer" who warns Guy against parachutists with machine guns but
who "didn't wait to see" if there were casualties (p. 273). Hound's selfish "They
say it's *sauve qui peut* now" (p. 239) belongs in the "Memorandum" to a cowardly Presbyterian minister. Many other episodes are paraphrased: the ditching
of the radio transmitters, the road which the sappers blow up too soon, and the
soldier with the hot-potato voice whom Guy suspects of being a spy. Unlike Guy,
Waugh did not escape in an open boat, and for this episode Waugh uncharacteristically borrowed the experiences of another man. He was "Pattison, of the
intelligence section" (*Diaries*, p. 510), who escaped to Egypt in a motorized landing craft. Waugh altered Pattison's story by changing the MLC to an open wooden
boat infested with bugs, and by adding the fictitious Ludovic.

   13. *Diaries*, p. 502.
   14. The felonious father-figure's Eastern garb recalls the oriental trappings of
other modern infidels, like Ivor Claire and Julia.
   15. *Diaries*, p. 728. Interview with Lady Diana Cooper, 11 March 1969. Critics differ: for example, Alan Watkins argues that Lovat is the model for Trimmer
(*Observer*, 29 October 1978, p. 48).
   16. In a letter to Nancy Mitford about the nuances of suicide, Waugh wrote,
"Oates just went for a walk in the snow. There was a very high probability that he
would not come back, but that is not the same as taking poison or shooting oneself the nature of which acts is lethal." See *Letters*, p. 595.
   17. Interestingly, Waugh deletes this important passage from the new Uniform
Edition of 1965. While I realize that divergent conclusions may be drawn from
this fact, my own view is that Waugh decided to depict Guy in a more favourable
and less ambiguous light and therefore removed the incriminating passage. This
is in keeping with other deletions concerning Guy; for example, in *Unconditional
Surrender* Waugh deletes the English composer who insists that Guy has "the
death wish." Since the present study investigates the way Waugh's fiction reflects
his state of mind at the time it was written, I have thought it best to retain first
edition readings, except for the reworked conclusion. See the Textual Note and
chap. 17 in this volume.
   18. *Letters*, pp. 443, 585.
   19. "Guy's silence in the hospital is all part of the strain that works out vari-

ously in the members of the family" (*Letters*, p. 444).

20. The passage calls to mind Cleopatra's flight at the Battle of Actium—another moment of betrayal. See Stopp, *Evelyn Waugh*, p. 177.

21. Evelyn Waugh, *Scott-King's Modern Europe* (London: Chapman and Hall, 1947), p. 5.

## Chapter 20

1. Evelyn Waugh, *Unconditional Surrender* (London: Chapman and Hall, 1961), p. 4. Subsequent page references appear in parentheses following each quotation.

2. *Diaries*, p. 530.

3. Ibid.

4. Ibid., p. 536.

5. Ibid., p. 556.

6. With the assistance of Joan Saunders, who often helped him in such matters, Waugh carefully researched the "state sword." He was interested in "the actual spectacle—dates, time, weather, etc." and the "wave of popular sentiment culminating in its ecclesiastical status. . . . E.g. was it blessed?" (*Letters*, pp. 532, 539).

7. The wedding is probably that of the Hon. Diana Mitford to Bryan Guinness, later the second Baron Moyne. Lady Perdita is Diana, "lost" because of her leftist sympathies. In *Work Suspended* Roger and Lucy Simmonds are modelled on the Guinnesses.

8. In some remarkable annotations in his copy of *The Unquiet Grave*, by "Palinurus" (pseudonym of Cyril Connolly), Waugh writes, "Why should I be interested in this book? . . . because Cyril is the most typical man of my generation. There but for the Grace of God, literally . . . [Waugh's ellipsis]. He has . . . the authentic waste-land despair . . . the ills he suffers from are theological, with the vocabulary of the nonsense-philosophy he learned holding him back" (rear endpapers). . . . "Palinurus seems never to have learned anything of the Fall of Man. It is his failure to take in the aboriginal calamity which is the dead rot putrefying his will" (p. 5). Waugh's relationship with Connolly was highly ambivalent, and helps explain his equally ambivalent attitude to aestheticism. The book is at the Humanities Research Center Library, University of Texas at Austin.

9. The "Loot" is modelled on Sergeant Stuart Preston, "an art historian serving in the American army. . . . Enjoyed an astonishing social success in wartime London" (*Letters*, p. 182n).

10. In his Preface to the new Uniform Edition *Sword of Honour* Waugh says: "I had written an obituary of the Roman Catholic Church in England as it had existed for many centuries. All the rites and most of the opinions here described are already obsolete. . . . It never occurred to me, writing *Sword of Honour*, that the Church was susceptible to change. I was wrong and I have seen a superficial revolution in what then seemed permanent" (p. 9).

11. It is certainly arguable that by refusing to believe he can help "all those others" Guy is even more defeatist than the "quantitative world," which at least

tries. Unsympathetic readers might easily construe Guy's argument as the reverse of admirable and see it as Waugh's defence of his own limited capacity for charity.

12. *Diaries*, p. 591.

13. Ibid., p. 587.

14. Ibid., p. 585.

15. Ibid., p. 587.

16. Randolph Churchill, "Evelyn Waugh: Letters (and Postcards) to Randolph Churchill," *Encounter* 31 (July 1968), p. 4. Churchill has no counterpart in *Unconditional Surrender*, where Guy's companion in Croatia is the Communist sympathizer, Frank de Souza.

17. After Waugh left Yugoslavia, he composed a report assessing the plight of Croatian Roman Catholics. The report was so critical of the British government's alleged failure to protect Croatian Catholics that some officials spoke of catching Waugh under the Official Secrets Act and charging him with treason if he published it. The report, along with the extensive correspondence it occasioned, is preserved in the Public Record Office in a folder bearing registration number R 5927/1059/92, dated 30 March 1945 and entitled "Church and State in Liberated Croatia." Among those involved in the controversy were Douglas F. Howard, Edgeworth Johnstone, John M. Addis, Fitzroy Maclean, Sir Anthony Eden, and the then British ambassador in Belgrade, Sir Ralph Stevenson. See also Sykes, pp. 272–81.

18. *Letters*, p. 134.

19. Evelyn Waugh, "Compassion," *Month* n.s., 3 (August 1949): 98.

20. See also Frederick J. Stopp, *Evelyn Waugh: Portrait of an Artist* (London: Chapman and Hall, 1958), pp. 173, 198, and Jerome Meckier, "Evelyn Waugh," *Contemporary Literature* 18 (Winter 1977): 108. I had the pleasure of reading the latter only after the present chapter was in manuscript form.

21. "For one who values privacy there is no keener pleasure than the feeling of isolation as you float down, but it is all too short-lived" (*Letters*, p. 181).

22. Evelyn Waugh, *Ninety-Two Days* (London: Duckworth, 1934), pp. 12, 11.

23. *Letters*, pp. 347, 351.

24. Alexander McLachlan in real life.

25. Evelyn Waugh, "Kicking Against the Goad," *Commonweal*, 11 March 1949, p. 534.

26. In Waugh's early conception of the novel, Mr. Crouchback did know; he was not to have died until after the adoption of little Trimmer. See *Letters*, p. 446.

27. Compare with this the parallel of Lucy's baby and John Plant's mature love in *Work Suspended*.

28. Evelyn Waugh, "The American Epoch in the Catholic Church," *Life*, 19 September 1949, p. 135.

29. John Bannerman, ed., and Nathan Cohen, interviewer, "A Profile of Evelyn Waugh," CBC "Tuesday Night," 28 October 1969.

30. See Winnifred Bogaards, "The Conclusion of Waugh's Trilogy: Three Variants," *Evelyn Waugh Newsletter* 4 (Autumn 1970): 6–7; Joseph F. Mattingly,

"Guy Crouchback's Children," *English Language Notes* 6 (1968–69): 200–201; Robert Murray Davis, "Guy Crouchback's Children—A Reply," *English Language Notes* 7 (1969–70): 127–129.

31. Christopher Tietjens is not unlike Guy Crouchback. He is a martyr of progress, a romantic, feudal in outlook, a Tory in politics, a humanist by upbringing, and a Christian in religion. He is "an eighteenth-century figure of the Dr. Johnson type," the "last stud-white bulldog . . . of the Groby Tory breed," the English public schoolboy incarnate, the only sane man in a crazed world. He envisions himself as a seventeenth-century Anglican parson; in particular he reveres the memory of the reclusive George Herbert in his parsonage near Salisbury. Betrayed by bunglers and "boodlers" in war and in marriage, Tietjens leaves Groby in the hands of his destructive wife, Sylvia, who is responsible for cutting down Groby Great Tree and contaminating the tradition it represents. Tietjens establishes a liaison with Valentine Wannop, a suffragette, and as the tetralogy ends, Tietjens and Wannop retreat to a cottage to establish a small world of order apart from the larger chaos. Their plight seems grave, but Ford hints that they or their descendants will emerge in the future from their ark. Tietjens' vision of himself as "an Anglican Saint" in a refuge is very close to Guy's view of himself at the end of *Unconditional Surrender*. Like Guy, Tietjens is a younger brother and an idealist; he too believes in a Providence which draws good out of evil and like him (though, of course, his marital circumstances are different) he has a child who will carry on his line: "George Herbert, Rector of Bemerton . . . That was what Chrissie was to be like." Despite superficial differences, there are many similarities between Waugh and Ford. They both hated modernity and loved privacy; they shared a vision of cultural decline, as well as the ideals of faith, order, and good taste. Like Ford in his tetralogy, Waugh in his trilogy chronicles the disastrous effects of war upon traditional morality; but each writer provides a glimmer of hope in the luminous figure of the newborn child.

32. Evelyn Waugh, *Men at Arms* (London: Chapman and Hall, 1952), p. 147.

33. An early version of Goodall's story can be found in Waugh's 1934 short story, "Period Piece," the story of Billy Cornphillip, his wife, Etta, and his brother-in-law, Ralph Bland. Ralph stands to inherit the Cornphillip fortune if Billy has no male heir. Time passes with no sign of a child; then, after Ralph and Billy quarrel, Etta runs away to Venice with Ralph. When she returns to Billy she is pregnant. "It was a son. Billy was very pleased about it." Ralph's adultery costs him his inheritance. In *Vile Bodies* a similar situation arises: Adam Symes, the only character with the slightest moral worth, provides his vacuous rival with an heir. We might notice that there is a marked contrast between Waugh's use of succession in his early and late fiction. In the early novels lineages are perverted and die out through unexpected misfortune—note, for example, the opening pages of *Black Mischief*—but in the novels after *Work Suspended* they are preserved through the unexpected intervention of Providence.

34. "American Epoch in the Catholic Church," p. 135.

## Chapter 21

1. *Diaries*, p. 769.
2. Ibid., p. 728.
3. *Letters*, p. 421.
4. Ibid., p. 426.
5. Ibid., p. 468.
6. Ibid., pp. 493–94.
7. Margaret Morriss, "Prejudice and Partiality: Evelyn Waugh and his Critics 1928–1966" (Ph.D. diss., University of Toronto, 1980), p. 332. Dr. Morriss's dissertation contains many excellent critical insights and a meticulously thorough survey of Waugh criticism. I did not have the opportunity to read her study until my own book was completed, but am very pleased to see that we are in agreement on several central points.
8. Interview with Henry Yorke (Henry Green), 23 February 1969.
9. *Letters*, pp. 176, 191.
10. Ibid., p. 315.
11. Waugh to Peters, 1 August 1953, A. D. Peters file, Humanities Research Center Library, University of Texas at Austin.
12. *Letters*, p. 410.
13. Waugh to Peters, 2 February, 10 November 1956, A. D. Peters file.
14. Waugh to Peters, 16 October 1957, and Waugh to Margaret Stephens, n.d. [1957], A. D. Peters file.
15. Waugh to Peters, 18 April, 27 June 1958, A. D. Peters file.
16. Waugh to Peters, n.d. [1960], A. D. Peters file.
17. Waugh to Peters, 29 March 1955, A. D. Peters file.
18. Waugh to Peters, 13 October 1956, A. D. Peters file.
19. Waugh to Peters, 24 February, 7 March 1957, A. D. Peters file.
20. Evelyn Waugh, *The Ordeal of Gilbert Pinfold* (London: Chapman and Hall, 1957), p. 3. Subsequent references appear in parentheses following each quotation.
21. "Frankly Speaking," BBC radio, 16 November 1953. Mark Amory (*Letters*, p. 546) identifies Black as Angel.
22. The five letters to Laura which Mark Amory incudes in the *Letters* show that Waugh did not exaggerate in *Pinfold*. One of them reads, "As I write this I hear the odious voices of the psychologists repeating every word in my ears" (p. 420).
23. In a letter to Ann Fleming (1 September 1952) Waugh writes, "My sexual passion for my ten-year-old daughter is obsessive" (*Letters*, p. 380). It is interesting to notice that Margaret Waugh's engagement triggered *Basil Seal Rides Again*, in which Basil prevents his daughter from marrying because he loves her too much. He claims that her marriage would be incestuous.
24. Initially Waugh wanted to disown responsibility for the "voices." In letters to Laura he wrote, "I know it sounds like acute p.m. but it is real and true", "it is a huge relief to realize that I am merely the victim of the malice of others, not mad myself as I really feared for a few days" (*Letters*, pp. 419, 420).

25. Interestingly, Francis Crease lived at "Lychpole."
26. In actual fact it was named MV *Staffordshire.*
27. *Diaries*, p. 781.
28. Sykes, pp. 364, 365.
29. "I do not absolutely exclude the possibility of diabolic possession" (*Letters*, p. 494).
30. J. B. Priestley, "What Was Wrong With Pinfold," *New Statesman*, 31 August 1957, p. 224.
31. Waugh's "biographical note" for the Spanish combined edition of *Black Mischief* and *A Handful of Dust* (1943); Evelyn Waugh, "General Conversation: Myself . . . ," *Nash's Pall Mall Magazine* 99 (March 1937): 11.

## Chapter 22

1. Father Martin D'Arcy, "The Religion of Evelyn Waugh," in *Evelyn Waugh and his World*, ed. David Pryce-Jones (London: Weidenfeld and Nicolson, 1973), p. 76.
2. Anthony Powell, "Waugh's Unvarnished Self-Portrait," *Daily Telegraph*, 2 September 1976, p. 10.
3. *Diaries*, p. 550.
4. Christopher Sykes, ed., "Evelyn Waugh—a Brief Life," *The Listener*, 24 August 1967, p. 229.
5. Sykes, pp. 290–92.
6. Dom Hubert van Zeller, "The Agreeable Mr. Waugh," *The Critic* 35 (Fall 1976): 38.
7. Peter Buckman, interviewer, "I Was Evelyn Waugh's Batman," *Punch*, 19 November 1975, pp. 960–61.
8. Kevin Burns, ed., "A Report on Evelyn Waugh," CBC "Nightcap," 9 November 1978.
9. *Letters*, p. viii.
10. Ibid., p. 141.
11. Ibid., p. 161.
12. Ibid., p. 324.
13. Ibid., p. 402.
14. Ibid., p. 422.
15. Ibid., p. 474.
16. Ibid., p. 469.
17. Ibid., p. 490.
18. Ibid., p. 344.
19. *Diaries*, p. 661.
20. Ibid., p. 690.
21. Interview with Sir Cecil Maurice Bowra, 24 January 1969.
22. Interview with Lady Diana Cooper, 11 March 1969.
23. *Diaries*, p. 747.
24. Ibid., p. 791.

25. Ibid., p. 758.

26. Evelyn Waugh, "Changes in the Church: Questions for the 'Progressives'," *Catholic Herald*, 7 August 1964, p. 4.

27. *Letters*, p. 638.

28. *Diaries*, p. 557.

29. Sykes, p. 445.

30. *Letters*, p. 636.

31. "The Agreeable Mr. Waugh," p. 41.

32. Sykes, p. 446.

33. Interview with Lady Diana Cooper, 11 March 1969. Sykes (p. 446) says that Waugh had his last Mass at a chapel near Combe Florey.

34. J. B. Priestley, "What Was Wrong with Pinfold," *New Statesman*, 31 August 1957, p. 224.

35. *Letters*, pp. 580, 635.

36. Ibid., pp. 296, 522.

37. Ibid., p. 588.

38. *Diaries*, p. 662.

39. Evelyn Waugh, *A Little Learning* (London: Chapman and Hall, 1964), p. 44.

40. Evelyn Waugh, "The War and the Younger Generation," *Spectator*, 13 April 1929, p. 570.

41. *Letters*, p. 639.

42. *Diaries*, p. 793.

43. Evelyn Waugh, *The Ordeal of Gilbert Pinfold* (London: Chapman and Hall, 1957), p. 6.

## Textual Note

1. Accessible manuscripts exist for all of Waugh's novels except *Vile Bodies* and *Put Out More Flags*. Only a partial typescript of the former is available. The manuscripts are at the Humanities Research Center Library, University of Texas at Austin. Waugh gave the manuscript of *Vile Bodies* to Diana Mitford and the manuscript of *Put Out More Flags* to Sir Robert Abdy.

2. Alexander McLachlan to Peters, 6 July 1931, Waugh to Peters, n.d. [early 1946], A. D. Peters file, Humanities Research Center Library, University of Texas at Austin.

3. Longmans Green published *Waugh in Abyssinia*; Chapman and Hall published *A Tourist in Africa*. (Longmans Green also published *Edmund Campion*.)

4. See Paul A. Doyle and Alan Clodd, "A British *Pinfold* and an American *Pinfold*," *Evelyn Waugh Newsletter* 3 (Winter 1969): 1–5.

5. Waugh to Peters, 9 June 1959 (postcard), A. D. Peters file. See also Robert Murray Davis, "'Clarifying and Enriching': Waugh's Changing Concept of Anthony Blanche," *Papers of the Bibliographical Society of North America* 72 (3rd quarter 1978): 305–20.

6. Evelyn Waugh, *Sword of Honour* (London: Chapman and Hall, 1965), p. 9.

7. *Letters*, p. 639.
8. Waugh to Peters, 9 June 1959 (postcard), A. D. Peters file.
9. Peters to Waugh, n.d. [1961], A. D. Peters file.
10. Waugh to Montgomery, n.d. [1962], A. D. Peters file.

# Index

Abyssinia: Waugh as reporter in, 25, 55, 91, 121, 124–25, 198; as seat of heresy, 93–94, 242
Academy of Carpentry, London, 25
Accidie, 218
Acton, Harold, 18, 21, 28, 29, 34, 42, 43, 55, 63, 80, 157; *Memoirs of an Aesthete*, 18, 48, 174; *More Memoirs of an Aesthete*, 52; *Aquarium*, 301n11
Aestheticism, 18, 37, 41, 42, 43, 178, 316n8; in *Put Out More Flags*, 154–60 passim; in *The Loved One*, 195
Amis, Kingsley, 58, 314n2
Amory, Mark, 267
Anglican Church: in Waugh's novels, 65–79 passim, 80–90 passim, 107, 109, 117, 162, 164–83 passim, 224, 247; related to Roman Catholicism, 31–36, 172
Anglo-Catholicism: Waugh's attraction to, 30–31, 172
Apollonian and Dionysiac. *See* Self, divided
Aquinas, Saint Thomas, 218, 280n15
Arius, 201
Arnold, Matthew, 73
Arnold House, 21–23
Art, 23, 37–46, 103; false, 188–97 passim; immature, 138, 139–51 passim; uncommitted, 152–60 pas-

sim; true, 161–83 passim
Aston Clinton, 23–24
Auden, Wystan Hugh, 144, 158
Augustine, Saint, of Canterbury, 30
Augustine, Saint, of Hippo, 43, 176, 306n26; and the two Cities, 2, 5, 116, 120, 201, 202, 209, 272, 310n13; *The City of God*, 7–8, 74, 190
Authority. *See* Fathers
Auty, Susan Ganis, 305n6

Baillie-Hamilton, Wanda (née Holden), 101, 297n9
Balfour, Patrick, 3rd Baron Kinross, 85, 125
Balston, Tom, 28
Barbarism: and the artist, 38; civilized, 104; figurative and actual, 122; Grimes as embodiment of, 64–65; order and, 65, 93–103 passim; Pinfold and, 261, 262
Beaton, Cecil, 10, 281n27, 294n18
Beauchamp, 7th Earl, 179
Beckett, Samuel: *Waiting for Godot*, 113
Beebe, Maurice, 44
Beerbohm, Sir Max, 41, 42, 43, 143, 268
Belloc, Hilaire, 225
Bergson, Henri, 17
Best, Edna, 133

Betjeman, John, 32, 260
Betjeman, Penelope, 203
Birkenhead, 2nd Earl of ("Freddie"), 249
Black, Stephen, 33, 39, 261, 310n1, 319n21
Blackstone, Sir William, 73
Boethius: *The Consolation of Philosophy*, 294n22
Bogus. *See* Fraudulence
Booth, Wayne, 59
Bourchier, Basil, 30, 32
Bowra, Sir Maurice, 49, 269
Boyle, Stuart, 189
Bracken, Brendan, 210
Bradbury, Malcolm, 58, 105
Brandt, Carl, 51
Breit, Harvey, 119, 310n1
Bright Young People, 82, 85
Brooke, Mrs. Charles Vyner, 26
Browning, Robert, 73; *Pippa Passes*, 77
Brummell, Beau, 42, 286n32
Bunyan, John, 311n7
Burgess, Anthony: *A Clockwork Orange*, 311n11
Burghclere, Lady, 25, 27, 28
Butler, Samuel, 73
Byron, Robert, 28

Cabell, James Branch: *Jurgen*, 294n23, 299n13
Caraman, Fr. Philip, 264, 270
Carens, James F., 58
Carew, Dudley, 8, 15, 17, 20, 32, 103; *A Fragment of Friendship*, 26
Carroll, Lewis: *Alice in Wonderland*, 63
Catholicism. *See* Roman Catholic Church
Chamberlin, C. L., 15
Chance. *See* Fortune
Channon, Sir Henry ("Chips"), 48
Chapman and Hall, 28, 51, 275, 277
Charity: as theme, 177, 213, 219,
221, 238, 250, 254, 255; Gilbert Pinfold and, 260, 262, 265; Waugh and, 213, 266, 310n4, 316n11; Waugh's gifts to, 213
Chesterman, Hugh: *The New Decameron*, 24
Chesterton, G. K., 32; "The Queer Feet," 176; "Wine and Water," 293n6
Child motif, 101, 106, 109, 111, 122, 127, 147, 220, 254–58
Chivalry, 111, 219, 237, 241, 243, 248
Churchill, Randolph, 8, 50, 159, 210, 245, 249, 317n16
Churchill, Sir Winston, 210
Cockburn, Claud, 23, 32
Combe Florey House, 1, 121, 270, 272, 273
Comfort, Alexander, 267
Commandos, 229–43 passim
Connolly, Cyril, 49, 52–53, 247; introduction to *The Loved One*, 189; *The Unquiet Grave* annotated by Waugh, 316n8
Conrad, Joseph: *Heart of Darkness*, 119; *Lord Jim*, 142
Consecutiveness. *See* Routine
Continuity. *See* Descendants
Cooper, Lady Diana, 50, 133, 136, 148, 158, 178, 240, 269, 270, 298n17, 301n13, 314n11
Cooper, Duff, 1st Viscount Norwich, 133, 158, 298n17, 314n11
Corpse Club, 14
Cory, W. J.: "Heraclitus: Paraphrase from Callimachus," 195, 235
Counter-Reformation, 36, 299n11
Crease, Francis, 1, 13, 15, 40, 42; *The Decorative Designs of Francis Crease*, 41
Crete, 210, 235–43
Croatia, 210, 249–51, 317n17
Cruttwell, C. R. M. F., 294n23
*The Cynic*, 11

Dandyism, 41–45. *See also*
Aestheticism
Dante Alighieri: *The Divine Comedy*,
31
D'Arcy, Fr. Martin, S. J., 33, 55, 179,
266, 280n15
D'Avanzo, Mario, 163–64, 172
Davie, Michael, 267, 289n48
Davies, Robertson, 256
Davis, Robert Murray, 208, 302n4,
303n6, 305n4, 309n27, 321n4
Delasanta, Rodney, 163–64, 173
Dennis, Nigel, 66, 144, 267,
304n10
Descendants: spiritual, 182, 202, 257;
bodily, 254, 256, 318n33
Design, 7, 8, 35, 61, 95–96, 161
Dickens, Charles, 53, 67, 73, 116,
118; *Dombey and Son*, 116; *Mar-
tin Chuzzlewit*, 116; *David Copper-
field*, 262
Dilettanti Club, 14, 15
Dionysus, 64, 70, 73, 76, 266
Discipline, 6, 65, 68, 231, 266
Dobson, Austin, 12, 13
Donatus, 201
Doppelgangers: escape from, 17,
46–47; in Waugh's novels, 71, 99,
119, 145–46, 153, 167–83 passim,
202, 203, 223–37, 241, 258,
299n16. *See also* Anglican Church;
Fraudulence; Heresy; Uniqueness
Dostoievsky, Feodor: *The Brothers
Karamazov*, 125, 294n23
Doubles. *See* Doppelgangers
Douglas, Keith, 177
Driberg, Tom, 15, 31, 85
Dru, Alick, 270
Duggan, Alfred, 267
Duggan, Hubert, 180, 266
Dyson, A. E., 60

Eaton, Dr. Hubert, 189, 308n11
Eliot, T. S., 292n81; *Ash-Wednesday*,
5; *The Waste Land*, 9, 18, 88–103,

113, 120, 158; "The Love Song of
J. Alfred Prufrock," 81, 132; "Frag-
ment of an Agon," 88; *Burnt Nor-
ton*, 113; *Little Gidding*, 183
Ellis, Havelock, 70
Ellmann, Richard, 43

Faith: and taste, 8, 34, 35, 36, 47, 77,
103, 105, 114, 122, 130, 168, 176,
199, 204, 234, 247, 256, 262; as
touchstone, 55, 105. *See also*
Fraudulence; Heresy; Taste; Right
reason
Family: as refuge, 254; in War Trilogy,
214, 221, 245; Waugh's letters to,
267
Farr, Paul, 131
Farrar, John, 51
Fathers: as irresponsible authorities,
2, 12, 13, 34, 64, 65, 66, 72, 74,
80, 104, 108, 118, 122, 123, 159,
166, 172, 174–75, 181, 195, 236;
Waugh's changing view of, 142–51
passim; Waugh's affirmative view
of, 162, 181–82, 183, 220, 235.
*See also* Waugh, Arthur
Faulkner, William: "The Bear," 257
Firbank, Ronald, 42, 60, 61, 68, 81,
123, 227, 296n29, 297n14; *Ca-
price*, 296n29; *The Flower Beneath
the Foot*, 296n29
Fitzgerald, F. Scott, 8; *The Great
Gatsby*, 257
Fleming, Ann, 52, 240, 267, 270
Fleming, Peter: *Brazilian Adventure*,
116
Ford, Ford Madox (Hueffer): *Parade's
End*, 256
Forest Lawn, Calif., 189
Forster, E. M.: *A Passage to India*, 34,
299n17; *Howards End*, 179, 182,
256, 257; "The Machine Stops,"
312n13
Fortune, 4, 25, 29, 36, 122, 318n33;
in *Decline and Fall*, 65, 67, 68,

70–71, 74–75, 294n22; in *Vile Bodies*, 81–90 passim; in *Black Mischief*, 98–99; in *A Handful of Dust*, 112–13; in *Scoop*, 133–38 passim; in *The Loved One*, 196; in War Trilogy, 220, 222, 230, 234, 245, 247, 250, 314n2

Franco, Francisco, 49

Fraudulence, 19, 34–35, 46, 60–61, 122; in *Decline and Fall*, 67; in *Vile Bodies*, 83, 86; in *A Handful of Dust*, 108; in *Black Mischief*, 95; in *Scoop*, 126–38 passim; in *Put Out More Flags*, 154, 156; in *Brideshead Revisited*, 167–83 passim; in War Trilogy, 222, 225–26, 229–30. *See also* Anglican Church; Doppelgangers; Heresy; Uniqueness

Frazer, Sir James, 73; *The Golden Bough*, 63, 70, 294n23

Freeman, John, 31, 33, 41, 45, 199

Fry, Althea, 27

Frye, Northrop, 123

Fulford, Roger, 15

Gardner, Evelyn, 18, 121, 133, 136; Waugh's relationship with, 25–29, 80, 83, 283n96

Gaudi, Antonio, 61

Gerson, Mark, 42

Gibbon, Edward, 33, 73, 200–201

Gifford, Barry, 26

Goulden, Mark, 51

Grace, divine, 34, 100, 155, 168, 182–83, 190, 220. *See also* Providence

Graham, Alastair, 18, 20, 21, 23, 43, 64, 68, 91, 96, 177, 178, 297n14

Graham, Mrs. Jessie, 23, 68, 177

Grahame, Kenneth: *The Wind in the Willows*, 23, 70

Green, Henry. *See* Yorke, Henry

Green, Martin, 58

Green, Peter, 59

Greene, George, 59

Greene, Graham, 206, 272, 314n2; *British Dramatists*, 60; *The End of the Affair*, 206

Greenidge, Terence, 18

Gropius, Walter, 294n23

Guinness, Bryan, 2nd Baron Moyne, 316n7

Guinness, Diana. *See* Mosley, Lady Diana

Gunther, John, 158

Guthrie, James, 21

Hardy, Thomas, 73, 294n25; *The Return of the Native*, 74; *Tess of the D'Urbervilles*, 295n25

Hartley, L. P., 60

Haynes, E. S. P., 29, 302n20

Heath Mount School, 10, 11, 13

Heatherley School of Fine Art, 20, 61

Henley, W. E.: "To W. A.," 294n19

Herbert, George: "The Pulley," 220

Heresy: as theme, 5, 6, 38; in *Decline and Fall*, 3, 35, 69, 76, 273; in *Vile Bodies*, 81; in *Black Mischief*, 94, 100; in *A Handful of Dust*, 167, 175; in *Helena*, 203; in War Trilogy, 234. *See also* Anglican Church; Doppelgangers; Fraudulence; Uniqueness

Herrick, Robert: "Corinna's Going a-Maying," 130, 137

Heygate, John, 28, 80, 84, 283n96

Higham, T. M., 293n10

Hill, Carol, 51

Hitler, Adolf, 48

Hodges, Lucy, 10, 11, 30

Hodgson, Ralph: "The Bells of Heaven," 162

Hogarth, William: *The Rake's Progress*, 311n7

Hollis, Christopher, 301n17

Hope, Bob, 52

Horace: *Odes*, 281n51

Hordern, Michael, 265

Howard, Brian, 303n13, 310n16

Hügel, Baron Friedrich von, 32
Hugo, Howard E., 49
Humanism, 105
Hunt, William Holman, 179, 297n14
Huxley, Aldous, 123, 209; *Antic Hay*, 70, 287n48, 299n17; *After Many a Summer*, 189; *Brave New World*, 207, 312n13
Hypocrites' Club, 43

Individuality, 66–67, 79, 126, 134, 142, 190, 295n28. *See also* Vocation; Uniqueness
Isherwood, Christopher, 158
Izzard, Percy W. D., 136

James, William: *The Varieties of Religious Experience*, 24
Jebb, Julian, 80, 232, 310n1, 314n2
Johnson, Samuel, 73
Joyce, James, 11–12, 56; *A Portrait of the Artist as Young Man*, 162; *Ulysses*, 257
Joynson-Hicks, Sir William, 295n26
Jungman, Teresa ("Baby"), 117, 133, 135

Kaufmann, Angelica, 159
Keats, John: "Ode on a Grecian Urn," 172
Kinross, 3rd Baron. *See* Balfour, Patrick
Kipling, Rudyard, 12, 44
Knightley, Phillip: *The First Casualty*, 125, 128
Knox, Msgr. Ronald, 50, 59, 102
Korda, Alexander, 51, 121

Laking, Sir Francis, 23–24
Lamb, Henry, 27
Lamb, Lady Pansy, 25, 48, 53, 283n96, 289n47, 303n13
Lanchester, Elsa, 20
Lancing College, 1, 162, 163, 266; *Lancing College Magazine*, 14, 54

Latimer, Hugh, 185, 235
Lavery, Lady Hazel, 50
Lawrence, D. H.: *Lady Chatterley's Lover*, 257, 263; *Women in Love*, 294n23
Laycock, Maj. Gen. Sir Robert, 210, 238–40, 244
Lewis, Rosa, 83
Lewis, Wyndham: *The Doom of Youth*, 3, 54
Lin, Yutang: *The Importance of Living*, 157
Little, Brown and Company, 51
Longfellow, Henry Wadsworth, 73
Longford, 7th Earl of. *See* Pakenham, Frank
Lovat, 17th Baron ("Shimi"), 211, 240
Luce, Henry, 51
Lygon, Lady Dorothy, 50, 59, 267, 289n47
Lygon family, 179
Lygon, Hugh, 20, 177
Lygon, Lady Mary, 50, 52, 129, 267, 289n47

Macaulay, Rose, 49
MacDougall, John, 277
Mackenzie, Compton: *The Lunatic Republic*, 312n13
McLachlan, Alexander, 317n24
Maclean, Fitzroy, 210, 249, 317n17
McPherson, Aimée Semple, 82, 201
Mansfield, Katherine, 15
Maritain, Jacques, 280n15
Martin, Graham, 58
Matson, Harold, 51, 260
Maturity, 8, 17, 181. *See also* Means and ends
Maugham, Somerset: *Sheppey*, 299n19
Means and ends, 5, 7–8, 74, 169–83 passim, 254, 310n16. *See also* Doppelgangers; Fraudulence
Meckier, Jerome, 298n7, 313n5

Merton, Thomas, 267
Mikes, George, 58
Milbanke, Lady (Princess Dmitri of
    Russia), 189
Mills, Clifford: *Where the Rainbow
    Ends*, 191
Milton, John, 4
Ministry of Information, 152, 154,
    157–58, 210
Mitford, Diana. *See* Mosley, Lady
    Diana
Mitford, Nancy, 27, 49, 52, 60, 212,
    223, 267, 272, 306n24, 313n6,
    315n16
Moers, Ellen: *The Dandy*, 42
Molson, Hugh, 15
Moncrieff, C. K. Scott, 21
Montgomery, John, 49, 267, 278
Morford, Brig. St. Clair, 251
Morris, William, 73
Morriss, Margaret, 259
Mosley, Lady Diana, 148, 277, 316n7
Mountbatten, Earl, 211
Muggeridge, Malcolm, 49, 59

Nabokov, Vladimir, 296n29
Newman, Evelyn, 15
Newman, John Henry, 31
Nicolson, Sir Harold, 158, 246
Nollekens, Joseph, 159
Nightingale, Ronald, 283n96

O'Brien, Conor Cruise (Donat
    O'Donnell), 58
Ohmann, Richard, 60
Oldmeadow, Ernest, 101–2
Olivier, Sir Laurence, 51–52
Orthodoxy. *See* Anglican Church;
    Discipline; Doppelgangers; Fraudu-
    lence; Heresy
Orwell, George, 158, 207, 306n21;
    *Nineteen Eighty-Four*, 209, 312n13

Pakenham, Frank, 7th Earl of Long-
    ford, 40, 205, 212

Pakenham, Lady Pansy. *See* Lamb,
    Lady Pansy
Palladio, Andrea, 6, 37, 61, 266. *See
    also* Discipline
Pares, Richard, 18, 177
Pater, Walter, 43; *The Renaissance*,
    64, 174, 184, 307n4
"Pervigilium Veneris" (Anon.), 71
Phillips, Sir Percival, 125
Picasso, Pablo, 38, 41
Picturesque, the, 1, 127, 129, 180,
    297n14
Piers Court, 121, 125, 139
Peters, A. D., 271, 275, 277, 282n78,
    297n11, 299n22, 305n1; Waugh's
    correspondence with, 51–52, 80,
    125, 139, 189, 198, 213, 260.
Pistol Troop, 10
Pixton Park, 130
Plato: *Republic*, 17; *Symposium*,
    294n23
Plunket-Greene, Elizabeth, 23
Plunket-Greene, Gwen, 32, 179
Plunket-Greene, Olivia, 21, 27, 33,
    179
Plunket-Greene, Richard, 23, 179
Ponsonby, Elizabeth, 177
Ponsonby, Matthew, 177, 282n69
Pope, Alexander, 31, 58, 73
Powell, Anthony, 60, 266, 293n2
Preston, Sgt. Stuart, 316n9
Priestley, J. B., 264, 271
Providence, 4, 255, 318n31; in *De-
    cline and Fall*, 67, 75; in *Brideshead
    Revisited*, 161–83 passim, 199; in
    *The Loved One*, 196–97; in War
    Trilogy, 225, 227, 247, 252, 255,
    256. *See also* Grace, divine
Pryce-Jones, Alan, 59
Pye, Sybil, 283n83

Quennell, Peter, 19

Ramsay, John: *Where the Rainbow
    Ends*, 191

Raschid, Haroun al-, 124

Reformation: effect on Britain, 33, 34, 35, 36; in *Vile Bodies*, 86, 87; in *A Handful of Dust*, 109, 118–19; in *Brideshead Revisited*, 116, 173, 183

Reith, Sir John, 1st Baron Reith of Stonehaven, 283n96

Rickett, F. W., 125

Right reason, 35, 77, 95. *See also* Faith; Taste

Rogers, Will, 52

Roman Catholic Church, 2, 33, 36, 65, 254–55, 258; Waugh's entry into, 29; innovations in, 269, 270, 271, 273

Rosten, Leo, 48

Rossetti, Dante Gabriel, 43, 171–72

Roughead, A. N., 139

Routine, 97, 118, 119, 134, 171. *See also* Water motif; Doppelgangers

Roxburgh, J. F., 16, 40, 293n15

Ruskin, John, 35

Sanctuaries, 1, 2, 12, 19, 45, 272–74; in *Decline and Fall*, 71–72, 74; in *Black Mischief*, 97, 100; in *A Handful of Dust*, 106, 116–17; in *Work Suspended*, 140, 141, 142, 144, 146, 149; in *Put Out More Flags*, 154, 155, 157, 159; in *Brideshead Revisited*, 166–67, 173, 182; in *Scott-King's Modern Europe*, 184–85; in *Helena*, 200, 202; in *Love Among the Ruins*, 207; in War Trilogy, 219, 236–37, 251–52; in *The Ordeal of Gilbert Pinfold*, 263

Sartre, Jean-Paul: *No Exit*, 272

Sassoon, Siegfried, 111

Selassie, Haile, 91, 124, 298n16

Self, divided, 1, 5, 9, 11, 13, 15, 16, 40, 43–45, 123, 297n14; in "The Tutor's Tale," 24, 135; in *Decline and Fall*, 75; in *Vile Bodies*, 84; in *Scoop*, 103; in *Work Suspended*, 140, 150; in *Put Out More Flags*, 152, 153; in "Charles Ryder's Schooldays," 163; in *Brideshead Revisited*, 178; in War Trilogy, 212–13, 215; and Waugh's renunciation of public self, 9, 57, 103, 205, 212, 271

Shadows. *See* Doppelgangers

Shakespeare, William: *Hamlet*, 70, 73; *The Merchant of Venice*, 73; *Richard II*, 88; *Two Gentlemen of Verona*, 150; *King Lear*, 259, 261, 263; *The Tempest*, 262

Sharp, William, 43, 287n40

Shaw, George Bernard, 58; *Saint Joan*, 204; *Misalliance*, 299n17

Shelley, Percy Bysshe, 190

Sherman, Richard, 51

Sidney, Sir Philip, 229; *Defense of Poesy*, 311n11

Silenus, 18, 21, 63; in *Decline and Fall*, 69, 70, 73, 76

Sin, original, 207, 209, 268, 311n11

Sitwell, Dame Edith, 42

Skinner, B. F.: *Walden II*, 312n13

Sloth, spiritual, 218

Smiles, Samuel: *Self-Help*, 73

Solitude, 2, 38, 40, 47, 212, 272, 317n21; in *A Handful of Dust*, 107; in *Put Out More Flags*, 157; in *Brideshead Revisited*, 176; in *Helena*, 200; in War Trilogy, 213, 217, 242; in *Pinfold*, 260, 263. *See also* Doppelgangers; Sanctuaries

Spain, Nancy, 41, 260

Spark, Muriel, 267

Spenser, Edmund, 299n13

Split self. *See* Self, divided

Stanley, Arthur Penrhyn: *The Eastern Church*, 73, 77, 93

Stannard, Martin, 303n19

Stein, Gertrude, 38

Stephens, Margaret, 260

Stevenson, Robert Louis: *Dr. Jekyll and Mr. Hyde*, 43, 162
Stirling, Col. William, 210
Stopes, Marie, 95
Stopp, Frederick J., 291n58; *Evelyn Waugh: Portrait of an Artist*, 58, 214, 313n12, 314n2
Strauss, Dr. Eric, 264
Strauss, Ralph, 28
Sturge Moore, T., 283n83
Style, 37, 41, 46, 60–61, 78, 129, 198, 200, 204
Sutro, Charles, 27
Sweet, Frederick D., 299n19
Swift, Jonathan, 58, 73, 293n15
Sykes, Christopher, 25, 28, 40, 53, 55, 63, 133, 148, 150, 179, 188, 199, 223, 267, 270

Tafari, Ras. *See* Selassie, Haile
Tanner, Ralph, 239, 267
Taste, 169, 311n11; and barbarism, 95–96; and fraudulence, 127–38 passim; as plot device, 66, 134, 143; in *The Loved One*, 190, 197; in *Helena*, 199–201, 204; in *Love Among the Ruins*, 207, 209. *See also* Faith; Fraudulence; Right reason
Thackeray, William Makepeace, 73
Tito, Josip Broz, 249
Tolerance, 104, 107–9, 114, 120
Trollope, Anthony, 39, 253
Tudors, 35–36, 69, 73, 94

Uniqueness: and doubles, 46–47, 154–56; and inspiration, 170–71, 172, 174; of vocations, 6–7, 204. *See also* Doppelgangers; Fraudulence; Heresy; Style; Vocation

Van Vechten, Carl, 40
Van Zeller, Dom Hubert, 267, 270
Vinci, Count, 125
Vitruvius, 37. *See also* Palladio, Andrea

Vittoria, Francisco de, 185
Vocation: uniqueness of, 6–7, 204; Augustine and, 7; acceptance and rejection of, 7–9, 161, 313n2; Waugh's sense of, 9, 15, 42, 47, 212, 265, 271; in *Brideshead Revisited*, 161–62; in *The Loved One*, 197; in *Helena*, 200–201, 204–5; in *Love Among the Ruins*, 209; in War Trilogy, 217, 219–20, 228, 236, 248. *See also* Design; Individuality; Uniqueness
Voltaire: *Candide*, 254

Wain, John, 58
Wasson, Richard, 279n1
Watkins, Alan, 315n15
Water motif, 105, 107, 126, 132, 149, 300n29
Waugh, Alec (brother), 11, 12, 17, 80; *Georgian Stories, 1926*, 23
Waugh, Arthur (father), 11–13, 16, 20, 30, 44, 87, 140, 171, 172, 180, 183, 211, 245; *One Man's Road*, 11; *Reticence in Literature*, 12; *The Lives of the Poets*, 59; The Nonesuch Dickens, 119
Waugh, Auberon (son), 8, 148
Waugh, Catherine (mother), 11, 13
Waugh, Evelyn
life:
    childhood, 1, 9–13, 30–31; at Lancing College, 1, 13–17, 31–32; at Oxford, 17–20, 32; from 1924 to 1928, 20–29, 32–33; as journalist, 25, 55, 91, 124–25; at Piers Court, 121; at Combe Florey House, 121, 270, 271, 273; as traveller, 124; in World War II, 139, 152, 205, 210, 244, 249; possible removal to Ireland, 152, 269, 272–73; withdrawal from the world, 1, 271–74; failing health and last days, 259–60, 268–74, 277–78

Waugh, Evelyn (*continued*)
  appearance and characteristics:
    physical appearance, 10–11, 14,
      18, 48, 174; as spokesman for
      youth, 34; as aesthete, 41–45;
      taste for lawsuits, 41, 54; per-
      secution mania, 46, 94, 258–
      59, 270; limited capacity for
      charity, 45, 213–14, 310n4;
      love of making scenes, 49–53;
      as convert, 50; fear of change,
      54; death wish, 55; self-hatred
      and despair, 55; boredom, 116,
      171, 212, 244, 269; enthusi-
      asm for war, 152; gloom after
      1945, 152, 184; writer's voca-
      tion, 161, 264, 271; sense of
      world as prison, 184, 272; per-
      fectionism, 188, 210; false vo-
      cation as soldier, 205; end of
      enthusiasm for war, 210–12,
      245; self-awareness, 266–67;
      response to Vatican II, 269,
      270, 273; handwriting, 275,
      289n48
  theory and technique:
    role of discipline in creative pro-
      cess, 5–6, 36–37, 61–62; use
      of actual experience in fiction,
      9, 39–40, 140, 205, 228,
      230–32, 235–36, 238–41,
      252, 258, 259–65, 314n12;
      vision of history, 35–36, 122;
      as responsible satirist, 55–
      62; communication of values
      through charged language, 55,
      57, 59–60, 77–78, 83, 105,
      123, 134, 175, 237–38,
      314n12; flat and round charac-
      ters, 56, 123, 143; cruelty, 58;
      fictional universe, 66; develop-
      ment of tone and narrative
      voice, 105, 123; early tech-
      niques, 121–23, 149, 220,
      303n21; later techniques, 149,
      182, 189, 308n14; revisions,

253, 276; novelty and tradi-
      tion, 292n81; unity of War
      Trilogy, 314n2
  works:
    "The American Epoch in the Ro-
      man Catholic Church," 255
    "Antony, Who Sought Things
      That Were Lost," 19–20
    "The Balance," 20, 22–23, 35,
      46, 62, 79, 98, 117, 135
    *Basil Seal Rides Again*, 4, 45, 99,
      278, 311, 319n23
    *Black Mischief*, 4, 51, 75,
      91–103, 121, 134, 297n11,
      298n5, 301n11, 318n33; com-
      pared with *Scoop*, 136, 270,
      275
    *Brideshead Revisited*, 161–83;
      sanctuary in, 2; as pivotal
      novel, 3, 9, 121, 136, 151, 175,
      177, 180–83; maturation in,
      17, 32, 46, 47, 138, 161–83
      passim, 193, 298n5; and reli-
      gious art, 35, 194, 271; ex-
      plicitness about Catholicism in,
      58, 59, 123; misanthropy in,
      160; theme of, 163, 168; man-
      uscript and variant editions of,
      163, 276–77; MGM "Memo-
      randum" on, 164–65; inspira-
      tion in, 170, 172; attempt to
      film, 188; parodied in *Uncon-
      ditional Surrender*, 216, 253;
      compared with War Trilogy,
      220, 257; marine imagery in,
      301n11
    "Captain Hance Saga," 136
    "Charles Ryder's Schooldays,"
      162, 198
    "Church and State in Liberated
      Croatia," 317n17
    "Come Inside," 33
    "Commando Raid on Bardia,"
      230
    "Compassion," 251, 274
    "Conversion," 15

Waugh, Evelyn (*continued*)
  "Death in Hollywood," 192–93
  *Decline and Fall*, 63–79; 310n4;
    sanctuary and prison in, 2–3,
    272; manuscript of, 6, 295n28;
    and decay of personality, 17;
    Waugh begins, 25; sales of, 28,
    80; religion in, 32, 35, 81, 87,
    90, 190; and Waugh's persona,
    46; as satire, 57; authorial
    presence in, 59; and Fortune,
    68, 70, 71, 74, 75, 134; taste
    and style in, 77–78, 88; and
    *Black Mischief*, 102; revisions
    to, 273, 277; original title,
    293n2
  *The Diaries of Evelyn Waugh*,
    13–14, 17, 53–55, 266, 267
  *Edmund Campion*, 35–36, 69,
    121
  "Edward of Unique Achieve-
    ment," 47
  "Fan-Fare," 6, 51, 56, 141,
    299n22
  "Foreword," *The Autobiography
    of an Elizabethan*, 285n25
  *A Handful of Dust*,
    104–23,282n78; sanctuary
    and prison in, 3; doubles in,
    47; Fortune in, 99, 134; per-
    sonal responsibility in, 253, 264
  *Helena*, 198–205; hidden
    humour in, 59; vocation in,
    197, 200–205; parallel of
    Waugh and Helena in, 271; not
    in new Uniform Edition, 276,
    277
  "The Holy Places," 204
  *Labels*, 28, 29, 35, 41, 82, 118
  *The Letters of Evelyn Waugh*,
    267–68
  *The Life of the Right Reverend
    Ronald Knox*, 260, 277
  *A Little Learning*, 10, 12, 13, 14,
    17, 19, 20, 178, 179, 278

  *Love Among the Ruins*, 4,
    206–9, 214, 276, 277
  *The Loved One*, 4, 38, 180–97,
    213, 271, 310n4
  "The Man Who Liked Dickens,"
    116, 275
  "Memorandum on Layforce,"
    235
  *Men at Arms*, 217–77, 314n2;
    revisions in 1965 edition,
    215–16. *See also* War Trilogy
  "Mr. Loveday's Little Outing,"
    276, 277
  *Mr. Loveday's Little Outing and
    Other Sad Stories*, 121
  *Ninety-Two Days*, 39, 115
  "Noah: or the Future of Intoxica-
    tion," 24, 64
  *Officers and Gentlemen*, 46, 190,
    202, 214, 215, 228–43,
    314n2. *See also* War Trilogy
  "An Open Letter to His Eminence
    the Cardinal Archbishop of
    Westminster," 101–2, 117
  *The Ordeal of Gilbert Pinfold*,
    12, 41, 55, 214, 258–65, 266,
    274, 276, 277, 310n1; personal
    responsibility in, 4, 262, 263;
    divided self and poses in, 43,
    44; lack of charity in, 260,
    262, 265; taste and faith in,
    262–63
  "Out of Depth," 2
  "Period Piece," 318n33
  "Portrait of Young Man with Ca-
    reer," 20
  "Preface," *The Decorative De-
    signs of Francis Crease*, 41
  "The Pre-Raphaelite Brother-
    hood," 23
  *Put Out More Flags*, 3, 46, 98,
    121, 138, 145, 152–60,
    301n11, 321n1; and life of ac-
    tion, 150, 270–71
  *Remote People*, 38, 40, 92, 275